T0311734

MODERN DEVELOPMENTS IN BEHAVIORAL ECONOMICS

SOCIAL SCIENCE PERSPECTIVES ON CHOICE AND DECISION MAKING

MODERN DEVELOPMENTS IN BEHAVIORAL ECONOMICS

SOCIAL SCIENCE PERSPECTIVES ON CHOICE AND DECISION MAKING

JOHN MALCOLM DOWLING

Singapore Management University, Singapore

YAP CHIN-FANG

World Scientific

NEW JERSEY • LONDON • SINGAPORE • BEIJING • SHANGHAI • HONG KONG • TAIPEI • CHENNAI

Published by

World Scientific Publishing Co. Pte. Ltd.

5 Toh Tuck Link, Singapore 596224

USA office: 27 Warren Street, Suite 401-402, Hackensack, NJ 07601

UK office: 57 Shelton Street, Covent Garden, London WC2H 9HE

Library of Congress Cataloging-in-Publication Data
Dowling, J. Malcolm (John Malcolm)
   Modern developments in behavioral economics : social science perspectives
on choice and decision making / by John Malcolm Dowling & Yap Chin-Fang.
      p. cm.
   ISBN-13 978-981-270-143-5
   ISBN-10 981-270-143-5
   1. Economics--Psychological aspects. 2. Economics--Decision making.
3. Decision making. I. Yap, Chin-Fang. II. Title.

HB74.P8 D69 2007
330.01'9--dc22

                                                                2006048910

British Library Cataloguing-in-Publication Data
A catalogue record for this book is available from the British Library.

First published 2007 (Hardcover)
Reprinted 2016 (in paperback edition)
ISBN 978-981-3203-37-2

Typeset by Stallion Press
Email: enquiries@stallionpress.com

Printed in Singapore

The Road Not Taken

Two roads diverged in a yellow wood,
And sorry I could not travel both
And be one traveler, long I stood
And looked down one as far as I could
To where it bent in the undergrowth;   5

Then took the other, as just as fair,
And having perhaps the better claim,
Because it was grassy and wanted wear;
Though as for that the passing there
Had worn them really about the same,   10

And both that morning equally lay
In leaves no step had trodden black.
Oh, I kept the first for another day!
Yet knowing how way leads on to way,
I doubted if I should ever come back.   15

I shall be telling this with a sigh
Somewhere ages and ages hence:
Two roads diverged in a wood, and I—
I took the one less traveled by,
And that has made all the difference.   20

— Robert Frost (1874–1963)

To Gurumayi and our families

Acknowledgments

This book has been several years in the making. In 2002, we worked on a project together which eventually led to the publication of a book on economic development in Asia. The final chapter of that book dealt with cooperation, altruism, ethics and corruption. Subsequently, one of us developed a course that was offered at Singapore Management University, titled "The Economics of Ethics and Happiness". This course dealt with these and other decision making issues. The notes for this course eventually became the first draft of this book. Both of us then worked to expand and deepen our understanding of the issues underlying the decision making process and expand the range of coverage of topics to include decision making by large groups and the government.

In the course of the preparation of the book, we benefited from the comments of many people. Maribeth Boritzer-Dowling read the entire manuscript. She suggested improvements in writing style and syntax, spotted inconsistent arguments and made useful suggestions for reworking the narrative. Her input significantly raised the quality and logic of the entire book. The students in the "Ethics and Happiness" course at Singapore Management University also made many valuable suggestions and were willing guinea pigs for a number of experiments, some of which are reported in the book. The Dean of the School of Economics and Social Science at Singapore Management University, Roberto S. Mariano, provided support and encouragement throughout the duration of the project.

We thank Colin Ash, Vincent Chua, Ilya Farber, Helena-Ann Glamheden, John Helliwell, Marcus Karner, Mark Nowacki, Y. Kwang Ng, Jennifer Tang, Ruut Veenhoven, Marco Verweij and Ana Wozniak for their helpful comments and suggestions. We thank Leung Hing Man who brought us together for this project. We thank the participants at the 2005 Happiness Workshop convened at Reading University. We thank Ms Helen Choo, Mrs Goh Hwee Choo, Mrs Loh Mui Eng and friends at Tampines Junior College for their kind support. We thank our editor, Yvonne Tan, who supported and encouraged through the entire writing and editing process. We also want to thank an anonymous reviewer who made many useful suggestions for strengthening the manuscript. We are responsible for any errors or omissions that remain.

John Malcolm Dowling
Yap Chin-Fang
April 2007

Contents

Chapter 1

Introduction

Economic theory begins with certain general assumptions. People are purely rational. They maximize utility whenever possible. General rules are established without making interpersonal comparisons or moral judgments. It is assumed that people are basically selfish. It assumes that there is competition and in order to make decisions, everyone is able to gather economic information easily, quickly and without cost. Economists also have developed methods for dealing with situations where information required to make decisions is not exact. Risk and uncertainty abound in the real world and economists factor this into their models by using what is called expected utility, i.e., the utility multiplied by some probability of the event occurring. This enables economists to factor out risk by being able to equate the expected utility of different outcomes.

The assumptions of economic theory and economics in general is that all people are similarly rational and self-interested. Many other social scientists, such as sociologists and political scientists, have a different view. They contend that such generalizations ignore the uniqueness of people and culture. The best we can do is describe each individual and community or perhaps derive some structural relationships that apply locally but certainly not globally.

This book takes the point of view that there is merit in both of these approaches. The "truth" lies somewhere in between. There are many economic relationships that do seem to have universal (or nearly universal) features such as the law of demand, diminishing returns or the tendency of competitive markets to allocate resources efficiently. However, there are many other circumstances where the generalizations of economics break down and are more consistent with actual behavior.

This book looks beyond the standard assumptions of economics in the following ways:

- It examines the field of behavioral economics and discusses instances when bounded rationality may lead to decisions that are not consistent with standard economic assumptions.
- It considers altruistic and cooperative behavior as alternatives to competition.
- It considers game theory as a way to explore motives of cooperation versus competition.
- It discusses the determinants of happiness and the relationship between utility and well-being.
- It discusses the concept of social capital including motivations for charity, being a responsible citizen, and the relationship between social capital and economic efficiency.
- It looks at the ethical concepts such as trust and fairness and how they relate to economic actions and the motivation to cooperate rather than compete.
- It analyzes risk and the processes by which investors and consumers make decisions.
- It looks at the concept of justice and income distribution from an ethical point of view.
- It explores the interaction of individuals within groups and the interaction of groups with the rest of society with regard to cooperation and trust.
- It looks at behavior such as crime, corruption and bribery from ethical, social and economic points of view.
- It considers the formation of "social capital" and its impact on the economic system.
- It looks at the ethical and behavioral patterns with respect to cooperation, trust and ethical behavior.
- It discusses possible ways that ethical and virtuous behavior, along with the formation of social capital, can be encouraged in economies.

Our approach is more eclectic than doctrinaire. In many cases, economic analysis makes useful contributions to understanding these different issues. In other cases philosophy, psychology, sociology and political science have also made important contributions to our understanding. By widening the scope of inquiry beyond a narrow interpretation of economic theory, we are able to better understand the motivations of "economic actors".

In the remainder of this chapter, we outline some of the basic features of the following chapters, including a short discussion of some of the issues covered. We begin with a short introduction to scientific method as it relates to economics.

Mainstream or orthodox economic theory likes to think of itself as being "scientific". As part of the scientific method, neoclassical economics is careful to draw a distinction between positive and normative statements. By taking opinions out of the picture through the use of positive logic, it hopes to make economic analysis rational and subject to the process of scientific verification. It strives to examine "what is" rather than "what should be".

Economics is willing to incorporate theories from other disciplines that it believes to be valid, such as attitudes toward risk or aspects of sociobiology which allow individuals to treat relatives differently from others with whom they share fewer genes. However, the general thrust of economic analysis remains focused on positive analysis. Judgments and normative analysis are relegated to the branches of economics where public goods and the role of the government are discussed.

Economists make a number of assumptions about how economic agents assemble and analyze information and how they make choices. These assumptions lead to certain theoretical constructs and certain conclusions about economic behavior flow from this analysis that is deductive in nature. Over time, these theoretical models have been modified and extended based on observations of actual behavior of economic agents. Throughout their analysis, economists are particularly emphatic in stressing the rational behavior of economic agents and the importance of competition and economic efficiency against a background of positive analysis.

Consideration of Pareto optimality is a feature of much economic analysis. Policy makers are often presented with a variety of possible choices to make, each of which has the characteristics of being efficient and optimal in some sense. The relationship between the public and these decision makers is the subject of considerable economic analysis within the neoclassical framework. Within this framework, economists assume that the public is also aware of the options presented to policy makers and is sufficiently informed to make their voice heard through the ballot box.

Economic theory is also based on the general assumption that all individuals are "rational", insofar as their economic decision making goes. They do not reverse their decisions quickly from one period to another without good reason. They follow the transitive laws of mathematics: if A is preferred to B and B is preferred to C, then A is preferred to C. Economists believe that every person when faced with similar circumstances will make the same basic decision, assuming that their tastes are similar. People are similarly rational and follow self-interest.

Actual decisions may differ because each individual has different tastes. These tastes may change and influence behavior accordingly. However, the basic calculus for making decisions remains the same for all individuals everywhere and anytime. Tastes are ordinarily assumed to be fixed and given, and the motivation for changes in taste is not explored systematically in most areas of standard economic analysis. It is assumed that economic agents have access to all the information they need to make decisions and that this information is, for all intents and purposes, costless. In the rest of this introductory chapter we explore ways that the parameters of the economic model have been questioned and replaced by more general behavioral assumptions which incorporate other aspects of behavior besides pure rationality. This includes exploring the role of emotions and incorporating other ways in which agents arrive at decisions as part of their general behavioral pattern.

1.1 A Model of Individual Decision Making — Bounded Rationality and the Inclusion of Emotions

In recent years, standard economic assumptions have been challenged on several different fronts. Proponents of what has become known as "bounded rationality", beginning with Herbert Simon (1972, 1982) and continuing through to Daniel Kahneman (2003), have stressed the importance of emotion as a strong input into decision making along with the notion that agents know, can know or choose to know only a limited number of possible options available to them when they make decisions. Decisions are often made using intuition and a variety of short-cut methods that sometimes violate the assumptions behind the rationality calculus that is the foundation of economic decision making. Focusing on the behavior of individuals, this approach suggests a variety of alternatives to the mechanistic, mathematical, detached view of economic agents as rational actors evaluating all sensory inputs objectively and then proceeding methodically to make an objective decision.

Both Simon and Kahneman won the Nobel Prize for economics, more than two decades apart. Simon was an economist while Kahneman was trained as a psychologist. Kahneman argues that by ignoring a wide variety of anomalies in the way people behave, economists are missing out on many aspects of behavior that do not fit into their neat little package of neoclassical inferences. He stresses the fact that people's emotions play a role in decision making: "Findings about the role of optimism in risk taking, the effects of emotion on decision weights, the role of fear in predictions of harm and the role of liking and disliking in factual predictions — all indicate that the traditional separation between belief and preference in analyses of decision making is psychologically unrealistic" (Kahneman, 2003, p. 1470).

1.2 An Extended Model of Decision Making — via Interactions with Others

In a broader sense, a new breed of interdisciplinary economist is also looking at the role of emotions and value in decision making processes where economic agents interact with other agents in society. The role of emotions and decisions to cooperate with others or to compete with them are important components of these interactions. These behavioral economists are often interested in more interdisciplinary approaches and believe that anthropology, psychology, political science, sociology, ethics and moral philosophy have an important contribution to make to economic analysis. They are not tied to a fine distinction between positive and normative judgments. They acknowledge the interdependence between economics, psychology, ethics and politics. They also acknowledge the need to make normative judgments in a more general way than strict neoclassical economists do.

These economists also relate well to social scientists in other disciplines such as anthropology, sociology and psychology where individual motivations can differ and where culture plays an important role in decision making. Douglas, Thomson and Verweij (2003) construct a diagram (see Figure 1.1) which relates an axis of competitiveness and cooperation (which they call low group and high group) against an axis of low versus high social mobility (which they refer to as high grid and low grid). The authors go on to indicate that in a low mobility/high grid environment, there are many rules that prescribe people's roles in society. Conversely in a low grid/high mobility environment, there are fewer rules to conform to group behavior and

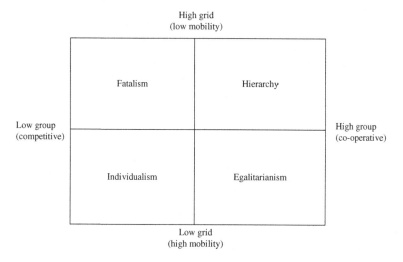

Figure 1.1 Axis of Competitiveness and Cooperation

Source: Douglas, Thomson and Verweij (2003, Figure 1).

Note: Some modifications to the title of the original figure have been made by the authors.

which constrain action. For example, the Mormons have specific and rigid rules that constrain the members of the religion. Similarly, in monasteries, the military and other rigid organizations, there are many rules that constrain behavior.

As a result of these rules, members will have different demands for goods and services than the "average" person. Mormons do not drink or use alcohol; they tithe and follow other codes. These rules constrain their consumption patterns. Monks take vows of poverty and chastity which constrain their participation in the market for goods and services.

Combined with tendencies toward competition or cooperation, we can group behavior according to four categories described in the four quadrants of Figure 1.1. These groupings and the names associated with them can be used to categorize different attitudes that members have toward different public issues as well as describing how they develop preferences for goods and services. The typical agent as described by conventional economic theory will fall in the lower left quadrant designated as "Individualism". Economic man is selfish and competitive; he values free choice and is also quite mobile physically, economically, socially and psychologically. Those with similar attitudes toward social mobility but with greater emphasis on social justice would fall in the lower right hand quadrant labeled "Egalitarianism". In the upper right hand quadrant labeled "Hierarchy" we have members of the religious and militaristic organizations. Those in the upper left hand quadrant are constrained by social laws and customs and at the same time are very competitive. This is a rather strange group and the authors have labeled them "Fatalists". Perhaps the existentialists of the French school such as Camus and Satre would fit into this category.

The introduction of these different categories at this juncture in this book is meant to give the reader some idea of possible alternatives to the standard model of economics. To break out of the narrow box that economists have drawn for themselves with their restrictive neo-classical economic theory, economists need to consider what happens when they move out of the lower left hand quadrant. Kahneman *et al.* (1986a, b) noted, for example, that there is no role for generosity and social conscience or even goodwill or indignation in economic theory. They also note that it is embarrassing to the economics profession that people vote, give to charity, take altruist actions, and do not always free ride or apply rules of equity when allocating resources between themselves and others, rather than following a "take it all" strategy.

All of these behaviors are left unexplained by conventional neo-classical analysis. There are many other examples including the role of trust, fairness, revenge and other emotions in decision making. Kahneman and his colleagues are among a group of social scientists (see Kahneman, 2003, for references) who are questioning whether other approaches are needed to explain these sorts of behavior (see also Camerer *et al.,* 2004).

These social scientists realize that to obtain better insights into behavior we need to expand our scope of reference to include topics which are normally considered to be beyond economics, such as fairness, happiness, trust and justice. In this new approach to decision making and economic analysis, we can still apply some of the tools of economics. However, we have to develop a different platform to analyze and evaluate what generally motivates human behavior. Much of this analysis has to do with how individuals interact with others in an economic setting and how these actions depend upon emotional factors and ethical value systems. Looking at how people make decisions from such an expanded perspective also enables us to explain aspects of behavior which are hard to understand using conventional tools of economic analysis.

1.3 Taste

In one way these aspects of behavior go beyond conventional analysis by looking at the concept of "taste" in a more detailed way. Broadly, taste reflects a predisposition toward buying and consuming particular goods or services. It can also be associated with emotional attitudes toward different people or social situations. Taste is widely used by economists to describe the utility or satisfaction derived by behavior or consumption patterns. While taste may influence decision making, such as having a taste for discrimination or cooperation in the ways described by Becker (1981), there have been limited consideration of how tastes are formulated and adjusted. A perspective that considers taste in a more systematic way allows us to look at normative questions that economics ordinarily shy away from.

1.4 Ethics and Happiness

There are emotional as well as ethical, moral and cooperative/altruistic factors that play a strong role in motivating human behavior. For example, we can explore fairness and what people view as fair and unfair decisions and practices. Trust and justice can be viewed from both a behavioral and ethical standpoint while using tools of economic analysis. The concept of happiness or subjective well-being is important and we discuss what factors increase well-being. We can also explore the issue of the provision of public goods from an ethical perspective and consider the provision of some goods which we call "merit goods" from a normative point of view. These "merit goods" are essentially private goods that are important enough to society that the wishes of consumers are over-ruled and more of these goods are provided than would occur under consumer sovereignty. The decision to supply merit goods is a matter of judgment and another area where ethical considerations are involved.

1.5 The Road Ahead

We begin the substantive discussion of these issues in Chapter 2, with a short introduction to the standard neoclassical description of the theory of the consumer and how this relates to the theory of markets and of the efficiency of an economic system in allocating resources in production through competition. This discussion is at an elementary level and is not mathematical in nature. However, it does give the reader an important background glimpse of the values, methods and approach of economic analysis.

In doing so, we recognize the importance of the concept of utility and satisfaction in the formulation of economic models of behavior, the role of competition, the importance of making rational choices and the elevation of economic efficiency to a position of prominence in decision making. This chapter also provides the reader with an ability to move on to discuss other aspects of economic behavior from the platform of "conventional" utility maximization. We begin with the standard analysis of the economic solution to utility maximization to show the importance that some economists put on subjective views of utility aside from pure utilitarianism. The importance of normative as well as positive judgments is discussed. Utility maximization and Pareto optimality are also briefly reviewed.

Chapter 3 looks more closely at the way in which decisions are affected by perception and interpretation. The chapter examines individual decision making within the context of bounded rationality and the psychology of behavioral economics. Often, conventional analysis of decision making using expected utility theory has to be augmented by new concepts such as prospect theory and the framing of choices developed by Kahneman and others. The chapter also investigates the pivotal role of emotions. It looks at attitudes toward risk and how attachment to possessions influences behavior. Using various psychological approaches, we discover that knowledge or information that is more accessible is valued and acted upon more systematically than information that is less accessible. We also learn that changes or departures from equilibrium or a given situation are often more important than the levels of attainment or the absolute size of variables. This is important in the analysis of many economic phenomena including the pursuit of happiness. Further, the chapter explores the use of heuristics to evaluate the likelihood of various uncertain outcomes. Prospect theory looks at the way agents make decisions in terms of the context, or what Kahneman calls "framing". This methodology leads to a number of surprising conclusions that are often at odds with conventional economic analysis. Sometimes, conventional expected utility analysis can be replaced by evaluation of alternatives that takes cognizance of other factors such as the size of the probabilities of alternative outcomes and the way that problems are framed with reference to probabilities of success and failure. They also include a possible reversal of a decision when only the wording of a problem is changed. Prospect theory throws new light on the risk return trade-off and it shows behavior is sensitive to the probabilities of different patterns of outcomes. The subject of risk and the process by which consumers and investors make decisions in a sequential manner is also considered within the general framework of prospect theory.

In Chapter 4, our attention shifts from the individual to decision making in a societal context. We first discuss game theory as a tool for exploring the relationship between self-interest and cooperation as they relate to how economic agents interact with others. Cooperation and self-interest is discussed within this game theoretic context. Various strategies are discussed for resolving conflicts including win/win and lose/lose games. We begin with an intuitive introduction to game theory and the concept of Nash equilibrium. Ways to break out of lose/lose situations are also discussed and strategies for bargaining are explored.

The concepts of trust, fairness and social pressure are also examined within the game theoretic context. The situations in which people tend to cooperate and how these situations differ from more competitive environments are then reviewed. The range of inquiry is extended to a broader understanding of motivations for actions, including the role of emotions and a sense of ethics and morality. Pressure from society, including friends and associates, is considered within the context of ultimatum and dictator games as well as the standard prisoner dilemma and public goods games. The concept of a "warm glow" arising from altruistic actions is also discussed within the context of game theory. How are motivations altered by the recognition of this "warm glow" that arises from a selfless or charitable or cooperative action? These kinds of altruistic or cooperative actions or tendencies are then related to other topics that are covered in subsequent chapters including public choice, charity and family exchanges and bequests.

Chapter 5 extends the analysis begun in Chapter 4 to the subject of altruism. The concepts of "pure" and "conditional" altruism are considered along with a number of exceptions and extensions to the "standard" economic maximization model that may be explained by altruistic or cooperative motives. An expanded framework that includes cooperative as well as competitive motives can explain these "exceptions". Characteristics of the products we buy and our attitudes toward them as well as the social context and developments in the workplace have a direct bearing on prices and economic choices. These include decision making within the family that involves aspects of cooperation rather than competition. This chapter draws on the work of Becker (1981) and Stark (1989) among others to explore a number of cases where altruistic and cooperative motives lead to results that differ from the standard neoclassical economic models.

In Chapter 6, we explore the general field of happiness or subjective well-being. We consider the question, "Does *utility* bring happiness?" We explore research which suggests that happiness is often not directly equated with the economist's concept of utility maximization. The chapter explores happiness and how it relates to the utilitarian concepts of economics that stress the accumulation of goods and services subject to constraints on income. Much of the research in this area suggests that the economic calculus of the utilitarian school needs to be modified to take into account a number of other factors, including leisure and social relationships, as determinants of happiness and social well-being. Within this context we then explore different aspects of happiness including the relationship between income and happiness, the role of trust, the importance of social interaction as a determinant of happiness, how fairness enters into establishing a social environment where happiness can flourish, and the role of government policy in formulating policies that can increase the level of happiness in society. In this section, we draw on the work of Lane (2000), Frank (1999) and Layard (2004) among others. There is also reference made to the historical literature including Scitovsky (1976) and early work by Veblen (1899). One objective of this chapter is to show that the concept of happiness is complex and depends upon many aspects other than "utility" in the economic sense. It is demonstrated that often, the concept of "relative utility" is more important than "absolute utility". It is also the purpose of this chapter to show that happiness requires a broader definition of welfare economics than we usually see in economics courses. Emotions often intervene to cause changes in behavior and possible reversal in decisions typified by the term "buyer's remorse". Other behavioral anomalies are also observed such as valuing the present more than the future and the importance of comparisons with others. The importance of leisure and spending time with family and friends is highlighted and found to be very important in many societies. On the other hand, unemployment and poor health have strong negative impacts on happiness. This ties in with the topics discussed previously regarding the importance of ethical virtues and the value of cooperation and building of social capital. The inability of most people to judge when others are happy and to determine what makes them happy is also discussed. Social ramifications of breakdown in family and kinship groups, and the lack of or deterioration in social capital that leads to crime, corruption and other antisocial behavior are investigated. The research in this area suggests reasons for valuing high status in one group and unwillingness to move to a lower status in another group, even though monetary rewards are higher. Discrimination among social groups and the theory of lemons by George Akerlof (1970) is also reviewed as it relates to the emotional content of economic decision making.

We introduce ways to increase happiness by increasing the opportunity for forming cohesive social groups and creating social capital. Making sound choices to maximize the chance of happiness are covered. This chapter also discusses differences between traditional and modern societies and the way societies and people change as development takes place, and as they have more money. Suggestions for changing the incentive system include the role of government to intervene when people generally make poor choices like providing for their own retirement.

In Chapter 7, we extend our analysis further to consider how societies create social systems where formation of social capital can take place. We study aspects of cooperation and altruism as contrasted with competition and narrow self-interest, and how these different perspectives influence participation and integration into the social capital network. "Social capital" can more generally be defined as the ethical and socially responsible actions of individuals as well as the ability of people to work together for common purposes in groups and organizations. See Putnam (1995, 2000) and Temple and Johnson (1998) for discussion of definitions of social capital.

We argue that the formation of "social capital" — broadly defined to include trust, fairness and collective action flowing from cooperation and social cohesion — are important components of the social and economic fabric of societies. In this view, the social virtues and ethical attitudes that promote the development and nurturing of social capital contribute positively to both income growth and the feeling of well-being and happiness in the general population.

Ethical issues for the individual as well as societies are discussed within the broader context of economic efficiency and operation of cooperative behavior and the formation of social capital. Market failure, public goods, free riders, principal agent, tragedy of the commons, overexploitation of resources, moral hazard, corruption, ethics and economic decision making are all touched upon. How these issues relate to the propensity for cooperation and competition is also explored. The potential benefits that accrue from cooperative action and the development of social capital are explained and discussed. Fairness, trust and social isolation are also discussed within the context of the formation of social capital and participation in social capital networks. Furthermore, the material presented ties into other topics discussed in particular field courses in economics such as altruism and the general case of market failure including the environmental literature, as well as selective readings from welfare economics.

Welfare economics and collective action are considered in more detail in the next two chapters. In Chapter 8, we take into account the collective action which occurs when individuals decide as a group to take actions that increase the collective benefit of the group. This could take the form of private clubs and institutions. Clubs provide a private alternative to the provision of public goods and the challenges clubs face in such provision of goods is further explored using game theory. In addition, the reasons why clubs are formed, persist and dissolve are explored. The ramifications of club actions on the general public are also discussed along with numerous examples of how clubs work to further the interests of their members to the detriment of overall welfare. The work of Olson (1965) plays a critical role in this chapter.

In Chapter 9, we consider the general question of public goods. We discuss the nature of public goods including what kind of goods are provided by the public, why they are provided and how the provision of such goods is influenced by motives such as altruism and selfishness. Analysis of public choice decisions, particularly charitable giving and role of private versus public charity, are explored. The importance of motives for charitable giving and how these motives interact with the supply of public goods by the government are reviewed. The work of Warr (1982), Andreoni (1988) and Akerlof (1970) among others are discussed. Emphasis is placed on how particular motivations for private giving would influence charity when public goods are introduced or when the supply of public goods is increased. Substitutions between public and private giving is also discussed and analyzed, as well as motivation for private charity. As an undesirable aspect of public choice, we also look at the topic of corruption, graft and bribery in this chapter. We explore motives for corruption and how these motives are influenced by the economic and ethical environment. Incentives for corruption and how they relate to cooperative and altruistic motives and economic incentives are also explored. Several country examples are presented. In concluding this chapter, we discuss how altruism fits in the picture and also how the allocation and provision of merit goods requires ethical analysis and careful consideration of public policy.

In Chapter 10, we consider income distribution, the theory of justice and how decisions are made to allocate public resources to redistribute income. The philosophy of social justice is discussed, including the work of John Rawls (1993), James Buchanan (1976a), Robert Nozick (1977) and Amartya Sen (1995). Different approaches to the concept of social justice and the way in which the market interacts with the government are also discussed. Values such as efficiency, equity and social context are explored to see how they inform the discussion of income distribution and justice. The philosophy of Buchanan

(1976b) and Nozick (1977) places particular emphasis on the process by which decision making is carried out by the government, while Rawls (1993) and Sen (1995) emphasize the outcomes of the process. The importance of fairness in determining justice is discussed along with the motivation for adjusting the distribution of income. The importance of achieving an ethical stance and how to incorporate the views of a wide variety of public opinion are explored along with the difficulties in arriving at a solution that values the opinions of both the minority and the majority. Different ways of achieving social justice including capitalistic and socialist solutions as well as different forms of government are also analyzed. The importance of fairness, justice and happiness are incorporated into the discussion.

Bibliography

Akerlof, G.A. (1970) The Market for 'Lemons': Quality Uncertainty and the Market Mechanism. *Quarterly Journal of Economics*, 84(3), 488–500.

Andreoni, J. (1988) Privately Provided Public Goods in a Large Economy: The Limits of Altruism. *Journal of Public Economics*, 35, 57–73.

Becker, G.S. (1976) Altruism, Egoism and Genetic Fitness: Economics and Sociobiology. *Journal of Economic Literature*, 14(3), 817–826.

Becker, G.S. (1981) Altruism in the Family and Selfishness in the Marketplace. *Economica*, 48(189), 1–15.

Buchanan, J.M. (1976a) Barro on the Ricardian Equivalence Theorem. *Journal of Political Economy*, 84(2), 337–342.

Buchanan, J.M. (1976b) A Hobbesian Interpretation of the Rawlsian Difference Principle. *Kyklos*, 29(1), 5–25.

Camerer, C.F., G. Loewenstein and M. Rabin (eds.) (2004) *Advances in Behavioral Economics*. Princeton, New Jersey: Princeton University Press.

Douglas, M., M. Thompson and M. Verweij (2003) Is Time Running Out? The Case of Global Warming. *Daedelus*, 132(1), 98–107.

Drèze, J. and A.K. Sen (1989) *Hunger and Public Action*. Oxford: Clarendon Press.

Frank, R.H. (1999) *Luxury Fever: Why Money Fails to Satisfy in an Era of Excess*. New York: Free Press. (Princeton University Press, paperback edition.)

Kahneman, D. (2003) Maps of Bounded Rationality: Psychology for Behavioral Economics. *American Economic Review*, 93(5), 1449–1475.

Kahneman, D., J.L. Knetsch and R.H. Thaler (1986a) Fairness and the Assumptions of Economics. *Journal of Business*, 59(4), S285–S300.

Kahneman, D., J.L. Knetsch and R.H. Thaler (1986b) Fairness as a Constraint on Profit Seeking: Entitlements in the Market. *American Economic Review*, 76(4), 728–741.

Lane, R.E. (2000) *The Loss of Happiness in Market Democracies*. New Haven, CT: Yale University Press.

Layard, R. (2004) *Happiness: Lessons from a New Science*. New York: Penguin Press.

Ng, Y.K. (2002a) The East-Asian Happiness Gap: Speculating on Causes and Implications. *Pacific Economic Review*, 7(1), 51–63.

Ng, Y.K. (2002b) Economic Policies in the Light of Happiness Studies with Reference to Singapore. *The Singapore Economic Review*, 47(2), 199–212.

Ng, Y.K. (2003) From Preferences to Happiness: Toward a More Complex Welfare Economics. *Social Choice and Welfare*, 20, 307–350.

Nozick, R. (1977) *Anarchy, State and Utopia*. New York: Basic Books.

Olson, M. (1965) *The Logic of Collective Action*. Cambridge: Harvard University Press.

Putnam, R. (1995) Bowling Alone: America's Declining Social Capital. *Journal of Democracy*, 6, 65–78.

Putnam, R. (2000) *Bowling Alone: The Collapse and Revival of American Community*. New York: Simon and Schuster.

Rawls, J. (1993) *Political Liberalism*. New York: Columbia University Press.

Scitovsky, T. (1976) *The Joyless Economy: In Inquiry into Human Satisfaction and Dissatisfaction*. Oxford: Oxford University Press.

Sen, A.K. (1970) *Collective Choice and Social Welfare*. San Francisco: Holden-Day. Republished Amsterdam: North-Holland.

Sen, A.K. (1984) *Resources, Values and Development*. Oxford: Blackwell; Cambridge/Mass.: Harvard University Press.

Sen, A.K. (1985a) *Commodities and Capabilities*. Amsterdam: North-Holland.

Sen, A.K. (1985b) Well-being, Agency and Freedom: The Dewey Lectures 1984. *Journal of Philosophy*, 82(4), 169–221.

Sen, A.K. (1990) Justice: Means versus Freedoms. *Philosophy and Public Affairs*, 19(2), 111–121.

Sen, A.K. (1995) Rationality and Social Choice. *American Economic Review*, 85(1), 1–24.

Sen, A.K. (1999) *Development as Freedom*. New York: Alfred A. Knopf.

Simon, H. (1972) Theories of Bounded Rationality. In R. Radner and C.B. McGuire (eds.), *Decision and Organisation*. Amsterdam: North-Holland.

Simon, H. (1982) *Models of Bounded Rationality*. Cambridge, MA: MIT Press.

Stark, O. (1989) Altruism and the Quality of Life. *American Economic Review*, 79(2), 86–90.

Temple, J. and P.A. Johnson (1998) Social Capital and Economic Growth. *Quarterly Journal of Economics*, 113, 965–990.

Tversky, A. and D. Kahneman (1986) Rational Choice and the Framing of Decisions. *Journal of Business*, 59(4), S251–S278.

Veblen, T. (1899) *The Theory of the Leisure Class: An Economic Study of Institutions.* New York: The Macmillan Company.

Warr, P. (1982) Pareto Optimal Redistribution and Private Charity. *Journal of Public Economics*, 19, 131–138.

Warr, P. (1983) The Private Provision of Public Goods is Independent of the Distribution of Income. *Economics Letters*, 13, 207–211.

Chapter 2

The Standard Model of the Household — Microfoundations of Consumer Behavior

In this chapter, we build a model of decision making by individuals and household based on the standard assumptions of utility maximization. In this model, consumers face an indifference map when considering purchases of commodities and maximize utility subject to an income constraint. The choice process assumes that preferences are fixed and information about relative prices is known by everyone. There are no risks and uncertainties. Furthermore, there are assumed to be no costs to acquiring this information. In such a world, consumers maximize their satisfaction by equating the marginal satisfaction across all goods so that no increase in utility can be achieved by changing the mix of goods purchased. Adjustments in demand arise from changes in taste or changes in relative price. The aspects of this model are addressed briefly and the exposition is illustrated by a series of diagrams.

2.1 In Pursuit of Happiness

Traditional economics has described economic agents as rational beings who strive to maximize their happiness or utility per se. Happiness and utility are interchangeable in this model. Happiness arises from the purchase of goods and services. Other possible sources of happiness or utility are ignored in this narrow version of what has become known as the neoclassical model of consumer choice. In simple layman terms, individuals strive to maximize happiness from their choice of consumption of goods and services, given the limitations on income and relative prices. Individuals are assumed to be completely rational in the sense that reversal of preferences is not allowed and the transitive laws of mathematics hold for everyone. For example, if *A* is preferred to *B* and *B* is preferred to *C*, then *A* is preferred to *C*. Consumers are assumed to act exclusively in their own interests. Behavior motivated by other factors such as altruism is not taken into account, although such actions are not explicitly prohibited.

Consumption of goods and services would apparently satisfy the individual's need for satisfaction and increase his level of happiness in a monotonic way. The more goods and services an individual consumes, the greater his level of happiness. In this chapter, we only concentrate on consumption goods and ignore investment goods where current consumption is foregone in favor of consumption sometime in the future.

2.2   Utility: The Economics Profession's Name for Happiness

"That which we call a rose, By any other name would smell as sweet."

William Shakespeare, 1564–1616
Romeo and Juliet, II, ii.43

Individuals pay for the stream of satisfaction that goods and services provide. Economists call this level of satisfaction "utility". The satisfaction or utility derived from the good can be measured in terms of what economists call "utils". The higher the level of utils, the higher level of satisfaction that is derived from it. Perishable goods provide utils over a short period of time. A loaf of bread has a certain number of utils and they are exhausted when the final slice is consumed. A car or a house, on the other hand, supplies services for many years. Note that the level of utils assigned to a particular good is just based on the subjective evaluation of the individual's satisfaction from consuming the good. This may vary from individual to individual and also over time for the same individual.

Because wants are unlimited and our resources are limited, people have to make choices all the time. In making these choices, individuals will have to rank the utility of the different consumption items in order to be able to make rational choices. Therefore, one of the most important tasks confronting consumers is how to order these choices. How wants are ordered would depend on the varying level of utility assigned to different goods. A higher level of utility would imply a higher level of want, thus being higher up the scale and vice versa.

For instance, if Mr X, who does not own a car, wants to travel from Bugis to Tampines in Singapore, he has the choice of taking a bus, train or cab. Each option offers the utility of satisfying his want. Each involves different sacrifices of money and time and offer different associated utilities of convenience and comfort. Thus, his choice would depend on whether he is in a hurry or whether he wants to spend the extra money on the cab, or if he prefers to take the bus. It may also depend on whether he prefers to enjoy an air-conditioned taxi ride or squeeze in a bus or train with other passengers.

2.3 Total Utility and Marginal Utility: What Goes Up Must Come Down

The greater the number of goods and services an individual consumes, the greater his level of total utility (refer to Figure 2.1). However, the increase in the level of utility gained by the individual from consuming an additional unit of the same good will eventually be less and less. Economists call this diminishing marginal utility. Marginal utility (MU) is the increment to total utility (ΔTU) resulting from the consumption of an extra unit of good (ΔQ). It is defined as the change in the total utility for a good when the quantity purchased is changed:

$$MU = \frac{\Delta TU}{Q}. \qquad (1)$$

This general observation that consumers derive less satisfaction from additional consumption is called the Law of Diminishing Marginal Utility. Suppose an individual is consuming chocolates. Initially, the marginal utility from consuming the first chocolate is very high. The marginal utility from the second, third and successive chocolates diminish. If he is so greedy that he finishes the entire box of chocolates, he might be sick and get negative marginal utility. This is demonstrated graphically in Figure 2.2 by the declining height of the vertical utility lines with additional consumption of chocolates. In this

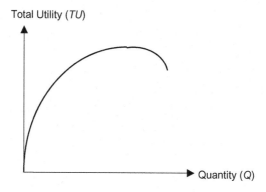

Figure 2.1 Total Utility

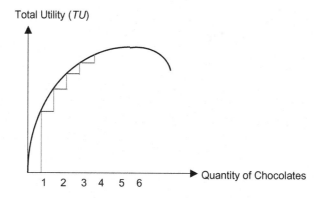

Figure 2.2 Marginal Utility

example, after around five to six chocolates, total utility begins to fall and the marginal utility declines instead of increasing.

Other things being constant, as more and more units of a commodity are consumed, the additional satisfaction or utility derived from the consumption of each successive unit will eventually decrease. In simple layman terms,

- The *less* of the good which I possess, the *more* I value it and the *higher* the level of marginal utility.
- The *more* of the good which I already possess, the *less* I value it and the *lower* the level of marginal utility.

Hence the individual, with fixed income and a given market price of goods, will attain maximum utility only when the marginal utility (*MU*) of the last dollar spent on each good is equivalent to that spent on any other good:

$$\frac{MU_x}{P_x} = \frac{MU_y}{P_y} = \frac{MU_z}{P_z}. \tag{2}$$

2.4 Utility Maximization

The rational individual will always act in his self-interest; hence he will always choose the consumption bundle that maximizes his utility given the prevailing market prices and his limited income. The following property is thus satisfied:

$$\max\ u(x) \text{ such that } px \le m, \tag{3}$$

where *u*: utility,

      x: consumption bundle,

      p: vector of prices of goods,

      m: fixed amount of money available to a consumer.

Graphically, this may be illustrated by the intersection of the individual's indifference curve, which represents his choice of consumption bundle for a certain level of utility, and budget constraint, which represents the level of purchasing power of the individual.

2.4.1 *Indifference curves*

An indifference curve is a graph linking all the combinations of two goods (consumption bundles) which provide the same level of utility for an individual, group of people or community. It is called an indifference curve because the people are indifferent to which combination of goods they consume since the level of utility for both combinations are the same. Individuals would be indifferent between points *a*, *b* and *c* on indifference curve U_1 (see Figure 2.3). Also, since individuals are rational, they would prefer more of a good than less of

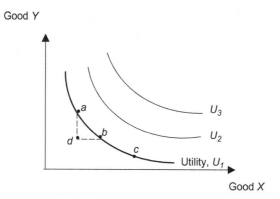

Figure 2.3 Indifference Curve

a good (non-satiation). The higher the indifference curve, the greater the level of utility enjoyed. Indifference curve U_3 has greater level of utility than U_2 and U_1.

The rate at which an individual is willing to exchange one unit of a good for units of another *without changing total utility* is known as the marginal rate of substitution (*MRS*). *MRS* is measured by the slope of the indifference curve:

$$MRS = \frac{MU_x}{MU_y}. \tag{4}$$

By referring to Figure 2.3, we see that *MRS* measures the amount of Good Y that the individual is prepared to sacrifice in return for one additional unit of Good X *without changing total utility*. Alternatively, it could measure the amount of Good X that the individual is prepared to sacrifice in return for one additional unit of Good Y *without changing total utility*. In moving from *a* to *b*, the *MRS* is *bd/ad*.

Individuals exhibit diminishing marginal rate of substitution all the time. In order to obtain an additional unit of one good, individuals would only be prepared to give up less and less of the other good (diminishing quantities) when the level of utility is held constant; the rationale being that once they obtained more units of one good, the less they would value it, and thus they would not be prepared to sacrifice as many units of Good Y as before. This behavior is consistent with the law of diminishing marginal utility.

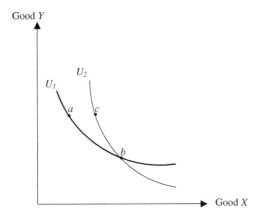

Figure 2.4 Why Indifference Curves Should Not Intersect

Indifference curves exhibit certain properties. Firstly, they slope downwards from the left to the right. Since individuals are assumed to be rational, if they give up some quantity of Good Y, they will want more of Good X in order to keep utility unchanged. This will therefore imply a negative, or inverse, slope for the indifference curve. Secondly, indifference curves are convex and bend inwards towards the origin. Lastly, indifference curves cannot intersect as this would violate the principle of transitivity. If they intersected, the individual should be indifferent between a and b on the indifference curve U_1 and between b and c on U_2, and hence he should also be indifferent between a and c (see Figure 2.4). But this reasoning does not hold as c offers more quantities of both goods than a.

2.4.2 Budget constraint

Note that the indifference curve is not a demand curve, thus it does not tell us how much of a good individuals are likely to buy. The indifference curve only indicates the relative preferences between different goods, and this indifference curve may extend as far as we like as the amount of the two goods increases. In order to find out the total quantities of a good that individuals are likely to buy with this level of income, we will have to apply the budget constraint.

The budget constraint describes the various combinations of the two goods that the individual can purchase with *a given level of income*. The total amount of goods that the individual is able to purchase depends on the price of the good itself (P) and amount of income available (m):

$$P_x X + P_y Y = m. \qquad (5)$$

For instance, if an individual has an income of $40, he can spend his income on having a hamburger at McDonald's and/or going to the cinema. Suppose the price of a hamburger is $4 and the price of a cinema ticket is $8. If the individual does not consume any hamburgers at McDonald's, he can spend all of his income on the movies. This way, he would be able to see five movies (Income/Price of a cinema ticket = $40/$8). At the other extreme, the person may not go to the movies and spend all his income at McDonald's. In this case he can buy 10 McDonald's meals (Income/Price of McDonald hamburger = $40/$4).

Alternatively and (perhaps) more sensibly, he could have a hamburger as well as go to the movie. For instance, he could go to the cinema twice ($8 × 2) and also consume six McDonald meals [($40 – $16)/$4 = 6].

The budget line in Figure 2.5 shows the maximum quantities of two good that can be afforded given the budget (income) available for spending. Points above the budget line are unaffordable. Points below the budget line would allow the consumer to move up to the budget line and undertake additional spending.

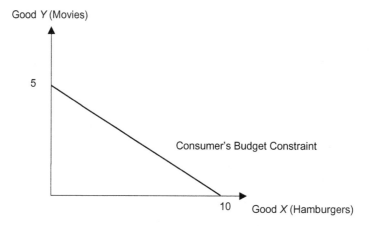

Figure 2.5 Budget Constraint

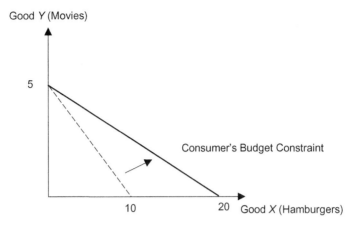

Figure 2.6　Effects of a Fall in Price X

The slope of the budget constraint depends on the *ratio of the prices of the two goods* (Px/Py). Px represents the price of Good X and Py represents the price of Good Y. Therefore,

$$\text{Slope of budget constraint} = Px/Py.$$

For instance, in our example of hamburgers and movies, the slope of the budget constraint = Price of hamburgers/Price of cinema tickets = \$4/\$8 = 1/2.

A change in the price of any of the goods will cause the budget constraint to pivot along the axis, and will change the slope of the budget constraint (Px/Py). Given that the price of movies remains unchanged, suppose the price of a McDonald's hamburger falls from \$4 to \$2, the individual will be able to afford double the number of McDonald hamburgers than before (Income/Price of McDonald's hamburger = \$40/\$2). As shown in Figure 2.6, the budget constraint pivots along the y-axis and becomes gentler.

A change in the level of income will not affect the slope of the budget constraint; it will lead to a parallel shift of the budget constraint instead depending on the amount of increase or decrease in income. An increase in the level of income of the individual will shift the budget constraint to the right, as the individual can buy more units of both Good X and Y than before (see Figure 2.7). On the other hand, a decrease in the level of income of the individual will shift the budget constraint to

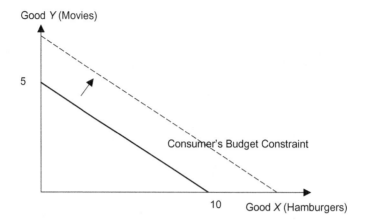

Figure 2.7 Effects of an Increase in Income

the left, as the individual is poorer than before, so he is no longer able to afford the amount of Good X and Y that he used to consume.

2.4.3 *Consumer equilibrium*

The budget constraint shows the various consumption bundles that the individual can afford with his given level of income. The indifference curve shows the various consumption bundles that give the individual the same level of utility. Hence, the individual will choose the consumption bundle that maximizes his utility with a given level of income. This is shown by the intersection of the indifference curve and the budget constraint line at point *b* in Figure 2.8. Note that points *a* and *c* are on the budget constraint but on a lower indifference curve. The consumer will maximize his utility by moving to a higher indifference curve which is just tangent to the budget line at *b*. At consumer equilibrium, the slopes of the indifference curve and the budget constraints are equivalent. This happens when choosing a new combination of X and Y places the consumer on a higher indifference curve, giving him a higher level of satisfaction:

$$\frac{MU_x}{MU_y} = \frac{P_x}{P_y}. \tag{6}$$

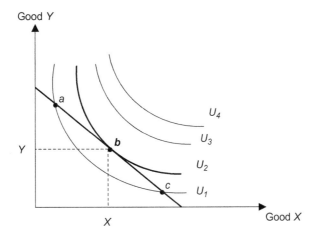

Figure 2.8 The Optimal Consumption Point

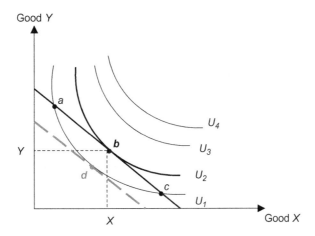

Figure 2.9 Effect of a Fall in Income

2.4.4 *Effect of a change in income*

Assume there is a change in the level of income of the individual. This would lead to a corresponding parallel shift for the budget constraint. For instance, if the individual's income declines, his budget constraint would parallel shift inwards, thus his optimal consumption of Goods X and Y would be less than before (at point d in Figure 2.9) and vice versa.

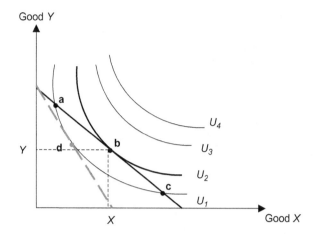

Figure 2.10 Effect of a Rise in the Price of Good X

2.4.5 *Effect of a change in price*

Assume there is an increase in the price of Good X. Hence, Good X is more expensive than before and the former consumption equilibrium at point b is no longer attainable. The budget constraint pivots inwards with its intercept on the y-axis unchanged. The amount of Good Y is unchanged since the price of Good Y remains constant. The new tangency point is at point d in Figure 2.10.

2.4.6 *Demand and supply curves*

When the preferences of many people are added together, we can arrive at a demand curve for a good. The demand curve relates the price and quantity combinations for a particular good aggregated over all the individuals who might buy or demand the good (see Figure 2.11).

When quantity demanded is unresponsive to changes in price, then demand is said to be inelastic. Can you think of commodities where the demand is inelastic? Conversely, when the demand is very responsive to changes in price, then demand is said to be elastic. Similar definitions are made for supply curves (see Figures 2.12 and 2.13).

A rational individual will choose to undertake an activity if the gain exceeds the cost of doing so. Hence, consumers will choose to

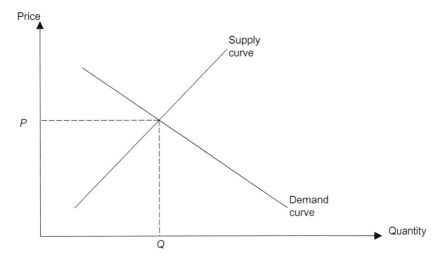

Figure 2.11 Intersection of Demand and Supply Curves

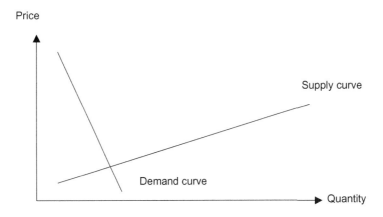

Figure 2.12 Inelastic Demand and Elastic Supply

consume as long as marginal benefits exceed marginal costs. The marginal benefit of consuming is the consumer's marginal utility (MU) and the marginal cost is the price (P) that he has to pay to consume the good. So he will consume until $MU = P$ (see Figure 2.14). A customer going to McDonald's will continue buying burgers as long as his MU is greater than the cost of the burger. Likewise, producers will

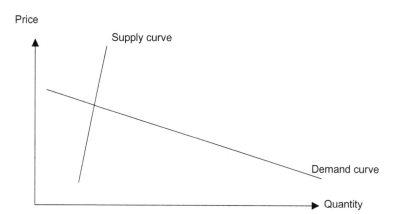

Figure 2.13 Elastic Demand and Inelastic Supply

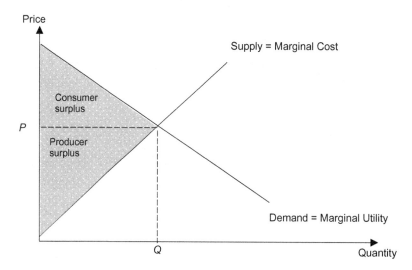

Figure 2.14 Demand and Supply in the Perfect Market

produce as long as their marginal benefits exceed their marginal cost. Their marginal benefit is the marginal revenue they get from selling an additional unit. Hence, they will continue to produce as long as P exceeds their marginal cost (see Figure 2.14).

Consumer surplus is the economic gain accruing to a consumer when they engage in trade. The gain is the difference between the price they are willing to pay and the actual price. If someone is willing to pay more than the actual price, their benefit in a transaction is how much they saved when they did not pay that price. The aggregate consumer surplus is the sum of the consumer surplus for each individual consumer. This can be represented on a supply and demand figure. If demand is given as the diagonal line from the price axis to the quantity axis, then the consumer surplus, where Supply = Marginal Cost in Figure 2.14, is the triangle above the line formed by price P to the intersection of demand and supply curves (bounded on the left by the price axis and on the top by the demand line). Similarly, the producer surplus is the amount that producers benefit by selling at a market price that is higher than they would be willing to sell for. In Figure 2.14, it is the area in the triangle bounded by the price axis, the Supply = Marginal Cost curve and the price line drawn from P to the intersection of demand and supply curves.

2.5 An Efficient Market — The Invisible Hand Adjustment

Changes in demand or supply will automatically cause markets to adjust to a new equilibrium. This is what Adam Smith (1776) termed the market economy. Since participants act in their self-interest, the market will attain equilibrium as if guided by an "invisible hand". The following is his description of the interaction of supply and demand:

> Man has almost constant occasion for the help of his brethren and it is vain for him to expect it from their benevolence only. He will be more likely to prevail if he can interest their self-love in his favour, and show them it is for their own advantage to do for him what he requires of them... It is not from their benevolence of the butcher, the brewer, or the baker that we expect our dinner, but from their regard to their own self-interest.

> Every individual...neither intends to promote the public interest, nor know how much he is promoting it... He intends only his own gain, and his is in this, as in many other cases, led by an invisible hand to promote an end which was no part of his intention. Nor is it always worse for the society that was no part of it. By pursuing his own interest he frequently promotes that of the society more effectually than when he really intends to promote it.

The price mechanism guided by the invisible hand of individual's self-interest will ensure the efficient allocation of resources. Whether the price is high or low will depend on the demand for and supply of the good.

The principles of economics can thus be summarized as:

(1) The rational man acts in his self-interest to maximize expected utility;
(2) By acting on his self-interest, he also promotes the self-interest of the society through an efficient market.

2.6 Conclusion

This is a very general introduction to the forces of microeconomics and markets. We have not discussed any details such as the forces of competition and aspects of monopoly or oligopoly or how they influence the efficiency of markets. Nor have we gone into situations where private competitive markets do not exist or when agents do not have all the information at hand that they need to make decisions in the market. What we have done is set the stage for going beyond the assumptions of the model described in Sections 2.1–2.5, and look at what happens when we relax the various assumptions.

This book will attempt to analyze its validity by incorporating issues like irrationality, attitudes towards risk and other variables that have a motivating factor on decision making such as altruism, ethics, trust, fairness, justice and the role of emotions. By widening the scope of inquiry beyond a narrow interpretation of economic theory, we are able to better understand the motivations of "economic actors", how people make choices and how it affects their well-being and happiness.

Bibliography

Samuelson, P.A. and W.D. Nordhaus (2005) *Microeconomics*. Boston, Massachusetts: Irwin/McGraw-Hill.
Sloman, J. and M. Sutcliff (2003) *Economics*. New York: Prentice Hall.
Smith, A. (1776) In E. Cannan (ed.), *An Inquiry into the Nature and Causes of the Wealth of Nations*, 5th Ed. London: Methuen and Co., Ltd., 1904.

Chapter 3

Bounded Rationality and Decision Making

The models of economic choice that we use today and which were reviewed in Chapter 2 were developed by economists building upon the foundation of utility maximization, beginning with Adam Smith and continuing on through William Stanley Jevons, John Stuart Mill and the other utilitarians. As they believed they could never measure the emotional side of behavior, utilitarians gave up trying. Instead, they sought to eliminate the necessity of considering these feelings and emotions by going directly to behavior and revealed preference. These tools gave economists a way to side-step the psychological factors underlying utility and the process of decision making. Further developments such as expected utility, Bayesian revision of preferences and subjective utility further refined this framework, which essentially portrays the economic agent as a decision maker who carefully deliberates among various options and considers constraints on time and money to make decisions that maximize satisfaction/utility/well-being.

Beginning in the 1950s, economists and psychologists began investigating the process of decision making within a larger context that includes variables and situations usually ignored by economists working within the framework of neoclassical economic theory. These investigations have demonstrated that people often violate the assumptions of the neoclassical model as they make everyday decisions. Instead of acting as economically "rational" (as economists define rationality) agents that behave according to the axioms of transitivity of preference and time consistency, most people often make decisions based on simple rules that use limited information; they violate transitivity by reversing preferences as the context changes; or they mix preferences by putting money into separate mental categories which have different consumption properties. Research has also shown that individuals sometimes do not maximize utility and when outcomes are uncertain, often follow courses of action that do not maximize expected utility.

Herbert Simon (1979, 1983) was one of the leaders of this new group of social scientists who had begun to question the fundamental rationale underlying this microeconomic foundation. This new tradition of behavioral economics grew alongside the conventional model without much interaction with it. The key to this parallel development was the gradual rejection of psychological factors by the establishment of neoclassical economics, and a corresponding welcoming of psychology by behavioralists. Simon was joined by George Katona, Harvey Leibenstein and Tibor Scitovsky, among others. Behavioral science became a more integrated and well-established field in its own right, without influencing the fundamental direction of economics. The work of Daniel Kahneman and Amos Tversky and the growth of prospect theory which culminated in the awarding of a Nobel Prize in economics to Kahneman, a psychologist, served further notice that people often follow courses of action that violate the fundamental assumptions upon which decision theory was narrowly built.

As a result of their work and the work of other economists, psychologists and behavioral scientists, a body of knowledge has evolved that analyzes how people actually make decisions in real life. A concept called "mental accounting" arose from the idea that people place different values of utility on shorter- and longer-term goals. These investigations also showed that using expected utility as a descriptive tool often leads to incorrect predictions of people's behavior. An alternative line of argument called prospect theory has been developed that asserts that individuals have asymmetrical value functions which treat loss and gain differently. For example, experiments showed that gamblers treat winnings differently from their own money and are much more willing to gamble with these winnings — the so-called *house money* effect. These results and others that focus primarily on decision making of individuals are reviewed in the remainder of this chapter. They have been confirmed in a number of different experiments in laboratory conditions and also by observations of people's behavior in everyday life.

In Section 3.1, we begin by describing a few of the ways decisions are made and how this process differs from the way economists have modeled behavior. The remaining sections of the chapter explore these behavioral patterns in more depth.

3.1 Bounded Rationality and Utility Theory

A fully rational model of behavior would require the decision maker to sift through all the available information before making a choice or taking a decision. Observations of agents making decisions suggest that this is not the case. Researchers studying bounded rationality have found that decisions are often based on shortcuts, heuristics and intuition rather than well-thought out rational choices. A component of this bounded rationality decision making process is that the individual does not necessarily make decisions based on expected utility that can be derived from the expected value of different outcomes. For example, the expected value of a game where I get \$100 if a coin comes up heads and \$10 if it comes up tails is $(1/2 \times \$100) + (1/2 \times \$10)$, or \$55. Some decisions may be made on the basis of this kind of reasoning but many others involve different kinds of logic.

If we acknowledge these additional aspects of decision theory, we are able to view how decisions are made within this wider context of "bounded rationality". Nobel Prize winner Herbert Simon (1979, 1983) introduced this concept many years ago. Since then there have been many extensions and developments both in business and economics as decision theory, and in the theory of choice by individual economic agents. Simon postulated that most decisions are made on the basis of limited information operating within the context of the individual and the decision making environment. He developed a theory of "satisficing" in which economic agents look for acceptable, not maximizing, solutions, where the cost of information and the time needed to collect it are considered. This process involves looking for a good cost/benefit solution. Once an economic agent finds an acceptable solution, the search stops: "Taking into account the actor's bounded rationality; the first solution the actor finds is generally adopted as there is no guarantee that a radical change would provide better results, the actor knowing that research cost will then be higher" (Forest *et al.*, 2001, p. 601).

The search for such decision making systems and decision criteria came to be known as decision theory or decision science. Although there have been many new developments in this field in the past few decades, Simon, as the founder of this field, is still the source of much wisdom regarding decision theory. His formulation of a decision making process did not require the unrealistic assumption of universal knowledge of alternatives and an ability to choose quickly from a seemingly limitless list of possibilities. Furthermore, it allowed practitioners to develop rules to stop searching for maximizing solutions and "settle" for "satisfying", while balancing the costs and benefits of further analysis.

This method of analysis proved very beneficial at the practical level when businessmen were looking for easily implemented ways of decision making in a variety of different circumstances that required quick, yet powerful methods of analysis. In the next section, we explore a few of these methods. Many others are discussed in courses in management and decision science in business school curricula.

3.1.1 *Heuristics*

As a component of the way decisions are made using bounded rationality, various "heuristics" have been developed. A heuristic strategy is a methodology for making decisions that simplifies the problem by eliminating many possible solutions. Heuristics do not necessarily reach an optimal solution, but they are good satisfying tools. For example, Tversky and Kahneman (1974) suggest that people follow a general heuristic to solve classification problems by using past experience. While useful shortcuts, these heuristics can be misleading and result in costly errors. For example, when a pattern of successive throws of the dice prevails for some time, there is a tendency to believe that the next sample observation will be different. As a roulette player you have seen the last nine spins of the wheel come up black. The tendency is to bet on a reversal to red whereas, if the wheel is fair, black and red are equally likely no matter how often black has come up in the past. As a gambler there is a tendency to ignore statistical probabilities, realizing that the roulette wheel has no memory. The same is true of coin tosses. This tendency is called the *gambler's fallacy*.

Another fallacy, called the *conjunction fallacy*, occurs when judgments are made about unlikely events. This fallacy is committed when ranking the likelihood of statements about people where two events are linked. One example would be that a person is more likely to be a policeman and a man than just a policeman, or more likely to be a nurse and a woman than being a nurse. From probability theory, we know that the probability of events A *and* B happening together is always less than or equal to the probability of A. However, general heuristics may neglect this seemingly obvious observation (we might believe that being a policeman and a man is more likely than just being a policeman), thus creating the fallacy.

There are other heuristic fallacies that arise such as the *availability heuristic*. Here, people become prone to overestimating the probability of noteworthy events such as floods, tornados and spectacular air disasters, while underestimating the probabilities of less noteworthy events such as diabetes, stroke and tuberculosis.

3.1.2 *More on heuristics — status quo effects, uncertainty aversion and analysis of fairness and justice*

One simple decision heuristic is to try and not modify behavior by sticking to the same pattern of action. Individuals often do not change behavior and stick with past solutions. Inertia prevails. We stick with past behavior even though it looks like the decision costs of making a change are small (Samuelson and Zeckhauser, 1988). On the other hand, some problems that seem simple may require much analysis unless rules can be devised to simplify the problem. Consider the problem of selecting the appropriate outfit to wear to the office. If I have 10 shirts, 10 pairs of pants and 10 ties along with one jacket, six pairs of socks and four pairs of shoes, there are 24,000 possible combinations which would take four hours to make if each choice was considered for only 0.6 seconds. If we add 10 jackets, the time rises to 40 hours and 240,000 choices. Whew!!!

In such a situation, we immediately make some choices that eliminate certain alternatives right off the bat. How do we do it? Can we describe the decision process? Lots of combinations are discarded at the outset. Experiments that I ran in one of my classes showed that students regularly wore a small proportion of the clothes in their closet and they tended to rotate their "favorites" in a fairly routine and predictable pattern. This pattern ensured that they did not have to "think" much about making these choices at the beginning of the day. After having established this pattern, they repeated it without much change. Others had fewer clothes, which also simplified the decision making process.

In the opening pages of Malcolm Gladwell's (2005) bestseller *Blink*, he relates how art antiquities experts had misgivings about the authenticity of certain Greek sculpture when they first laid their eyes on it, at a time when all other evidence favored its authenticity. The experts turned out to be correct. Gladwell describes this as an example of rapid cognition where a person reaches a conclusion without needing all the available information. He describes such a decision making process as "thin-slicing" — individuals thin-slice through whatever information they have and arrive at their conclusion. Thin-slicing occurs whenever we meet someone for the first time or see something unusual. We arrive at a conclusion quickly within a few seconds. Gladwell does not characterize it as intuition; rather, he suggests that some thinking can be done within two seconds. Doctors do it, economists do it, managers do it — we all do it. However, we are not aware of how we do it. It is an innate function of the human being. As such, it defies one of the critical economic assumptions that rational human beings calmly and logically sieve through all available and relevant information to arrive at an informed conclusion — most of the time we do not.

Thin-slicing allows us to eliminate some alternatives immediately and greatly simplifies the decision making process. Gladwell

(2005) gives an example of the decision making process in Cook County Hospital in Chicago, where doctors were advised to gather *less* information on their patients, just to focus on the critical pieces of information and diagnose. According to Gladwell, this is one of the most successful hospitals in the US in diagnosing chest pains. Of course, he does acknowledge that snap judgments are not necessarily always better; they could be worse. But in *Blink*, Gladwell is able to illustrate that heuristics are in place so people can make accurate decisions under stressful conditions in split-seconds with minimal information.

Heuristics can also be developed reflecting emotional reactions to situations. For example, loss and gain are not treated equally and decisions can take into account aspects such as fairness and justice. Generally, behavior suggests that foregone gains are less painful than perceived losses, and decisions are colored by the perceived fairness of the outcomes. Losses are usually judged as less fair than gains. Kahneman, Knetsch and Thaler (1991) report telephone interviews with respondents whose interview results were grouped into acceptable (including "completely fair" and "acceptable" categories) and unfair (which was a grouping of "somewhat unfair" and "very unfair"). Perceptions of fairness were highly correlated with whether the question was framed as a reduction in a gain or as an actual loss.

The two questions were framed as follows with the resulting percentages for acceptable or unfair judgments:

Question 1. A shortage has developed for a popular model of automobile and customers must now wait two months for delivery. A dealer has been selling cars at list price. Now the dealer prices this model at $200 above list price. The responses were largely negative, acceptable 29 percent and unfair 79 percent.

When the question is rephrased slightly (changes in italics), the results are much different.

Question 2. A shortage has developed for a popular model of automobile and customers must now wait two months for delivery. *A* *dealer has been selling these cars at a discount of $200 below list price. Now the dealer sells this model only at list price.* Now the acceptable percentage increases to 58 percent while the unfair falls to 42 percent.

A similar result is reported when a company located in a community experiencing a recession is making a small profit and decides to reduce wages. When it reduces wages by seven percent in a noninflationary environment, this action was judged unfair by 63 percent of respondents. When salaries were increased by five percent while inflation was 12 percent, this was judged to be acceptable by 78 percent of respondents. This result is surprising to economists who realize that both alternatives are identical — a cut in real wages by seven percent. However, the lay public viewed the cut in wages as much worse than a small increase in a period of high inflation.

3.1.3 *Do individuals maximize utility?*

Aside from the use of heuristics to make decisions, there are many other circumstances where people do not maximize utility. In this section, we review some such examples of suboptimal decision making.

- *People are myopic*

When groups of people were offered a choice of $1 today or $1.20 tomorrow, they took the $1.20. This is sensible because a daily interest rate of 20 percent works out to nearly 1,000 percent per year compounded. However, when the same offer was made at the end of a month instead of tomorrow, many people decided to take the dollar today rather than waiting a month. Even though the interest rate is lower because of the longer one month time horizon, the interest rate is still over 100 percent on an annual basis, much higher than they could get by investing the dollar they get today.

Why would consumers make such an irrational decision? Time preference is the logical answer — an almost absurd inability to wait for interest to accrue. Possibly the result is also because the amounts involved were small. If the amounts were $1 million and $1.2 million, the results may have been different.

The standard model of discounting suggests that utility is discounted at a constant rate over time (the discounted utility model was originally formulated by Paul Samuelson, 1937). This accounts for the reason why a dollar now is worth more than a dollar sometime in the future and explains why this relationship is quite regular.

There have been many studies of this relationship which show that time discount is often not that simple. For instance, the kind of myopia described above is typical of decisions made where rewards vary over time. We can see this in the research by Thaler (1981), who asked subjects to specify the amount of money they would require at different future times in order to make them indifferent between that amount and $15 received now. He found that the average response implied an extremely high average annual discount rate of 345 percent for a one month time horizon compared with a relatively modest 19 percent rate for a ten year time horizon. The discount rate declines as the time period increases. This suggests that the constant discount rate assumption may be incorrect.

A number of other explanations and considerations have been taken into account to explain such myopic behavior (see Frederick *et al.*, 2005). For example, Loewenstein *et al.* (2001) suggest that three interrelated emotional factors are responsible for differences in discounting behavior. They are impulsivity, compulsivity and inhibition. Impulsivity is the degree to which actions are unplanned and spontaneous. Compulsivity is the characteristic of making plans and sticking to them. Inhibition is the ability to inhibit or control the tendency to act impulsively. Someone whose behavior is impulsive will likely have more trouble balancing expenditures and have myopic time preferences. Such individuals will be unable to postpone consumption and will have a low saving propensity. Those with stronger compulsive and inhibiting instincts are likely to be better planners and save for retirement. A high degree of impulsiveness explains why many people do not save throughout their working life, arriving at retirement with very little savings. This systematic tendency for many people to underestimate the monetary burden in the future may also be one reason why governments have seen fit to introduce social security or other compulsory saving plans. Can you think of other instances where individuals are prone to consume now and not worry about the future? How do individuals approach consumer credit and time payments for consumer durables? Do you think this kind of consumer orientation has anything to do with the rate of saving in a society?

- *Attitudes toward risk depend upon loss or gain*

The fear of loss prompts people to act in a risk averse manner. The fear of financial insolvency is often far greater than the attractiveness of becoming rich. This risk aversion can be easily demonstrated by asking someone if they would be willing to bet a substantial amount of money on the outcome of a coin toss. If the payoff for losses and gains are equal, few people will take the gamble. Some students in my class were unwilling to gamble even if the payoff was 50 percent higher for gain. Some of this behavior could be the result of the declining marginal utility of money, but the evidence suggests that behavioral changes are more dramatic than a subtle reaction to the changing value of money.

- *Shoppers generally do not explore different options and alternatives*

If consumers did undertake extensive search for the lowest price, then there would be a tendency toward the law of one price to hold. However, surveys of price variation within local markets done by Lester Telser some years ago (1973) and referred to by Etzioni (1988) showed variations in the prices of aspirin and tape recorders of over 200 percent, and an average price differential of over 50 percent for the majority of 25 products sampled. While the internet and the growth of large retail discounters may have changed this pattern somewhat in recent years, there are undoubtedly still very large variations in retail prices for standard goods. These variations persist only because consumers are unwilling or do not have the time to search for the lowest price.

- *Rules of thumb are used in place of utility maximization*

A good example of a rule of thumb is price setting by business firms. In the theory of the firm in microeconomic theory, we assert that the firm maximizes profit by pricing so that marginal cost equals marginal revenue. However, much of the literature on firm pricing suggests that firms use full cost pricing rules (see Hall and Hitch, 1939; Cyert and March, 1963). This rule of thumb adds a predetermined rate of profit to estimated unit cost to establish a product's price. This rate of profit may be related to a target rate of return on capital invested in the firm (Lanzillotti, 1958). Sometimes the rule of thumb is adjusted in cases of sales or markdowns, when sales were poor or inventories had built up. These studies also reflect that pricing was based nearly completely on costs and not on demand, except to the extent that high inventories may signal that prices are out of line. Katona (1975) studied investment decisions and found rules of thumb were widely used such as "follow the leader". A recent example of the latter is the move to internet ordering, marketing and use of IT to maintain inventory and get best deals from suppliers (B2B and B2C). Often these rules of thumb or adjustments to these rules are biased toward a set of narrow alternatives (Cyert and March, 1963, p. 121).

Psychologists Chaiken and Stangor (1987) have shown that people often evaluate the validity of information using such rules as "consensus implies correctness", "experts' statements can be trusted" and "length implies strength". Taller political candidates win a disproportionate number of elections, perhaps because "height makes right". (Recent econometric research also suggests that taller people make more money than shorter people, other things being equal.) Many rules have been etched into our awareness and often they are contradictory (e.g., "turn the other cheek", "an eye for an eye", "look before you leap" and "he who hesitates is lost"). "When in Rome do as the Romans do" and "to thine own self be true" are examples of pithy rules of thumb that serve to confuse rather than lead to rational choices.

There are many rules of thumb for the proportion of cash, equities, bonds and real estate we should have in our portfolio and these rules of thumb will vary by the investment counselors and the economic era. In the present low inflation environment, the threat of losing capital value by a conservative strategy are minimal compared to the high inflation environment that prevailed in the 1970s.

- *People have difficulty in assessing their future tastes and preferences*

People are able to adapt to changing circumstances such as higher income, divorce and deterioration in health. They are unable to predict such adaptive behavior before the fact. Lottery winners are very happy initially, but their level of happiness reverts back to original levels in a few weeks (Brickman, Coates and Janoff-Bulman, 1978). Those who become disabled adapt quite well psychologically, although most people predict that they would be in constant despair when asked to contemplate becoming disabled. This adaptation mechanism also results in a disconnect between higher incomes and elevated levels of happiness and well-being (see Chapter 6).

- *People are generally overly optimistic (and overconfident) about the future*

People underestimate the probability of many possible future events. Many of these underestimations involve unpleasant or unwanted outcomes such as getting cancer, heart disease, other illness or death. People usually do not contemplate their own death and do not make wills, creating difficulties for their surviving children, spouses and other relatives. This certainty illusion, a belief in their own infallibility, results in a bias in assessing the likelihood of future events. This results in underinsurance and unnecessary risk taking. On the other hand, people want to believe they are better than others or that they are at least above average. We all think we are better than average drivers, more "street smart" than others and above average workers (see Meyer, 1975). We do not ever think that our marriages will end in divorce or that our children will turn to drugs (see Frey and Eichenberger, 2001).

- *People make incompatible short-run and long-run decisions*

People make spur-of-the-moment decisions that they regret once they realize the longer-term implications of these decisions. Addictive behavior is the most blatant and obvious example of this kind of irrational behavior. Impulse buying is a more benign yet very common example. How many people have bought on impulse only to regret the purchase once they get home and open their shopping bags? The risk of this kind of behavior is one reason why shoppers are warned not to go to the supermarket when they are hungry. Emotion will outweigh reason. In the real estate business, where the stakes are higher than buying a loaf of bread, a reversal in sentiment is called "buyer's remorse". Many potential homebuyers make a commitment to buy, then change their mind and even change it back again. Uncertainty and fear of making the wrong decision seem to be directly proportional to the size of the purchase involved.

Generally, this bias toward the present is reflected by time inconsistencies when considering the dynamics of behavior. We are more averse to delaying today's gratification until tomorrow, than delaying gratification from 30 days from now to 31 days from now. Our decision now would be different from our decision a month from now simply because of the passage of time. We feel that today is different from tomorrow, yet we do not feel that 30 days from now is different from 31 days from now. The lens of time changes our perceptions (see Rabin, 2004, for more examples). This also relates to the discussion of myopia and the rate of discount above.

3.1.4 *Decision making and risk*[1]

How can we develop a theory of decision making that incorporates some of the evidence from the use of heuristics, rules of thumb and emotions? One approach is to examine the relationship between risk and expected utility. At one level, expected utility is simply the application of the laws of probability to the analysis of events. However, in many circumstances, we do not know the probability of certain events, whereas we do know the probability of others. When these two situations are merged, strange results are sometimes observed that cannot be explained by the conventional expected utility arguments, yet are consistent with many of the decisions discussed in

---

[1]This section is based on material in http://www.gametheory.net/Mike/applets/Risk/.

Sections 3.1.2 and 3.1.3. We will return to this point momentarily after some grounding in conventional analysis of risk and uncertainty.

Why are some people willing to buy lottery tickets, but at the same time insure themselves against theft, death or property damage? The cost of a lottery ticket is substantially less than the average winnings one can expect to get. If everyone purchased lottery tickets every week over one's entire life, the odds suggest that few people would come out ahead. On the other hand, the premium we pay for insurance is substantially greater than the average cost of claims. If everyone carries car insurance, relatively few people will file claims in a given year above the cost of their premiums. There are, of course, catastrophic accidents where claims are extremely large.

People differ in how much risk they are willing to take and what is worth the risk. The expected benefits and losses play an important role in this decision. A lottery ticket costs only a dollar, and a dollar lost has little impact on our lifestyle, while the potential multi-million dollar payoff from winning would impact our lives greatly. Paying a thousand or two thousand in insurance premiums for a house or car is costly, but perhaps is worthwhile if it protects us from the unlikely but costly lawsuits resulting from our accidents or the chance that our house will be burned down or torn apart in a storm. These losses are all the more devastating when we recognize the asymmetric nature of loss and gain.

Economists often express one's willingness to take risks through a utility function of money. To understand the notion of "utility over money", consider the following illustration. A "prize patrol van" pulls up in front of your house. When you open the door, the representative of the state lottery announces that you have won one million dollars. As you scream in glee, a decibel meter records the volume (loudness) of your scream. Now imagine the same scenario, only you are told that you have won *two* million dollars. Do you scream twice as loud? The answer is probably not!! Winning a million dollars probably makes you very happy. Winning two million also makes you happy, but not *twice* as happy as one million dollars.

To fix these ideas more firmly, consider the utility function in Figure 3.1.

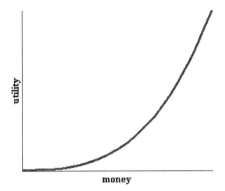

Figure 3.1 Risk Taking Utility Function

The horizontal axis represents the amount of money a person has, and the vertical axis represents "utility" or how much that money is worth to us. Note that the utility function is convex (loosely, this means that it increases slowly initially, and then faster). What does this utility function say about risk? It implies that a person is *risk-seeking*, or likely to take gambles such as buying lottery tickets. To see why, consider a struggling college student with a $2 bank balance at the end of the month, the day before $100 rent is due. If the student gave up a dollar, his condition would be little changed. His "utility" of one dollar or of two dollars is almost the same, since neither is enough to pay the rent. However, $100 is worth substantially more to the student. Therefore, he may be willing to buy a lottery ticket with one or both of his two dollars, thinking "even if I lose, I am still in trouble with the landlord, but if I win, I am saved!" The convex utility function represents this — small increases in money above zero wealth have little impact on one's utility, but larger increases make one substantially better off. Risk takers are ready to gamble on the large payoff.

Now consider the utility function in Figure 3.2.

This utility function is concave — it increases quickly initially and then flattens out. This implies that money, initially, is more valuable than additional sums of money once we are already rich (this explains why we do not scream twice as loud when we win twice as much). The utility function represents a person who is *risk averse* or prefers

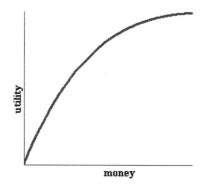

Figure 3.2 Risk Averse Utility Function

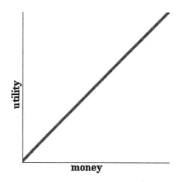

Figure 3.3 Risk Neutral Utility Function

not to take risks. In the case of the struggling college student who is risk averse, he will hunker down and save the money he could have spent on the lottery ticket and put it toward purchasing another book or his next meal.

A third type of utility function is shown in Figure 3.3.

This utility function simply represents that every dollar is worth to us as much as every other. Such a person is deemed *risk neutral.* In the case of the struggling college student, he might buy a couple of lottery tickets if he really believes that the expected gain (probability of winning × the lottery purse) is the same for winning as the utility of the $2 spent on the lottery ticket. This brings us to the concept of certainty equivalents.

- *Certainty equivalents*

Why the shapes of the utility functions pictured above represent risk seeking, risk aversion and risk neutrality can be made clearer by considering a certainty equivalent (CE). A CE represents the maximum amount of money we are willing to pay for some gamble. Alternately, a CE is the minimum premium we are willing to pay to insure us against some risk. Imagine that I offer you the following bet: I will flip a coin and if it lands *heads* you win nothing, but if it lands *tails* I award you $100. How much would you be willing to pay for this chance? If I set up a shop on a street corner and offer passersby this gamble for $10, it is likely that most would take it (wouldn't you?). As I increase the price to $20 and then $30 and $40, fewer and fewer people would accept. To see why, consider the three utility functions below in Figure 3.4.

The first is a risk seeker, the second is risk averse and the third is risk neutral. In each case, the utility of winning $0 and the utility of winning $100 is denoted on the vertical axis. Since each outcome (*heads* and *tails*) is equally likely, I am just as likely to get the happiness of $0 as I am of gaining the happiness of $100. This is expressed below.

My *expected utility*, or the happiness I expect to earn from this gamble *on average* is halfway between my utility from winning $100 and my utility from winning $0, since each is equally likely. The horizontal line in each panel of Figure 3.5 represents the utility that this gamble will bring me, on average. The interesting question, however, is not how happy this gamble makes me, but how much I am willing to pay for it.

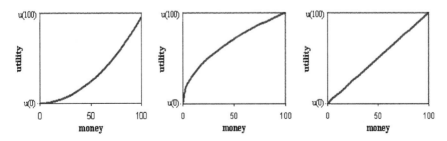

Figure 3.4 Three Risk Scenarios

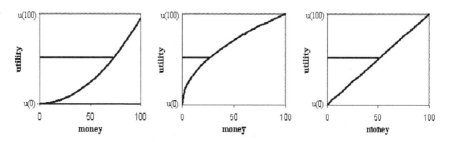

Figure 3.5 Utility from a Gamble

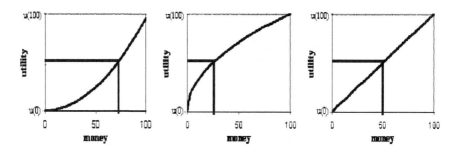

Figure 3.6 Value of the Gamble

Notice that in the first panel of Figure 3.6, the gamble between $0 and $100 is worth about $75. The person is a risk taker. This means that the person would be willing to pay me up to $75 for the right to win $100 based on a coin toss. Certainly, this is a "bad bet" since the average winnings are only $50. However, just like some are willing to make bad bets by playing the lottery or entering a casino, this person likes to take risks.

In the second panel, the person would not be willing to pay anything over $25. Even though the coin toss, on average, pays $50, the extra risk is not worth it to that person. He is risk averse. This can be understood in the context of insurance. Consider a person with $100,000 net worth. Some accident, which has a 50 percent chance of happening, could cost the person his entire net worth. Therefore, this individual could end the year with a net worth of either $0 or $100,000. Because ending the year without any money is too great a risk, the person purchases insurance against the risk at a cost of $75,000. This way, he is certain to end the year at a net worth of $25,000 regardless of whether or not the accident occurs.

The person in the third panel is risk neutral. Since the *expected value* of the bet is $50 (1/2 chance at 0, 1/2 chance at 100), the person is willing to pay only up to $50 for the bet. This defines risk neutrality — a person who is risk neutral is concerned only with the actual expected value. These numbers that the three individuals are willing to bet ($75, $25 and $50) are called *certainty equivalents.*

Definition: A certainty equivalent is the minimum amount of money one would rather have for certain instead of taking some risk. The more risk averse a person is, the lower is his or her certainty equivalent.

3.1.5 *Expected utility and three paradoxes*

In this section we look at some cases where the standard expected utility calculations do not fit into how people actually make decisions.

- *St. Petersburg paradox*

This paradox was first suggested by Nicholas Bernoulli and Gabriel Cramer and solved by Bernoulli's cousin, Daniel Bernoulli, in 1738. The paradox resurfaced in the classic work on game theory by Von Neumann and Morgenstern (1944). The game involves a coin flip and a payoff when the first head appears. The game continues until the coin lands head up. The payoff increases as the number of tosses without a head increases. This payoff is directly related to the number of tosses by the following relationship — the payoff on the nth toss is 2^n. So the expected return from this game is:

$$(1/2)(2) + (1/4)(4) + \cdots + (1/n)n + \cdots$$
$$= 1 + 1 + 1 + 1 + \cdots = \text{infinity.}$$

However in the real world, no one would be willing to pay an infinity amount of money to play this game. For example, in experiments where subjects were offered $40 or a lottery ticket that pays off according to the game just described, the average person is quite happy to take the $40 rather than the lottery ticket. Why?

Daniel Bernoulli's solution to this problem involved two ideas which were to become extremely important to economists in the future. The first was the introduction of the idea of diminishing marginal utility. Secondly, there is a proposition that a person's valuation of a risky venture is not necessarily the expected utility from that venture. If we introduce diminishing marginal utility into the above equation, then it may be possible to have a finite return to the game. However, the decrease in marginal utility of the money payoff would have to be bounded and decrease rapidly approaching zero so that the sum is not infinite.

For our purposes, however, the relationship between expected utility and risk is of equal if not greater importance. Most people would not put a lot of money if they suspected they would get a head on the first toss. So when people are risk averse they will not play a game where the risks outweigh the expected future utility, even when that utility is very high.

- *Allais paradox*

To appreciate the St. Petersburg paradox, we turn to the second paradox first suggested by Maurice Allais in 1953. A version of this paradox was suggested by Kahneman and Tversky in 1979 and discussed further by Robert Sugden (1986). We will follow the Kahneman and Tversky example as articulated by Sugden, with a few minor modifications for clarity. We are asked to consider a number of "prospects". These prospects or alternatives involve various options, some involving sure outcomes and other unsure outcomes (see Table 3.1).

First, consider two possible alternative prospects, p_1 and p_2. The first prospect, p_1, gives $2,400 with certainty and the second prospect, p_2, gives $2,500 with probability 0.33, $2,400 with probability 0.66 and $0 with probability 0.01. So the expected utility using our usual formulas would be $2,400 for p_1 and $(0.33)($2,500) + (0.66)($2,400) = $2,417$ for p_2. If we are risk neutral and we maximize expected utility, we would pick p_2.

Table 3.1 Expected Payoff for Alternatives p_1, p_2, p_3 and p_4

Alternative	Payoff	Probability	Expected Return	Kahneman and Tversky's Experiment
p_1	$2,400	1	$2,400	Preferred choice
p_2	$2,500 $2,400 $0	0.33 0.66 0.01	$2,417	
p_3	$2,400 $0	0.34 0.66	$816	Preferred choice
p_4	$2,400 $0	0.33 0.67	$792	

Subjects were then asked to pick between two other alternatives, both with some risk involved. p_3 gives a return of $2,400 with probability 0.34 and $0 with probability 0.66, while p_4 gives a return of $2,400 with probability 0.33 and $0 with probability 0.67. Doing the math, we see that the expected value of p_3 = $816, while the expected value of p_4 = $792. In terms of higher expected return we should pick p_3.

Combining the two alternative choices, the logical solution would be to pick p_2 and p_3. However, the majority of subjects in an experiment by Kahneman and Tversky picked p_1 (82 percent) and p_3 (83 percent). This reversal in preference is called the Allais paradox or common consequence effect. In the Allais paradox, a person chooses a sure thing even when the expected payoff for a more risky venture is higher.

Recently, psychologists and brain researchers have examined the Allais paradox as an example of *ambiguity*. Smith *et al.* (2002) consider two lotteries where lottery A guarantees a payment of $10, while lottery B pays $20 if a red ball is pulled from an urn which contains 90 balls and at least 50 of these balls are red. In expected probability terms, we should choose B because the expected payoff is higher than A, i.e., (5/9) × $20 > $10; however subjects tended to choose A. Smith *et al.* (2002) discovered that different parts of the brain are activated as these decisions are made. They found that more primitive areas of the brain were activated by losses, while gains stimulated parts of the brain associated with logical reasoning.

Research in this new area called *neuroeconomics*[2] suggests that the very presence of ambiguity alone tends to activate the limbic system which is associated with emotional decision making (rather than logical reasoning). This neural explanation also helps us to begin to understand why some people may take more risk than others. There are a number of areas where *neuroeconomics* can help us to better understand decision making behavior. We will refer to them again later in this chapter and in Chapter 4 when we discuss aspects of game theory.

We continue with the Kahneman and Tversky examples to demonstrate another example of preference reversal (see Table 3.1a). Consider four more alternatives p_5, p_6, p_7, p_8, where p_5 gives \$3,000 with certainty, p_6 gives an 80 percent chance of winning \$4,000, while p_7 gives a 25 percent chance of winning \$3,000 and p_8 a 20 percent chance of winning \$4,000. The payoffs are \$3,000, \$3,200, \$750 and \$800 respectively for p_5, p_6, p_7 and p_8. As expected, 80 percent of subjects chose p_5 and 65 percent chose p_8.

As a variation of these prospect experiments, participants were asked to choose between prospects that involved losses. This experiment is identical to the previous experiment except that instead of having possible gains of \$3,000, \$3,200, \$750 and \$800 for the four prospects, we now have four possible loss scenarios (see Table 3.1b).

Table 3.1a Expected Payoffs for p_5, p_6, p_7 and p_8

Alternative	Payoff	Probability	Expected Return	Kahneman and Tversky's Experiment
p_5	\$3,000	1	\$3,000	Preferred choice
p_6	\$4,000	0.80	\$3,200	
	\$0	0.20		
p_7	\$3,000	0.25	\$750	
	\$0	0.75		
p_8	\$4,000	0.20	\$800	Preferred choice
	\$0	0.80		

[2]This is an exciting field which blends economics, decision science and neural analysis of the brain.

Table 3.1b Expected Payoffs for p_9, p_{10}, p_{11} and p_{12}

Alternative	Payoff	Probability	Expected Return	Kahneman and Tversky's Experiment
p_9	−$3,000	1	−$3,000	
p_{10}	−$4,000	0.80	−$3,200	Preferred choice
	$0	0.20		
p_{11}	−$3,000	0.25	−$750	Preferred choice
	$0	0.75		
p_{12}	−$4,000	0.20	−$800	
	$0	0.80		

p_9 is the certainty of losing $3,000, p_{10} is the 80 percent chance of losing $4,000, p_{11} is the 25 percent chance of losing $3,000, while p_{12} is the 20 percent chance of losing $4,000.

What happened here demonstrates the opposite effect of preference reversal when losses are involved. Nearly all subjects picked the risky alternative p_{10} in the choice between p_9 and p_{10}, while they chose the lower loss p_{11} in the second option between p_{11} and p_{12}. In the first set of choices, subjects picked the "irrational" alternative of p_{10} giving a higher expected loss of $3,200, while in the second set of choices they acted rationally, picking the alternative of a smaller loss.

• *Ellsberg paradox*

In a similar vein to the Allais paradox, Ellsberg (1961) shows that when outcomes are uncertain, subjects show that they are more averse to the *ambiguous* decision.

Consider an urn containing 90 balls. Ellsberg asked subjects to choose from alternatives in two experiments. In the first experiment (I), payoffs come from a draw of one ball from an urn containing 30 red balls and 60 balls whose color is either black or yellow (see Table 3.2). We do not know how many black balls or yellow balls there are; the proportion of black and yellow balls is unknown. If you select a red ball you will get $100 and nothing for selecting the other colors. Assuming a ball is selected randomly from the urn, the expected payoff

Table 3.2 Expected Payoffs for Experiment I

Options	30 Balls	60 Balls (either black or yellow)	
	Red	Black	Yellow
1	$100	$0	$0
2	$0	$100	$0

Table 3.3 Expected Payoffs for Experiment II

Options	30 Balls	60 Balls (either black or yellow)	
	Red	Black	Yellow
3	$100	$0	$100
4	$0	$100	$100

for a red ball in option 1 is $1/3 \times 100 = \$33$. In option 2, the subject gets $100 if he selects a black ball from the urn containing 90 balls and nothing if he selects either of the other colors. The expected payoff in option 2 is also $33 if we assume that the number of black and yellow balls in the urn is equal. In both cases, the expected payoff is $33 if we assume that black and yellow balls are equally likely in option 2. However, most people picked the option with less uncertainty, i.e., option 1. The uncertainty has to do with the number of black and yellow balls in the urn.

The second experiment (II) involved the same 90 balls, 30 of which were red (see Table 3.3). In option 3, a red ball pays $100 and so does a yellow. So the expected payoff (assuming black and yellow are equally likely) is $1/3(\$100) + 1/3(\$100) = \$66$. In option 4, both black and yellow balls pay $100. In the comparison of these two cases, option 4 has less uncertainty since we know that the chance of their being black or yellow is $2/3$, while in option 3 there is still uncertainty about the probability of yellow. Indeed, subjects picked option 4 more often.

If we used expected utility, we would assign some probability to black and yellow. If it is greater than $1/2$ for black, we would pick options 2 and 4. If yellow is more likely, we would pick options 1 and 3. But this is not how the world works in real life. There is a cost to the uncertainty that occurs in this situation, which is why respondents usually pick what they believe to be the more certain outcome.

The Ellsberg, Allais and St. Petersburg paradoxes demonstrate that there are definite flaws in the expected utility theory that flow from the introduction of uncertainty and ambiguity in the decision making process. Nevertheless, no one has yet discovered a more general global theory that can replace expected utility theory. What we are left with is a series of insights that augment expected utility, some of which involve emotional and psychological factors. We explore these further in the next section.

3.2 Expected Utility, Decision Making and the Role of Emotions

In Section 3.1, a number of cases were reviewed where individuals did not make rational decisions. In this section, we provide an alternative explanation for this behavior. This explanation involves the role of emotions in decision making. Instead of looking at heuristics, the various paradoxes and inconsistencies from a logical point of view, consider an alternative where individuals make decisions taking into account both rational as well as *emotional* considerations. In psychological parlance, these emotional considerations are also referred to by psychologists as passions or affective states.

While the role of emotions has often been viewed as being counter to logic and reason, the current view in psychology is that emotions are a central aspect of motivation and are necessary to energize people to work towards achieving life objectives. However, there should be moderation. An individual can become disorganized and inefficient if too much emotion is involved, or lethargic and lacking interest if too little emotion is involved — the so-called Yerkes–Dodson law (see Kaufman, 1999, for details). Very low levels of arousal or emotional intensity are characteristics of people who are bored or depressed. With too much intensity, people lose their ability to make reasoned judgments and are unable to remember important facts or ideas to the point of becoming paralyzed into a state of inaction.

Neuroscientists and economists are working to better understand the role of emotions and feelings in decision making (see Glimcher and Rustichini, 2004; Loewenstein, 2004). Loewenstein argues that some kinds of baser visceral drives such as hunger, thirst and sexual drives as well as emotional factors can cause people to act in ways that are detrimental in the long-term. Loewenstein (2004) distinguishes these emotional states from tastes, which he contends are smoother and evolve slowly over time. Damasio (2003), arguing from the point of view of a neuroscientist, concludes that emotions and feelings are different. Emotions involve the brain while feelings engage the entire system, including the body and the brain. We know from many neurological experiments that emotions work with the higher cognitive areas (those stressed by conventional decision making analysis) to affect behavior. Exactly how this process takes place in different circumstances and with different individuals is still not well understood.

However, recent work in neuroeconomics suggests ways in which this interaction works. Using functional magnetic resonance imaging (fMRI) and other techniques for analyzing how the brain works, decision making neuroscientists have discovered that often the cognitive and emotional centers of the brain work together to make decisions (see for example Hanoch, 2002; Damasio, 1994, 2003).

We know that attitudes toward loss and gain are strongly influenced by emotional factors that complement the mechanisms which determine the calculation of expected utility. Overoptimism and assessment of future tastes is an emotional reaction rather than a cognitive one. By the same token, buyers' remorse can be caused by a change in the relative intensity of emotional and cognitive factors. Pressure from salesmen and flights of fancy can result in impulsive decisions that individuals regret later.

Emotions often work to supplement cognitive factors in a model of bounded rationality. Consider the clothes selection problem. It may be restricted by emotional attachment to some clothes and not to others. In this way the emotions help us discriminate among the various types of information we encounter, and they help us generate alternatives as well as signals to stop gathering information and start making decisions. The emotions also help us to focus attention on matters that need our attention and to disregard irrelevant alternatives. They also allow us to shift gears and react to unanticipated events.

Without the thrust of emotions, it is extremely hard to make decisions. Damasio (1994) examined patients who have sustained damage to the frontal lobes of the brain, where many emotional reactions are housed. As a result, these patients have become emotionally flat even while retaining all of their cognitive abilities. One manifestation of this loss of emotional content was that the patients could not assign any emotional value to future events, either to value or discount them. In one instance a patient could not decide when to set his next appointment with the doctor. He evaluated many different alternatives including possible weather conditions, but could never reach a conclusion. It was only Damasio's intervention that stopped the process. There was no stop/start switch activated by the emotions or the need to get on with the next order of business. Generally, obsessing about making the right decision is not an efficient use of time.

Emotions also help us to focus on the information we need to make decisions in a myriad of mundane circumstances from what we wear, to shopping for groceries or buying a house. The set of variables we focus on is determined by the emotions and not the cognitive sectors of the brain. In addition, intuition plays a role in decision making. Some things just seem "right" and others just seem "wrong". Sometimes intuition can lead us down a dead end, but it is critically important in an uncertain world. The great economist Joseph Schumpeter said, "The success of everything depends on intuition, the capacity of seeing things in a way which afterwards proves to be true, even though it cannot be established at the moment" (Schumpeter, 1934, p. 85). Emotions attach value to the array of information that we have to process and therefore allow us to cut down the range of options.

The economist puts all of these intuitions and emotional variables into something he calls "tastes", which are assumed to be constant for most decision making purposes. In reality, these tastes change all the time and color our decision making process. Loewenstein (2004) suggests that emotions result in short-term perturbations that affect decisions, while tastes are longer-run in nature. We hear a particular Chinese restaurant is good and we develop a sudden craving for Chinese food (emotions). We go to a particular Chinese restaurant because we like Chinese food (taste). Our choice may have been based on the recommendation of a friend and not on any cognitive analysis of costs, scope of the menu and well-researched investigation into the quality of the food. In other circumstances, decisions may have been arrived at from memory, the sight of an old friend or something we saw on TV, read about in the newspaper or downloaded from the Internet.

On the other hand, a slavish commitment to rationality can lead to bizarre and sometimes horrific results. The case of the production of the Ford Pinto is instructive. Instead of recalling or reengineering the car so that its gas tank would be less likely to explode, the company let it go to market after they calculated that the cost of law suits due to wrongful death and injury would be less than the costs of reworking the car's fuel system (Ritzer, 1993).

As we will discuss in future chapters, how we think and act is dynamic and ever-changing and is partly the result of experience. It is also the result of changes that take place in the brain as a result of this experience. In the remainder of this chapter, we will discuss a particularly important aspect of bounded rationality that involves certain widely documented psychological factors that depart from the standard economic model. Some of the decisions discussed in Section 3.1 can be analyzed using this framework, which leads to very powerful results about behavior. While these results do not necessarily depend upon the incorporation of the role of emotions, emotional factors certainly play a role in determining the ultimate decision. We return to the role of emotions in decision making in Chapter 4.

3.3 Prospect Theory — an Introduction

We continue this chapter by reviewing the experimental work of psychological and economic pioneers in a field that has come to be known as *prospect theory*. This work throws further light on the role of the emotions and the interaction between logical thinking and the physical, emotional and cultural conditions that help to frame decisions. Many of the issues raised in Sections 3.1 and 3.2 can be further analyzed using this analytical framework. Prospect theory gets its name from the investigation of how people view future prospects, opportunities or outcomes when these prospects are presented in different languages. This process of presenting alternatives in different contexts or with different languages is called *framing*.

Daniel Kahneman, who won the Nobel Prize for economics in 2001, is one of the leaders in prospect theory. Working with his colleague Amos Tversky, he published a series of influential papers in the *Journal of Business* and *Econometrica* in the early 1980s.

The thrust of their work has shown that people make decisions and choices in ways that are not directly considered by neoclassical theory. John List (2003a, b, c) has carefully reviewed many of Kahneman and Tversky's (KT) papers and describes how people actually make choices. We summarize the major features of the KT theory here and further details in subsequent sections of this chapter. Our discussion expands on some of the decision making characteristics discussed in Section 3.1, using a number of examples.

Endowment effect and status quo bias. The endowment effect says that people value what they have more than what someone else has. This is true even if the ownership is short-lived. Gilbert (2006, p. 160) lists a number of examples where people find ways to view purchases or actions positively once they own them (household appliances, political candidate voted for, university where applicant has just been admitted and so on). It is even possible that an object that was not desired before a person received it could be highly desired once it comes into an individual's possession. This has important implications for behavior of participants in equity markets who may hold on to assets when logic suggests they should sell. The endowment effect has also been called status quo bias — a situation where individuals want to maintain the status quo rather than change their behavior or pattern of decision making. This desire to maintain the status quo and one's personal belief system remains fixed and persists despite contrary evidence (see Slovic *et al.*, 1982). This may have to do with such diverse behavior like still favoring a discredited political figure, keeping your lemon of a car that has cost you a fortune in repairs, or a romantic relationship that has gone sour.

Economic agents fear loss more than they crave gain. We have come across this behavior already when discussing risk taking earlier in Section 3.1. For example, when presented with two equally likely alternatives, one negative and the other positive, most people will require a greater payoff for the positive outcome in order for them to take the gamble. This asymmetry is widely observed in a variety of different contexts and has implications for a variety of situations where public choice and the allocation of resources is involved. For example, people who have just made a big gain tend to be risk taking in the next round of decision making, while losers may be generally more cautious in the next round.

Context or how choices are presented affects consumers' decisions. The same choice, couched in a slightly different way using different terminology, leads people to draw different conclusions and make different decisions. KT call this process of presenting alternatives "framing". For example, when a doctor presents alternative medical procedures in such a way that highlights the possibility of a negative outcome, patients will tend to veer away from these alternatives. Conversely, when the frame is presented in a positive light, patients will shift their perspective and choose to maximize the probability of the positive outcome.

Probabilities of likely and highly unlikely events are weighted differently. Consider events that have a very low probability of occurring. Evidence suggests that people give a higher subjective weight to unlikely events than is warranted by the historical record. One reason why rare events are given a higher psychological weight relative to other, more likely events, is that they are given lots of press coverage so people will remember them. Fatal air crashes are a good example of an unlikely event and people tend to think air travel is more risky than traveling by automobile, when statistics have proven that air travel is safer than ground transport per mile traveled. Similarly, likely events are underweighted. The probability of contracting AIDS is quite high yet many people do not take necessary precautions and/or preventative measures to avoid contracting the disease.

There are time dependence and time diversification effects. These two possible effects combine risk aversion with a finite time horizon in assessing the returns of different assets. One aspect of these effects is that investors with a shorter time horizon will invest in a narrow portfolio of assets (less diversification) with a more reliable earnings stream, while those with more diverse holding longer-term assets will be willing to take more risk. Also, discounting will be lower for longer-term assets.

People adopt mental accounting to categorize different expenditure categories. This phrase, mental accounting, describes a mental process whereby consumers categorize expenditures into different categories. Consumers created these artificial categories to "protect" themselves from unwanted future actions and expenditures, or to earmark money for some extravagance like buying an expensive birthday present. Alternatively, consumers with undesirable habits such as gambling, drugs or alcohol will take care not to spend any money on these products for fear of falling back into the addiction.

Decisions are often based on relative rather than absolute utility. People tend to make choices relative to what other people are making and judge utility in this relative way rather than in absolute terms. In this sense, utility and happiness come from the relative value placed on goods which then provide greater satisfaction or utility in addition to the absolute value that consumers placed on the product or service. Conspicuous consumption of everyday products that are homogenous and bland will not create much utility or happiness. Products which are more heterogeneous and which have status value will contain both intrinsic value as well as snob appeal. We return to the topic of conspicuous consumption when we discuss happiness and well-being in Chapter 6.

We turn next to a deeper analysis of prospect theory.

3.4 Elements of Prospect Theory — "Endowment Effect", "Status Quo Bias" and "Myopic Loss Aversion"

List (2003c) presents an experiment where two gifts of equal value are distributed randomly among a group of individuals. Assuming that each of the gifts is preferred by an equal number of these individuals, i.e., half prefer gift one and the other half prefer gift two, then it is likely that a lot of trading would go on after the gifts were distributed randomly, as each person would have only a 50 percent chance of getting the gift he preferred.

But something else happened in experimental situations. In an experiment I conducted in one of my classes, I distributed two different colored pens. Almost no trading occurred even when students knew that the pen they got randomly cost less than the other pen. Kahneman and Tversky (see Kahneman, Knetsch and Thaler, 1991) dubbed this the "endowment effect" and they believe that it is a general characteristic of people's behavior.

The endowment effect manifests in many situations. The endowment effect could be one explanation why people hold on to stocks longer than they should if they are only interested in making a profit. In looking at the volume of stock market transaction, the volume of shares traded where shares have declined in value is nearly always lower than the volume of shares that are traded where shares have increased in value. This happens in spite of the tax benefit that accrues to losers versus winners. The endowment effect also explains why people are reluctant to return defective merchandise or Christmas gifts they would never buy for themselves or why many garages and storage closets are filled with junk. How many of you have "stuff" that you never use? The endowment effect can extend to ideas and behavior as well as patterns of behavior. Individuals are reluctant to give up established beliefs even when confronted with new evidence. This idea is considered further in Section 3.13 on memory and bounded rationality.

Luckily, research also shows that the endowment effect cycle can be broken. Agents can learn to let go of their attachments and minimize the endowment effect. List (2003c) shows that ownership is strong for uninformed or less informed new traders in the stock market. However, the attachment of ownership dies out as traders become more experienced. As a result, List suggests that more experienced "traders" are less susceptible to the endowment effect. They are more able to buy and sell without getting attached to their "portfolio" of assets.

Joel Chernoff (2002) considers another aspect of the endowment effect. He notes that investors may suffer from "myopic loss aversion". Investors lose money because they refuse to cut losses and reinvest money elsewhere. Another aspect of the endowment effect is that investors expect the past to repeat itself and so tend to look at history in making forecasts of the future. So they buy assets they wished they had invested in last year. This could lead to further run-ups in prices that may not be justified by fundamentals. This same principle applies to losses. If there has been a string of losses, this investor would hold on to stocks for sentimental value only. This myopic loss aversion is also sometimes called "fear of regret" because investors do not want to face the regret they will feel when they sell stocks at a loss.

In a related article, Kahneman, Knetsch and Thaler (1991) present a variety of evidence that support the endowment effect and what they call the "status quo bias". They provide the results of an experiment where mugs and pens (rather than mugs and candy bars or two different kinds of pens) were distributed at random and little trading took place. Based on their theory of status quo bias, they suggest that departures from the status quo are risky and the compensation required to dislodge people from the status quo can be very high.

Another piece of evidence to support the existence of status quo bias comes from an insurance case in two adjacent states of the US — New Jersey and Pennsylvania. In New Jersey, the car insurance default option provides for cheap insurance coverage with an expensive option as an alternative, which allows more opportunity to file a legal suit for damages. In Pennsylvania, the default is the higher cost policy that includes coverage for damages. In both states, most vehicle owners took the default option.

Again, you would expect some switching away from the default option in both states since some drivers would not be willing to sue for damages resulting from an accident (New Jersey) or some drivers would be more optimistic that they would not have any accidents involving damages (Pennsylvania). This was not the case. The status quo bias overwhelmed any variation in behavior toward risk.

In another experiment, two groups of consumers were asked to choose between two service providers. One gave reliable service and high electricity rates as the default, and the other less reliable service and lower electricity rates as the default. The two groups had distinctly different records of service reliability yet both picked the status quo, even though the low reliability group could have increased the reliability of service with an increase in rates of 30 percent. Almost none of the first group picked a low reliability option even though it came with a 30 percent reduction in rates.

In the financial world, status quo bias relates to the predisposition of investors to hold on to losers too long and sell winners too early. In this context, status quo bias has been called the "disposition effect". The disposition effect has been studied in a number of markets and found to be generally valid. There are a number of recent papers on the subject. See, for example, Weber and Camerer (1998), Barber and Odean (1999), Shefrin and Statman (1985) and Shefrin (2002).

3.5 Elements of Prospect Theory — Risk Taking after Profit

Risk taking after profit is an interesting component of prospect theory that is also considered by List (2003a) and others. It has been widely observed that people take more risks on subsequent transactions after making a profit on a transaction than they would have taken if they had not made the profit. A gambler who may have bet conservatively when losing or breaking even, will bet more and take more risks after winning. This leads to a bubble mentality and can explain why gamblers often bet away their winnings and leave the table penniless.

Santos (2001) argues that people are less risk averse following prior gains, a behavior called the "house money effect", and more risk averse after prior losses. This behavior has been called the house money effect because it is reminiscent of the expression "playing with the house money", used to describe gamblers' increased willingness to take risks when ahead. It is also argued that in financial markets, investors are "loss averse", meaning they become very conservative and try to avoid making more losses. The amount of loss aversion depends on their prior investment performance. Big losers are gun shy. In this way, volatility is built into stock returns. Stocks are bid up and down based on past experience. Wins result in more speculation. When luck changes, the spiral reverses itself and investors are reluctant to get into the market again. Markets do not seem to have a natural self-correcting mechanism that comes into effect quickly.

Sometimes there are complications and the attitude toward risk after a loss becomes less predictable. For example, consider the research of Thaler and Johnson (1990), who investigated the house money effect in a detailed way, focusing on behavior over time. They report a number of different experiments that test the house money effect. In particular, they explore whether subjects in the experiments spread or segregate gains and whether they consolidate/integrate/compress losses. They also investigate whether they segregate or spread small gains from larger losses and finally, whether they integrate or cancel small losses against larger gains. The major conclusion they draw from these experiments is that subjects tend to spread out gains so that they can experience the emotional high of a gain many times. They do, however, generally tend to consolidate losses so that they do not have to experience the sting of defeat more than once.

Thaler and Johnson (1990) go on to explore the house money effect from a different perspective. In general, the house money effect has to do with the sequential pattern of behavior from gains and losses, risk taking and the sequence of gains and losses. First of all, they show that history does matter. They conclude that previous losses and gains do affect subsequent behavior, unlike the assumption of economics that suggests that history is not important. In the case of a gamble after a gain, there is usually an increased tendency to take risks. The reason is that losing the "house money", money you have just won, is not as painful as losing your own money that you came to the table with. Therefore, you are willing to take more risks because the pain of losing is lower when players are using the house money. However, if the decision or game is compressed into a one-stage game, then risk seeking falls. The sense of "being ahead" is lost. Risk taking in the case of the house money effect is not as much about the decreasing marginal utility of money as the "ownership" or "lack of ownership". The gambler seems to segregate the money he came to the table with from the money won. The latter has less utility, perhaps because it was obtained without any work effort.

According to Thaler and Johnson (1990), the question of whether a prior loss induces risk seeking will depend on the reference point and the size of the loss and expected gain. They argue that "while an initial loss may induce risk aversion for some gambles, other gambles, which offer the opportunity to get even will be found acceptable" (Thaler and Johnson, 1990, p. 658). They explain this result by looking at the tendency of bettors at horse races to play long shots as the day progresses.

Kahneman and Tversky (1979) argue that this kind of behavior supports the hypothesis that a failure to adapt to losses or to attain an expected gain induces risk seeking. However, Thaler and Johnson (1990) say this depends on the background conditions of the bettor. A risk seeking bettor who is losing $30 could bet $30 on the even money favorite as a method of recovery. However, the increased loss aversion produced by prior losses renders this strategy unappealing, in which case a $2 bet on a long shot offers a more attractive chance at recovery because "it does not risk a significant further loss". This kind of behavior also explains why many people bet on "the numbers". It is highly risky but the stakes are low. This suggests that there may be some threshold level of loss that can be incurred without much loss in utility. Once this threshold is passed, additional losses may bring significant loss in utility. That could be why gamblers bet on long shots toward the end of the day or end of the racing day if they are at the race track. They are trying to get even, i.e., get back to where they started the day.

Thaler and Johnson (1990) also explore the outcomes of these different strategies in terms of risk taking and risk aversion in the context of framing of decisions. In particular, they are concerned with the effect of the timing and sequence of loss and gains on behavior. The hypothesis that people take risks following a loss may not always be true if people are not given an opportunity to break even in the next round. They suggest that prior losses may sensitize people to subsequent losses. In one experiment, subjects reported that a $9 loss hurt more following a $30 loss than if it had occurred by itself. This increased loss aversion would tend to produce risk aversion in gamblers from risking additional losses. They also argue that the house money effect is strong but tends to diminish as the new stake approaches the level of previous winnings. The break even effect noted above demonstrates that unless there is an opportunity to get back to a break even point, then losers may remain risk averse. The tendency to hope to break even can also explain why loss-making enterprises still remain in business hoping to somehow "right the ship" and become profitable again.

3.6 Elements of Prospect Theory — Loss/Gain Asymmetry

The loss versus gain asymmetry is related to risk taking after a loss. It is more universally distinguished by the sequential attitudes toward risk following losses and gains, and it has been verified by a number of experiments. In one experiment, students were asked to play a series of games with different expected returns. They were asked if they were willing to play a "fair" game, a game where the probability of winning and losing a particular amount was the same (using the expected utility argument) — win or lose $100 by guessing the result of a coin toss. The students refused to play unless the odds were much more favorable for winning. In many experiments, this tradeoff is valued at two (or more); people would risk losing a dollar only if there is an equal probability of winning two dollars (see also Section 3.1.4 on certainty equivalents for more discussion of this point). These results also show that the certainly equivalent is low and that people are generally risk averse. In a test conducted by Olsen (1997), given a series of possible outcomes couched in vague terms, subjects gave large losses much higher weight than large gains (see Table 3.4).

The loss/gain asymmetry was also mentioned when we were analyzing the Allais paradox in Section 3.1.5. We saw that subjects were more likely to choose the riskier option when faced with a loss, whereas they chose a sure option when faced with a gain.

As a further insight into risk and choice, Kahneman, Knetsch and Thaler (1986a, b) argue that in situations involving risk, "choices are best explained by assuming that the significant carriers of utility are not states of wealth or welfare, but changes (in utility) relative to a neutral reference point" (1986a, p. 199). This situation is depicted in Figures 3.7 and 3.8. The slope of the value function for small gains and losses is about two to one.

Table 3.4 Rating of Outcomes

Attribute Rating	Rating
Chance of incurring a large loss relative to what is expected	2.2
The chance that the assets will earn less than the minimum needed to meet client's needs	2.6
The overall variability of assets' return over time	4.0
The chance that the assets will earn less than expected	4.1
The chance that the assets will earn less than it has historically	4.7
The chance of obtaining a large gain relative to what is expected	5.7

Note: 1 is very important, 7 is not important at all.
Source: Olsen (1997).

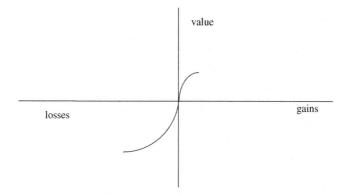

Figure 3.7 Value Function for Gains and Losses

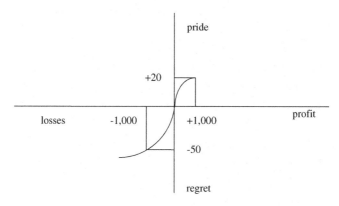

Figure 3.8 Value Function for "Pride" and "Regret"

In a series of experiments dealing with different initial positions, they discovered that experimental subjects were "more sensitive to the dimension in which they were losing relative to their reference point" (Kahneman, Knetsch and Thaler, 1986a, p. 201). For example, when subjects were asked to choose between two alternative jobs that had different amounts of social interaction and commuting time, they tended to select the new job that was more similar to the present job. Furthermore, loss aversion pertains more strongly to affect owners of goods that have been bought for personal use rather than those that are to be traded as we saw in the "endowment effect" discussion above. People are much less willing to give up a personal possession than an item to be traded. Stock traders who work in the market every day are much more willing to sell a loser than a private investor who has a stake in "his portfolio" and is reluctant to sell.

The emotional intensity of a loss is greater than for a gain. This aspect of behavior and emotional reaction can be seen by redrawing Figure 3.7, renaming the vertical axis as "pride" for positive gains and "regret" for losses as shown in Figure 3.8. We can see from this new Figure 3.8 that a gain of $1,000 and a loss of $1,000 have much different emotional value. The loss is felt two and half times more strongly than a gain, −50 versus +20. Regret is a more powerful motivator than pride. These results show a strong loss aversion — people are generally reluctant to accept losses.

A further example of this loss aversion is reflected by the disposition effect among stock traders. Traders hold losers too long and sell winners too early. It also manifests in what stock traders call the sunk cost effect. This behavior results in traders taking even greater chances by buying more risky stocks when losing in order to recoup losses. Gamblers do the same thing.

3.7 Elements of Prospect Theory — Framing Effects and Risk

Laury and Holt (2000) revisit the framing paradox in the context of risk. This paradox states that the way a problem is framed will result in a dramatic shift in choice, even when the underlying expected probabilities are the same in both alternatives. When negative payoffs replace positive payoffs while the expected gains/losses remain identical, decisions are essentially reversed.

For example, given a 90 percent chance of getting $3,000 (expected value of $2,700 gain) and a 45 percent chance of gaining $6,000 (again yielding an expected value of $2,700 gain), then the vast majority of subjects (around 90 percent) chose the first option, the one with less risk. On the other hand, when the "frame" is reversed and the choice is put in the negative, the decision is reversed. For example, the first option is replaced by a 90 percent chance of losing $3,000 (again the expectation is $2,700, but now for a loss) and the second option is replaced by a 45 percent chance of losing $6,000 (again a $2,700, loss). The replacement of gain with loss resulted in a change in risk taking. Now the majority of people (close to 90 percent) picked the second option, the more risky option, despite the fact that the expected value remained at a negative $2,700. The only change is the expectation for a loss of $2,700, not a gain of $2,700. The intuitive explanation for this shift in behavior is that because the loss "hurts more", people pick the option with the lower probability, despite the fact the expected payoffs are the same.

Laury and Holt (2000) consider the implications of such behavior for the Coase theorem. The Coase theorem is a powerful theorem in public choice economics that says we can compensate losers from the gains of winners. If preferences are not symmetric, the Coase solution would not lead to a Pareto optimum, since the losers will be more adversely affected than the winners. Winners are not able to "compensate" losers as Coase suggests because dollar losses are more "valuable" than dollar gains.

A notable and robust example of this kind of framing effect was illustrated by Tversky and Kahneman (1981) using the "Asian disease problem".

3.7.1 *Problem 1 (N = 152)*

Imagine that the US is preparing for the outbreak of an unusual Asian disease, which is expected to kill 600 people. Two alternative programs to combat the disease have been proposed. Assume that the exact scientific estimates of the consequences of the programs are as follows:

Program A: If Program A is adopted, 200 people will be saved (72 percent).

Program B: If Program B is adopted, there is 1/3 probability that 600 people will be saved, and 2/3 probability that no one will be saved (28 percent).

Which of the two programs would you favor?

Tversky and Kahneman (1981) found that the majority choice in this problem was risk averse: the prospect of saving 200 lives with certainty was more promising than the probability of a one-in-three chance of saving 600 lives. This risky prospect B was of equal expected value as the first prospect A.

A second group of respondents were given the same story of the Asian disease problem, but were provided with different program options.

3.7.2 *Problem 2 (N = 155)*

Program C: If Program C is adopted, 400 people will die (22 percent).

Program D: If Program D is adopted, there is 1/3 probability that nobody will die, and 2/3 probability that 600 people will die (78 percent).

Which of the two programs would you favor?

The majority choice of respondents in the second problem was risk taking: the certain death of 400 people is less acceptable than the two-in-three chance that 600 people will die. Even though the alternative programs in Problem 2 are identical to the first set of alternatives in Problem 1 in the sense that the probabilities of success and failure are the same, the vast majority (nearly 80 percent) picked Program D. In the second scenario, the respondents rejected the sure solution and accepted the choice where this is "hope of survival".

Because the outcomes are stated in lives lost in the second case, the majority choice is risk seeking. In the first case, the alternatives are put in positive terms and the result is risk averse. The prospect of saving 200 lives is more attractive than a risky prospect of equal expected value. The same result has been shown in many other experiments and reflects the risk taking attitudes to avert a bad situation and risk aversion attitudes to maintain a good situation.

3.8   Elements of Prospect Theory — Risk and Return

We address the standard finance problem of risk and return to assets by using the results of prospect theory. Placing the risk-return issue in perspective of prospect theory, some research has uncovered a negative relationship between risk and return (Fiegenbaum and Thomas, 1988). They build on the observation by Bowman (1982) that there is indeed a negative relationship between risk and return. Bowman's analysis results in a U-shaped risk-return relationship with the inflection point being around the target rate of return (see Figure 3.9). Fiegenbaum and Thomas' study of US firms confirms this relationship between risk and return. To the far left of the inflection point, firms will be risk taking in order to get back to a target rate of return. Firms will also take risk once they have gone substantially above the target rate to the right of the inflection point. Near the inflection point firms will be risk averse, not wanting to disturb their target equilibrium. How do you think mergers and acquisition are affected by such behavior?

Another aspect of risk and return relates to behavior that has been dubbed "risk homeostasis". This behavior implies that there is an optimum or equilibrium level of risk that people are generally comfortable with. If this is true, then efforts to decrease risk may be met by riskier behavior. Consider the case of farm tractors and road design. When tractors were designed for greater stability, farmers used them on steeper slopes and the accident rate tended to remain constant. When highways were designed to be safer, drivers increased their speed and took more risks and the accident rate tended to return to previous levels (see Slovic, 1984, for details).

Figure 3.9 Risk-Return Tradeoff

Source: Fiegenbaum and Thomas (1988, p. 98, Figure 1).

3.9 Elements of Prospect Theory — Rare and Nearly Sure Events

As noted in Section 3.1, many experiments have shown that there are dramatic changes in the weighting of risks when the probability of the event under question is very low or very high (see Figure 3.10). The psychological reasons for these adjustments are unclear. It could be that people give these events probabilities of zero and one and only adjust the probabilities when the likelihood of the event departs from very unlikely or very likely by a significant amount. Rottenstreich and Hsee (2001) argue that this behavior could also be a result of the introduction of fear (or hope) to the outcome being different from zero or one, sure or not possible. Rottenstreich and Hsee label this response as an affective or emotional factor that biases the weights near zero or one. They also contend that the strength of this emotional reaction will have an impact on the shape of the weighting function.

In general, people either ignore low probability events or fail to react logically to low probability events. This inhibits their ability to conceptualize or imagine events that have not occurred. Hurricane Katrina in the US demonstrates this by way of the lack of appropriate flood planning in New Orleans, Louisiana. This is partly a result of the future being perceived as a mirror of the past. When the immediate past does not contain a catastrophic or massive natural or manmade disaster, we do not have any way of dealing with it in a probabilistic sense.

Another perspective on rare events is provided in experiments conducted by Shanteau (1992). Students were told that a natural disaster had occurred last year. They were then asked whether they would be willing to pay more for insurance. The results suggest that respondents felt once a rare event had occurred, they were somehow inoculated against a repeat in the coming year. As a result, most respondents were not willing to pay more for insurance. This could explain why residents in flood-prone areas are willing to move back into their homes following a major flood without insurance (see Kunreuther and Slovic, 1978).

Another interesting observation arises in the study of disease. Schneiderman and Kaplan (1992) look at two diseases, HIV and Hepatitis B, in terms of probabilities of contracting the diseases and of dying of the disease once it has been contracted. In the case of Hepatitis B, the probability of getting the disease was 25 percent and five percent of those who contract the disease die. On the other hand, the chance of getting HIV is calculated at one percent with death certain. In an expected utility sense, the probabilities of dying in the general population are the same for both diseases — about one percent (25 percent × five percent is 1.25 percent) for Hepatitis B, which is nearly the same as the probability of dying from AIDS.

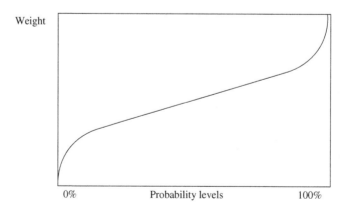

Figure 3.10 Weights of Unlikely and Nearly Sure Events

Nevertheless, the concern over HIV is much greater than over Hepatitis B. Why? The authors suspect that it is because of the certainty of death in the HIV case:

> Fear of living for any length of time infected with a virus for which the outcomes are always fatal apparently overrides the concern that the initial chances of being infected are small.... Who would not prefer to live, no matter how long or short a time, in a state of hopeful uncertainty when it comes to death (as most of us do every day) than to be forced to alter our perception and live in a state of dismal certainty (Schneiderman and Kaplan, 1992, p. 586).

This intuition is confirmed by experiments with students who were asked a question about being stung by insects in a jungle that mirrored the probabilities of Hepatitis B and HIV. They tended to prefer the option where death was not certain and the probability of getting stung was higher.

The logic of these alternative choices is similar to the fear of an airplane crash versus an automobile crash. There are always many fatalities when an airplane crashes, yet there are very few plane crashes per mile traveled relative to fatal accidents per mile when traveling by car. Many people have been involved in a car accident in their lifetime. Using expected utility formulas, the per mile risk of dying in a car crash is much higher than in an airplane crash. Nevertheless, air travel is more feared than car travel probably because the perceived risk of dying in an airplane crash is so much higher.

3.10 Elements of Prospect Theory — Time and Diversification Effects

The time diversification effect can be best explained by an example. Consider the problem posed by Paul Samuelson (1963b) to a colleague. He asked a colleague if he would accept a bet given a 50 percent chance of winning $200 and a 50 percent chance of losing $100. His colleague replied that he would not accept this bet but he would be happy to accept a series of such bets.

Why did the colleague suggest this alternative? Consider a weighting function which translates the expected utility into actual utility.

If $U(x)$, actual utility, is a function of the outcomes of winning or losing and their probabilities such that winning is weighted by the actual amount won but losing is weighted by 2.5 times the amount won, then the colleague is right to decline the bet. Samuelson expressed his colleague's feelings thus: "I won't bet because I would feel the $100 loss more than the $200 gain." Using our weighting function, he would feel an equivalent loss of $100 × 2.5 = $250.

But see what happens when we consider two sequential bets with the same weighting function and the same probability law. There are four sequences of possible outcomes with associated probabilities of 0.25: $200, $200; $200, –$100; –$100, $200; –$100, –$100. Adding all of these expected outcomes together, we get the overall expected outcome of two bets:

$$\$400(1/4) + \$100(1/4) + \$100(1/4) - \$200(1/4)$$
$$= \$100 + \$25 + \$25 - \$50 = \$150 - \$50.$$

If we weight the loss by 2.5 times the gain, we have $150 – (2.5 × $50) = $150 – $125, which is positive. This explains why the colleague would accept the two-bet alternative but would not accept the one-bet alternative. Of course, the actual outcome will depend upon the actual sequence of events and could lead to a loss. However, the expected value of the bet sequence will continue to get larger as the number of trials increases. The three-bet sequence will give an even higher return.

This simple example leads to a general idea that the longer the time horizon, the more attracted investors will be to risky assets. Risk is an increasing function of time in the prospect theory framework and flows from the higher value put on negative outcomes.

A combination of short time horizon and risk aversion leads to myopic loss aversion, a concept discussed in Section 3.4. Benartzi and Thaler (1995) contend that myopic loss aversion may help to explain the low return on bonds versus equities in the US over the last 100 years or so. Investors place more importance on short-term goals. They feel compelled to hold bonds which perform better in the short-run rather than stocks which perform better in the long-run. Investors demand a very high stock premium to shift from bonds to stocks. In Section 3.4, we looked at myopic loss aversion as another aspect of the endowment effect. Joel Chernoff (2002) notes that investors may suffer from myopic loss aversion, which results in investors taking losses because they refuse to sell bonds and look into long-term stock investment alternatives.

3.11 Aspects of Prospect Theory — Mental Accounting

There is a range of behavior that has been grouped under the heading of "mental accounting". Mental accounting describes a mental process that categorizes expenditures into different categories, sometimes on the basis of generalizations about how the individual expects to act in the future. These future actions are anticipated and so current actions are taken to protect against how the formation of undesirable future decisions. For example, a gambler or heavy drinker will shy away from the craps table or the gin mill for fear of falling into a future cycle of bad habits. While this may apply to potential addiction, it may not apply to benign behavior. A person acting in the present moment makes the generalization that he/she will act the same way in the future even though there is no logical reason for believing this to be true.

In a sense, this is an intertemporal example of Kant's categorical imperative (see also the discussion in Chapter 5 on altruism). Kant's idea is that all future actions will be the same as the present action or that others are assumed to follow our course of action. This assumption can lead to decisions that are not strictly rational in the usual sense of the word. Take, for example, the spending pattern of unexpected income. Milton Friedman (1957) divided permanent and transitory income into two groups and formulated the hypothesis that consumption decisions would be made on the basis of permanent income. All transitory income would be saved. Another possibility is that it is easier to spend windfall gains while constraining spending out of permanent income. Consumers may reason, "It's okay to spend windfall gains which occur infrequently rather than to be always spending a lot of money".

In any event, this categorizing of income flows requires a mental accounting of where the money came from to justify either spending or saving it. In general, people manage money differently depending on their mental accounting. This mental accounting incorporates both the goals of the individual and the source of the money.

Consider the example of a man who goes into a store and admires a cashmere sweater (Thaler, 1985). He does not buy it because it is too expensive — say $300. Later on, his wife buys it for him for his birthday and he is overjoyed. He and his wife share the same bank account. What is the rationale for this change in attitude? Why does he not ask his wife to return the sweater because it costs too much? Let us assume that it is not because he does not want to irritate his wife. Thaler gives several possibilities for this change in attitude. First, as his wife bought the sweater for his birthday, he could argue it is a one-time expense and he does not have to worry about becoming an extravagant spender. Second, since it is a special occasion and special occasions occur infrequently, it is okay to splurge once in a while.

Consider a second example (Thaler, 1980). A family pays $100 for tickets to a baseball game to be played 50 miles from home. On the day of the game, the family goes to the game despite a snowstorm. However, if the tickets had been given as a gift they would probably have stayed home. What is the logic behind this decision? If they had stayed home after paying for the tickets they might have thought, "We always buy tickets and don't use them", which is not a desirable pattern of behavior as it is wasteful.

In the second case of gift tickets they might have thought, "We often don't use tickets that are given to us". This is acceptable because they are not wasting their own money. The first pattern of behavior is undesirable, particularly if it is repeated. If we make the overgeneralization implied by Kant's categorical imperative, we would be very distressed by this because of the impact it would have on our future lifestyle.

Self-signaling is another way of understanding the behavior in these and other similar circumstances. The family going to the game wants to prove to themselves that they are not the kind of people who do not use what they buy. The man going into the store is trying to prove to himself that he has restraint by not buying the expensive sweater on impulse. However, he might have acted differently had he just gotten an unexpected windfall! Viewed in this way, the purchase of the sweater is similar to the house money effect in gambling. Extravagant spending exhibits a similar mindset to taking greater risks with a windfall.

3.12 Alternative Theories

Beside prospect theory which allows for myopia and emotion into the economic equations, other behavioral theories have also arisen to explain the workings of individual decision making. In this section, we include discussion of models which attempt to relax the key assumptions behind Samuelson's (1937) discounted utility model. Key assumptions behind Samuelson's model include: (i) positive time preference — consumers prefer to receive a good sooner than later; (ii) constant discount rate — preferences over time are consistent; (iii) independence of utility; (iv) independence of consumption; (v) stationary instantaneous utility; and (vi) independence of discount rate.

Several alternatives to the Samuelson model are also suggested. They include how emotional anticipation affects decisions, the possibility of discount rates that are not constant over time such as models with hyperbolic discounting, and the multiple selves model (Loewenstein, 1987, 2006; Laibson, 1994, 1997; Ainslie and Haslam, 1992).

3.12.1 *Utility from anticipation*

Individuals derive pleasure from current consumption and anticipation of future consumption. In real life, decision makers sometimes prefer to delay consumption for future benefits. This violates one of the assumptions in Samuelson's discounted utility model that decision makers prefer to receive the good "sooner than later" and that immediate gratification of desires is more desirable than gratification later on. Loewenstein (1987) captures the anticipation of future outcomes into the standard utility function in intertemporal choices of individuals by assuming that instantaneous utility of the individual is the sum of the utility from present consumption plus some function of the discounted utility in future periods. The existence of the additional incentive — anticipated utility of future consumption — could explain why individual agents could prefer to delay gratification rather than just enjoying consumption in the present moment. For example, an individual could defer his holiday plans, preferring to take his vacation at the end of the year during Christmas when work obligations are minimal and he can enjoy his vacation without worrying about what is happening at the office while he is away. In this way, the Loewenstein approach incorporates farsightedness into the model and the pleasurable emotions that arise from anticipation of a future event.

On the other hand, frustration could arise when immediate gratification of desires overcomes the anticipation of future benefits. Other anticipatory emotions such as anxiety and fear could also enter into and affect people's choices. Caplin and Leahy (2001) point out that anxiety help to explain the equity premium puzzle of why investors generally prefer low risk bonds to more risky assets such as stocks. Anxiety over the possible volatility of stock prices and the fear of loss overcomes their higher expected future income relative to bonds.

In the evolving literature on neuroeconomics (see also the discussion of the Allais paradox in Section 3.1.5), researchers looking at brain functions discovered that choosing between immediate and delayed gratification constitutes a battle between limbic structures that invoke more primitive and emotional reactions based on immediate gratification, and more newly developed cortical regions of the brain that rely on reason and the evaluation of tradeoffs. As opposed to instant gratification, Berns *et al.* (2006) conduct an interesting experiment on immediate and delayed pain. Rationally we do not expect people to choose more pain in the short-run. Rational people should delay events with unfavorable outcomes for as long as possible. However, results of this pain experiment found a different outcome. In a brain imaging study of 32 participants to detect brain activity in responses to pain, a series of brief electronic shocks was applied to the top of the left feet of the participants. Participants were provided with options involving various combinations of the amount of voltage (pain) they were going to experience and the time they had to wait for it. For instance, one option may be 90 percent of maximum pain after three seconds or 60 percent after 27 seconds. Brain scanners were used to detect the "dread response", i.e., the anticipation of the pain. Two-thirds of the participants generally chose as short a delay as they could with a given level of pain suffered, and one-third even willingly accepted highest voltage sooner than later. These "extreme dreaders" were willing to accept the pain as soon as possible to avoid a long dread response.

The notion that information directly confers pain or pleasure to the individual is interesting because it seems to offer an explanation to an observed anomaly as to why individuals prefer improving sequences to declining sequences. Researchers such as Hsee *et al.* (1991) have reported preferences for an increasing salary sequence rather than a decreasing sequence, even if the latter has greater total monetary value. In another study, Varey and Kahneman (1992) reported that participants surveyed reported strong preference for streams of decreasing discomfort over streams of increasing discomfort, even though the overall sum of discomfort was equal for both streams.

These developments in the ordering of preferences along with recent advances in neuroeconomics open an exciting new window for researchers to investigate and better understand interactions between expectations, emotions and decision making that have long baffled economists, psychologists and other social scientists.

3.12.2 *Hyperbolic discounting*

Hyperbolic discounting has been applied in a variety of areas in recent years. It has been used to model a variety of empirical observations in the consumption-saving literature (Laibson *et al.*, 1998; Angeletos *et al.*, 2001), problems of addiction (O'Donoghue and Rabin, 2000; Gruber and Koszegi, 2000) and principal-agent model with procrastination (Fischer, 1999; O'Donoghue and Rabin, 2001).

First, recall the standard Samuelson (1937) model of discounting that assumes utility is discounted at a *constant* rate over time.

It also implied that time preferences of the individual are consistent through time.[3] Strotz (1955–1956) questions this assumption. He notes that preferences are not always consistent at different points in time. For instance, individuals usually prefer to take $1.00 now rather than wait for a delayed reward of $1.20 at the end of the month. Similarly, when faced with the choice between $100 now and $110 tomorrow, individuals usually prefer to take $100 now. However, consider what happens when individuals are offered the same monetary choices with an identical one day delay at *different points of time in the future*. When individuals were offered the choice between *delayed rewards* at the end of a month's time, either $100 in 30 days or $110 in 31 days, they picked $110 after 31 days rather than $100 after 30 days. There was a reversal in preferences over time.

Such a preference reversal trend is well-documented and evidenced by studies (for example, Green *et al.*, 1994; Kirby and Herrnstein, 1995). Some economists feel this phenomenon could be explained by the individual's declining discount rate over time. The concept of declining discount rate or rather, hyperbolic discounting,[4] has received renewed interest with Laibson's (1994, 1997) papers. This behavior implies that the individual has asymmetric weights between choices yielding utility in the near-term compared with choices yielding utility in the longer-term.

Hyperbolic discounting means that the discount rates do not remain constant. They are greater in the near-term than in the long-run. Future outcomes generally tend to be valued lower. An outcome becomes more and more attractive as the time approaches when decisions have to be made.

---

[3]An individual is said to have consistent time preferences if his preferences remain consistent through time. Say if an individual prefers to have A in Day 1 than B in Day 2, he would also prefer to enjoy A in 30 days as compared to B in 31 days.

[4]Hyperbolic discounting is but one of the family of discount functions to explain intertemporal inconsistency. Quadratic hyperbolic discounting with its biases on the present is another (see Frederick *et al.*, 2005, and Soman *et al.*, 2005, for a review of time preference and time discounting).

People find it hard to resist rewards and yet can behave patiently in the long-run. With hyperbolic discounting, Laibson (1997) suggests that individuals respond to immediate cost and benefits. He illustrates this by noting that credit card debt is large in the US, even though interest rates are extremely high (18 percent or more). He suggests this is because individuals place such a high value on immediate gratification and are willing to incur high interest charges. Placing higher value on the immediate short-run and lower value on the long-term future is consistent with hyperbolic discounting. It explains why households are impatient in the short-run, chalking up expensive credit card debts with high interest rates, and yet patient in the long-run, buying illiquid assets such as homes and long-term investment packages with low interest payouts.

Hyperbolic discounting has also been used to explain substance abuse by addicted individuals. Studies by O'Donoghue and Rabin (2000) and Gruber and Koszegi (2000) found that hyperbolic discounting can lead people to overconsume addictive substances by overweighing the immediate gratification of needs. Madden *et al.* (1999) pose two scenarios to empirically investigate delayed reward discounting of drug addicts using the exponential constant discount function and hyperbolic discount function. In the first scenario, participants chose between immediate and delayed hypothetical monetary rewards of $1,000. In the second scenario, participants chose between immediate and delayed amounts of what drugs $1,000 could buy. Madden *et al.* (1999) found that the hyperbolic discount function was a better model of behavior than constant discounting. Addicts chose the immediate option.

Are there any ways to get around the problem implied by hyperbolic discounting? At the country and global level, the future impact of current environmental policies is difficult to predict, yet will be experienced for many years to come. At the individual level, Laibson (1997) assumes that individuals are sophisticated enough to know that "later" selves may not honor the well-meaning intentions of "early" selves. Most individuals have self-control problems. To get around this problem of lack of self-control, he proposes the use of binding personal commitments that would commit individuals irrevocably towards some preferred course of action both in the present and the future. For instance, to prohibit individuals from spending excessively and using credit card debt while ending up with little savings in the future, irrevocable commitments can be made to save by contributing to saving schemes, retirement programs or by buying less liquid assets such as houses. Commitments to strengthen self-resolve are discussed in the next two sections.

Why are people patient in the long-run? One approach to this question is to look at coupon clipping. People clip coupons regularly in anticipation of cashing them in at some future time. However, they do not mail the coupon because they are too busy with other things. Nevertheless, they still cut the coupons.

Psychologists have a theory to explain why time changes the utility of an outcome which is consistent with hyperbolic discounting — they call it temporal construct theory (Trope and Liberman, 2003). Immediate outcomes are dominated by low-level attributes, whereas future outcomes are dominated by high-level attributes. Low-level attributes focus on the task required to attain the desired outcome. High-level attributes relate to the longer-run outcome underlying the choice. For instance, learning a new language is associated with high-level attributes of enhanced communication skills and the joy of learning, while the lower-level attributes of learning a new language include going to class, doing homework and the difficulties encountered in mastering a new language.

Hence, when faced with the prospect of learning a new language in the immediate future, the outcomes tend to be dominated by low-level attributes and will appear unattractive. On the other hand, when viewed from a longer-term perspective, the prospect of learning a new language in the future is dominated by high-level attributes and the delayed outcome will be more attractive as the individual contemplates the activity which will take place sometime in the future (Soman *et al.*, 2005).

Why are people impatient in the short-run? Hyperbolic discounting does not seem to be able to fully account for the observed anomalies of instantaneous gratification. Why do people place higher value on choices with nearer-term outcomes? In a way, this behavior appears to be linked to what Loewenstein (2004) calls visceral effects such as hunger and greed. The visceral effects act as a cue or mechanism to trigger the immediate short-run response for satisfaction of desires. Impulsive behavior results in spur-of-the-moment actions. These decisions are often not in our long-run best interest and/or are inconsistent with rational judgment.

Gifford (2002) suggests a biology-based model of choice as an explanation. The brain is facilitated by both a lower-level system which assigns values and motivates action, and a higher-level system which is able to undertake deliberate thinking and process higher-order cognitive skills. The lack of self-control is due to an inability to control the emotions.

3.12.3 *Multiple selves model, self-control and self-reputation*

Another way to look at the discounting problems is to realize that individuals face internal conflicts when determining their choices in the future. This gives rise to the multiple selves model, where myopic selves are in conflict with farsighted ones (Ainslie and Haslam, 1992; Schelling, 1984). Individuals can try to resist temptation in order to build up future utility (the farsighted self) or give in to instant gratification (the shortsighted self). The two selves fight for control over decision making. The farsighted self would have the foresight to predict actions of the myopic self but not vice versa. Individuals are sophisticated enough to have the self-awareness to understand their actions will fall between the range of the myopic self and farsighted self. However, they may be powerless to take farsighted decisions when tempted by shortsighted alternatives.

Recall the discussion in Section 3.10 about how time diversification effects encourage investors to hold riskier assets such as stocks in the long-run. However, if bad news comes into play, say there is news of prices of stocks falling over the past two years, investors are very likely to "want out" *despite* having an initial long-term horizon mapped by the farsighted self. Would investors hold on despite the "pain derived from the information" and short-term mental accounting that leads to myopia? This arises due to cognitive error and lack of self-control (Fisher and Statman, 1999).

Psychologists and economists alike (Ainslie, 1975; Prelec, 1989; Loewenstein and Prelec, 1992) stress the importance of declining discount rates (hyperbolic discounting) on self-regulation problems. Rules and commitment devices are in place to foster self-control (Loewenstein, 2000; Bénabou and Tirole, 2004). Tying oneself to the mast such as Ulysses is an example of external commitment (see Box 3.1). Other external commitments include signing contracts with deadlines. Internal commitments could be in the form of rules and regulations such as diets, moral resolutions such as regular exercise one hour daily, writing a certain amount of pages daily, or for New York cab drivers to drive a certain number of hours daily (Camerer *et al.*, 1997).

Box 3.1 Ulysses' Adventure with the Sirens

In Homer's ancient Greece mythology, the adventurer Ulysses learns from Circes that he will pass near the island of the Sirens who have lured countless sailors with their sweet bewitching songs to throw themselves into the seas and ultimate death by drowning or sea monsters. Upon Circes' advice, he comes out with an ingenious solution to listen to the songs of the Sirens safely. He instructs his crew members to lash him to the ship's mast while advising them to fill their ears with wax so that they are unaffected by the Siren's beautiful but deadly cries. He advises them not to untie him until he gives them a pre-designated signal that they are far away from danger and away from hearing range of the Sirens' island. As they approached the island, there arose notes so sweet and enchanting that Ulysses forgot about all thoughts of danger in his struggle to get to the source of the music. He pleaded with his crew to release him. His crew, obedient to his previous orders, sprang forward and bound him tighter. They kept on course, and the music grew fainter and ceased to be heard. Then with joy Ulysses gave his companions the signal to unseal their ears; and they relieved him from his bonds. It is said that one of the Sirens, Parthenope, in grief at the escape of Ulysses, drowned herself. Her body was cast up on the Italian shore where the city of Naples now stands.

Source: Adapted from http://www.2020site.org/ulysses/sirens.html.

Building upon the work of Ainslie (1992, 2001), Bénabou and Tirole (2004) explicitly suggest a model of personal rules based on what they call "self-reputation". Individuals are assumed to have imperfect knowledge of their willpower and are assumed to have imperfect recall of past actions and motives. This is because it is difficult to recall the intensity of stress, temptation and other short-run visceral emotions. Furthermore, it is often selective and self-serving. People tend to recall successful outcomes more often than failed ones. People also tend to believe what they wish to believe, which easily distorts the decision making process. Finally, it is often difficult to differentiate why individuals act in certain ways — is it because of a well-defined belief system or is it a reaction to circumstances?

In Figure 3.11, the individual faces a horizon of two periods, subperiod I and subperiod II. He can choose the "no-willpower option" to satisfy his desire immediately by eating, drinking or smoking without resisting the urge. He obtains benefit a. Alternatively, he could pursue a "willpower dependent project" where he attempts to exercise his willpower or abstinence over immediate gratification. If he gives up halfway, he receives a delayed benefit $b > a$. If he proceeds with his intended course of action that his farsighted self has promulgated, he incurs a loss of craving cost c, but gains better benefit (better

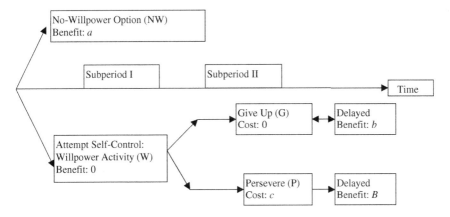

Figure 3.11 Willpower and Personal Rules

Source: Bénabou and Tirole (2004, p. 857, Figure 1).

health or career, higher consumption) $B > b$. The three selected courses of action — (i) non-resistance, (ii) trying but quitting, and (iii) perseverance — yield differing levels of utility. Internal commitments are more efficient than external commitments as they promote self-signaling, heighten self-confidence and strengthen the level of self-regulation. The fear of setting precedents that disrupt willpower and undermine self-control in the future preempts the individual from giving in to temptation. If he resists the temptation successfully, he sends a positive signal to himself. He feels good about his ability to practice self-control and may derive utility from self-reputation (Loewenstein, 2000).

On the other hand, external constraints are good for those who have low levels of self-confidence and need the external commitments to bind them to a pre-committed course of action. It is also possible that there could be individuals who place excessively high value on the future than the present, for example, workaholics and those suffering from anorexia. Workaholics go without leisure and feel compelled to work incessantly. Anorexic individuals severely deprive themselves of food in order to fulfill their wish of being slim in the future. For those who are anorexic, every single decision taken is a test of willpower and self-control. The regimen ends up being overly excessive and rigid with negative side-effects on utility.

Self-controls have been incorporated into more sophisticated hyperbolic discounting models (Laibson, 1994, 1997). In these models, agents with hyperbolic discounting can put more weight on the future relative to the present (Bénabou and Tirole, 2004). To complicate matters further, choices bring consequences, emotions and recollections of memories. Although individuals do not have perfect memory recall, their actions are based upon these memories of past experiences, motives and emotions. These memories and emotions provide a basis of self-signaling. Through this self-signaling process, individuals gain or lose self-confidence. This in turn has feedback effects on self-reputation and utility (Loewenstein, 2000). There is no guarantee that this process will be self-regulating and beneficial. If the workaholic gets positive feedback, he may continue to overwork himself and suffer burnout. If the anorexic gets positive feedback, the process can continue with detrimental impacts on health.

Information is one important determinant process. How to react to information gleaned from others and from one's actions is important. The multiple selves model and self-control model have been extended into interactions with others (Battaglini *et al.*, 2002). These models are discussed in greater detail in Chapter 4. In the next section, we continue with a discussion of memory.

3.13 Memory, Bounded Rationality and Prospect Theory

Researchers on memory and decision making have developed a simple description of the features of memories that can be related to bounded rationality and prospect theory. Mullainathan (2002) has developed a series of descriptors that relate memory to current assessment of probabilities and potentials for action.

Rehearsal is the process of recalling a memory. This process increases the probability of recalling the memory in the future and could bias the assessment of the likelihood of the event being repeated. Recall of events will differ on circumstances and the strength of the memory. A lover who has been rejected may recall it again and again, and this will bias the individual's assessment as to whether he/she will be rejected again if they enter another relationship, an assessment that may not be realistic. In another example, some family members get sick after going to a particular restaurant chain. As a result, the family avoids the restaurant chain. The same thing happened to me as a child and our family never went to any of the restaurants in that restaurant chain ever again.

Associativeness is the characteristic of memory that recalls events that are similar to the current situation. We may have had the experience of going to a resort and being reminded of other similar resorts or of a mall that reminds us of another mall. A man sees a woman and she reminds him of another woman that he met in a similar set of circumstances. Associativeness involves cues that bring back such memories. For example, things learned in a particular mood are better remembered in that mood. Students can remember lessons if they study in the same surroundings week after week. By the same token, associativeness can result in selective memory patterns leading to the conclusion that more easily remembered events are more probable. If a person loses at the race track he may be more likely to believe that he is going to lose again on his next visit. As a result, he reassesses the probability of loss and gain and changes his betting pattern.

Vividness is the characteristic of a seemingly random event that has many things in common with a commonly encountered event. Vividness results in that event being given a much higher probability of occurring, even though it is uncommon, because it has many features in common with commonly encountered events. Because the unusual event also maps easily with more commonly encountered events, it is more easily recalled and the probability of its recurring is also rated more likely than a less vivid event. Someone sees a plane crashing on the runway as it lands. This person has seen many planes land safely before. The vividness of this event is enhanced because much of what is happening as the plane lands and then crashes is embedded in his memory. Since the event is vivid and will be recalled through the association of the crash with airplanes and airports, the individual may be scared of both airplanes and airports.

Evocativeness is the measure of the information content of memory. Evocativeness influences what memories are triggered and also affects belief about the recurrence of events. For example, seeing a crime evokes other crime scenes whether they are real, from TV, from books or from imagination. Being involved in a natural disaster such as an earthquake, forest fire, tsunami or hurricane creates a pattern whereby the recurrence of these events may be reevaluated and given a different probability.

From an analysis of these factors, brain researchers have drawn several general conclusions:

- Easily remembered events are judged as being more probable.
- Beliefs persist even after original evidence has been discredited.
- Memorable events are given much higher probabilities of recurring.
- Beliefs adjust slowly. Old memories are discarded in a decay process.
- Greater vividness and evocativeness increase the probability of recall and, as a result, are given a higher probability of recurrence.
- Individuals overreact to new information.

Expanding on these ideas, Mullainathan (2002) suggests that evocativeness leads to an overresponse to new information and creates undue volatility in markets. Researchers have found that prices move even when there is no apparent news to justify price movement. These movements could be a reaction to previous news or other unexplained emotional reactions of market participants. When prices do change, the new information could further increase volatility due to the evocative reaction of participants. In the case of consumption, the same overreaction to unexpected news creates volatility in spending that is not warranted by an objective view of the information. When the boss gives an employee a pat on the back along with a raise, it can lead to an upward shift in spending because the employee thinks his permanent income has increased.

Established beliefs and attachments are hard to dislodge. Memories of a bad day at the race track or a good win at the roulette wheel could have a strong impact on risk behavior. Memories of accidents may affect travel behavior. Memories of a failed love affair may prevent an individual from taking any steps to establish another relationship. In the realm of public policy and general attitudes of the population toward controversial issues of gun control, the war in Iraq, abortion, gay marriage, etc., we are all influenced by sensory inputs. Our attitudes are framed and influenced by conversations with friends and family, what programs we listen to or watch and our general social environment.

Memories of Holocaust survivors and those suffering from post-traumatic stress disorder have been shown to have long-term impacts on attitudes toward taking risks and also general attitudes toward others in society. Studies have shown that those who experienced long-term food deprivation and suffering during war tended to save more and consume less. They fear a recurrence and take precautions. Other things equal, there is evidence that adult Japanese citizens who survived World War II as adults consume less and save more than other younger Japanese who were born after the war ended.

In the US, the media often portrays Blacks and Hispanics as dangerous and prone to committing crimes. TV viewers see them being arrested and pursued for violent crimes on shows such as Cops much more often than Orientals or Caucasians. As a result, it is not unlikely that Caucasians may come to view Blacks and Hispanics as dangerous people that they would not like to associate with or help. Caucasians might even imagine being attacked by them. They would thus be the victims of the rare event fallacy discussed in Section 3.9. They might go out and buy a gun to protect themselves against such an attack. This behavior is not rational, given the fact that such attacks are quite rare and considering that the overall crime rate in the US has been falling for some time. A similar pattern of behavior could result from the events of 9/11 and attitudes toward Arab terrorists. The account of looting in New Orleans reported in the *New York Times* and reproduced in Box 3.2 demonstrates how rumor and predispositional beliefs created a fearful environment in the city after Hurricane Katrina.

Box 3.2 Fear in New Orleans

After the storm came the siege. In the days after Hurricane Katrina, terror from crimes seen and unseen, real and rumored, gripped New Orleans. The fears changed troop deployments, delayed medical evacuations, drove police officers to quit, grounded helicopters. Edwin P. Compass III, the police superintendent, said that tourists — the core of the city's economy — were being robbed and raped on streets that had slid into anarchy.

The mass misery in the city's two unlit and uncooled primary shelters, the convention center and the Superdome, was compounded, officials said, by gangs that were raping women and children.

A month later, a review of the available evidence now shows that some, though not all, of the most alarming stories that coursed through the city appear to be little more than figments of frightened imaginations, the product of chaotic circumstances that included no reliable communications, and perhaps the residue of the longstanding raw relations between some police officers and members of the public.

Beyond a doubt, the sense of menace had been ignited by genuine disorder and violence that week. Looting began at the moment the storm passed over New Orleans, and it ranged from base thievery to foraging for the necessities of life. ......

In an interview last week with the *New York Times*, Superintendent Compass said that some of his most shocking statements turned out to

(*Continued*)

Box 3.2 (*Continued*)

be untrue. Asked about reports of rapes and murders, he said: "We have no official reports to document any murder. Not one official report of rape or sexual assault."

On Sept. 4, however, he was quoted in the *Times* about conditions at the convention center, saying: "The tourists are walking around there, and as soon as these individuals see them, they're being preyed upon. They are beating, they are raping them in the streets."

Those comments, Superintendent Compass now says, were based on secondhand reports. The tourists "were walking with their suitcases, and they would have their clothes and things taken," he said last week. "No rapes that we can quantify." ...

Rumors Affected Response

To assemble a picture of crime, both real and perceived, the *New York Times* interviewed dozens of evacuees in four cities, police officers, medical workers and city officials. Though many provided concrete, firsthand accounts, others passed along secondhand information or rumor that after multiple tellings had ossified into what became accepted as fact.

What became clear is that the rumor of crime, as much as the reality of the public disorder, often played a powerful role in the emergency response. A team of paramedics was barred from entering Slidell, across Lake Pontchartrain from New Orleans, for nearly 10 hours based on a state trooper's report that a mob of armed, marauding people had commandeered boats. It turned out to be two men escaping from their flooded streets, said Farol Champlin, a paramedic with the Acadian Ambulance Company.

On another occasion, the company's ambulances were locked down after word came that a firehouse in Covington had been looted by armed robbers of all its water — a report that proved totally untrue, said Aaron Labatt, another paramedic.

A contingent of National Guard troops was sent to rescue a St. Bernard Parish deputy sheriff who radioed for help, saying he was pinned down by a sniper. Accompanied by a SWAT team, the troops surrounded the

(*Continued*)

Box 3.2 (*Continued*)

area. The shots turned out to be the relief valve on a gas tank that popped open every few minutes, said Maj. Gen. Ron Mason of the 35th Infantry Division of the Kansas National Guard.

"It's part of human nature," General Mason said. "When you get one or two reports, it echoes around the community."

Faced with reports that 400 to 500 armed looters were advancing on the town of Westwego, two police officers quit on the spot. The looters never appeared, said the Westwego police chief, Dwayne Munch.

"Rumors could tear down an entire army," Chief Munch said.

During six days when the Superdome was used as a shelter, the head of the New Orleans Police Department's sex crimes unit, Lt. David Benelli, said he and his officers lived inside the dome and ran down every rumor of rape or atrocity. In the end, they made two arrests for attempted sexual assault, and concluded that the other attacks had not happened.

"I think it was urban myth," said Lieutenant Benelli, who also heads the police union. "Any time you put 25,000 people under one roof, with no running water, no electricity and no information, stories get told."

The convention center, without water, air-conditioning, light or any authority figures, was recalled by many as a place of great suffering. Many heard rumors of crime, and saw sinister behavior, but few had firsthand knowledge of violence, which they often said they believed had taken place in another part of the half-mile-long center.

"I saw Coke machines being torn up — each and every one of them was busted on the second floor," said Percy McCormick, a security guard who spent four nights in the convention center and was interviewed in Austin, Tex.

Capt. Jeffrey Winn, the commander of the SWAT team, said its members rushed into the convention center to chase muzzle flashes from weapons to root out groups of men who had taken over some of the halls. No guns were recovered.

Source: Dwyer, J. and C. Drew (2005) Fear Exceeded Crime's Reality in New Orleans. *New York Times*, 29 September.

Such social issues are of concern not only to social science researchers, but also to civil servants and elected government officials. It is incumbent upon the academic professions involved to explore how these issues can be developed and worked into a testable framework.

3.14 Conclusions

Thaler and Johnson (1990) conclude that it is difficult to make any strong inferences about risk taking preferences because subjects can reframe the problems they are confronted with in many different ways. This reframing is hard to explain or to model. As a result, many of the problems posed by prospect theory are still up in the air. One thing we do know is that the world is much more complicated than the neoclassical economic theory would lead us to believe. Kahneman (2003) puts it a bit more strongly: "The central characteristic of agents is not that they reason poorly but that they often act intuitively. And the behavior of agents is not guided by what they are able to compute but by what they see at a given time."

Thus, the emotions play a key role in decision making. Without analyzing systematically the role of emotions and how they are formed and retrieved from memory and vary with different circumstances, it will be impossible to develop rational models of behavior that can explain the widely varying number and variety of departures from the standard rational choice model. Cooperation between neuroscientists and economists has begun to deepen our understanding of the relationship between decision making and neural processes. We have briefly alluded to some of this work in Section 3.1.5 and in the discussion of framing in Section 3.3. We will refer to some other examples in Chapter 4.

Bibliography

Ainslie, G. (1975) Specious Reward: A Behavioral Theory of Impulsiveness and Impulse Control. *Psychological Bulletin*, 82(4), 463–496.

Ainslie, G. (2001) *Breakdown of Will.* Cambridge: Cambridge University Press.

Ainslie, G. and N. Haslam (1992) Hyperbolic Discounting. In G. Loewenstein and J. Elster (eds.), *Choice Over Time* (pp. 57–92). New York: Russell Sage Foundation.

Allais, M. (1953) Actions of Rational Agents in Risky Circumstances: A Critique of the Axioms of the American School. *Econometrica*, 21, 503–546.

Angeletos, G.-M., D. Laibson, A. Repetto, J. Tobacman and S. Weinberg (2001) The Hyperbolic Consumption Model: Calibration, Simulation, and Empirical Evaluation. *Journal of Economic Perspectives*, 15(3), 47–68.

Barber, B.M. and T. Odean (1999) The Courage of Misguided Convictions. *Financial Analysts Journal*, November/December, 41–55.

Battaglini, M., R. Bénabou and J. Tirole (2002) Self-Control in Peer Groups. CEPR Discussion Paper No. 3149.

Battaglini, M., R. Bénabou and J. Tirole (2005) Self-Control in Peer Groups. *Journal of Economic Theory*, 123(2), 105–134.

Bénabou, R. and J. Tirole (2004) Willpower and Personal Rules. *Journal of Political Economy*, 112(4), 848–886.

Benartzi, S. and R. Thaler (1995) Myopic Loss Aversion and the Equity Premium Puzzle. *Quarterly Journal of Economics*, 110, 73–92.

Bernoulli, D. (1738) Exposition of a New Theory on the Measurement of Risk. *Econometrica*, 22(1954), 23–36.

Berns, G.S., J. Chappelow, M. Pekic, C.F. Zink, G. Pagnoni and M.E. Martin-Skurski (2006) Neurobiological Substrates of Dread. *Science*, 312, 754–758.

Bowman, E.H. (1982) Risk-Seeking by Troubled Firms. *Sloan Management Review*, 23, 33–42.

Brickman, P., D. Coates and R. Janoff-Bulman (1978) Lottery Winners and Accident Victims: Is Happiness Relative? *Journal of Personality and Social Psychology*, 36, 917–927.

Camerer, C. (1998) Bounded Rationality in Individual Decision Making. *Experimental Economics*, 1(2), 163–183.

Camerer, C., G. Loewenstein and M. Rabin (2004) *Advances in Behavior Economics.* New York: Russel Sage Foundation.

Camerer, C., L. Babcock, G. Loewenstein and R. Thaler (1997) Labor Supply of New York Cabdrivers: One Day at a Time. *Quarterly Journal of Economics*, 112, 407–441.

Caplin, A. and J. Leahy (2001) Psychological Expected Utility Theory and Anticipatory Feelings. *Quarterly Journal of Economics*, 116(1), 55–79.

Chaiken, S. and C. Stangor (1987) Attitudes and Attitude Change. *Annual Review of Psychology*, 38, 575–630.

Chernoff, J. (2002) Mind over Money: Economics Award Seen Vindicating Validity of Behavioral Economics. *Pensions and Investments*, 30(21).

China's Coal, World's Peril: No Easy Solution. (2006) *International Herald Tribune*, 12 June, pp. 1–2.

Cyert, R. and J. March (1963) *A Behavioral Theory of the Firm.* Englewood Cliffs, NJ: Prentice-Hall.

Damasio, A. (1994) *Descartes' Error: Emotion, Reason, and the Human Brain.* New York: Putnam.

Damasio, A. (1999) *The Feeling of What Happens: Body and Emotion in the Making of Consciousness.* New York: Harcourt Brace.

Damasio, A. (2003) *Looking for Spinoza: Joy, Sorrow, and the Feeling Brain.* Orlando, Florida: Harcourt.

Dwyer, J. and C. Drew (2005) Fear Exceeded Crime's Reality in New Orleans. *New York Times,* 29 September.

Ellsberg, D. (1961) Risk, Ambiguity, and the Savage Axioms. *Quarterly Journal of Economics,* 75, 643–669.

Etzioni, A. (ed.) (1988) *The Moral Dimension: Toward a New Economics.* New York: Free Press; London: Collier Macmillan.

Fiegenbaum, A. and H. Thomas (1988) Attitudes Towards Risk and Risk Return Paradox: Prospect Theory Explanations. *Academy of Management Journal,* 31, 85–106.

Fischer, C. (1999) Read this Paper Even Later: Procrastination with Time-Inconsistent Preferences. Resources for the Future Discussion Paper No. 99–20.

Fisher, K.L. and M. Statman (1999) A Behavioral Framework for Time Diversification. *Financial Analysts Journal,* May/June, 88–97.

Forest, M., J.R. Commons and H.A. Simon (2001) Concept of Rationality. *Journal of Economic Issues,* 35(3), 591–605.

Frederick, S., G. Loewenstein and T. O'Donoghue (2005) Time Discounting and Time Preference: A Critical Review. In G. Loewenstein, D. Read and. R.F. Baumeister (eds.), *Time and Decision: Economic and Psychological Perspectives on Intertemporal Choice.* New York: Russel Sage Foundation.

Frey, B.S. and R. Eichenberger (2001) Economic Incentives Transform Psychological Anomalies. In B.S. Frey (ed.), *Inspiring Economics: Human Motivation in Political Economy.* Cheltenham, UK and Brookfield, USA: Edward Elgar.

Friedman, M. (1957) The Permanent Income Hypothesis: Comment. *American Economic Review,* 48, 990–991.

Gifford, Jr., A. (2002) Emotion and Self-Control. *Journal of Economic Behavior & Organization,* 49, 113–130.

Gilbert, D. (2006) *Stumbling on Happiness.* New York: Knopf.

Gladwell, M. (2005) *Blink.* USA: Time Warner.

Glimcher, P.W. and A. Rustichini (2004) Neuroeconomics: The Concilience of Brain and Decision. *Science,* 306(5695), 1–10.

Green, L., N. Fristoe and J. Myerson (1994) Temporal Discounting and Preference Reversals in Choice between Delayed Outcomes. *Psychonomic Bulletin & Review,* 1(3), 383–389.

Gruber, J. and B. Koszegi (2000) Is Addiction 'Rational'? Theory and Evidence. NBER Working Paper No. 7507.

Hall, R.L. and C.J. Hitch (1939) Price Theory and Business Behavior. *Oxford Economic Papers*, 2(12), 12–45.

Hanoch, Y. (2002) Neither an Angel nor an Ant: Emotion as an Aid to Bounded Rationality. *Journal of Economic Psychology*, 23, 1–25.

Hsee, C.K. and Y. Rottenstreich (2001) Money, Kisses, and Electric Shocks: On the Affective Psychology of Risk. *Psychological Science*, 12, 185–190.

Hsee, C.K., R.P. Abelson and P. Salovey (1991) Relative Weighting of Position and Velocity in Satisfaction. *Psychological Science*, 2, 263–266.

Kahneman, D. (2003) Maps of Bounded Rationality: Psychology for Behavioral Economics. *American Economic Review*, 93(5), 1449–1475.

Kahneman, D. and A. Tversky (1979) Prospect Theory: An Analysis of Decision under Risk. *Econometrica*, 47, 263–291.

Kahneman, D. and A. Tversky (1982) The Simulation Heuristic. In D. Kahneman, P. Slovic and A. Tversky (eds.), *Judgement under Uncertainty: Heuristics and Biases* (pp. 201–208). New York: Cambridge University Press.

Kahneman, D. and A. Tversky (1984) Choices, Values and Frames. *American Psychologist*, 39, 341–350.

Kahneman, D., J. Knetsch and R. Thaler (1986a) Fairness as a Constraint on Profit Seeking Entitlements in the Market. *American Economic Review*, 76, 728–741.

Kahneman, D., J. Knetsch and R. Thaler (1986b) Fairness and the Assumptions of Economics. *Journal of Business*, 59, S285–S300.

Kahneman, D., J. Knetsch and R. Thaler (1990) Experimental Tests of the Endowment Effect and the Coase Theorem. *Journal of Political Economy*, 98(6), 1325–1348.

Kahneman, D., J. Knetsch and R. Thaler (1991) The Endowment Effect, Loss Aversion, and Status Quo Bias: Anomalies. *Journal of Economic Perspectives*, 5(1), 193–206.

Kahneman, D., P. Slovic and A. Tversky (1982) *Judgment under Uncertainty: Heuristics and Biases* (pp. 84–98). Cambridge: Cambridge University Press.

Katona, G. (1975) *Psychological Economics*. Amsterdam: Elsevier.

Kaufman, G. (1999) Emotional Arousal as a Source of Bounded Rationality. *Journal of Economic Behavior and Organization*, 38, 135–144.

Kirby, K.N. and R.J. Herrnstein (1995) Preference Reversals Due to Myopic Discounting of Delayed Reward. *Psychological Science*, 6(2), 83–89.

Kunreuther, H. and P. Slovic (1978) Economics, Psychology and Protective Behavior. *American Economic Review*, 68, 64–69.

Laibson, D. (1994) *Essays in Hyperbolic Discounting*. Ph.D. dissertation, MIT, USA.

Laibson, D. (1997) Golden Eggs and Hyperbolic Discounting. *Quarterly Journal of Economics*, 12, 443–477.

Laibson, D., A. Repetto and J. Tobacman (1998) Self-Control and Saving for Retirement. *Brookings Papers on Economic Activity*, (1), 91–196.

Laibson, D., A. Repetto and J. Tobacman (2003) A Debt Puzzle. In P. Aghion, R. Fyrdman, J. Stiglitz and M. Woodford (eds.), *Knowledge, Information and*

Expectations in Modern Economics: In Honour of Edmond S. Phelps (pp. 228–226). Princeton, NJ: Princeton University Press.

Lanzillotti, R.F. (1958) Pricing Objectives in Large Companies. *American Economic Review*, 48(5), 921–940.

Laury, S.K. and C.A. Holt (2000) Further Reflections on Prospect Theory. Dept. of Economics, Georgia State University, Atlanta, GA.

List, J. (2003a) Does Market Experience Eliminate Market Anomalies? *Quarterly Journal of Economics*, 118(1), 41–71.

List, J. (2003b) Economic Focus, to Have and to Hold. *Economist*, 30 August.

List, J. (2003c) Neoclassical Theory versus Prospect Theory: Evidence from the Marketplace. NBER Working Paper No. 9736.

List, J. (2004) Neoclassical Theory versus Prospect Theory: Evidence from the Marketplace. *Econometrica*, 72(2), 615–625.

Loewenstein, G. (1987) Anticipation and the Valuation of Delayed Consumption. *Economic Journal*, 97(387), 666–684.

Loewenstein, G. (2000) Emotions in Economic Theory and Economic Behavior. *American Economic Review: Papers and Proceedings*, 90, 426–432.

Loewenstein, G. (2004) Out of Control: Visceral Influences on Behavior. In C. Camerer, G. Loewenstein and M. Rabin (eds.), *Advances in Behavior Economics*. New York: Russel Sage Foundation.

Loewenstein, G. (2006) The Pleasures and Pains of Information. *Science*, 312, 704–706.

Loewenstein, G. and D. Prelec (1992) Anomalies in Intertemporal Choice: Evidence and an Interpretation. *Quarterly Journal of Economics*, 107(2), 573–597.

Loewenstein, G., R. Weber, J. Flory, S. Manuck and M. Muldoon (2001) Dimensions of Time Discounting. Paper presented at the Conference on Survey Research on Household Expectations and Preferences, Ann Arbor, Michigan.

Madden, G.J., W.K. Bickel and E.A. Jacobs (1999) Discounting of Delayed Rewards in Opiod-Dependent Outpatients: Exponential or Hyperbolic Discounting Functions? *Experimental Clinical Psychopharmacology*, 7(3), 284–293.

Meyer, B.J.F. (1975) *The Organization of Prose and its Effects on Memory*. New York: American Elsevier Publishing Company, Inc.

Moore, D.A. and G. Loewenstein (2004) Self-Interest, Automaticity, and the Psychology of Conflict of Interest. *Social Justice Research*, 17(2), 189–202.

Moore, D.A., G. Loewenstein, L. Tanlu and M.H. Bazerman (2004) Psychological Dimensions of Holding Conflicting Roles: Is it Possible to Play Advocate and Judge at the Same Time? Tepper Working Paper 2004–E40, Pittsburgh, PA.

Mullainathan, S. (2002) A Memory-Based Model of Bounded Rationality. *Quarterly Journal of Economics*, 117(3), 735–774.

O'Donoghue, T. and M. Rabin (2000) Addiction and Present-Biased Preferences. Cornell University and UC Berkeley. Center for Analytical Economics Working Paper No. 02–10, Cornell University.

O'Donoghue, T. and M. Rabin (2001) Choice and Procrastination. *Quarterly Journal of Economics*, 116(1), 121–160.

Olsen, R.A. (1997) Prospect Theory as an Explanation of Risky Choice by Professional Investors: Some Evidence. *Review of Financial Economics*, 6(2), 225–232.

Prelec, D. (1989) Decreasing Impatience: Definition and Consequences. Harvard Business School Working Paper No. 90-015.

Rabin, M. (2004) A Perspective on Psychology and Economics. http://repositories.cdlib.org/iber/econ/E02-03 [Retrieved 1 February 2006].

Ritzer, P. (1993) *The McDonaldization of Society*. California: Pine Forge Press.

Rottenstreich, Y. and C.K. Hsee (2001) Money, Kisses and Electric Shocks: Of the Affective Psychology of Risk. *Psychological Science*, 12(3), 185–190.

Samuelson, P. (1937) A Note on Measurement of Utility. *Review of Economic Studies*, 4, 155–161.

Samuelson, P. (1963a) Discussion Contribution. *American Economic Review*, 53(2), 231–236.

Samuelson, P. (1963b) Risk and Uncertainty: A Fallacy of Large Numbers. *Scientia*, 98, 108–113.

Samuelson, W. and R. Zeckhauser (1988) Status Quo Bias in Decision Making. *Journal of Risk and Uncertainty*, 1, 7–59.

Santos, J. (2001) Prospect Theory and Asset Prices. *Quarterly Journal of Economics*, 116(1), 53–67.

Schelling, T.C. (1984) Self-Command in Practice, in Policy, and in a Theory of Rational Choice. *American Economic Review*, 74(2), 1–11.

Schneiderman, L.J. and R.M. Kaplan (1992) Fear of Dying and HIV Infection vs Hepatitis B Infection. *Public Health Briefs*, 82(4), 584–586.

Schumpeter, J.A. (1934) *The Theory of Economic Development*. Cambridge: Harvard University Press. (New York: Oxford University Press, 1961.) First published in Germany, 1912.

Scitovsky, T. (1992) *The Joyless Economy*, Revised Ed. New York: Oxford University Press.

Shanteau, J. (1992) Decision Making Under Risk: Application to Insurance Purchasing. *Advances in Consumer Research*, 19, 177–181.

Shefrin, H. (2002) *Beyond Greed and Fear: Understanding Behavioral Finance and the Psychology of Investing*. New York: Oxford University Press.

Shefrin, H. and M. Statman (1985) The Disposition to Sell Winners Too Early and Ride Losers Too Long: Theory and Evidence. *Journal of Finance*, 40(3), 77–782.

Simon, H. (1979) Rational Decision Making in Business Organizations. *American Economic Review*, 69(4), 493–513.

Simon, H. (1983) *Reason in Human Affairs*. Oxford: Basil Blackwell.

Slovic, P. (1984) Facts vs Fears: Understanding Perceived Risk. Science and Public Policy Seminar, Federation of Behavioral, Psychological and Cognitive Sciences, Washington, DC.

Slovic, P., B. Fischoff and S. Lichtenstein (1982) Facts versus Fears: Understanding Perceived Risks. In D. Kahneman, P. Slovic and A. Tversky (eds.), *Judgment under Uncertainty: Heuristics and Biases*. Cambridge: Cambridge University Press.

Smith, K., J. Dickhaut, K. McCabe and J. Pardo (2002) Neuronal Substrates for Choice under Ambiguity, Risk, Certainty, Gains and Losses. *Management Science*, 48, 711–718.

Soman, D. (1998) The Illusion of Delayed Incentives: Evaluating Future Effort-Monetary Transactions. *Journal of Marketing Research*, 35(4), 427–437.

Soman, D. (2004) The Effect of Time Delay on Multi-Attribute Choice. *Journal of Economic Psychology*, 25, 153–175.

Soman, D., G. Ainslie, S. Frederick, X. Li, J. Lynch, P. Moreau, A. Mitchell, D. Read, A. Sawyer, Y. Trope, K. Wertenbroch and G. Zauberman (2005) The Psychology of Intertemporal Discounting: Why are Distant Events Valued Differently from Proximal Ones? *Marketing Letters*, 16(3/4), 347–360.

Strotz, R.H. (1955–1956) Myopia and Inconsistency in Dynamic Utility Maximization. *Review of Economic Studies*, 23(3), 165–180.

Sugden, R. (1986) *The Economics of Rights, Co-operation and Welfare*. Oxford: Basil Blackwell, Inc.

Telser, L.G. (1973) Searching for the Lowest Price. *American Economic Review*, 63, 40–49.

Thaler, R. (1980) Toward a Positive Theory of Consumer Choice. *Journal of Economic Behavior and Organization*, 1, 39–60.

Thaler, R. (1981) Some Empirical Evidence on Dynamic Inconsistency. *Economic Letters*, 8, 201–207.

Thaler, R. (1985) Mental Accounting and Consumer Choice. *Marketing Science*, 4, 199–214.

Thaler, R.H. and E.J. Johnson (1990) Gambling with the House Money and Trying to Break Even: The Effects of Prior Outcomes on Risky Choice. *Management Science*, 36, 643–660.

Trope, Y. and N. Liberman (2003) Temporal Construal. *Psychological Review*, 110, 401–421.

Tversky, A. and D. Kahneman (1974) Judgment under Uncertainty: Heuristics and Biases. *Science*, 185, 1124–1130.

Tversky, A. and D. Kahneman (1981) The Framing of Decisions and Psychology of Choice. *Science*, 211, 453–458.

Tversky, A. and D. Kahneman (1983) Extension versus Intuitive Reasoning: The Conjunction Fallacy in Probability Judgment. *Psychological Review*, 90, 293–315.

Tversky, A. and D. Kahneman (1986) Rational Choice and Framing of Decisions. *Journal of Business*, 59, S252–278.

Ulysses and the Sirens (2006) http://www.2020site.org/ulysses/sirens.html [Retrieved 3 June 2006].

Varey, C. and D. Kahneman (1992) Experience Extended Across Time: Evaluations of Moments and Episodes. *Journal of Behavioral Decision Making*, 5, 169–185.

Veblen, T. (1899) *The Theory of the Leisure Class: An Economic Study of Institutions.* New York: Macmillan.

Von Neumann, J. and O. Morgenstern (1944) *Theory of Games and Economic Behaviour.* Princeton: Princeton University Press.

Weber, C. and M. Camerer (1998) The Disposition Effect in Securities Trading: An Experimental Analysis. *Journal of Economic Behavior and Organization*, 33(2), 167–184.

Zak, P.J. (2004) Neuroeconomics. *Philosophical Transactions of Royal Society Biology*, 359(1451), 1737–1748.

Zauberman, G. and J.G. Lynch, Jr. (2005) Resource Slack and Discounting of Future Time versus Money. *Journal of Experimental Psychology: General*, 134(1), 23–37.

Chapter 4

Cooperation and Defection in a Game Theoretic Context

4.1 Introduction

To get a better idea of how people follow their own self-interest in some situations and cooperate in others, it is useful to consider some aspects of game theory. The mathematician John Von Neumann and the economist Oscar Morgenstern developed game theory over 50 years ago (1944). In its most esoteric and mathematical form, game theory developed as a mathematics that looks at how players make decisions in sequences of moves in structured game situations. These games can be designed in many different ways employing a variety of rules and number of players.

We begin our study of game theory by looking at the Prisoner's Dilemma, a simple game involving two people that got its name from a situation where two prisoners are held in separate cells for a crime that they commited. (This game was originally devised by Merrill Flood and Melvin Dresher in about 1950.) The prosecutor, however, has only enough evidence to convict them of a minor crime that carries a light sentence — that is unless one of them confesses to the more serious crime. If that happens, the sentences change. Each prisoner is told that if he confesses while the other remains silent denying the crime, the confessor will go free while the other will spend 20 years in prison. If both prisoners confess, they will each get an intermediate sentence of five years in prison. If both remain silent, they each get a sentence of only six months. The two prisoners are not allowed to communicate with each other. Table 4.1 summarizes these various options in what is called the "payoff matrix".

Table 4.1 The Prisoner's Dilemma

Prisoner X	Prisoner Y	
	Confess	Remain Silent
Confess	Five years for each prisoner	20 years for Y and X is set free
Remain Silent	20 years for X and Y is set free	Six months for each prisoner

If we analyze these choices, we see that the preferred strategy is for each prisoner to confess to the serious crime. No matter what Y does, X gets a lighter sentence by confessing. If Y remains silent, he goes free. If Y also confesses, he gets a five-year sentence. The same is true for X. However, if they both confess they get a five-year prison sentence, while in the case that they both remain silent, they each get only six months.

The fact that they are not allowed to communicate may seem like it should affect the decision to confess or not, that is to defect or cooperate. (To simplify further analysis, let us denote that cooperation is to remain silent and to defect is to confess in the Prisoner's Dilemma game.) The problem is more fundamental. If X agrees with Y to remain silent, sealing the bargain that they both get a very short-term sentence for a very big crime, he can still do better if he defects and confesses while Y remains silent.

So the crux of the Prisoner's Dilemma puts the issue of cooperation and competition in bold relief. It also highlights the issue of trust, which is fundamental to whether cooperation will take place between parties in any economic or social situation. In general, the Prisoner's Dilemma model is described in terms of whether there is co-operation or defection/competition. We will deal with these kinds of problems in many different contexts as we work through this chapter and in subsequent chapters of this book.

We mention the Prisoner's Dilemma version of this decision problem only because it is a classic example of a dilemma that people face when they are in situations where they can choose to defect or cooperate. It is also a "situation" game that has been the subject of numerous experiments by many researchers over the years.

Carrying the discussion of decision making in the Prisoner's Dilemma a bit further and generalizing its conclusions, we can say that it is more likely people will cooperate with those they know and love, and compete with those they do not know. Gary Becker (1981) uses the phrase "cooperate at home and compete at work". In what follows in subsequent sections of this chapter, we will look at various aspects of this dilemma of whether to cooperate or compete.

4.2 Some General Examples of Cooperation versus Competition

Creating an atmosphere of cooperation and harmony within a firm can foster a cooperative environment. The practice of lifetime employment, singing company songs early in the morning and a "bottom-up" management style were studied closely by Western management experts when the Japanese economy was growing fast in the 1980s. These Western managers were used to a competitive work-place where employees were pitted against each other for promotion, and management and labor were trying to get the competitive advantage in every bargaining situation. Strikes were common in the West and unheard of in Japan.

While the appeal of the Japanese management system has dissipated since the stock and real estate bubble burst in the late 1980s and Japan experienced slow growth for the next decade, the advantages of cooperation to achieve better corporate results and raise labor productivity cannot be denied. It is a course of action that is still followed by many companies around the world.

In situations where people can either cooperate or compete, various research studies have shown that the chances of cooperation rise when the two parties know each other. One reason is that emotional factors enter into the picture, giving rise to a more cooperative attitude. It is often harder to compete with a friend than with someone you do not know. Furthermore, in cases where situations reoccur as in Prisoner's Dilemma-type games, cooperation is more likely because a cooperator has a chance to retaliate if his partner defects and follows a self-interested strategy. Once it becomes obvious that defection invites retaliation, then the players settle into a pattern of mutual cooperation. This pattern is also observed among siblings, although often the older sibling will be willing to put up with retaliation since the younger ones cannot mete out as much physical punishment as the older sibling.

Andreoni and Miller (1993) manipulate the reputation of opponents so that it pays for a player to build a cooperation reputation if the opponent is also believed to be cooperative. In actual experiments, it was also found that there are genuinely altruistic people playing the game as well as those who wish to build reputations so that they can eventually defect. They propose a payoff matrix where both players get seven if they cooperate and four if they both defect. The payoff is zero if the player remains silent and the other player defects. A defector gets 12 when the other player cooperates and gets nothing.

So the Andreoni and Miller payoff matrix is similar in structure to the Prisoner's Dilemma matrix discussed in Table 4.1. The incentives for competiton/defection are such that both players will defect unless they are quite sure their cooperation will be matched by their opponent.

4.3 Extension of the Prisoner's Dilemma

The idea of cooperative strategies can be explored further within the context of game theory by extending the Prisoner's Dilemma a bit further. Game theory provides a promising approach to understanding strategic problems of all sorts, and the simplicity and power of the Prisoner's Dilemma and similar examples make them a natural starting point.[1] But there will often be complications we must consider in a more complex and realistic application.

Let us see how we might move from a simpler to a more realistic game model in a real-world example of strategic thinking: a firm choosing a new information system. For this example, the players are a company considering the choice of a new internal e-mail or intranet

---

[1]This example is drawn from the Drexell University website of William King (williamking.www.drexel.edu/top/eco/game/nash.html).

Table 4.2 Coordination Game

		User	
		Advanced	Proven
Supplier	Advanced	20, 20	0, 0
	Proven	0, 0	5, 5

system, and a supplier who is considering producing the system. The two choices are to install a technically advanced or a more proven system with less functionality. We will assume that the more advanced system really does supply a lot more functionality, so that the payoffs to the two players are as shown in Table 4.2.

We see that both players can be better off, on net, if an advanced system is installed. (We are not claiming that is always the case! We are just assuming it is in this particular decision.) But the worst that can happen is for one player to commit to an advanced system while the other player stays with the proven one. In that case, there is no deal and no payoffs for anyone. The problem is that the supplier and the user must have a compatible standard in order to work together, and since the choice of a standard is a strategic choice, their strategies have to mesh.

Although it looks a lot like the Prisoner's Dilemma at first glance, this is a more complicated game. Looking at it carefully, we see that this game has no dominant strategies. The best strategy for each participant depends on the strategy chosen by the other participant. Thus, we need a new concept of game-equilibrium to allow for this added complication. When there are no dominant strategies, we often use an equilibrium conception called the *Nash equilibrium*, named after Nobel Memorial Laureate John Nash. In its basic form, the Nash equilibrium is a pretty simple idea: we have a Nash equilibrium if each participant chooses the best strategy, given the strategy chosen by the other participant. A Nash strategy is defined as the best strategy that a player can play, given the strategy chosen by the other player and a "Nash equilibrium" is the equilibrium achieved when both players follow a Nash strategy. If both players believe that the opponent may be altruistic, then both players may "pretend" to be altruistic until the final rounds of a repeated Prisoner's Dilemma game when mutual defection becomes more likely. Andreoni and Miller (1993) note that defection in the Prisoner's Dilemma game is a unique dominant-strategy Nash equilibrium.

In the case of the proven and advanced systems, if the user opts for the advanced system, then it is best for the supplier to do that too. So (Advanced, Advanced) is a Nash equilibrium. But, hold on here! If the user chooses the proven system, it is best for the supplier to do that too. There are two Nash equilibria! Which one will be chosen? It may seem easy enough to opt for the advanced system that is better all-round. However, if each participant believes that the other will stick with the proven system, then it will be best for each player to choose the proven system.

This is a decision making pitfall that is typical of a class of games called coordination games — and we see that the choice of compatible standards is a coordination game. Another coordination game that shows the importance of social convention is the decision of which side of the road to drive on. There are two win/win possibilities. Both drivers agree to drive on the left-hand side or the right-hand side. Both of these are Nash equilibrium strategies. If one driver picks the left and the other the right, there will be big trouble on the road and many accidents. Whether to pick the right or the left will depend upon social convention. We see from driving around the world that many countries have adopted different conventions — some drive on the left and some on the right. Both are Nash equilibria.

4.4 The Most Beautiful Number Game

To give us a better insight into Nash equilibrium and the uncertainties associated with playing games with several other players, consider what is called "the most beautiful number game". The most beautiful number game is derived from a game that J.M. Keynes is said to have suggested in his general theory in 1936. He suggested that the public vote for the most beautiful woman from a series of 100 photos of beautiful women. The most beautiful number game turned the beautiful faces into numbers. Subjects were asked to pick the most beautiful number. In the game, the most beautiful number is found by multiplying the average of the numbers selected by all the contestants by a constant. This value of the constant has to lie between zero and one. It adjusts the average of the beautiful numbers picked by contestants. For example, if the average of numbers picked by a group of subjects is 60, then to find the most beautiful number, we multiply this number by a constant. The experimenter picks the constant. Suppose the constant is $2/3$, then the most beautiful number is $60 \times 2/3 = 40$.

We are fortunate to have many experimental results, often with many participants. The game has been played and studied by a number of academics and there are several papers written about it where the results from various studies are compiled and analyzed.

Why has so much effort been exerted in studying this game? We study it because it is a very interesting example of Nash equilibrium which helps us to see if it works or not. It also demonstrates that if we consider the idea of Nash equilibrium clearly, we are led to think about the strategy of others playing this game.

Now that we have the elements of the game fixed in our heads, let us see what the results of this game show us. The most beautiful number game has been played by newspaper readers in several different countries. In some cases, the payoff offered to newspaper readers playing this beautiful number game was quite high and people would spend considerable time on it in hopes of winning the prize.

The conventional constant used in the most beautiful number game was $2/3$, which we will also use here. Let us go through a thought experiment and see if we can come up with the most beautiful number using the Nash equilibrium solution. If you know a bit about probability theory, you would say initially that the most beautiful number is $2/3 \times 50$, because 50 would be the midpoint in a uniform distribution. It would be the mean of the distribution of a sample drawn, where all the integers between 0 and 100 are equally likely. This would be the sample mean without any further knowledge of people's preferences for individual numbers. So the initial answer for the most beautiful number is $2/3 \times 50 = 33.3$, rounded to 33.

Does the story necessarily stop here? No!! If you think that everyone else has also picked $2/3 \times 50 = 33$ as the most beautiful number, what would they all do? They would multiply this number again by $2/3$ so that the most beautiful number now becomes $2/3 \times 2/3 \times 50 = 22.2$.

Is this the end? Not necessarily — not if you follow through on your logic. There is no reason to stop here, so that in the next step we have $2/3 \times 2/3 \times 2/3 \times 50$ and so on. This is an infinite series that regresses to zero as we raise $2/3$ to higher and higher powers. (Now you see why the constant chosen has to be less than one! If it were greater than one, we would have an explosive solution.) Did all the people in all the samples in all the countries and classrooms around the world that have played this game come up with the number zero as the most beautiful number?

No, not all picked zero. Why? After all, this is the logical Nash equilibrium. Recall that the Nash equilibrium is the best strategy given the strategy chosen by the other participants. They all did not pick zero because they were not sure what strategy other people were going to follow. Imagine yourself as a newspaper reader and being asked this question. Will other readers be as "smart" as you? Will they know about the uniform distribution? Will they make the infinite regress connection? So there are many uncertainties.

What happened in the real world as the newspapers and academics conducted these experiments? You can read the papers for yourself. The general result was that some people picked numbers at random, usually somewhere in the range of zero to 60 because of the need to multiply the average by $2/3$. Some thought it through so that there were spikes at $2/3 \times 50 = 33$ and $4/9 \times 50 = 22$. Beyond that there were sometimes spikes around zero, as if some people believed that most other contestants would think the problem through but were not sure that *all* would.

The overriding conclusion in this case of the most beautiful number game is we are never sure of the other participants' strategy! In my classes at the university level where we have been studying probability and game theory, the average response was similar to the newspaper answers, e.g., a few spikes around $2/3 \times 50$ and $2/3 \times 2/3 \times 50$

and another spike around zero. The results of this exercise points to a general weakness of the Nash equilibrium approach in some circumstances. It also highlights the general weakness in economic theory which assumes that individuals know or can predict well what other people are going to do in particular circumstances. The most beautiful number game's results prove this assumption is erroneous.

In one sense the beautiful number game is an example of "bounded rationality", a topic we have discussed in Chapter 3 on prospect theory and the role of emotions in decision making. Not everyone is completely rational in the narrow sense that economists use this term. In this instance, rationality would imply a movement to the Nash equilibrium. People generally do not make the infinite regression required to come up with the choice of zero as the most beautiful number. They stop after one or two iterations (or three) and implicitly assume that everyone else will also. These results are fairly robust across a wide range of experiments including several carried out by newspapers in the UK. Some game theorists and science students may go a bit further and even arrive at the Nash equilibrium, but their numbers are small (see Nagel *et al.*, 1999).

An interesting, challenging and complex application of game theory that involves many players is the stock market. While the efficient market theory of price determination in securities markets is widely accepted by most financial economists, these same economists are at a loss to explain the periodic development of stock market bubbles which arise when stock prices reach levels that far exceed their economic value. There are many examples including the tulip bubble in Holland in the 16th century when the price of tulips skyrocketed; the South Sea bubble in 1720 when a company trading in South America convinced investors to put up large sums until there was a crash; the dot com boom in the US in 2000, when the Nasdaq index hit 5,000 in March and then plummeted 70 percent two years later.

The efficient market hypothesis cannot explain these bubbles and economists warn that bubbles create many problems. Investors get a false feeling of wealth and security and as a result, capital can be misallocated. In the modern world, more effective disclosure rules that include information on short positions can induce speculators to attack bubbles before they get out of hand. However, from the point of view of game theory and the uncertainties that arise from playing games with several players, bubbles point to the general problem that investors cannot predict what other investors are going to do. As long as the bubble is growing, everyone benefits. Putting it another way, no one wants to be the first to leave a good party even if the party is overrated. However, there is no way to effectively predict when a large enough number of investors will take a profit to tip expectations and cause the market to collapse and the bubble to burst. So the efficient market theory has to be augmented by these game theoretic considerations (for more on speculative bubbles, see Shiller, 2005).

4.5 Sequential Prisoner's Dilemma Games and Tit for Tat[2]

In this section, we consider repeated games. We can imagine an extended Prisoner's Dilemma game which is played repeatedly over time. Whether the number of rounds a game is played is known or unknown has an important influence on its outcome. Let us assume that the payoff matrix in Table 4.1 remains unchanged, and the players have an opportunity to choose to cooperate or defect over an extended time period. Indeed, they could cooperate by remaining silent upon realizing that cooperation gives the highest payoff, but a lot would still depend on the belief that the other player would also cooperate.

If the number of rounds in which they repeat the game were *known*, say, 100 times, it would be in their interest to defect in the last game, which yields a strategy identical to the one-shot Prisoner's Dilemma game. Each would know that defecting is the best strategy, and defecting is the only credible strategy they would believe the other would follow with each player knowing that the ideal strategy is to defect in the last period. Going backwards to the 99th round

---

[2]The first part of this section on tit for tat is taken from the website: http://www.globalideasbank.org/BI/BI-36.html.

(also known as backward induction), it is best to defect now in the 99th round too. Since this applies in the *n*th period, it also applies in the *n* − 1 period and so on. Thus, backward induction deduces that each player will defect in every single period. The reasoning is somewhat similar to the beautiful number game. Of course, defection in this way means that neither player gets to enjoy the fruits of cooperation. They always defect by confessing. This is the backward induction paradox. Games that are repeated infinitely (unknown number of rounds) are exempt from this paradox and therefore more receptive to the sustenance of repeated cooperation between players.

Box 4.1 shows another example of backward induction in a game called fairmen or gamesmen.

Box 4.1 Backward Induction Game: Fairmen or Gamesmen

We illustrate how backward induction can be utilized in games of finite sequential periods. There is a sum of money to be divided between two parties, namely Ann and Ben. As can be seen below in the tree diagram, initially there is 100 pence to be divided in Stage 1. Ben can either accept or reject Ann's division of the money. If he rejects, they move onto Stage 2, whereby the money is reduced to 25 pence and Ben now is in charge of the division of the money.

Going by backward induction, given that they have arrived at Stage 2 with only 25 pence, the best strategy for Ann is to accept any sum of money greater than zero pence than if she had rejected Ben's proposal. Hence her possible payoff in Stage 2 if she accepted Ben's proposal would be between $0 < y < 25$. If Ben were rational, he would offer her the bare minimum, i.e., one pence with him garnering 24 pence. If Ann is able to rationally anticipate the outcome of Stage 2, she would offer Ben a payoff of $24 < x < 100$ in Stage 1 to preempt Stage 2 from occurring. Since Ann is also rational, the bare minimum to keep Ben happy would be 25 pence, i.e., one pence more than his best outcome in Stage 2.

Thus, backward induction inferred that if Ann and Ben behaved like gamesmen, Ann would have received 75 pence and Ben 25 pence

(*Continued*)

Box 4.1 (*Continued*)

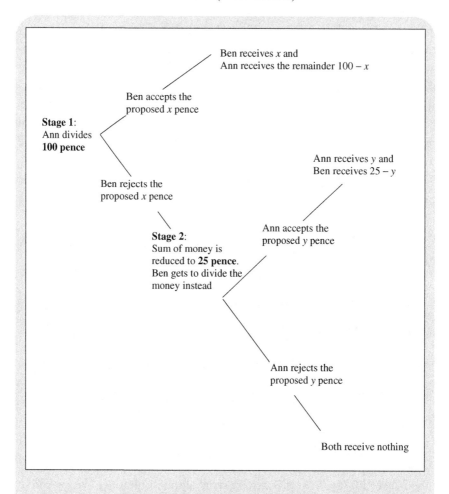

respectively. On the other hand, if they behaved like fairmen, Ann should have agreed to an equal division of the 100 pence in Stage 1. Hence this game exemplifies the issue of fairness which does occur at times, and which results in a different outcome from the rational gamesmen theory.

Source: Adapted from Binmore, Shaked and Sutton (1985) in Heap *et al.* (1992, p. 141).

Another simple example of backward induction is the centipede game. In this game, players A and B play a sequential game where a dime is put on the table by the experimenter and A has the option to take the dime or leave it. If A takes the dime, the game is over and B gets nothing. If A leaves the dime, the experimenter adds another dime. B has the option to take the 20 cents. If B takes the 20 cents, the game is over and A gets nothing. The game proceeds in this way as A and B alternate and a dime is added each time there is a refusal to take the money. The pile of money payoff grows until the last round. Assume there are 10 rounds, so a dollar is the payoff for the 10th and final round where it is B's decision. Of course he will take the money for sure since this is the final round. A, knowing this, will take the money on the 9th round, and B, knowing this, will take the money on the 8th round, and so on until the first round. By backward induction, the Nash equilibrium is for A to take the dime on the first round. Since this game only involves two players and the logic is straightforward, students in experiments often arrive at the Nash equilibrium solution.

An interesting result from one experiment is that both players waited until the last round. B took the dollar and split it with A. The subjects said there was no collusion. However, this is a viable strategy with a higher payoff for both players if there is trust that B will divide the money. Even if there is a chance he will not, it may still pay A to wait since the potential payoff is five times what he would get if he chose the Nash equilibrium and took the dime on the first round.

4.5.1 *Tit for tat*

Robert Axelrod (1984) came up with an interesting strategy to tackle the issue of cooperation and competition in a repeated game setting. He named it "Tit for Tat". The beauty of the strategy is its simplicity and appeal to the human emotions for reciprocity and perhaps revenge against defectors. Axelrod begins his analysis by explaining a variation of the Prisoner's Dilemma game. In this game, which involves a group of people who play each other in turn, players are awarded differing points according to whether they cooperate or defect, with the overall aim being to amass the most points from all the games. (As we defined earlier, to defect means not to cooperate, i.e., to compete.)

The game works like this. Let two players of the group be A and B. If A and B cooperate, they both get three points. This outcome for both players is called R, the reward for mutual cooperation. If A cooperates but B defects, then A gets zero points and B gets five points. A's outcome is called S, the sucker's payoff. Finally, if A and B both defect, they get one point. This outcome for both players is called P, the punishment for mutual defection.

Obviously, if the game involved just two players (with the aim of one winning or at least not losing), the safest strategy would be to defect all the time, since, if your opponent cooperated, you would get five points and if not, you would both get only one point. However, in a group of players where the aim is to win the most points, the strategy of defection is likely to fall victim to a low point count.

Axelrod organized several computer tournaments in which the participants' computer programs were to play this game of Prisoner's Dilemma on a round-robin basis, i.e., every computer program was to play every other program and was also to play against a copy of itself. The winner was to be the program which amassed the greatest number of points summed over all interactions. The program which won the main tournaments was the simplest and shortest program of all.

The program always initially offered cooperation, but would respond to a defection move with its own defection move. For this reason, it was called Tit for Tat.

The broad conclusions for behavior which Axelrod draws from this analysis are as follows:

(1) Cooperation can get started even in a world of unconditional defection (everyone following a policy of always defecting). It can evolve within small clusters of individuals who base their cooperation on reciprocity and only have a small proportion of their interactions with each other. But it cannot emerge if such individuals are too scattered and have a negligible proportion of their interactions with each other.

(2) A strategy based on reciprocity can thrive in a world where many different kinds of strategies are being followed (robustness).
(3) Cooperation, once established, can protect itself from invasion by less cooperative strategies (also robustness).

Axelrod then shows how these theoretical arguments can be applied to various social and biological settings. One example he describes is the Live-And-Let-Live system of trench warfare during World War I. This is a particularly illuminating example since here we had cooperation between groups who were most definitely *not* supposed to cooperate since they were at war with each other! Axelrod explains how the conditions of trench warfare met the technical conditions of the Prisoner's Dilemma.

What made trench warfare different from most other combat was that the same small units faced each other in immobile sectors for extended periods of time. It is this fact that makes the Tit for Tat strategy viable. Axelrod describes how both sides did indeed follow a Tit for Tat strategy, which meant that both sides tended to cooperate, but would respond to a defection by the other side. Both sides tended to cooperate by not fighting, but would return fire from the other side. This behavior of mutual cooperation tended to occur despite the best efforts of the opposing high commands to prevent it.

Axelrod provides four suggestions for doing well in an iterated Prisoner's Dilemma:

(1) Do not be envious of the other player.
(2) Do not be the first to defect.
(3) Reciprocate both cooperation and defection.
(4) Do not be too clever.

With *both* conscious foresight *and* the ability to shape our environment, human beings can actively promote cooperation. Axelrod gives five broad ways in which we can do this:

(1) Enlarge the shadow of the future. In other words, arrange things so that possible future interactions are sufficiently important.

(2) Change the payoffs so that consequences of defection (e.g., fines or imprisonment) are not as attractive as would be the case if the laws were absent. Thus, cooperation is induced.
(3) Teach people to care about each other.
(4) Teach reciprocity.
(5) Improve recognition abilities. An example of poor recognition abilities hampering cooperation in a human social environment is the case of superpower arms negotiations. In this case, the difficulty has more to do with recognizing what the other player has done, rather than in failing to recognize the other player.

Other interesting work on the Prisoner's Dilemma has been carried out by Nowak, May and Sigmund (1995). They report the results of two sets of Prisoner's Dilemma experiments they had performed. In the first, they provided their computerized players with longer memories, a statistical propensity to cooperate or defect, and the ability to mutate. They found that the population as a whole tended to either cooperate or to defect, but as the rounds wore on, the trend was to cooperate. They also discovered that the population would change its tendencies precipitously, moving from the propensity to cooperate to the propensity to defect (or vice versa) within just a few generations — a phenomena very suggestive of punctuated equilibrium in biology.

Nowak, May and Sigmund (1995) observed the same Tit for Tat strategy which won Axelrod's tournament; they also observed a variation called *generous Tit for Tat* in which a player occasionally failed to retaliate against defection. They observed yet another, more common, strategy as well — one they called *Pavlov*.

In this approach, a player repeats moves which provide rewards and steer away from moves for which they were punished in the previous move. For example, a player might repeat a defect move if its opponent had cooperated against the defect, but if such a move brought a low reward, the player would switch on the next move. This, of course, is similar to the "stimulus-response" behavior that B.F. Skinner observed in animal behavior. The Pavlov strategy tends to encourage cooperative societies. However, it discourages the emergence of players who always cooperate and who never defect because it can maximize its returns by defecting on these "good guys". Pavlov does not do well against chronic defectors because, on every other move, it attempts cooperation and loses big time against its opponent's defection. However, Pavlov will protect a cooperative environment against the invasion of exploiters by retaliating against the exploitation.

Tit for Tat strategy, on the other hand, supports cooperation and is likely to breed a large colony of unconditional cooperators. The downside of this strategy, however, is that it leaves the population defenseless against unscrupulous exploiters, like a naive group of carnival show attendees.

Nowak, May and Sigmund's second simulation functioned much like a biological phenomena known as cellular automata. In the cellular automata program, players interact with other players on what looks like an extended chess board. Players (cells) live or die based on the status of their neighbors. In this Prisoner's Dilemma simulation, competitors play against eight contiguous players in the same way those cellular automata units interact with their neighbors. After each round of play, cells are occupied by the players who accumulated the most points. The authors created two types of players: pure cooperators and pure defectors. They found that lone cooperators are exploited by neighboring defectors, but that four or more cooperators can hold their own in many situations. Lone defectors fare pretty well, but if a number of defectors clump together, they work to their mutual detriment. After a number of generations, the relative number of cooperators and defectors stabilize, thus mimicking the pattern of host and parasites or prey and predators in the biological world, or the mix of honest people and cheaters in worldly economic and social environments. This also has implications for the problem of corruption which is discussed further in Chapter 8.

In another experiment, Clark and Sefton (2001) discuss a Prisoner's Dilemma coordination game whereby the second player moves only after the first person has moved. This allows for choice on the part of the second player, whose move is conditioned by the move of the first player. The analysis of the various choices suggests that if the first player defects, then the second player will also defect. This is a lose/lose situation and, as we saw in Section 4.3, is also a Nash equilibrium. If the first player's choice is to cooperate, then the second player is in a dilemma. If he is selfish, he will defect after the first player has opted for cooperation. However, if he defects, he risks having the first player also defect in the next round, which will give a worse outcome than the win/win situation which arises if they both cooperate. So, in sequential coordination games, there are aspects involved such as trust and building consensus that influence the choice to defect or cooperate.

4.5.2 *Altruism and defection — crime and punishment*

There is another aspect of cooperation and defection that has been studied which has to do with the concept of altruistic punishment. When norms of society are broken, people derive satisfaction from punishing the perpetrator. Consider the case of a driver who has been waiting in a long line of traffic for a while. A red sports car speeds by on the shoulder. Eventually, the sports car driver has run out of shoulder and signals to get back in front of you. Instead of letting him in, you drive up very close to the car in front of you. You successfully cut him off and as you edge by you smile. This is a case of altruistic punishment. Models that incorporate these motives, interpreted as including fairness into the utility function, seem to describe behavior in certain circumstances such as the one described. They are characterized by a belief that defection has "social value" and will "teach a lesson".

Why do people punish those they believe have violated a basic social norm such as road courtesy, honesty in financial transactions or other economic exchanges, even when they receive no benefit for themselves? Neuroeconomics research using brain scans analyzes decision making in a simple game to investigate this kind of unfair behavior. Two players (A and B) interact anonymously with each other (de Quervain *et al.*, 2004). They each know that they are playing against another person but there is no eye or other physical contact. Each player has 10 monetary units and they can increase their income substantially if A trusts B.

The game is started when A has the choice of sending his endowment of 10 units to B. If he sends the endowment to B, then B quadruples his endowment to 40 units plus 10 units to a total of 50 units. B has the choice of keeping the sent 10 units or returning half of his total of 50 to A. In the event he does not return anything, A winds up with nothing and B has 50. If he returns half, they both have 25. If A decides not to send, they both have 10.

de Quervain *et al.* (2004) study the case where B keeps it all. They predict that A will want to punish B for being unfair. A is given the option of deducting up to 20 units of B's current endowment. By observing the pattern of activity (blood flow) in the brain of participant A, the research was able to conclude that parts of the brain associated with rewards (caudate nucleus) were activated. Put simply, those in the A group that punished those in B were being rewarded psychologically for withholding return of 25 monetary units. Those with stronger activation in the caudate area also punished more strongly. This experiment shows the importance of emotional factors, in this case a lack of perceived fairness, in decision making.

These results support research that suggests strong reciprocity, including both altruistic rewards and punishment, was critical in the evolution of human cooperation (see Bowles and Gintis, 2004; Fehr and Gachter, 2002; see also the discussion of altruism and cooperation in Chapter 5). There is also evidence that mutual cooperation and trust in the Prisoner's Dilemma-type game activates parts of the brain associated with reciprocity and the level of oxytocin, a hormone important in social bonding, creating a "warm glow" often referred to by people making altruistic decisions (see Rilling *et al.*, 2003; see also Chapter 5 for further discussion of warm glow). There are competitive and cooperative forces at play in these games and resolution will depend upon the relative strength of the forces as they are interpreted by the brain, which then makes a decision to act. Individual behavior will vary depending on the wiring of the brain, which is in turn dependent upon experience and genetic factors. Those who are prone to cooperate might have benefited from cooperative behavior in the past and/or were taught to cooperate at home or at school.

4.5.3 *Learning in a game theory context*

Much of the discussion in the previous section demonstrates that learning can take place, particularly when games are repeated. Much of this learning has to do with positive reinforcement (see Camerer and Ho, 1999). It also has to do with understanding that others are also learning and therefore it is important to build reputation and establish trust, particularly in games which are repeated (see Camerer, 2003, and the next section on trust). Trust is also important in other contexts (see, for example, the discussion in Chapters 6 and 7). However, there is considerable evidence that players in games which require foresight do not look more than one or two moves ahead. Only those that do look far ahead conform to the rational game theory prediction that anticipates infinite regress and smooth movement toward a Nash equilibrium in interactive games.

4.6 Dictator and Ultimatum Games

Dictator or ultimatum games also involve two players. They differ from the Prisoner's Dilemma in terms of context. In the dictator game, the first player is given a sum of money to divide between himself and the other player. Several variations of dictator games have been investigated. In one variation, the second player has a choice to either accept or reject the offer. Very often the first player (the dictator) offers the second player nothing or very little.

In an alternative form of the dictator game, the second player can reject the offer and then neither player gets anything. In this form called the ultimatum game, there is the threat of reprisal on the part of the second player. The second player can refuse the offer, suffering a loss in order to punish the first player. The results of ultimatum game trials by Kravitz and Gunto (1992) show that the self-interest strategy of offering nothing or very little does not hold up. They suggest that a more equal split is the result of fairness or reflects the fear that the offer will be rejected. Statistical evidence from their paper supports the fear hypothesis which is prompted by the revenge of the other player. We return to the motives of fairness and revenge in Chapter 7.

In a twist on the ultimatum game, Nowak, Page and Sigmund (2000) show that a fair solution tends to evolve if the dictator obtained some information on what type of deals the responder has accepted in the past. Hence, the authors conclude that the evolution of fairness, similar to the evolution of cooperation, is linked to reputation.

The result that outcomes are linked to reputation is consistent with other studies reviewed below with respect to the discussion of fairness. For example, Bolton and Zwick (1995) show that in a dictator game where the dictator decides how to distribute a fixed amount of money between himself and one other person, he can elect to give the other person nothing and keep it all for himself. But this does not usually happen because the dictator does not want to be viewed as greedy, even though both players are anonymous. However, when given the option of giving a small or large amount, the dictator usually chooses the small amount. Bolton and Zwick call this the impunity game, a game where the dictator has to split the money equally or give a small amount to the other player. The other player can reject the offer; however, rejection of the offer does not affect the amount given to the dictator. In these experiments, the dictator always gives the smaller amount, even as the arbitrator of the game observes the dictator making this selfish decision. When there is complete anonymity in a double blind experiment and the recipient's refusal had no impact on the actions of the dictator, fully two-thirds of the dictators did not leave anything to the other player, and only six percent left half. *If there is no threat of reprisal, people are generally selfish.*

There is little evidence to support the anonymity hypothesis, i.e., that a dictator will give less if nobody knows what they are giving. However, the issue of anonymity is still unresolved in the literature. The result depends upon circumstances and the attitudes of those who "know" that the dictator is giving very little to the other player. Experimental studies that allowed for anonymity of players show that time does appear to play a factor — fairness appeared to be more dominant in one-off games (Roth, 1995). With repetition of the game over time, as players became more familiar with its structure and payoff, there was a greater tendency for players to move towards their own advantage. Yet three out of 20 people in Roth's experiments would still fail to come to agreement with the terms of the deals despite complete information on each other's payoffs and strategy. The aforesaid players simply declined to accept the "advantageous but unfair deals".

The Roth game illustrates the importance of acceptable thresholds and threats. Credibility of the second player to take action if the dictator does not keep his promise is essential. The second player might threaten that he would only agree to the deal if he is given a certain proportion of the sum of money (say 35 percent). If the dictator believes him, it would be in the interest of the dictator to offer at least 35 percent share of the money to the second player for fear of the deal falling through. 35 percent is thus the acceptance threshold of the second player. Bargains are often made on the premise of what the other party would accept (acceptance threshold), given that both parties would benefit from the bargain.

See Box 4.2 for an interesting twist on bargaining games with an acceptance threshold. Games of this type also involve reprisal so that if the offer is not accepted, neither player gains anything.

4.6.1 *Importance of reputation*

Reputation can play a critically important factor in game theory (as mentioned earlier in Section 4.2). In the dictator/ultimatum game, the dictator has gathered information about what offers the second player has accepted in the past. Based on this knowledge, the dictator is able to propose a division of money that the second player will accept. If the second player has a reputation of being unwilling to accept less than a certain sum of money, the dictator would have to compromise in his allocation of the money. It may also be advantageous for the second player to have the reputation of being irrational so that other players cannot use backward induction to deduce his or her strategy in sequential games. At times, depending on the situation, it may pay to have a reputation for cooperation, or even a reputation for trustworthiness.

Box 4.2 Bargaining with an Acceptance Threshold

Below is an excerpt from the novel by Lloyd Alexander, which narrates the adventure of Taran the Wanderer who comes across two feuding lords, Lord Goryon and Lord Gast, warring over the division of their herd of cows which has strayed from their pastures and are now thoroughly mixed on the fields. They each own half of the 1,000 cows. Our young hero, Taran, comes up with an ingenious method to aid King Smoit in resolving the problem.

"And what of my herd?" cried Goryon.

"And mine!" cried Gast. "They're so mixed together no man can tell his own from another's."

"Lord Goryon shall divide the herds in equal portions", Taran said.

"He shall not!" Lord Gast broke in. "He'll give me all the scrawny ones and keep the fat for himself. It's I who'll divide them!"

"Not so!" shouted Goryon. "You'll fob off none of your rawboned creatures on me!"

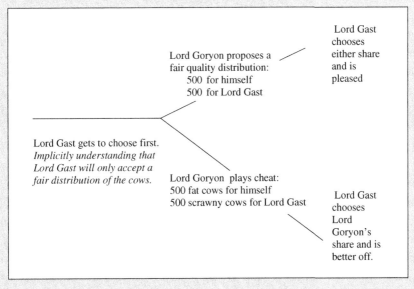

(*Continued*)

Box 4.2 (*Continued*)

"Lord Goryon shall divide the herds", Taran repeated. "But Lord Gast shall be first to choose his half".

"Well said!" Smoit burst out, roaring with laughter. "My breath and blood, you have them there! Goryon divides and Gast chooses! Ho, oho! It takes two thieves to strike an honest bargain!"

This tale illustrates an interesting twist to the acceptance threshold in bargaining games. It is implicit that Lord Gast would only accept a fair division of the cows and since Lord Gast gets to choose his share first, it is in Lord Goryon's best interest to divide the herds equally (both in terms of quantity and quality). If Lord Goryon tried to cheat in the process by allocating better quality cows to himself, it is obvious that Lord Gast would simply choose Lord Goryon's share. See the decision tree.

Source: Novel extract from Alexander (1967, p. 57).

Akerlof (1970) has shown that owing to asymmetric information between the buyers and the car salesman in the used car market, buyers are unable to determine the quality of the used car and hence, sales transactions are unlikely to take place. Buyers can only take the word of the salesman regarding the quality of the used car. It is highly likely that there is a bias toward selection of lemons (i.e., inferior cars), particularly if the car is relatively new. The question arises in the mind of the buyer, "Why would anyone sell a brand new car?" The answer arises, "Only if it is a lemon". This is one reason why used cars, even nearly new models, have such a big discount in the market.

Using game theory, Dasgupta (1988) shows that this difficulty could be circumvented if the salesman enjoys a reputation for being trustworthy (a probability of being trustworthy must be more than 1/3 in one-off games in the Dasgupta exercise). The probability of being trustworthy could be less in sequential games, since repeated interaction in subsequent games would provide the incentive for the

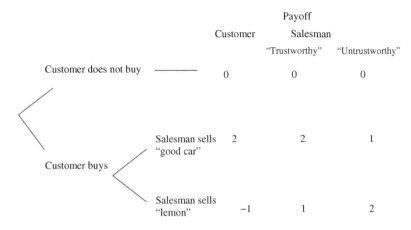

Figure 4.1 Second-Hand Car Salesman and "Lemon"

Source: Heap *et al.* (1992, p. 152, Figure 9.3).

salesman to behave as if he were trustworthy. The reputation for trustworthiness would thus allow the salesman to generate greater car sales. Therefore, the reputation for trustworthiness does appear to have its own valuable payoffs, provided it is recognizable. See Figure 4.1 for an example (see also Frank, 1988; Akerlof, 1983).

Hence, it is possible that some people have deliberately cultivated a certain reputation in order to earn material gains or other possible benefits. If they are able to successfully mimic that needed trait or characteristic, they would be able to gain access to the same benefits enjoyed by people who have the genuine traits. For instance, recall the players in Box 4.2 — if Goryon and Gast managed to successfully mask their true traits of being "thieves", it would not have been necessary to mandate that Goryon divide and Gast choose. If Goryon could successful pass himself off as being honest, he could have been given entire authority over the division and allocation of the cows and he could have had his pick of the herd. However, it must be realized that such mimicking may require time and cost, so it might not be that easy to achieve. Furthermore, once the dishonest character has been discovered, he will have to go elsewhere to try his luck at masquerading as an honest person.

4.6.2 Neuroeconomics and decision making in the ultimatum game

We have seen that different emotions play a role in whether players accept or reject offers made in the ultimatum game. As we know, the standard economic solution to the ultimatum game is for the proposer to offer the smallest sum possible and for the responder to accept this offer. Any monetary amount is preferable to nothing, according to standard theory. However, in several experiments (Thaler, 1988; Bolton and Zwick, 1995; Henrich *et al.*, 2001), average offers were around 50 percent of the maximum amount that could be offered. Low offers (say less than 30 percent) were rejected about half the time. These results do not vary much across countries sampled. Furthermore, many subjects turned down (unfair) monetary rewards even when there was no punishment of the proposer.

How can we determine that offers are unfair and are there some ways to explore this seemingly "emotional" decision? Researchers into the neural basis of these decisions, using neuroeconomics, looked at the ultimatum game by using functional magnetic resonance imaging (fMRI) to examine what is happening in the brain during rounds of the ultimatum game (Sanfey *et al.*, 2003; McCabe *et al.*, 2001).

Sanfey *et al.* (2003) discovered that three parts of the brain were involved in the decision making processes of responders. When offers were judged to be unfair (and therefore usually rejected), a part of the brain associated with negative emotional states (bilateral anterior insula) was active. When offers were deemed acceptable, another area of the brain associated with cognitive process such as "goal maintenance and executive control" was more heavily involved (dorsolateral prefrontal cortex) (Sanfey *et al.*, 2003, p. 1757). This region of brain activity is consistent with the economic incentive to accumulate money. It was also reasonably active in assessing negative offers, although the authors concluded this was to note the loss of money involved by rejection and to offer resistance in rejecting the offer. The third area (anterior cingulated cortex) identified in other studies is a region of the brain where cognitive conflicts are detected (and perhaps resolved). From this analysis, we can conclude that the cognitive and emotional aspects of decision making are processed in different parts of the brain and also that there is another area of the brain that mediates these two conflicting motives.

McCabe *et al.* (2001) discovered a part of the orbitofrontal cortex (called BA10) which allows gratification delay in order to obtain larger rewards through cooperation. This area of the brain is active in game theoretical situations where a trusting player can receive greater reward by making a sequential choice to give his money to another player (see McCabe *et al.*, 2001, and also Zak, 2004, for details).

This analysis of brain activity by Sanfey *et al.* (2003) and McCabe *et al.* (2001) illustrates that complex process of evaluation of monetary reward and the unfairness of the offer is carried out in the brain. This process leads to a decision. Since people are different, decisions are not uniform. Those who have been cheated in the past may have a tendency to reject low offers more than those who have a strong sense of the value of money. Sanfey *et al.* (2003, p. 1758) conclude that "Models of decision making cannot afford to ignore emotion as a vital and dynamic component of our decisions and choices in the real world."

Experiments carried out by McCabe *et al.* (2001) show that activation of areas of the brain that invoke trust is required for cooperation. This process requires the mediation of the conflicting concerns of making more money and behaving in socially unacceptable ways. Different parts of the brain appear to be responsible for the activation of these different functions and some of these responses reflect the importance of establishing and maintaining social reputation.

In both the Sanfey *et al.* (2003) and McCabe *et al.* (2001) studies, the complexity of the decision making process is highlighted. Through the use of fMRI, researchers are beginning to better understand the areas in the brain that interact and the factors being considered in simple games that lead to a final decision being taken.

4.7 Cooperative Games and Going Beyond the Laboratory

In the experiments reviewed so far, we have assumed that the payoffs in Prisoner's Dilemma or dictator games are known and certain. In the real world, every strategic decision is risky. For example, in choosing between proven and advanced information systems, to choose the advanced system is likely to be riskier than choosing the proven system. Thus, we would have to take into account the players' subjective attitudes toward risk — their risk aversion — to make the example fully realistic.

Remember the discussion of risk in Chapter 3? We will not attempt to incorporate risk in this discussion of game theory, but we must keep it in mind. The examples introduced in this chapter assume that payoffs are measured in money. Thus, we are not only leaving risk aversion out of the picture, but also any other subjective rewards and penalties that cannot be measured monetarily. Economists have ways of measuring subjective rewards in monetary terms. Sometimes they work and sometimes they do not. Nevertheless, we are going to skip over that problem and assume that all rewards and penalties are monetary and transferable from the user to the supplier and vice versa.

Furthermore, looking at the choice of technology example, real choices of information systems are likely to involve more than two players, at least in the long-run — the user may choose among several suppliers, and suppliers may have many customers. That makes the coordination problem harder to solve. Suppose, for example, that "Beta" is the advanced system and "VHS" is the proven system, and suppose that about 90 percent of the market uses "VHS"; then "VHS" may take over the market even though "Beta" is the better system. Many economists, game theorists and others believe this is a main reason why certain technical standards gain dominance. How about Macintosh/Apple and the IBM Windows-based operating systems? Or the fight for the music market between Apple's IPOD and other vendors such as Microsoft? Or the current struggle in the high-definition DVD formats between Sony-led Blue-ray and Toshiba-led HD-DVD systems?

On the other hand, the user and the supplier does not have to just sit back and wait to see what the other person does — they can sit down and talk it out, and commit themselves to a contract. In fact, they have to do so, because the amount of payment from the user to the supplier — a strategic decision we have ignored until now — also has to be agreed upon. This could be very tricky if users and suppliers have opposing views and cannot come to an agreement. For instance, if we just look at the high-definition DVD, it looks quite messy (*International Herald Tribune*, 2006, June 14). Blue-ray has garnered the support of consumer electronics such as Sony and Dell and major movie studios such as Disney and 20th Century Fox. HD-DVD has its own camp of supporters from Toshiba, Microsoft and Universal. Consumers are faced with a dilemma. Shall they buy now and commit themselves to the HD-DVD players, or wait for the Blue-ray machines? Consumers eventually risk ending up with an obsolete player, should one side triumph over the other. On the other hand, it could take some time for the winner to emerge. The prospect of buying 2 DVDs in order to view favorite movies that play in one format but not the other does not seem appealing. There does not seem to be a win/win situation in sight yet.

This is an example of a *cooperative game*, unlike the Prisoner's Dilemma. It makes the problem of coordinating standards easier, at least in the short-run. On the other hand, cooperative games call for a different approach to the solution.

In the real world, the payoffs and available strategies available to players are often uncertain as well. People generally have incomplete information. One good example is the most beautiful number game, where spikes randomly occurred around zero and multiples of $1/2 \times 2/3$, since people were not all perfectly sure if everyone could and would apply the same strategy of backward reasoning to the Nash equilibrium of zero. Hence, incomplete information could create this lack of consistency in backward induction games.

In some cases, information is asymmetrically distributed among the players. Some players would have more precise information than others, and players could still estimate other players' payoff matrix with a subjective probability distribution p (such games are termed "asymmetric information games"). Bayes' rule[3] takes into account

---

[3]Bayes' Theorem states that the probability of A is conditional on the occurrence of B. It is defined as $P(A|B) = P(B|A) P(A)/P(B)$.

such probability distribution when incorporating new information with processing past information, enabling the player to maximize the expected value of each set of strategies, given the strategy pursued by the other players. Thus, the player can eliminate strategies which are not credible in the future.

There are myriad possible applications of game theory ranging from war strategies to labor/management contract negotiations to how to win a sports match. Since we are primarily interested in the nexus between cooperation and selfish or self-centered competitive behavior, we have focused on what happens in situations when there is a possibility of cooperation or competition in a game-type situation and the possible dynamics of these interactions. In general, people will cooperate with those they know and trust and also if they are hoping to build a lasting relationship with their opponent in the game. On the other hand, there is always the temptation to defect and make a "sucker" of your opponent in, say, the last round of a game. For example, some people are able to locate those who are willing to cooperate in real world situations. For those looking to cooperate, it pays to look for like-minded people. On the other hand, those unwilling to cooperate may pretend to cooperate until they get a chance to defect (see Frank, 1988).

4.8 Memory, the Categorical Imperative and Game Theory[4]

The game theoretic problem of finding like-minded players can be put in another context. Consider the statement by the German philosopher Immanuel Kant that has come to be known as the "categorical imperative". This dictum states:

> "Individuals should behave in a way that one would like everyone to behave."

---

[4]This line of reasoning is related to the mental accounting problem discussed in Chapter 3 and also to the most beautiful number game.

This is a normative statement and can also be seen as an overgeneralization, in the sense that we know some people will not behave in the way we would like them to. Furthermore, each of us would put a different spin on this statement. In its pure ethical form, the idea is that a decision maker would decide on a course of action, assuming all other players acted in the same way, and that this course of action would be the most ethical course of action.

In the Prisoner's Dilemma, this means that cooperative individuals would act in this way because they believe others would also be cooperative. We know that cooperative behavior leads to a win/win situation in simple games like the Prisoner's Dilemma and also in some other game contexts. If a society thinks that cooperation is a better strategy for the betterment of its citizens, then it will have to change the game by changing the payoff matrix for the players by education, inducing a feeling of guilt if they do not cooperate and by setting an example through public policies that support cooperation where it serves the public interest. In later chapters, we will discuss some of these circumstances such as situations when free riding is an issue, in general ethical issues or in a discussion of altruism.

Another situation where game theoretic ideas can come into play is when players have faulty memories. Consider the scenario of a driver who has to get off a freeway at exit two to get to her destination (see Gilboa and Gilboa-Schechtman, 2001; Piccioni and Rubenstein, 1997). However, when she gets to exit two she does not remember whether she has already passed the first exit.

Let us assume that she is now starting all over again and has to develop a strategy for exiting. The losses and gains associated with exiting at the first or second exit or continuing on are given in Table 4.3. Consider two pure strategies. One pure strategy is to exit whenever an exit comes up. This leads her to leave at the first exit. The payoff is zero. Another pure strategy is to keep on going past both exits. This results in a loss of one. So the best pure strategy is to get off early. In my real life experiences with driving, this is usually the best alternative. Get off early when unsure when to get off.

Table 4.3 Exit Strategies with Imperfect Memory

Strategy	Payoff
Leave freeway at exit one	0
Leave freeway at exit two	1
Continue on freeway past exit one and exit two	−1

4.9 Games and Collective Action

Game theory has a number of applications in the field of collective action. This is an extensive field and space does not permit more than a brief introduction. The reader is referred to Olson (1965) and Sandler (1992) for further details. See also the discussion in Chapter 8 for further analysis of clubs.

Collective action takes place when individuals coordinate their actions within a group context so as to further their collective well-being. Many of the problems and challenges of how to achieve satisfactory outcomes when working as a group can be demonstrated by using game theory. For the Prisoner's Dilemma-type situation, imagine that instead of two individuals we are dealing with two groups of advocates. In a Prisoner's Dilemma-type situation, we can see that when prisoners refuse to cooperate, they arrive at a strategy that yields an outcome that is less satisfactory than if they had both cooperated.

Taking this logic to the field of welfare economics and the provision of public goods, where the state is one player and the general public is the other player, the general public will often elect to free ride on the efforts of others and use public services without paying for them. It defects. As the state gets less revenue than it would if everyone in the general public agreed to pay for public services by cooperating, it provides less than the optimal amount of public service. This means that the Nash equilibrium is different and less than the Pareto optimal solution. Too little of the public service is provided, although it could result in a higher level of satisfaction for some without reducing the satisfaction of anyone else (see Chapters 5 and 9 for further discussion of free riders).

However, when the assumptions of the standard game theoretic or public goods model are violated, then Nash equilibrium need not be suboptimal. This can occur when public goods are "impure", i.e., their use cannot be excluded or they are jointly produced (not nonrival). This is where collective action and the theory of clubs come in. Clubs are a private alternative to the provisioning of public goods by the government.

Olson (1965) defines two kinds of clubs based on the concept of rivalry. In the first instance, a club is nonrival in the sense that the crowding costs are zero regardless of the number of members. Allowing in everyone who wants to join can expand the size of the club and will cut the costs of the club since the average cost will decline as the club size increases without reducing the club's benefits. Clubs where rivalry exists cannot expand membership without reducing the benefits of existing members. Therefore, there will be some size restriction. Using economic tools, the marginal benefits and costs of an additional member are equated and that determines the total membership.

The collective action literature spends considerable time looking into club membership, whether any of the collective good will be provided (and also whether the club will actually be formed) and the payoff matrix for games like the Prisoner's Dilemma. We return to this subject in Chapter 8.

Privilege: The concept of privilege is important in determining whether clubs are formed or not. Privilege is defined as "when at least one individual derives sufficient net benefits from the collective action to go it alone" (Sandler, 1992, p. 35). For example, in a "normal" Prisoner's Dilemma version of an option to join or not join a collective, the rational action is to defect and so the group would not be formed (Sandler, 1992, p. 40). However, if the payoff matrix is changed to what Sandler calls the "chicken game", then some collective good will be provided. The term "chicken game" comes from the scenario when two cars speed toward each other at breakneck speed and the first one to swerve (collude/cooperate) is a chicken. If they both keep going, they have a head-on collision and die. So the lower right-hand element in the payoff matrix of the Prisoner's Dilemma is a very big negative number, as indicated by $-x, -x$ in Table 4.4.

Table 4.4 Chicken Game

	Cooperate	Defect
Cooperate	4, 4	−1, −5
Defect	5, 1	−x, −x

Note: x indicates a very large number.

Table 4.5 Assurance Game

	Cooperate	Defect
Cooperate	4, 4	−3, −3
Defect	−3, −3	0, 0

In this case, since the cost of defection is so high, there will be some cooperation to provide the public good. This is the kind of situation that arises in mutual defense and nonproliferation treaties where governments agree to provide mutual security and some smaller nations benefit from the umbrella provided by major powers in these kinds of situations.

Olson (1965) and others have shown that the weaker/smaller members can take advantage of the dominant member of the club. Sandler (1992) provides a number of examples of such club behavior including the minor states of Greece being protected by Athens and Sparta, and the current example of NATO, where smaller European countries fall under the US military umbrella. Another variation of a two-person non-cooperative game is called the assurance game, where a minimal effort must be exerted to obtain any benefit. In this game, there is a strong incentive to cooperate and a big penalty if either defects (see Table 4.5).

Size and design of payoff matrix: As the examples in the previous section demonstrate, the Prisoner's Dilemma structure will go a long way toward determining the decisions that the players make. If there is a large negative or even zero reward to defecting versus cooperating, then the cooperative solution will be more likely. However, in many real life situations, clubs may not form and the problem of free riders may be substantial. In these circumstances, win/win solutions may be more difficult to ensure and may, in some circumstances, depend upon the emotional and psychological propensities of participants to cooperate rather than defect. We return to these issues in Chapter 8.

4.10 Summary — What are the Important Factors in Determining People's Actions in a Game Theoretic Setting?

What are the important factors in determining people's actions in a game theoretic setting? The answer is, as always, "it depends". However, research seems to suggest that there are several key factors that play a role.

Firstly, the size of the relative payoff plays a big role in wooing cooperators into the defector camp. This is evident from the results of game theory simulations and also from the common sense point of view.

Secondly, the social milieu is important. If one is operating with many defectors around, the benefits to cooperation will be small. However, if cooperators can generate a critical mass, then it is likely that win/win situations will be more widely observed. This will in turn have a demonstration effect for other participants in similar situations.

Thirdly, cooperation is more likely among friends and associates with some history and some experience with bonding. Trust builds more quickly in such environments and becomes resistant to the occasional defection that might otherwise lead to a breakdown in cooperation. In this regard, trust and fairness play a key role in building cooperation. At the same time, we have to recognize that there is always a risk of defection, particularly if the price is right. The role of public policy, as we will discuss subsequently in Chapter 8, is to devise mechanisms that reduce this temptation to defect.

Fourthly, the role of emotions and previous conditioning that manifests through these emotions can play an important role in the decision to cooperate or defect. Societies and groups where cooperation is taught and practiced widely have a better chance of developing win/win scenarios.

Finally, we also have to recognize that cooperation can be a guise for possible defection after a trusting environment has been established. In many forms of the Prisoner's Dilemma and public choice games, defection is observed on the last round of repeated games, suggesting that the veil of cooperation can be very thin.

In economic theory, Adam Smith has stated that (i) as the individual pursues his or her own self-interest, (ii) it would lead spontaneously to the emergence of the market clearing as if through an invisible hand, which would be to their collective benefit. In equilibrium, consumers would have maximized their utility and firms maximized their profits.

Rational action by individuals would lead to Pareto optimal solution whereby it is unable to make anyone better off without making someone worse off. However, as we have shown, individual rationality might not always lead to collective efficiency. We will discuss its implications on the evolution of social order, organizations and government in the later chapters.

But before going into that, let us move on to the other component, the antithesis of self-interest — altruism. How does that fall into place in economic context? We have stressed the importance of social milieu. In our interactions with one another in the real world, we are well aware that there are other emotions beside self-interest that govern our behavior. Frequently, we do not operate as coolly and detached as a rational economic agent does. Emotions and feelings do play a role. Altruism, sympathy, jealousy and other emotions impact the decision making process.

Going back to the game theoretical setting, Heap *et al.* (1992, pp. 176–178) suggest there is a relationship between altruism and backward and forward induction. In the former, we are acting in the stance of moral certainty. Kant proposes that we only look at the best outcomes for all. Hence, looking backwards, our best action is to cooperate. In terms of the latter, we are looking forward to what we are going to receive in terms of recognition and verification from the community or society; hence we behave the way we do. Both lead to the same cooperative outcome despite differing reasoning. For instance, in the Prisoner's Dilemma, if the players could pause to think of each other and of their end consequences, they might decide to cooperate since it is in all their best interests. Whether they do or not will often depend on other factors as we have discussed.

Cooperation may also enable players to break out of powerful lose/lose situations like feuds between neighbors or between neighboring countries (Palestine and Israel, Catholics and Protestants in Northern Ireland, India and Pakistan in Kashmir, North and South Korea, US and Iraq). Breaking loose from this cycle in a national or geopolitical setting may include considering alternatives like offering amnesty, working toward a ceasefire or cessation of hostilities, pursuing a policy of nonviolence even though there is a threat of being attacked, bringing in an outside arbitrator or changing the payoff matrix to reward cooperation and punish defection. For example, the threat of nuclear war and the large negative payoff to such action has, in the view of some observers, kept the world from another world war.

In these situations, it is important to realize the gains that can be made from cooperation as opposed to the losses that will be sustained by defection. We have to consider seriously the possibility that in many situations, individuals and societies actually gain utility by acting altruistically. We will discuss these issues further in Chapter 5.

Bibliography

Akerlof, G.A. (1970) The Market for 'Lemons': Quality Uncertainty and the Market Mechanism. *Quarterly Journal of Economics*, 84(3), 488–500.

Akerlof, G.A. (1983) Loyalty Filters. *American Economic Review*, 73(1), 54–63.

Alexander, L. (1967) *Taran Wanderer.* New York: Holt, Rinehart and Winston.

Andreoni, J.A. and J.H. Miller (1993) Rational Cooperation in the Finitely Repeated Prisoner's Dilemma: Experimental Evidence. *Economic Journal*, 103, 570–585.

Axelrod, R. (1984) *The Evolution of Cooperation.* New York: Basic Books.

Becker, G.S. (1981) Altruism in the Family and Selfishness in the Marketplace. *Economica*, 48, 1–15.

Binmore, K., A. Shaked and J. Sutton (1985) Testing Non-Cooperative Bargaining Theory: A Preliminary Experiment. *American Economic Review*, 75(5), 1178–1180.

Bolton, G.E. and R. Zwick (1995) Anonymity versus Punishment in Ultimatum Bargaining. *Games and Economic Behavior*, 10(1), 95–121.

Bolton, G.E., R. Zwick and E. Katok (1998) Dictator Game Giving: Rules of Fairness versus Acts of Kindness. *International Journal of Game Theory*, 27(2), 269–299.

Bowles, S. and H. Gintis (2004) The Evolution of Strong Reciprocity: Cooperation in Heterogeneous Populations. *Theoretical Population Biology*, 65, 17–28.

Camerer, C.F. (2003) *Behavioral Games Theory: Experiments in Strategic Interaction.* Princeton: Princeton University Press.

Camerer, C.F. and T.-H. Ho (1999) Experience-Weighted Attraction Learning in Normal Form Games. *Econometrica*, 67(4), 827–874.

Clark, K. and M. Sefton (2001) The Sequential Prisoner's Dilemma: Evidence on Reciprocal Altruism. *Economic Journal*, 111(468), 51–68.

Dasgupta, P. (1988) Trust as a Commodity. In D. Gambetta (ed.), *Trust: Making and Breaking Cooperate Relations.* Oxford: Blackwell.

de Quervain, D.J.-F., U. Fischbacher, V. Treyer, M. Schellhammer, U. Schnyder, A. Buck and E. Fehr (2004) The Neural Basis of Altruistic Punishment. *Science*, 305, 1254–1258.

Dresher, M., A.W. Tucker and P. Wolfe (eds.) (1957) *Contributions to the Theory of Games*, Volume III (Annals of Mathematics Studies, 39). Princeton: Princeton University Press.

Fehr, E. and S. Gachter (2002) Altruistic Punishment in Humans. *Nature*, 415, 137–140.

Flood, M. (1958) Some Experimental Games. *Management Science*, 5, 5–26.

Frank, R. (1988) *The Passions within Reason: Prisoner's Dilemmas and the Strategic Role of the Emotions.* New York: W.W. Norton.

Gilboa, I. and E. Gilboa-Schechtman (2001) Mental Accounting and the Absentminded Driver. Tel Aviv Working Paper No. 2001–20.

Heap, S.H., M. Hollis, B. Lyons, R. Sugden and A. Weale (1992) *The Theory of Choice: A Critical Guide.* Oxford, UK and Cambridge, Mass.: Blackwell.

Henrich, J., R. Boyd, S. Bowles, C. Camerer, H. Gintis, R. McElreath and E. Fehr (2001) In Search of Homo Economicus: Experiments in 15 Small-Scale Societies. American Economic Review, 91(2), 73–79.

Keynes, J.M. (1936) *General Theory of Employment Interest and Money.* New York: Harcourt Brace.

King, W. (2006) Nash Equilibrium. http://williamking.www.drexel.edu/top/eco/game/nash.html [Retrieved 28 January 2006].

Kravitz, D.A. and S. Gunto (1992) Decisions and Perceptions of Recipients in Ultimatum Bargaining Games. *Journal of Socio-Economics*, 21, 65–84.

McCabe, K., D. Houser, L. Ryan, V. Smith and T. Trouard (2001) A Functional Imaging Study of Cooperation in Two-Person Reciprocal Exchange. *Proceedings of the National Academy of Science*, pp. 11832–11835.

Nagel, R., A. Bosch-Domènech, A. Satorra and G. Montalvo (1999) One, Two, (Three), Infinity: Newspaper and Lab Beauty-Contest Experiments. Economics Working Papers 438, Department of Economics and Business, Universitat Pompeu Fabra.

Nowak, M.A., R.M. May and K. Sigmund (1995) The Arithmetics of Mutual Help. *Scientific American*, 272, 50–55.

Nowak, M.A., K.M. Page and K. Sigmund (2000) Fairness versus Reason in the Ultimatum Game. *Science*, 289, 1773–1775.

Olson, M. (1965) *The Logic of Collective Action*. Cambridge: Harvard University Press.

Piccioni, M. and A. Rubenstein (1997) On the Interpretation of Decision Problems with Imperfect Recall. *Games and Economic Behavior*, 20, 121–130.

Rilling, J.K., D.A. Gutman, T. Zeh, G. Pagnoni, G.S. Brms and C.D. Kilts (2003) A Neural Basis for Social Cooperation. *Neuron*, 35, 395–405.

Roth, A.E. (1995) Bargaining Experiments. In J.H. Kagel and A.E. Roth (eds.), *The Handbook of Experimental Economics*. Princeton, NJ: Princeton University Press.

Sandler, T. (1992) *Collective Action: Theory and Applications*. Ann Arbor: University of Michigan Press.

Sanfey, A.G., J.K. Rilling, J.A. Aronson, L.E. Nystrom and J.D. Cohen (2003) The Neural Basis of Economic Decision Making in the Ultimatum Game. *Science*, 300, 1755–1758.

Shiller, R. (2005) *Irrational Exuberance*. Princeton: Princeton University Press.

Skinner, B.F. (1938) *The Behavior of Organisms; An Experimental Analysis*. New York and London: D. Appleton-Century Company.

Skinner, B.F. (1974) *About Behaviorism*. New York: Knopf.

Thaler, R.H. (1988) Anomalies: The Ultimatum Game. *The Journal of Economic Perspectives*, 2(4), 195–206.

von Neumann, J. and O. Morgenstern (1944) *Theory of Games and Economic Behavior*. Princeton: Princeton University Press.

Zak, P.J. (2004) Neuroeconomics. *Philosophical Transactions of the Royal Society Biology*, 359, 1737–1748.

Chapter 5

Altruism

What aspects of human behavior can be considered as alternatives to the narrow self-interest used in orthodox economic analysis? There is much discussion of how behavior violates the pure self-interest assumptions of the neoclassical model. This aspect of behavior was discussed in the previous chapter when we discussed games such as the Prisoner's Dilemma and dictator games. We observed that in certain circumstances, people would choose the opportunity to cooperate rather than defect. In this chapter, we delve further into cooperative behavior, looking at several additional factors that might motivate people to be cooperative rather than competitive.

Altruism and charity are two aspects of behavior that are widely observed but do not easily fit into the hedonistic framework. When economic agents are charitable or altruistic, they act on the base motive of treating others as more or less equal to themselves. Acts of heroism such as saving a drowning person or rescuing someone from a burning building at the risk of personal safety are extreme examples. But there are many other subtle acts of altruism and charity which take place in day to day life. How do you treat your family members and work associates? Are you charitable and cooperative or are you penny pinching and uncooperative? Do you follow acceptable road etiquette and behavior or do you cut people off when you have a chance to get ahead in the queue? Are you a good sport? Do you hold a grudge when you are passed over for promotion or do you congratulate the other person who got it? These are all instances where we act either in a selfish or cooperative manner.

Ethics enters the discussion when actions require upholding implicit and often unenforceable contracts or social norms of behavior. Upholding these norms are consistent with a cooperative and generous point of view. Free riders, moral hazards and principal-agent problems are all circumstances where conflicts in ethical versus pure economic self-interested behavior arise.

An honest and ethical person would be less likely to take advantage of these situations for his own narrow self-interest. Rather, the ethical individual would comply with both the spirit and letter of the law and regulations. He would do that because he realizes that when he takes advantage of the system, he raises costs and reduces welfare of others. By complying with the spirit and letter of the law and regulations, the ethical person is also following a cooperative or altruistic course of action.

Most of us seesaw back and forth between cooperation and competition. As a result, Etzioni (1988) suggests that economic behavior is a combination of neoclassical utilitarian and ethical motives, which he characterizes as deontology, "the notion that actions are morally right when they confirm to a relevant principle or duty" (p. 12). Further, "Deontology uses as the criterion for judging the morality of an act, not the ends it aspires to achieve nor the consequences, but the moral duty it discharges or disregards" (p. 13).

Etzioni (1988) discusses at length these two principles at work in economic decision making. We will refer to many of his and similar arguments involving the emotions and ethical considerations as we move through the chapters of this book. The role of charity is discussed in greater detail in Chapter 9, where issues of market failure are taken up. In this chapter, we focus on the role of altruism and cooperation.

5.1 The Altruist's Dilemma

One way to relate material in game theory as discussed in Chapter 4 to altruism is to think of the Prisoner's Dilemma as the Altruist's Dilemma (Grant, 2004). Consider, for example, the case of two students, say they are girls, who are accused of a crime by their teacher. The teacher leaves a coffee mug on the edge of her desk when she leaves the room. She slams the door behind her as she leaves the room and the mug falls to the floor and breaks. When she returns she accuses the two children, who had been left alone in the room, of breaking the mug. The mug cost $10. If one girl confesses, then she will have to pay the $10 and the other girl is not penalized. If both

Table 5.1 Altruist's Dilemma

		Student 2	
		Does not confess	Confesses
Student 1	Does not confess	Both students miss recess	Student 2 pays $10 and Student 1 pays nothing
	Confesses	Student 2 pays nothing and Student 1 pays $10	Both students pay $5

confess, they each will pay $5. If neither confesses, they will have to stay in the class and miss recess. The children are best friends and each is concerned about the other. They are altruistic in the sense that they are equally or even more worried about their friend than they are about themselves. The payoff matrix for this "Altruist's" Dilemma situation is shown in Table 5.1.

Consider the reasoning of both Student 1 and Student 2. Each student thinks, "If my friend confesses then I should confess. If I do not confess then my friend will have to pay $10. I, should confess and then we will both only have to pay $5. If my friend does not confess, I should still confess because my friend can go out and play and I will willingly pay the $10 to replace the mug." The Nash equilibrium is that they both confess (defect) and both pay $5. If they had both kept quiet, they would have only missed recess and would have had a chance to be together too. Even if the children had been put in separate rooms and asked to confess, the fact that they are friends would have prompted them both to confess.

Is this the end of the story? What if the friends were so close that they could imagine what the other was thinking? In that case, they might have opted to keep their mouths shut, since missing recess was a better option for both than having to pay $5.

This kind of Altruist's Dilemma continues to pit cooperation against competition. However, it is possible that altruism involves more complex issues than simple decision making in a Prisoner's Dilemma game. It may be that altruistic actions touch on a concern for the human condition and not just self-interest. To explore altruism at this more fundamental level, we need to ask questions about how cooperation begins as well as how it is sustained.

In the Tit for Tat strategy discussed in Chapter 4, cooperation begets cooperation. It begs the question of how cooperation gets started in the first place. If we study altruism from this deeper vantage point, we can explore the behavior horizons that lead to cooperation or competition from a broader perspective.

5.2 Religious and Spiritual Traditions

The model of self-interest receives no support from the world religious and spiritual traditions. "Love your neighbor as yourself" is a powerful dictum in the Judeo-Christian ethic. The golden rule of "Do unto others as you would have them do unto you" is an example of the spiritual or moral imperative to treat others as you would like to be treated.

To get a sense of how a truly altruistic individual might act, we can study the behavior of great saints and spiritual giants such as Buddha, Jesus, Moses, Mohammed, Ghandi, Confucius and a host of others from all the spiritual traditions. These sages lived in a purely selfless manner, following the golden rule and thinking of the welfare of others. They put these precepts into action in their daily lives. The lives of these few enlightened beings are the yardstick by which pure altruism or selfless action can be measured. These great beings truly viewed everyone as equal and treated everyone they met with great love and respect. They treated everyone as they would wish to be treated. They went beyond the pettiness of self-interest, seeing everything and everyone as being imbued with the same sacred origins. When we lose our ego, our narrow interest in our individual lives, we have the opportunity of finding unity with everything.[1]

---

[1]A cynic might point out that the golden rule might mean something different for a masochist or a sadist than a more "normal" person. What we are trying to get at here by invoking the golden rule is that one objective of human endeavor is to search for an ethical platform of behavior that is consistent with the actions of love, compassion and charity as exemplified and embodied by the spiritual figures that have been revered throughout history.

Getting rid of egoistic behavior requires putting other people on an equal footing with ourselves. Egocentric behavior is out. Egoism is self-defeating, while self-sacrifice eventually leads to the highest form of self-realization, love, joy and happiness. While it may seem impossible to achieve such a state of selflessness, there are enough examples over the centuries to give us concrete evidence that it is indeed possible. The question is: are we willing to forsake the worldly life by devoting ourselves completely to the path of spiritual devotion? The vast majority of us are not. Monks and mystics make up a small fraction of the world's population. Most of us are content to be arm-chair spiritualists — following their trials, tribulations and attainment by reading about them or watching movies that depict their lives.

5.3 Altruism, Reciprocity and Self-Interest

While we may strive to attain and understand the status of the great spiritual teachers and saints, we can also strive for an understanding of altruistic behavior at a more mundane level. We can ask the question that Etzioni (1988) has posed. Are we a mixture of self-interest and altruism? How do most of us act in our daily lives? Are we a mixture of higher and baser motives? Do we act with self-interest most of the time? Are there glimpses of the higher actions and motives of the saints in our own lives or the lives of our friends and relatives? Do we ride the trams for free when there is no one around to collect the fare? Do we tell a few lies now and then to make it easier to get our way? Do we ever go out of our way to help someone in trouble with no thought of getting "paid back"? How often are we selfish and how often do we put other people first?

In retrospect, we can probably conclude that for most people, actions are usually a combination of selfish and selfless behavior. Often we do not even think about it. We do not contemplate or consider what is the right or just thing to do in any particular circumstance. We are conditioned to act in a particular way. As a result, much of our behavior is based on habit and what we have learned from our parents, siblings, teachers and friends. We follow social norms by stopping at stop signs even when it is late at night and there is no one around. We pick up our clothes and make our beds. We clear up after eating. We greet our colleagues at work with a smile. We queue up to get tickets. We contribute to charity and we vote for candidates to public office. Much of this behavior is learned as socially acceptable and we do not even give it a thought. If there was a reward for following self-interest in any of these circumstances, would we think twice about breaking the rules and not cooperating? Would we stop at the stop sign if our pregnant wife was in the car ready to deliver? Would we be tempted to bribe someone at the front of the line if it was for a World Cup match that we were dying to see? Would our action depend upon how much we would be fined or chastised by following self-interest rather than cooperating?

There is clearly a need to examine our motives more carefully and to look at how these motives and actions are formed and altered. Whether we are following self-interest or looking out for others, it is important to recognize our motives and explore the consequences that these actions have for us, our friends, neighbors, society and the economy.

We begin by considering what we call "pure altruism" and "reciprocity", two fundamentally different concepts. There are many gradations between the two and many discussions dealing with the time frame of reciprocity (see Sesardic, 1995; Bercher, 1999). Without going into details of different subtle definitions, it is useful to note that the primary distinction between the two is that *when there is some self-interested motivation for an action, then the action is not altruistic in its pure sense.*

This includes what might look like seemingly altruistic actions such as contributions to private charities, donations of blood, volunteer work and so on. If the motivation for performing any of these actions is purely altruistic, then the individual would not tell anyone about his actions. Bercher (1999) asks, "How many of us keep blood donation a complete secret?" If the answer is none, then we are talking about indirect reciprocity and not pure altruism. Bercher argues there is a kind of social investment when we spread the word that we are performing charitable acts, wherein we can expect some form of reward in the future. Putting it another way, Sesardic (1995) says, "The human mind systematically and unintentionally leaks information about its content to the outside" (p. 151). Concern for "reputation" distinguishes altruism from reciprocity, wherein reciprocity is another form of self-interest — that of mutual back rubbing.

There are many cases of pure altruism. Some people are altruistic without any thought of mutual advantage. People give blood, contribute to charities, offer their services to the church and charitable organizations in a quiet and self-effacing way. In some cases, altruistic acts also involve risk. Examples that come to mind are acts of heroism or valor during armed conflict or acts of bravery by police, firemen or bystanders to rescue others from harm's way. These altruistic actions are taken at the spur of the moment, leaving no time for conjecture about the possible payback. Similar actions in the extreme or opposite direction such as cowardice and inaction are more likely made for reasons of self-preservation or fear of death or injury, which can overwhelm the social stigma attached to cowardice or inaction.

Acts of pure altruism are more of a mystery to economists and social scientists than acts motivated by reciprocity. They are particularly mysterious when carried out to save strangers rather than family members. In saving family members, we might be able to reason that some kind of Darwinian genetic mechanism is operating. Such arguments are less compelling when total strangers are involved. Nevertheless, these acts of heroism do occur. When interviewed afterwards, these heroes generally maintain that they did not think about the benefits and costs. There was no weighing of possible risk to life and limb against the benefits of saving others. These heroes just acted immediately in the face of danger.

Many authors have investigated the motivations for altruism or reciprocity. Sociobiology and psychology have made numerous contributions (see, for example, Wilson, 1978; Singer, 1981). From a genetic point of view, we are more likely to help close relatives and may even give up our own lives if it means survival of our offspring. However, when it comes to the general population, we are less likely to be altruistic. Close friends and associates come somewhere in between. Here, emotional attachment substitutes for the genetic imperative. Therefore, acts of heroism are even more inexplicable as expressions of the survival imperative.

5.4 Modeling Altruism

In defining altruism as "unselfish regard for or devotion to the welfare of others", economists have modeled this behavior within the conventional orthodox neoclassical framework in several ways.

5.4.1 *Altruism as a preference in the utility function*

In the simplest model there are two individuals, i and k, and i is an altruist. Then k's utility will be in i's utility function:

$$U_i = (1 - \mathbf{a})\, U_i(c_i) + \mathbf{a}\, U_k(c_k), \tag{1}$$

where $\mathbf{a}$ is a parameter $(0 < \mathbf{a} < 1)$ that weights the utility functions of the two individuals. If $\mathbf{a}$ is large, then individual i is a strong altruist. If $\mathbf{a}$ is close to zero, then i's altruism toward k is weak. Although this model is constructed for two individuals, it could be generalized so that k could be a representative of a group of people, all of whom altruist i favors, and $\mathbf{a}$ is a vector of altruism coefficients which relate to each of these people. Economists have modeled this kind of altruistic behavior by assuming that $\mathbf{a}$, the altruism parameter, is exogenously determined by taste. Just as people have a "taste" for discrimination, or sugar or whatever, so also they have a taste for altruism. When a person operates with pure selfishness toward all people, then $\mathbf{a}$ is zero. The motivation for a positive $\mathbf{a}$ is not discussed. These economic models generally assume that taste is fixed and predetermined.

We can speculate that by looking after others, the ith individual increases his own utility when he is being evaluated more positively by his boss, parents, etc. Parents can reward the charitable behavior of their children toward their siblings and discourage negative behavior.

Whatever the motivation, this model allows us to incorporate altruistic motives into behavior within the context of an optimizing framework. Mueller (1986) argues that if $\mathbf{a}$ is either zero or one, we are either selfish or altruistic if individuals are what he calls rational egoists. He argues that learned cooperative behavior leads to an $\mathbf{a}$ of one. **a** will be one if the rational egoist sees that his self-interest is served by cooperating in situations where the social norm requires it. The rational egoist will vote, even though he knows his one vote will count for nothing in the final outcome, or go to church even though he is an atheist.

The rationale egoist also treats some costs as sunk and not variable. However, as we saw in Chapter 3, this is not always the way people act. Mueller (1986) cites two experiments where students make vastly different decisions showing that they do not view sunk costs as truly sunk. In experiment one, imagine that you have decided to see a play where admission is $10 per ticket. As you enter the theater to buy a ticket, you find you have lost a $10 bill. Would you still go to the play? In experiment two, you have paid for the ticket but you realize you have lost the ticket and there is no way to recover the ticket or to be seated without it. Would you buy another ticket? Less than 46 percent of the 200 students in experiment two would buy another ticket as opposed to 88 percent of students in experiment one. Why should this be so since in both cases the student has lost $10 when entering the theater?

The answer is because the students in the second experiment did not realize that the ticket was a sunk cost that should be ignored in making the decision whether to buy another ticket. There are a number of other examples that we noted in Chapter 3, such as preference reversal, framing and analysis of situations with large and small probabilities that should convince us that to predict behavior, we need to know something about context, past experience and knowledge and how they are used in individual circumstances.

Alternatively, Mueller stresses the importance of social conditioning as a motive for cooperation. This includes many of the rituals we go through every day where cooperation makes life easier. It also relates to the social taboos that help to ensure that groups maintain social order like the Ten Commandments. Imagine a society that did not punish stealing, wife swapping, murder and the like. Mueller argues that these social and moral imperatives will dictate when **a** is zero and when it is one, and also circumstances where it can be another number between zero and one, for example offering a "little bit" of charity.

5.4.2 *Altruism as cooperative behavior*

In the case of a Prisoner's Dilemma game discussed in Chapter 4, both players can be better off if they cooperate. If altruism is viewed as cooperation, altruistic players are more likely to reach the cooperative solution. (However, recall the Altruist's Dilemma discussed above.) The more trust one player has in the cooperative instincts of others, the more likely a cooperative strategy will be the dominant strategy. Notice that when cooperative players meet those playing for self-interest, they are the losers in Prisoner's Dilemma games and generally in these kinds of real life situations. Frank (1988) discusses this issue, arguing that there are many situations when cooperation is observed and others where competition prevails.

Competition can have dire consequences not only for those directly concerned but for others as well. There is a legendary feud in US history between two families living in West Virginia, namely the Hatfields and the McCoys. After the initial fight between these two families began, each succeeding generation tried to wipe out the other clan, knowing that if any of the other clan survived they would continue to seek revenge. This feud was a "lose/lose" situation for both sides, yet it continued. Revenge was a powerful motive that dominated more beneficial strategies which could have resulted in a peaceful outcome. The continuing Arab–Israeli conflict in the Middle East and the dispute in Northern Ireland, which continued for centuries until a recent peace settlement was reached, are also examples where conflict, revenge and self-interest are so strong that the dispute continues on and on for years. It is fueled by murder, fear, anger and hatred — negativities that are passed on to generation after generation in an unending cycle of violence. Terrorism is another example of how hatred can infect others very quickly and lead to a rapid escalation in violence.

In all of these cases, the environment supports continued conflict and not cooperation. The challenge is how to sever the thread of violence. For example, should we consider amnesty for criminals? What other methods can be explored for reducing the motives for revenge and retribution?

On the other hand, there are many examples of cooperation that result in benefits to both sides. One can think of any number of examples such as:

- Keeping amicable relations between management and labor in wage bargaining situations;
- Maintenance of wildlife sanctuaries and other environmentally protected areas by private interest groups;
- Concerned citizens lobbying for just causes;
- Raising funds to fight disease, to help the homeless, the sick, the poor and the aged;
- Community service such as providing assistance for shut-ins.

Most economists prefer to believe that competition is more common than cooperation, particularly in the marketplace. Frank (1988) points out that this need not necessarily be the case. As we noted in the discussion of the Altruist's Dilemma, there are advantages to seeing altruism as the flip side of competition. On the other hand, there are other aspects of altruism that may go beyond this rather mechanical relationship. As Mueller (1986) suggests, we also need to look at the social context and whether cooperation is a trait that has survived because it is beneficial to society and its survival. Viewed in this way, cooperative and altruistic behavior can be considered hedonistic by society as a whole.

5.4.3 *Altruism as quid pro quo*

If we think of altruism as being conditional and based on reciprocity, one could argue that it is not really altruism. However, in the literature, this kind of behavior has been called conditional altruism or reciprocal altruism. A common case of this kind of altruism is family investment in children. Forget for the moment the pure altruism case where parents have no regard for payback in the future, being only interested in the welfare and happiness of their children. Childhood investment could be in exchange for implicit payback when the child grows up and enters the labor force, and the parents need financial and logistical support. A purist would argue that this is not altruism at all, but self-interest parading as altruism. But if the payback period is long and unsure, then the conditional relationship may be weak. In such cases, "quid pro quo" may have similar characteristics to a purer form of unconditional altruism.

5.4.4 Altruism as a genetically or inherited trait

The argument that in many situations people are more likely to cooperate than compete as proposed in Section 5.4.2 appeals to geneticists and biologists, particularly sociobiologists. When are people generally more likely to cooperate than compete? Geneticists suggest that there is more cooperative or altruistic behavior when genetic ties are strongest. Using genetic linkages, this argument can be extended to other relatives. The closer the genetic connection, the greater the chances are that we will observe cooperative or altruistic behavior. From this perspective, we are most altruistic toward those with whom we share a large gene pool. We may also consider the clan or village group, since there is mutual reinforcement for protection, gathering food and providing shelter. This expands the narrow definition of genetic fitness or survival of the fittest or strongest or most competitive, to include the survival of close kin and friends.

So self-interest and genetic selection in the narrow sense can exist and lead to altruism. Stark (1995) shows that even in situations where cooperative and altruistic behavior is penalized, such as the Prisoner's Dilemma, altruistic behavior can prevail when individuals that share the same role model of altruistic or cooperative behavior group together. Altruistic behavior can survive wherever altruistic people cluster. It may be for family or cultural reasons. The motivation is the important determinant of this beneficial behavior and relates closely to the motives stressed by Mueller (1986) and as noted above.

5.4.5 Altruism as a "Kantian" duty

The philosopher Immanuel Kant (1776, 1990) spoke of a "categorical imperative" whereby rational individuals decide to behave morally and ethically based on fundamental beliefs and their duty as human beings. There is much discussion about whether this moral duty is fully consistent with altruism. Nevertheless, it has been used by many writers as a justification for ethical and altruistic behavior. According to Kant, we have a duty as human beings to behave in a moral and ethical fashion. There can be no arguments about this and it is not subject to the analysis of utility maximization. The Kantian position is also reflected in the deontology argument of Etzioni presented earlier in this chapter. For further details, see Beauchamp (1982).

David Collard (1995) argues that a distinction should be made between the "categorical imperative" (CI), which is an inescapable moral duty to support certain causes, and a "hypothetical imperative" (HI), which depends upon context, particularly the expected outcome of the righteous action. By making this delineation, Collard suggests that the assembly of economic facts can be very useful in helping altruists to decide to support charitable works based on HI. Using logic from the theory of clubs (see Chapters 4 and 8), he shows that a Kantian group will only form if the group's willingness to pay is less than the individuals' willingness to pay.

Collard also introduces a number of possible examples of good works that might be supported by HI Kantians. He shows that in order to judge whether support is justified, the donor has to know something about the benefits that will accrue from the charitable action. In the case of support for immunization, he should know the effectiveness of the treatment, the nature of side effects and how well society can be expected to be protected as a result of the immunization program. This kind of economic analysis is required if HI Kantian altruists are to make cost-effective contributions that maximize the impact of their donations on society.

5.4.6 *Altruism as a social characteristic in a group context*

There was a highly publicized murder in New York City on 14 March 1964, when Kitty Genovese was killed by an assailant while many people either witnessed it from their apartment buildings or heard her screams. An article written by a *New York Times* reporter after that incident is reproduced in Box 5.1.

Box 5.1 Kitty Genovese Murder

Twenty-eight-year-old Catherine Genovese, who was called Kitty by almost everyone in the neighborhood, was returning home from her job as manager of a bar in Hollis. She parked her red Fiat in a lot adjacent to the Kew Gardens Long Island Railroad Station, facing Mowbray Place. Like many residents of the neighborhood, she had parked there day after day since her arrival from Connecticut a year ago, although the railroad frowns on the practice.

She turned off the lights of her car, locked the door, and started to walk the 100 feet to the entrance of her apartment at 82-70 Austin Street, which is in a Tudor building, with stores in the first floor and apartments on the second.

The entrance to the apartment is in the rear of the building because the front is rented to retail stores. At night the quiet neighborhood is shrouded in the slumbering darkness that marks most residential areas.

Miss Genovese noticed a man at the far end of the lot, near a seven-story apartment house at 82-40 Austin Street. She halted. Then, nervously, she headed up Austin Street toward Lefferts Boulevard, where there is a call box to the 102nd Police Precinct in nearby Richmond Hill.

She got as far as a street light in front of a bookstore before the man grabbed her. She screamed. Lights went on in the 10-story apartment house at 82-67 Austin Street, which faces the bookstore. Windows slid open and voices punctuated the early-morning stillness.

Miss Genovese screamed: "Oh, my God, he stabbed me! Please help me! Please help me!"

From one of the upper windows in the apartment house, a man called down: "Let that girl alone!"

The assailant looked up at him, shrugged, and walked down Austin Street toward a white sedan parked a short distance away. Miss Genovese struggled to her feet.

Lights went out. The killer returned to Miss Genovese, now trying to make her way around the side of the building by the parking lot to get to her apartment. The assailant stabbed her again.

"I'm dying!" she shrieked. "I'm dying!"

(Continued)

Box 5.1 (*Continued*)

Windows were opened again, and lights went on in many apartments. The assailant got into his car and drove away. Miss Genovese staggered to her feet. A city bus, 0-10, the Lefferts Boulevard line to Kennedy International Airport, passed. It was 3:35 a.m.

The assailant returned. By then, Miss Genovese had crawled to the back of the building, where the freshly painted brown doors to the apartment house held out hope for safety. The killer tried the first door; she wasn't there. At the second door, 82-62 Austin Street, he saw her slumped on the floor at the foot of the stairs. He stabbed her a third time — fatally.

It was 3:50 a.m. by the time the police received their first call, from a man who was a neighbor of Miss Genovese. In two minutes they were at the scene. The neighbor, a 70-year-old woman, and another woman were the only persons on the street. Nobody else came forward.

The man explained that he had called the police after much deliberation. He had phoned a friend in Nassau County for advice and then he had crossed the roof of the building to the apartment of the elderly woman to get her to make the call.

"I didn't want to get involved," he sheepishly told police.

Six days later, the police arrested Winston Moseley, a 29-year-old business machine operator, and charged him with homicide. Moseley had no previous record. He is married, has two children and owns a home at 133-19 Sutter Avenue, South Ozone Park, Queens. On Wednesday, a court committed him to Kings County Hospital for psychiatric observation.

When questioned by the police, Moseley also said he had slain Mrs. Annie May Johnson, 24, of 146-12 133d Avenue, Jamaica, on Feb. 29 and Barbara Kralik, 15, of 174-17 140th Avenue, Springfield Gardens, last July. In the Kralik case, the police are holding Alvin L. Mitchell, who is said to have confessed to that slaying.

The police stressed how simple it would have been to have gotten in touch with them. "A phone call," said one of the detectives "would have done it." The police may be reached by dialing "0" for operator or SPring 7-3100.

(Continued)

Box 5.1 (*Continued*)

Today witnesses from the neighborhood, which is made up of one-family homes in the $35,000 to $60,000 range with the exception of the two apartment houses near the railroad station, find it difficult to explain why they didn't call the police.

A housewife, knowingly if quite casually, said, "We thought it was a lovers' quarrel." A husband and wife both said, "Frankly, we were afraid." They seemed aware of the fact that events might have been different. A distraught woman, wiping her hands in her apron, said, "I didn't want my husband to get involved."

One couple, now willing to talk about that night, said they heard the first screams. The husband looked thoughtfully at the bookstore where the killer first grabbed Miss Genovese.

"We went to the window to see what was happening," he said, "but the light from our bedroom made it difficult to see the street." The wife, still apprehensive, added: "I put out the light and we were able to see better."

Asked why they hadn't called the police, she shrugged and replied: "I don't know."

A man peeked out from a slight opening in the doorway to his apartment and rattled off an account of the killer's second attack. Why hadn't he called the police at the time? "I was tired," he said without emotion. "I went back to bed."

It was 4:25 a.m. when the ambulance arrived to take the body of Miss Genovese. It drove off. "Then," a solemn police detective said, "the people came out."

Source: Gansberg (1964).

After this incident, a psychologist named Bibb Latané began a project that tried to explain how such an incident could have happened. He focused on the helping aspect of altruistic behavior. He asked when people help, whom they help and why they help. He focused initially on the work of another psychologist, Kurt Lewin (1935, 1951), who argued in the early 1930s and 1940s that human behavior is a function of both the person and the environment. Lewin concluded after much experimentation that social factors were much more important than personal factors. Latané and his co-author J.M. Darley (1970) developed a decision making model which was composed of five steps. The steps were as follows:

- *Notice the event.* People need to identify the party in need first before they can help.
- *Interpret the event as an emergency.* Ambiguity diminishes helping behavior. When others who are present do not act, then the situation may seem less critical. In experiments with smoke coming out from under a door, experimental participants did not raise an alarm immediately, particularly if others in the room did not respond.
- *Take responsibility for helping.* Even if there is a clear emergency, people may not help if others are around. This effect, called the bystander effect, seems to be stronger the greater the number of bystanders. This can also be termed the diffusion effect — someone else will help.
- *Must know how to give help.* If you do not know CPR, you may not be able to help a heart attack victim. If you cannot swim, how you can help a drowning person?
- *Must weigh the decision to help or not.* This involves weighing the costs and benefits of helping.

As part of the final decision whether to help or not, individuals will have to also consider:

- *Rewards for helping.* Some of the rewards include social responsibility, social approval, feeling good for doing it — sometimes called "warm glow" — and finally less guilt and distress for not helping.
- *Costs of helping.* Danger, time lost, the effort required to help, embarrassment at being a show-off or for other reasons.

In the Kitty Genevose case, an additional element was the anonymity factor. Most of the witnesses heard her but did not see her. Yet it remains a mystery why one of the more than thirty witnesses did not call the police.

Latané subsequently expanded his analysis to a number of situations where there is social interaction among groups of individuals which he called "social diffusion" (Latané, 1981). He discovered that generally when there are more people as bystanders, the less responsibility each individual feels. Further, in a generalized theory of social impacts, he theorized that the impact of an additional person on a situation has a declining marginal contribution. The sound of ten people clapping is not as loud as the accumulated sound of ten individuals clapping alone. When a person comes into your lecture as the fourth person attending versus the 44th, the impact is less. Also, tipping per individual declines as the size of the group increases. Large groups tip less per head than small groups. The classic example of smoke in a room has received considerable attention. It takes a single person a much shorter period of time to warn authorities that there is smoke coming out from underneath a door in a waiting room, than it does where there are a large number of people waiting. Furthermore, acts of heroism often occur when one person sees the need for heroic action. However, it is hard to generalize since heroic actions also occur in groups such as the actions by city firefighters during 9/11.

5.4.7 *Altruism as a characteristic of sympathy and empathy*

When we emotionally associate with others, we experience sympathy or empathy. When we empathize fully, it may become difficult to separate our emotions from those of the other person. When this is the case, then the parameter **a** in the utility function [Equation (1)] would be one — our utility and the other's utility are merged completely. While this might not generally be the case, the sympathetic and empathetic feelings we have toward others can motivate our actions. These actions bring with them a strong association with others and a boost in utility that is reflected by the good feeling we have inside when we help and relate to others. In the context of charity, this has been referred to as the "warm glow" of giving. Furthermore, the emotional bonds with others are important in achieving happiness and self-esteem. We explore these aspects further in the discussion on what activities result in a higher level of subjective well-being or happiness (see Chapter 6).

5.5 Advantages of Altruistic/Cooperative Behavior

There are many situations where unselfish or altruistic action leads to more satisfactory economic outcomes, as well as providing a more acceptable moral or spiritual foundation for behavior. However, in some of the models that economists have constructed using interactions between selfish individuals and altruists, those following self-interest dominate the altruists. The altruists are being taken advantage of and they feel like suckers. This leads to a lower social optimum and an inferior economic solution compared to one that favors pure self-interest. But such a solution does not take into account many of the side benefits of altruism or cooperative behavior. Some examples are discussed in the next few paragraphs.

Altruism can raise overall welfare of individuals or groups in society. In situations where other people's welfare is included in the utility function of an individual, the individual will be motivated to share his income and wealth with others. Under certain fairly general conditions, Stark (1995) shows that kind of behavior will lead to an increase in welfare. Bill and Melinda Gates and Warren Buffett appear to have given high consideration to the welfare of others in their utility functions. Bill Gates has pledged some US$26 billion of his personal wealth to the Gates Foundation for developing medical vaccines against malaria, HIV and AIDS. Analysts comment that only someone with Gates' stature is likely to succeed in his aim of fostering cooperation between scientists, drug companies, health groups and international governments, and is likely to change the very face of medical philanthropy (Bill Gates' World of Possibility, 2006). Bill Gates' close friend, Warren Buffett, has also jumped on the philanthropy bandwagon and announced that he would be giving away 85 percent of his US$44 billion fortune to charity (The Ultra-Rich Give Differently from You and Me, 2006). However, these appear to be the exception rather than the norm, with reports that the percentage of income given away by wealthy American millionaires has fallen from 4.1 percent (1995) to 3.6 percent (2003). The culture of giving in many other parts of the world, including Asia and other developing regions, has yet to be developed, with many of the rich still intent on accumulating wealth for their descendants.

5.5.1 *Altruism and family life*

Altruism can lead to better family interaction in terms of lower divorce rates, less substance abuse, limited social disintegration of families and less physical and psychological abuse of children. While altruism does not relate directly to emotional problems, it is likely that greater social responsibility will flow from situations where individuals are more caring about the welfare of others than in situations where individuals are pursuing pure self-interest. Some evidence of this has been developed by projects that stress cooperation and community action in inner cities. However, it is important to gather more information and evidence regarding these suspected benefits.

With respect to the general observation that altruism among family members helps to pool risk and also to provide moral and emotional support within the family, Gary Becker (1991) has made important contributions. He was one of the first economists to emphasize such cooperative behavior, particularly when markets for income transfer, including borrowing from financial institutions that would smooth out fluctuations in income, are underdeveloped. Several recent studies support Becker's conjecture including works by Rosenzweig and Stark (1989) and Rozenzweig (1988). Other works by Cox (1987) and Foster and Rosenzweig (2001) suggest that barriers to information flows within communities create problems of moral hazard, which are the primary reason for income transfers within the family. These transfers are not simply a result of altruism. They serve an economic function. Richer members of a family or clan lend money to poorer members who are unable to borrow from banks or other financial institutions. Often the money is paid back.

Information about the chances of repayment within the family is more easily obtained than it is in markets with incomplete information, as in many developing countries. The evidence suggests that both altruism and an insurance mechanism are at work when income transfers are made within the family. Other studies such as Diaz and Echevarria (2002) suggest that altruistic motives within the family are highest when relative consumption falls below a certain threshold. This kind of argument is reminiscent of poverty alleviation strategies to provide support to raise poor families' income above a poverty threshold level.

In one of his papers on altruism, Becker (1976) uses an analogy to illustrate the strength of relationships within the family. One of these relationships is between a selfish offspring and an altruistic parent. In this "rotten kid" syndrome, the altruistic parent makes transfers to the selfish "rotten kid". Becker shows that however selfish the "rotten kid" is, it is in his best interest to help his father maximize family income.

This result can be easily seen by considering a parent-child relationship, where the parental role is symbolized by p and the child by k. The parent's preferences depend upon the utility of the child and the parent makes transfers, t, to the child. If Y_p and Y_k are the exogenously determined incomes of the parent and child respectively, then the consumption levels of the parent, C_p, and child, C_k, are respectively $C_p = Y_p - t$ and $C_k = Y_k + t$. Ordinarily Y_p will be much great than Y_k and so the parent will essentially determine the income of the child. Intuitively, the child (k) will never take an action that lowers Y_p by more than it raises Y_k because that would cause the parent to lower transfers to the child (k) by an amount greater than the increase in Y_k. This line of argument necessarily assumes that t is an increasing function of $Y_p + Y_k$.

In a series of experiments conducted by Peters *et al.* (2004), with several families in a public goods experiment where both children and parents could contribute to a public good or free ride, they tested many conjectures of the "rotten kid" and other allocations within the family. Both parents and children tended to give more to their own families than when they were grouped with strangers, and the parents gave more to their own children than to children of strangers. Parents also tended to give, although not as much, when they were with strange children.

There was also evidence that parents trusted other parents to give, and so they tended to give more than expected when in a group with strange adults. While the results were not designed explicitly to test the "rotten kid" theory of Becker, there was evidence that children understood the basics of the game and figured they could make more by free riding if the parents kept on giving. There was no indication that they saw a parallel between parent's actions outside the experiment and the results of the game. That is, they did not envision the results of the relationships between Υp and Υk discussed in the previous paragraph. On the other hand, it was not clear whether any of the children in this family were "rotten kids".

The analysis of allocation of resources within families in an altruistic setting has a number of other possible applications including discrimination against girls within the family, intergenerational transfers (bequeaths) and the role of societal norms and reciprocal obligations. Much of this analysis is beyond the scope of narrow neoclassical analysis. For example, Purkayastha (2003) argues that intra-household altruistic norms have to be understood within the context of the religious, social, moral and ethical environment. Using this logic, the motive for bequeaths cannot be purely economic, since the consumption of the beneficiary only takes place, by definition, after the death of the benefactor.

5.5.2 *The aged*

Altruism is likely to result in better and more consistent care of grandparents and parents by their children and grandchildren. Within Asian families, there is a tradition of caring for aging parents and grandparents. In many Asian cultures, it is the responsibility of the eldest male child to provide for the parents. In recent years, this practice is sometimes augmented by sharing the responsibility among several siblings or by those children with the most money, or who have room in their house. In industrial countries, the extended family model is less prevalent and parents do not live with their children as often as they do in developing countries. In these situations, care of parents is often expressed by helping in care management and financial assistance.

5.5.3 *Intergenerational transfers and growth*

Under certain assumptions, altruism in the form of intergenerational transfers can increase the formation of human capital and therefore stimulate economic growth. If fathers are altruistic in the sense that they leave all their wealth to their children, then an increase in their own life expectancy will stimulate the children to become more educated (Stark, 1995). If the father dies at a young age and bequeaths his wealth to his children while they are still young, the incentive to seek more education can fall. For example, if a wealthy father dies at 40 and leaves his 20–year-old son all his wealth, there is no financial reason for the son to become highly educated. Therefore, an exogenous shock or better health measures resulting in an increase in life expectancy will create a virtuous cycle of growth, education and longevity.

5.5.4 *Savings and growth*

Altruism can, under certain circumstances, lead to a higher rate of saving and higher rates of growth. If altruistic people have stronger intergenerational motives to make bequeaths to their children and others, then saving rates could increase. In a variety of growth models (Harrod, 1937; Solow, 1957), altruism leads to an increase in the growth rate. If, however, the lack of individual altruism is offset by societies saving through social security systems, then altruism may have a limited effect (Kapur, 1999a, b).

5.5.5 *Moral hazard*

If a party to an agreement pledges to take certain actions which are hard to observe, it is just as difficult to enforce these pledged actions. Fire insurance is a good example. Once a building has been insured against fire, the owner will have little incentive to install and maintain costly maintenance equipment to prevent fire; similar results can be seen when there is a high level of insurance on deposits in commercial banks. Bank managers tend to make more risky loans. If people were altruistic, they would value the welfare of others as well as their own. Therefore, they would be less likely to act in such a way so as to present a moral hazard. We will revisit the discussion of moral hazard when we address public choice in Chapter 10.

5.5.6 *Principal-agent relationships*

Principal-agent theory relates a quasi-monopolistic buyer (the principal) to a variety of employees, borrowers, subcontractors, tenant farmers, potential borrowers from the bank and so on (the agents). Due to his quasi-monopoly power, the principal is in a position to be able to write performance contracts with the agents. There is a large body of economic theory that discusses how these contracts should be written so that the principal gets the most for his money. The general assumption is that the agent will withhold information that might have an adverse effect on the contract. For example, someone who has gone bankrupt will generally not disclose this information. There may also be hidden actions by the agents that subvert the goals of the principal. A contractor can use inferior material in a building; an automobile repair shop can charge for work not done or supply used instead of new parts. If a worker is working for a fixed wage, he may not exert as much effort as he would if he was paid on the basis of output. However, if the agent is altruistic, he is more likely to be cognizant of the rights of the principal under the contract and hence, abide by the stipulations in the contract.

5.5.7 *Asymmetric information*

When a party to a transaction or a party in a market has access to information that is not available to others, he can profit from it. One of the best examples of this is insider stock trading. This is illegal in most stock markets but hard to prove. Asymmetric information may also extend to substandard building or the fact that a used car which has been in an accident or has had its odometer turned back is being sold. Altruistic individuals are less likely to enter into these kinds of agreements since they harm the other party and create unethical gains.

5.5.8 *Corporate issues*

The free rider problem arises with regard to monitoring the decisions of corporate executives. If you own shares in a company, it is quite likely that due diligence to make sure the company is acting in the best interest of the shareholders is weak. This is because there is an overwhelming and irresistible temptation to free ride on the efforts of the few that are monitoring its activities. In the case of Enron and other recent cases of corporate malfeasance, there was a breakdown in the monitoring function. A combination of free rider problems, poor regulation and various instances of fraud resulted in the misuse of private information and corruption by the top executives.

5.5.9 *Business ethics and decision making*

In analyzing corporate behavior, we draw a distinction between two broad kinds of decisions. First, there are decisions that have a measurable external impact on the rest of society or the consumer himself, such as sales of tobacco, use of unsafe equipment, emitting pollutants into the environment, illegal disposal of hazardous waste, etc. Secondly, there are those decisions that have a direct impact on the firm and its employees, but the overall benefit or tax on the society is unclear. Corporate buyouts and restructuring/sale of assets might fall in the second category. There would be an increase in overall efficiency at the cost of job losses. The ethical principles hold more clearly in the first instance.

Cases which come to mind include the Pinto automobile recall, the tobacco industry in the US and the Exxon Valdez oil spill. Were there adequate safeguards? Was there a moral hazard? Were they random acts of incompetence? How would an altruistic and ethical person assess these situations compared with a more self-centered and profit maximizing individual? In some cases, the answer to this question is clear. The actions taken by the tobacco companies and the Ford motor company reflected their self-centered interests — tobacco companies tried to cover up the detrimental effects of smoking on health for many years, while Ford chose to continue sales of the Pinto despite its known defects. Both of these actions led to many legal suits. The cover up of the Pinto defect prompted consumer advocate Ralph Nader to write the bestselling book *Unsafe at Any Speed* in 1965. In both cases, Ford and the tobacco companies deliberately hid information that could have reduced sales at the cost of consumer health and safety. In other situations, the distinction between different courses of action may not be as clear. It does appear that taking a more ethical stance for general well-being and consumers would be more beneficial for society as a whole.

Nevertheless, there is also the risk that taking the "high ground" of ethics and altruism can lead to situations where the rights of others are ignored. For example, in the case of HIV/AIDS versus military spending, the implicit argument might be made by ethical consumers that more money should be spent on HIV/AIDS and less on the military. However, if the democratic process results in more military spending, then individual consumers that want more money spent on HIV/AIDS research have to surrender to the outcome of the political process, no matter how ethical their arguments seem to be. This leads to the next point.

5.5.10 *Governance*

An altruistic person would address governmental and civic issues from an equality-based perspective rather than from a narrow self-centered perspective. That way, the value to both those who benefit and those harmed by a particular policy or action can be evaluated more objectively than if the person has only his own self-interest in mind. Some instances which come to mind are discussed below.

• *Providing health care*

When expensive medical treatments have to be rationed, some method has to be devised to prioritize potential recipients. One way of making this judgment is to prioritize by expected years of healthy life. Then young healthy people would rank high, whereas frail, older people would rank low. Is this ethical or fair? Does it reduce the maintenance of human life to an emotionless equation? Is this the way you would like to be treated when you get old?

- *Criminal sentencing*

Society and the legal system have to make judgments regarding risks to society and the chance of rehabilitation for criminals. Society also makes decisions regarding the severity of crime. How are these decisions made? What are they based on?

- *Environmental issues*

Where possible, the polluter should pay for damages to the environment. This is the case where the polluter pays principle applies. But what about the case where the pollution goes across national boundaries, such as pollution of the ocean, acid rain and overfishing? In these cases, an altruistic individual is likely to evaluate objectively the damage to all countries than someone with purely nationalistic interests. Furthermore, an altruistic person is less likely to succumb to the free rider problem when it comes to voting and coming to informed positions on public and corporate issues related to the protection of the environment.

5.6 Education and the Role of Parents

Gary Becker developed models of altruistic behavior by parents on behalf of children (see Becker, 1981). In societies where schooling requires some sacrifice by the parents, either personally or through the political system, the role of altruism is critically important. In one particular model developed by Casey Mulligan (1997), altruism becomes endogenous, depending on the interactions within the family rather than an outside influence. In the model, the amount of altruistic behavior depends on the hours spent together between child and parent. The more time spent together, the stronger the altruistic bond between parent and child.

What would change in family life given the assumption of endogenous altruism? Consider the effect of an increase in income. Increasing leisure in the leisure/income choice would give the parent more time to spend with the child. This would increase the transfers of income to the child from the parent and also increase altruism. Consider a reduction in hours worked. Would it have the same effect? What about an increase in labor force participation of women? What would it do to altruism and income transfers from parents to children?

In any case, a model where more time spent together increases the possibility of altruism is in keeping with a model of altruism based on sociobiology or genetics. You usually spend more time with family members or people you know well and you form close bonds with them; therefore, you tend to be more altruistic toward them. As your associations with others become more at arms-length, tendencies of altruism become weaker. One exception to this rule is the hero syndrome. The fireman runs into a burning building to save a child. A soldier single-handedly risks almost certain death by attacking an enemy position or a bystander helps to detain a thief.

5.7 Nurturing Altruism

Much altruistic behavior takes place in the context of social interaction. By reinforcing altruistic or cooperative behavior, beneficial social outcomes can be supported. In an interesting set of experiments, Ernst Fehr (2003) shows the effect of external approval or disapproval on altruistic behavior. Using social dilemma experiments with 283 college students, Fehr shows that altruism based on a sense of what is fair is a powerful source of human cooperation. Actions which are selfish or greedy destroy altruistic cooperation almost completely, while actions perceived as fair and unbiased leave altruism and cooperation intact. Fehr says this result is useful in situations wherever voluntary compliance is important such as between spouses, in the education of children, in business organizations, in markets and in environmental issues. It is also important in resolving problems of free riders and other situations where cooperation leads to desirable outcomes.

5.8 Free Rider Problems

The general problem of free riding occurs in many different situations and leads to an inefficient level of production and consumption. The literature is replete with examples of the tragedy of the commons and moral hazard. However, these inefficiencies in production and consumption depend upon the assumption that agents maximize self-interest with regard to others. However, if altruism is common, various suggestions for provision of public goods may actually reduce voluntary contributions (see Andreoni, 1993, and discussion of charity in Chapter 9). By the same token, increased monitoring of business dealings to detect corruption may backfire by reducing the natural tendency for altruistic individuals to self-regulate (Schulze and Frank, 2003).

There is also evidence that people do not free ride to the extent predicted by economic theory (Dawes and Thaler, 1988). In one experiment, Gneezy *et al.* (2004) examined a family-type situation where diners split the bill for dinner. In the experiment, six students (three males and three females) who did not know each other were recruited and invited to a restaurant for lunch. Three different scenarios were programmed: (i) each student pays for his/her own lunch; (ii) the lunch is free; and (iii) the bill is split evenly.

When the bill is split and when lunch is free, Gneezy expected that the students would consume more. The results were as expected from the self-interest model. The average bill for the three experiments were 37.3 shekels for the individual pay meal, 50.9 for the even split and 82.3 for the free meal. (The experiment was carried out in Israel.) The bill for the free meal was more than double that of the individual pay meal.

When asked which option of the individual pay and split bill options they preferred, 80 percent answered the individual pay option. Yet when given the chance to free ride in the free meal option, they ate more because of the perceived advantage of being a free rider. Do you ever consider this type of behavior when dining out with friends? Do some people order the expensive wine and lobster thermador, while you order vegetables and a coke, then split the bill? We might conclude that there will be a limitation on free riding because of social pressure and retribution. Also, why would diners choose to subject themselves to possible free riding and a higher than desired lunch bill by choosing to divide the bill evenly? There are several possible answers including simplicity of calculating each diner's share and the implicit understanding among friends that no one would free ride "too much".

5.9 Altruism and Economic Efficiency

In Chapter 2, we discussed the standard assumptions and results of the neoclassical model. One of the results was that in a perfectly competitive market where individuals are following their self-interest, we obtain an efficient outcome. Efficiency in the Pareto sense is when we cannot increase the utility of any individual without diminishing the utility of someone else. Kolm (1983) asks the question, "What would the result be if we replaced self-interested egoists with altruists who were interested in the welfare of everyone, not just themselves?" (p. 36). He concludes, after careful analysis, that such a world would lead to a more equitable and efficient allocation of resources and distribution of income. This is primarily because the inefficiency in markets arising from market failures would disappear in a world inhabited by altruists. Market failures include free riding, use of hidden information, principal/agent problems and moral hazard. He contends, furthermore, that the allocation and distribution problems of a complex society do not require market competition to allocate resources efficiently. His reasoning is similar to the socialist argument about efficient resource allocation under a system without private property.

Kolm asks the question, "Why hasn't a social system featuring more cooperation and altruism, a social system that has the support of all spiritual and religious traditions, prevailed over the present system that idealizes competition and egoism?" De Botton (2004) suggests that the pressures of the modern world and the social, political and economic organization required of a technological world have created a strong need to compete for status in society. Competition and eventual triumph over others is a way to achieve that status, remove status anxiety and soothe the troubled ego. We shall see in the next chapter that competition may be a way to feed the ego. However, unfortunately, it does not always lead to happiness and well-being.

5.10 Conclusions

Those who have developed altruistic behavior, either naturally or by following some spiritual or religious path or by contemplating their own actions and motivations, are probably more likely to follow behavioral patterns that minimize confrontation with others and lead to more cooperative behavior. While such behavior is probably beneficial within family or community groups, it is still looked upon with some skepticism in the business world. Becker (1981) uses the phrase "cooperative at home, competitive at work". The great thinkers and spiritual leaders of all generations do not make such a distinction and there are business firms with a highly developed sense of social responsibility and a culture of looking out for the customer — putting the customer first. One of the first rules of doing business in Japan is to blindly follow the aphorism "The customer is always right". In retailing, this not only makes good sense, but it also makes good business sense generally. There is a saying, "What goes around comes around". A virtuous cycle is created when we treat others well. Somehow it makes us feel good and it also makes the other person feel good. Why not do it more often?

This brings up the question of competitors. What about competitors? How should they be treated? To cooperate with competitors is often illegal and against the tenants of competitive behavior that says that such collusion (monopoly/oligopoly) will lead to higher prices and a lower level of output. On the other hand, we do not have to trash our competitor. We can respect their rights to do business. We should simply try to attract customers away from them in a more ethical way. This may not be acting altruistically toward them, but it is also not overtly competitive either.

Bibliography

Andreoni, J. (1993) An Experimental Test of the Public-Goods Crowding-Out Hypothesis. *American Economic Review*, 83(5), 1317–1327.

Andreoni, J. (1998) Towards a Theory of Charitable Fund-Raising. *Journal of Political Economy*, 106(6), 1186–1213.

Beauchamp, T. (1982) *Philosophical Ethics: An Introduction to Moral Philosophy*. New York: McGraw-Hill.

Becker, G.S. (1976) Altruism, Egoism, and Genetic Fitness: Economics and Sociobiology. *Journal of Economic Literature*, 14(3), 817–826.

Becker, G.S. (1981) Altruism in the Family and Selfishness in the Marketplace. *Economica*, 48(189), 1–15.

Becker, G.S. (1991) *A Treatise on the Family*, Enlarged Edition. Boston: Harvard University Press.

Bercher, P. (1999) Human Altruism and Evolution. http://ucsu.colorado.edu/~becker/Sesardicarticle.htm [Retrieved 28 January 2005].

Bill Gates' World of Possibility (2006) *Washington Post*, 21 June. http://washingtonpost.com [Retrieved 21 June 2006].

Collard, D. (1978) *Altruism and Economy*. New York: Oxford University Press.

Collard, D. (1995) Love is Not Enough. In S. Zamagni (ed.), *Economics of Altruism*. London: Edward Elgar.

Cox, D. (1987) Motives for Private Income Transfers. *Journal of Political Economy*, 95(3), 508–546.

Dawes, R.M. and R.H. Thaler (1988) Anomalies: Cooperation. *Journal of Economic Perspectives*, 2(3), 187–197.

De Botton, A. (2004) *Status Anxiety*. London: Hamish Hamilton.

Diaz, A. and C. Echevarria (2002) Solidarity, Transfers, and Poverty. *Review of Development Economics*, 6(3), 337–350.

Etzioni, A. (1988) *The Moral Dimension: Toward a New Economics*. New York: The Free Press.

Fehr, E. (2003) Detrimental Effects of Sanctions on Human Altruism. *Nature*, 422, 137–140.

Foster, A.D. and M.R. Rosenzweig (2001) Imperfect Commitment, Altruism, and the Family: Evidence from Transfer Behavior in Low-Income Rural Areas. *Review of Economics and Statistics*, 83(3), 389–407.

Frank, R.H. (1988) *Passions within Reason: The Strategic Role of the Emotions*. New York: W.W. Norton.

Gansberg, M. (1964) Thirty-Eight who Saw Murder Didn't Call the Police. *New York Times*, 27 March.

Gneezy, U., E. Haruvy and H. Yafe (2004) The Inefficiency of Splitting the Bill. *Economic Journal*, 114(495), 265–280.

Grant, C. (2004) The Altruist's Dilemma. *Business Ethics Quarterly*, 14(2), 315–328.

Harrod, R.F. (1937) Mr. Keynes and Traditional Theory. *Econometrica*, 5, 74–86.

Kant, I. (1776, 1990) *Critique of Pure Reason*, English version. New York: Prometheus Books.

Kapur, B.K. (1999a) A Communitarian Utility Function and Its Social and Economic Implications. *Economics and Philosophy*, 15(1), 43–62.

Kapur, B.K. (1999b) Harmonization between Communitarian Ethics and Market Economics. *Journal of Markets and Morality*, 2(1), 35–52.

Kolm, S.-C. (1983) Altruism and Efficiency. *Ethics*, 94, 18–65.

Latané, B. (1981) The Psychology of Social Impact. *American Psychologist*, 36, 343–356.

Latané, B. and J. Darley (1970) *The Unresponsive Bystander: Why Doesn't He Help?* New York: Appleton-Century-Crofts.

Lewin, K. (1935) *A Dynamic Theory of Personality. Selected Papers.* New York: McGraw Hill.

Lewin, K. (1951) *Field Research in Social Sciences.* New York: Harper & Row.

Mueller, D.C. (1986) Rational Egoism versus Adaptive Egoism as Fundamental Postulates for a Descriptive Theory of Human Behavior. *Public Choice,* 51, 3–23.

Mulligan, C.B. (1997) *Parental Priorities and Economic Inequality.* Chicago: University of Chicago Press.

Nader, R. (1965) *Unsafe at Any Speed.* New York: Grossman.

Peters, H.E., S. Unur, J. Clark and W.D. Schulze (2004) Free-Riding and the Provision of Public Goods in the Family: A Laboratory Experiment. *International Economic Review,* 45(1), 283–299.

Purkayastha, D. (2003) From Parents to Children: Intra-Household Altruism as Institutional Behavior. *Journal of Economic Issues,* 37(3), 601–620.

Rosenzweig, M.R. (1988) Risk, Implicit Contracts and the Family in Rural Areas of Low-Income Countries. *Economic Journal,* 98(393), 1148–1170.

Rosenzweig, M.R. and O. Stark (1989) Consumption Smoothing, Migration, and Marriage: Evidence from Rural India. *Journal of Political Economy,* 97(4), 905–926.

Schulze, G. and B. Frank (2003) Deterrence versus Intrinsic Motivation: Experimental Evidence on the Determinants of Corruptibility. *Economics of Governance,* 4(2), 143–160.

Sesardic, N. (1995) Recent Work on Human Altruism and Evolution. *Ethics,* 106, 128–157.

Singer, P. (1981) *The Expanding Circle: Ethics and Sociobiology.* New York: Farrar Straus and Giroux.

Solow, R. (1957) Technical Change and the Aggregate Production Function. *Review of Economics and Statistics,* 39, 312–320.

Stark, O. (1995) *Altruism and Beyond: An Economic Analysis of Transfers and Exchanges within Families and Groups.* New York: Cambridge University Press.

The Ultra-Rich Give Differently from You and Me (2006) *New York Times,* 2 July. http://www.nytimes.com [Retrieved 2 July 2006].

Wilson, E.O. (1978) *On Human Nature.* New York: Bantam.

Chapter 6

Utility and Happiness

As discussed previously in Chapter 2, individuals maximize utility by allocating resources (income) in such a way that the marginal utility of all goods and services is maximized. Allocations among goods shift with prices, and tastes are assumed to be constant. Comparative statics are introduced to show what happens when income increases or when prices change. Changes in tastes can also be introduced but the analysis is complicated, as it requires shifting the utility mapping and the results are not as clear as when tastes are fixed. This model of utility maximization forms the cornerstone of microeconomic analysis of the consumers and also the choice between work and leisure. Consumers are assumed to be rational individuals who act in their own self-interest.

However, there are cases where individuals do not follow the self-interest model that economists have developed in the area of individual utility maximization. Robert E. Lane (2000)[1] explores various aspects of why this happens. He argues in a highly persuasive way that, aside from very low levels of income, greater income and higher levels of consumption do not generally result in greater happiness. To the contrary, he finds that in many situations, the focus on materialism leads to a decline in happiness or what he calls subjective well-being. There are a number of possible reasons for this, many of which are discussed in subsequent sections and chapters. In what follows, we outline the main reasons why the utility maximization model does not necessarily lead to increased happiness.

Despite the lack of a close relationship between happiness and utility, as narrowly defined by economists, there is a wider interest in the subject of happiness and well-being. There are aspects of happiness that cannot

---

[1]There have been many studies of the determinants of happiness and we will be referring to them in the rest of this chapter. These include, among others, Easterlin (2001a), Frey and Stutzer (2000, 2001), Frank (1999), Layard (2005a, b) and Helliwell (2003).

181

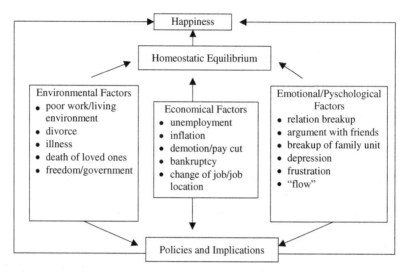

Figure 6.1 Flow Chart

be captured by statistical analysis. The fact that decision makers often regret their decisions after the fact and the seeming disconnect between accumulating income and the level of happiness suggest deeper and more subtle relationships between well-being and its determinants. A brief sketch of a model of well-being will be discussed to identify the factors that affect well-being and happiness. A flow chart representing the interaction of these factors in such a model is presented in Figure 6.1.

We begin with a definition of the term "homeostasis". Biological scientists define homeostasis as the maintenance of equilibrium in a biological system by means of automatic mechanisms that counteract influences tending toward disequilibrium. Homeostatic mechanisms are present in all levels of living systems, including the molecular and cellular level, as well as in organisms themselves and even in populations. In complex organisms, such as humans, it involves constant monitoring and regulation of oxygen and carbon dioxide levels, nutrients, hormones, and organic and inorganic substances. The concentrations of these substances in the bodily fluid remain unchanged, within limits, despite changes in the external environment.

Homeostasis in organisms is exemplified by the operations of the endocrine system. The hormone-synthesizing activities of the endocrine glands are regulated by events occurring in the systems that the hormones regulate. For example, a rise in blood glucose levels stimulates the pancreas to secrete insulin, which acts to accelerate the removal of glucose from the blood by conversion into storage products like glycogen and fat. The sensations of hunger and thirst are also homeostatic mechanisms; they help the organism maintain optimum levels of energy, nutrients and water.

Homeostatic mechanisms also operate to regulate the size of populations. An example is the relationship between the populations of predatory animals and their prey. If prey becomes abundant, so do their predators, until predation diminishes the supply of prey and causes a decline in the predator population. This allows the prey population to build up again, and the cycle is repeated. In this manner, the populations of both prey and predator oscillate around a mean.

The role of homeostasis presents a fundamental challenge for economists trying to show that humans are trying to maximize utility or satisfaction or happiness, even as these powerful forces dominate much of our behavior and are imprinted on our genetic material. If we consider homeostasis as a fundamental motivation for action, then pleasure, well-being and happiness may be only one of the many bits of informational inputs into the homeostatic regulatory system.

One aspect of homeostasis is that the regulatory system is sensitive to *changes* in stimuli and environments rather than to the maintained *level* of activity or equilibrium. For example, happiness indicators are not sensitive to levels of income and wealth, but rather to changes in income and wealth. These happiness indicators are also sensitive to changes in other life circumstances like marriage/divorce, work/unemployment, illness and death/good health, moving/not moving, stability of government/anarchy, vulnerability to disaster and so on. As will be presented in the remaining sections of this chapter, particularly the works of Layard (2005a, b), Helliwell (2003, 2005), Frank (1988, 1999) and others, these indicators are the key determinants of happiness. People have a strong desire to remain in homeostatic equilibrium, not only physically but also emotionally and socially. This may explain why risk aversion is so strong and why people become unhappy when this equilibrium is disturbed.

Research on happiness can aid in making better policy choices that will lift the level of well-being in society. Better knowledge of the determinants of happiness will allow policy makers to evaluate the tradeoffs between different policies, in terms of their impact on happiness and well-being.

Public policy should focus on ways to make everybody's life fulfilling, enjoyable and meaningful by using economic and other policies to achieve these goals. Raising standards of living in the traditional sense of raising income per capita ignores broader policy questions, which can be addressed by focusing on subjective well-being or happiness. For example, it is important to understand the relative impact of changes in unemployment and inflation on the level of happiness and subjective well-being. It is also important to understand the relationship between happiness, social capital and institutional conditions such as the quality of governance when evaluating tradeoffs, in evaluating the impact of different policies on welfare and happiness.

It is also important to understand the relationship between a gain in utility as measured by, for example, greater consumption, and its impact on happiness and subjective well-being. This relationship involves the psychology of memory, the apparent disconnect between living standards and aggregate measures of happiness as well as the importance of being a valued member of society. For example, there is evidence that there is a trend toward a higher incidence of depression and other forms of mental illness even as per capita income has been rising. A better understanding of happiness and the psychology and sociological framework within which people make economic decisions may also give us a better insight into issues of discrimination and the role of freedom and government in happiness.

6.1 Some History

Beginning with Adam Smith (1776) and then Veblen (1899), economists have been concerned about the broader issues of well-being.

By doing so, they went beyond the narrow definition of utility that was used by the followers of Bentham and J.S. Mill. More recently, economists and other social scientists have begun to focus on how to measure "utility". Some, such as Ng (2003), Lane (2000), Deiner and Seligman (2004), Easterlin (2001a, b, 2006), Frank (1988, 1999) and Scitovsky (1976) have shifted their concerns to other measures such as happiness and subjective well-being.

They have also investigated the process of decision making and how consumers adopt decision rules that are not rational in the conventional sense that economists use this term. To explain these seemingly "irrational" decisions, social scientists and economists have examined the role of the emotions and other factors outside the usual realm of economics.

By exploring various aspects of sociology, psychology, biology and political science, these writers have expanded the scope of economic inquiry into many areas of economics. In this chapter, we will focus on how consumers make decisions and how workers relate to each other and to their jobs in an expanded framework that considers interpersonal relationships, emotional issues and the general well-being or happiness of individuals. We examine some of these issues in order to know how to increase well-being and welfare in a broader sense. In addition to exploring the motivation for decision making and how they relate to well-being and happiness, we also look at how the misallocation of resources gives rise to a lack of well-being.

6.2 What is the Nature of Happiness?

We begin by trying to better understand happiness. Some psychologists and sociologists have developed the notion that happiness and unhappiness are fixed parameters that are an unalterable part of personality. People are born happy or unhappy. If happiness is not fixed at birth, it is at least formed as a component of personality at an early age. If this is true and happiness is a fixed parameter, then it is fruitless to study happiness as a possible variable that changes and is subject to social, political and public policy forces. Veenhoven (1994) investigates this proposition from several alternative points of view using data from a number of different sources. He looks at the temporal stability of happiness, the cross-sectional consistency and the inner causation of happiness. In all cases, he concludes that happiness is not an immutable trait, but rather a variable subject to empirical study with a view to improving the individual as well as aggregate level of happiness. He concludes that:

> Firstly, happiness is not temporarily stable. Individuals revise their evaluation of life periodically.... Average happiness of nations appears not immutable either. Though stability prevails, there are cases of change. Secondly, happiness is not situationally consistent. People are not equally happy in good or bad situations. Improvement or deterioration of life is typically followed by changes in the appreciation of it.... Average happiness is highest in the countries that provide the best living conditions. Major changes in conditions of the country affect average happiness of its citizens. Lastly, happiness is not entirely an internal matter. It is true that happiness roots to some extent in stable individual characteristics and collective orientations, but the impact of these inner factors is limited. They modify the outcome of environmental effects rather than dominate them (1994, pp. 145–146).

Renowned psychologist Seligman (2002) suggests that happiness is the simple sum of two components — a personal, unalterable constant, and another component that responds to different life situations and changes in individual circumstances.

Other psychologists suggest that there are two kinds of well-being — *psychological well-being* (also called *eudaimonic well-being*) and *subjective well-being* (*hedonic well-being*). Psychological well-being has to do with personal growth, purpose in life, positive relations with others and self-acceptance. Hedonic well-being, on the other hand, focuses on embracing positive affect such as satisfaction with work and life in general, and the frequency of pleasant emotions (or lack of unpleasant emotions) in the context of self-reporting. In the rest of this chapter, we explore subjective well-being to see what variables influence behavior. We also consider how public policy can be reoriented to raise levels of happiness and well-being. Much of the literature reviewed here focuses on subjective well-being as reflected by self-reporting responses to questions on surveys of well-being. These surveys have been conducted by various research institutes around the world over the past several decades (see Appendix for some sources).

6.2.1 *Are happiness and utility related?*

As we noted in Chapter 2, economic theory has been dominated by the positive approach. It puts great emphasis on the ability to observe objectively how behavioral choice is involved in economic decision making. Alternatively, many economists have approached microeconomic decision making using other approaches. Lane (2000) focuses on status and misallocation of resources as a result of conspicuous consumption. Others including Elster (1998) and Mullainathan (1998) discuss the role of emotions, while Kahneman *et al.* (1991) talk about psychological factors, as we have already discussed in Chapter 3 on prospect theory. There are also a number of puzzles and anomalies, some of which we have also discussed in Chapter 3, that make it difficult to believe that utility can be understood by looking at observed choices alone.

As an alternative to the standard economic approach or the psychological approach of Kahneman, we can adopt a normative and subjective view which takes a broader view of decision making and focuses on subjective well-being rather than objective measures of utility. This chapter explores why people are not "rational" in the narrow hedonistic definition of the term, when they make decisions and perform actions that do not necessarily lead to a greater level of satisfaction or well-being. It also allows us to see that many of the things we do and things we want such as job security, status, power, love and contentment as well as money, are desired because they make us happy and not for their own sake (see Frey and Stutzer, 2002b).

6.2.2 *Measuring utility*

Instead of looking at what people buy and the pattern of consumption and income, researchers on happiness rely on self-assessment questionnaires to determine whether people think they are happy. A term often used as a substitute for happiness is subjective well-being. This focus on

Table 6.1 Some Measures of Utility

Survey	Questions Asked of Respondents
General social surveys[1]	Taken all together, how would you say things are these days — would you say you are very happy, pretty happy or not too happy?
World values survey[2]	All things considered, how satisfied are you with your life as a whole these days?
Eurobarometer surveys[3]	On the whole, are you very satisfied, fairly satisfied, not very satisfied or not at all satisfied with the life you lead?
Satisfaction with life scale[4]	Five questions rated on a scale from one to seven

Sources: [1]Davis *et al.* (2001); [2]Inglehart *et al.* (2000); [3]Eurobarometer Surveys; [4]Pavot and Diener (1993).

the term "well-being" takes away some of the emotional content contained in the word "happiness" and allows people to evaluate their level of satisfaction relative to others, to their past levels of satisfaction and their expectations of the future (see Andrews and Robinson, 1991, for more discussion on different measures of subjective well-being).

Due to the subjective nature of surveys, there are many different approaches to deciding whether someone is happy or not. Four prominent measures and the questions asked by different survey groups are displayed in Table 6.1.

After delving into possible biases in responses, Frey and Stutzer (2002b) conclude that there may be some systematic biases that reflect socioeconomic characteristics. For example, people doing volunteer work seem to report higher life satisfaction. This could be because more extroverted people tend to volunteer and they may be happier people. Also, young people seem to record lower life satisfaction scores than older people. Are they really less happy or is it that older people have learned to respond to these questions in a particular way? Nevertheless, the economists who have been studying these surveys suggest that these problems are not a reason to dispute the conclusions from these surveys, many of which have been conducted over many years: "It is thus possible and worthwhile to study economic and institutional effects on happiness" (Frey and Stutzer, 2002b, p. 10).

6.3 What Determines Happiness?

In the next few sections of this chapter, we will discuss further the relationship between well-being and possible explanatory variables. These variables can help explain more fully the variation in well-being over time and between individuals and societies. Some of these variables are economic in nature and others relate to social and psychological factors. Suggestions for public policy are offered in the concluding section to the chapter. To begin the discussion, we turn to the variable that has historically been most closely associated with well-being or happiness, namely income.

6.3.1 *Income and happiness*

The relationship between happiness or subjective well-being and income has been studied by many researchers (see Lane, 2000; Frey and Stutzer, 2002a, b; Diener and Seligman, 2004). Up to a point, increasing income does result in a significant increase in happiness, but the relationship breaks down at higher levels of income.

Consider, for example, the relationship between well-being and income for a panel of countries displayed in Figure 6.2. At low levels of income, there is a loose but positive relationship between well-being and income. After income has reached about $8,000 or $9,000 per capita in purchasing power parity terms, countries exhibit similar levels of well-being.

Evidence shows that at a particular point in time, those who are better off may be somewhat marginally happier than those with lower income in a particular society. This result for the US is displayed in Tables 6.2 and 6.3. Those in the higher deciles or quartiles of the income distribution have somewhat higher levels of well-being than those in the lower deciles, and these conclusions do not change much between the 1970s and the 1990s. In fact, Table 6.2 and Figure 6.3 show that there has been a slight decline in the happiness curve in the US between 1972–1974 and 1994–1996. Furthermore, the curve flattens out at higher levels of income. There are decreasing returns to happiness given a dollar increase in income.

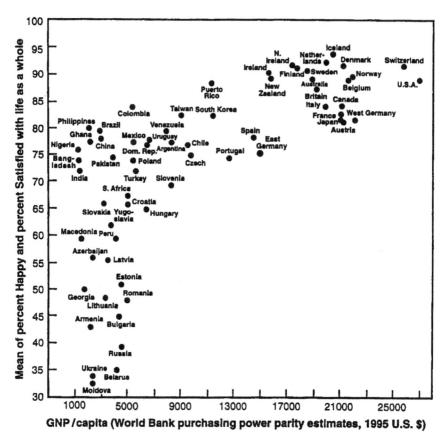

Figure 6.2 Income and Well-Being, 1995

Source: Inglehart and Klingemann (2000, p. 168, Figure 7.2).

The results shown in Table 6.2 and other research demonstrate that differences in income explain a small proportion of the variation in happiness. For example, results reported by Easterlin (2001a, p. 468) show a small correlation coefficient of 0.20 between subjective well-being and income.

Looking at time series for individual countries, there is compelling evidence that overall happiness in industrial countries has not increased much, if at all. This result holds despite a considerable increase in the level of disposable income. For example, Figures 6.4 and 6.5 show indices of income and happiness in the US and Japan

Table 6.2 Happiness and Equivalence Income in the US

Equivalence Income[a] (1996 US$)	Mean Happiness Rating[b]		Mean Equivalence Income		Number of Observations	
	1972–1974	1994–1996	1972–1974	1994–1996	1972–1974	1994–1996
Full sample	2.21	2.17	17434	20767	4214	5171
Decile						
1	1.92	1.94	2522	2586	421	499
2	2.09	2.03	5777	5867	419	528
3	2.17	2.07	8694	8634	417	497
4	2.22	2.15	11114	11533	416	542
5	2.19	2.19	13517	14763	391	512
6	2.29	2.29	15970	17666	460	500
7	2.24	2.20	18713	21128	393	527
8	2.31	2.20	22343	25745	447	529
9	2.26	2.30	28473	34688	427	472
10	2.36	2.36	46338	61836	423	565

Source: General Social Survey, National Opinion Research Center. Variables 34, 157 and 1028. "Don't Know" and "no answer" responses are omitted (Frey and Stutzer, 2002b, p. 53, Table 1). [a]Total household income divided by the square root of the total number of household members. [b]Based on score of "not too happy" = 1, "pretty happy" = 2 and "very happy" = 3.

Table 6.3 Happiness According to Income Position by Percentage of the Group Responding

Happiness	United States		Great Britain	
	Top Quarter	Bottom Quarter	Top Quarter	Bottom Quarter
Very happy	45	33	40	29
Quite happy	51	53	54	59
Not too happy	4	14	6	12
Total	100	100	100	100

Source: Layard (2005a, p. 8, Table 2).

respectively over a long time span. Income has increased fourfold since the end of World War II, while happiness has not changed much at all.

Putting these two results together, we see a possible contradiction. Individuals are happier when their income goes up relative to

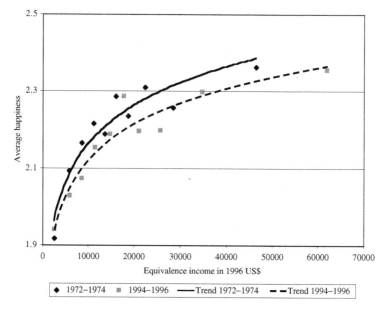

Figure 6.3 Happiness and Income in the US

Source: Frey and Stutzer (2002b, p. 54, Figure 1).

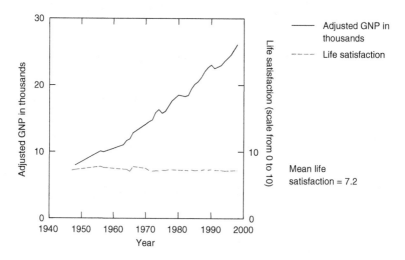

Figure 6.4 Mean Life Satisfaction and Gross National Product (GNP) in the US, 1947–1998

Source: Diener and Seligman (2004, p. 3, Figure 1).

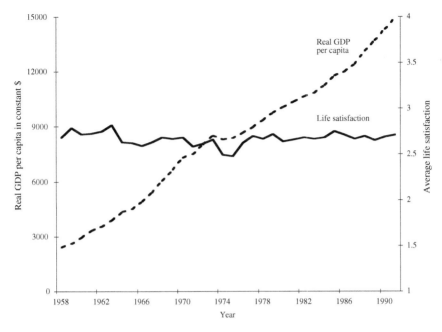

Figure 6.5 Satisfaction with Life and Income per Capita in Japan, 1958–1991
Source: Frey and Stutzer (2002b, p. 55, Figure 2).

others in the society, but the well-being of industrial societies has not changed much over the last 50 years. These seemingly contradictory results can be explained once we realize that changes in ranking in the income distribution cancel out over time. The fact that people generally experience an increase in subjective well-being (SWB) or happiness when their *ranking* in the income distribution improves need not affect the overall level of happiness, because at the same time others will fall in the rankings and their well-being will fall.

Generally, psychologists refer to this as a characteristic of *social comparison*, which will be discussed further in Section 6.5. More importantly, it is obvious from this time series evidence for industrial economies that the absolute level of money earned and spent does not tell us enough about well-being. Moreover, comparisons with others also have an impact on well-being, so we now turn to the relationship between relative income and happiness.

6.3.2 *Relative income and happiness*

As noted earlier, above a certain subsistence level, people seem to be more interested in relative income than absolute income. Economists have tried to explain this kind of behavior in another context by arguing that consumption depends on the level of current income relative to some historical average [the relative consumption hypothesis of Duesenberry (1949) or by habit persistence models of consumption (Friedman, 1957)].

In any event, happiness as a result of higher levels of consumption apparently "wears off" over time (see also Frey and Stutzer, 2002b). Satisfaction depends on change and disappears with continued consumption. This process or mechanism that reduces the hedonic effects of a constant or repeated stimulus is called *adaptation*. This process of hedonic adaptation also makes people strive for even higher aspirations. Alternatively, we could describe this process of relying on relative income rather than absolute income as incorporating interdependent preferences as part of an individual's objective functions. Since these aspirations can never be fully satisfied, we remain stuck, unable to realize a higher level of subjective well-being no matter how many goods we have accumulated. Also, as everyone else's income goes up, the linkage between the absolute level of income and subjective well-being is severed. This will be true so long as there are no significant changes in the relative position of the individual in the income distribution. In aggregate, the adjustments in well-being as people move up and down within the income distribution will tend to cancel out, leaving overall well-being unaffected.

Extending these arguments, Frank (1988) suggests that some goods, which Hirsch (1976) calls *positional goods*, are coveted only because most other people cannot purchase them. These goods such as yachts, hideaways on secluded islands and expensive jewelry are so costly that they are out of reach for most consumers. As an extension of the envy status that such positional goods hold, Clark and Oswald (1994) conclude that the higher the income of the reference group used by workers in the UK, the less satisfied people were with their own jobs. That is, when expectations far exceed a realistically attainable level of achievement, the level of frustration leads to a decrease in the level of well-being.

6.3.3 *Materialism and well-being*

We can pursue the relationship between relative income and well-being a bit further. For example, there is evidence that materialism, defined as placing a high value on income and material possessions, has a negative impact on well-being across countries, other things being equal. This result was obtained by comparing residents in the US and Singapore (see Kirkcaldy *et al.*, 1998, and also Swinyard *et al.*, 2001). Using a probability sample of adults in the US and Singapore, Swinyard *et al.* found that adults in Singapore are less happy and more materialistic than those in the US. Admittedly this result is only suggestive, since there could be other reasons for a lower level of happiness in Singapore.

Nevertheless, Kasser and Kanner (2004) show that materialistic individuals experience lower self-esteem, higher levels of narcissism and less empathy and greater conflict in social relationships. This could be because materialists tend to play down the importance of social interactions and relationships, which have been shown in other studies to be an important determinant of well-being. It is possible, however, that the flow of causation may run the other direction, i.e., that unhappiness forces people to focus on material goals.

Srivastava *et al.* (2001) found that materialism was most damaging to the psyche when it arose from a desire to gain power and influence as opposed to being secure and free to pursue different objectives. Emphasis on material objects is reflected also in the finding that higher-income communities in the US were less happy, other things equal, than middle-class neighborhoods (Hagerty, 2000; Putnam, 2001).

The negative impact of high levels of family income on happiness is also reflected in the work of Csikszentmihalyi *et al.* (2003), who found that adolescents in affluent suburbs were less happy and reported lower self-esteem than those from middle-class neighborhoods and urban slums in the US. Luthar (2003) suggests that this is because the wealthy kids were expected to achieve more and compete at school. They also reported a lower level of personal intimacy, which could have also led to a lower level of self-esteem.

Taken together, these research findings provide strong evidence that while well-being may be enhanced somewhat by moving up the income scale, there are also negative impacts on well-being if individuals place a high value on material objects.

6.3.4 *The importance of aspirations*

The research results reported above suggest that the search for well-being and happiness must move away from goods to something else. These arguments are reinforced by the work of Richard Layard (2005a, b). Layard summarizes research that reinforces the results which show that in developed countries people are not getting happier, despite rises in income. Individuals may express more happiness if their income rises up above the rest of society, that is their place in the income distribution goes up; but in aggregate there has not been a corresponding increase in happiness (see also Lane, 2000; Frank, 1999). Taking a slightly different approach to explain this phenomenon, Richard Easterlin (2001a) argues that as human *aspirations* grow, higher income does not bring further happiness.

Easterlin argues that people continually project that they will be happier in the future as their income increases, yet they are not. So there is a consistent bias in people's expectations according to Easterlin. He notes three facts relating to income and happiness as recorded from a variety of studies. First, as we have seen above, those with higher income are happier than those with lower incomes. Second, people expect to be happier in the future than they are now. Third, happiness tends to be constant over the lifecycle. These three facts are explained by the notion that *material aspirations change in proportion to income, and so people do not become happier over time even if they believe they will.*

Easterlin's evidence points to the persistence of materialism. Needs may be limited but "greeds" are not. In a related approach, Nettle (2005) argues that wants are strong, but once we have spent

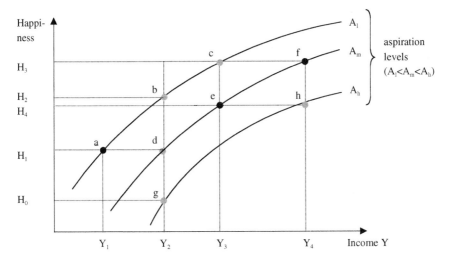

Figure 6.6 Happiness, Income and the Role of the Aspiration Level
Source: Frey and Stutzer (2002b, p. 56, Figure 3).

money and obtained the objects of our desire, we do not necessarily like them as much as we thought we would. To quantify this kind of psychology, Frey and Stutzer (2002a, b) suggest that rising aspirations nullify up to 70 percent of the rise in income. This can be illustrated by Figure 6.6. Initially, we assume that the individual has Y_1 income and H_1 level of happiness (at point *a* of the aspiration curve A_1). As his income increases from Y_1 to Y_2, his level of happiness increases to H_2 at point *b*. If his income continues rising, his happiness level should proceed to point *c*. However, over time, rising incomes lead to rising aspirations. This causes the aspiration curve to shift down to A_m. Hence in equilibrium, instead of observing *abc*, one could get *aef* instead, where an increase in income produces a smaller increase in happiness.

Finally, these findings of Easterlin and others challenge psychologist Abraham Maslow's "hierarchy of wants" as a reliable guide to future human motivation. Maslow (1968) suggests that once people's basic needs are satisfied, they seek to achieve nonmaterial or spiritual goals. The powerful force of aspirations suggests this is not the case.

6.3.5 *Affective forecasting and well-being*

Psychologists and economists have been studying the relationship between the actual and expected utility of a purchase. They call this gauge of how much satisfaction they will get out of something *affective forecasting*. People try to look into the future to predict how much they will like something new in their life — a new purchase, a new experience, a vacation, a new relationship or a promotion.

Research by a number of different psychologists (e.g., Gilbert and Wilson, 2000; Wilson and Gilbert, 2003; Gilovich, 1991) suggests that people generally overestimate the thrill, satisfaction and utility they will get out of a purchase. This psychological characteristic extends to negative events as well. Gilbert and Wilson (2000) show that academics getting tenure were not as gleeful as they expected to be and those who did not get tenure were not as devastated as they thought they would be. Lovers who are dumped do not feel as bad as they thought they would and supporters of political candidates who lost (won) are not as depressed (elated) as they thought they would be before the fact.

Wilson says that people recover very quickly from emotional news, good and bad. It is just that we do not expect to. And, surprisingly enough, there does not seem to be any feedback loop to tell us we will recover when the next similar event comes along. As a result, we continue to react in the same way. We have experienced most of the events in our lives that bring pain or pleasure many times before. Yet there does not seem to be much, if any, "learning by doing" when it comes to these emotional overreactions (see also Section 3.13).

Psychologists suggest that this systematic miscalculation is a way the brain has evolved to protect us from excessive volatility in our reactions to shifts in emotion. Part of this protective armor is that we develop rationalizations, justifications and self-serving logic that soothes our psyche during bad times.

A partial explanation for why there is a poor feedback loop could be that the psychological immune system is a subtle part of the intuitive section of the brain, which operates as a parallel network to the rational mind. When we imagine the feeling we are going to have after a pleasurable experience, we focus only on the event and not on the myriad of other stimuli that we experience all the time. These additional experiences dilute the impact of a single event. On the negative side, the reactions are similar. A romantic breakup is just one in a series of events that occurs in our life. You could meet a fabulous new person just a day after breaking up. Yet we focus on the breakup alone and project our feelings about it and nothing else.

This is not to say that the end of a romance is not upsetting. Rather, we all tend to overdramatize and overreact in our minds when we contemplate our reactions to events in the future. The actual experience is usually much less upsetting and emotionally draining.

Rationalization also sets in to dilute the experience. "She wasn't right for me", "I'm better off without her", "I'll now have a chance to meet my true soul mate", and so on. When people are asked how they would respond to losing a child to cancer or an accident, the uniform reaction is complete devastation for the foreseeable future. Yet the experience of parents who have lost children is gradual recovery to a state of well-being that is pretty similar to what they experienced before the loss of the child. There are those who grieve for a long time, but they seem to be the exception. We are all more resilient than we think we are.

This affective forecasting bias explains why income per capita can rise while well-being remains relatively unaffected. Is this emotional fail-safe method immune to adaptation? We are able to accommodate illness, emotional breakups and other emotional difficulties more easily than we expected.

Affective forecasting also demonstrates why people who have experienced devastating accidents or health problems are able to generally adapt and come back to a position of equanimity. It also explains why various studies show that people tend to overestimate how much their well-being will be affected by relocation, victory (loss) of political candidates or sports teams, losing weight, winning the lottery and more free time.

To get a better gauge of how we are going to react to a new experience, we can think about it and also ask others about their experience.

If you are interested in buying a new Mercedes, talk to the new Mercedes buyer. If you want to travel, talk to those who have traveled to the places you are interested in going to. Many travel books such as Arthur Frommer's travel guides and the Lonely Planet travel guides include personal experiences of other travelers. These can give us a better gauge as to whether we will enjoy a vacation.

However, many people do not seem to think this is a good course of action. They prefer to experience it themselves. For example, A asks, "How was that dentist?" B says, "He was great. Didn't hurt at all. You should go to him". A says, "Well maybe. Or I might go back to my old dentist. At least I know what to expect from him".

Some of these predictable overreactions have implications for public policy. Being tested for HIV brings up strong emotions. Yet people who tested positive were not as distraught as they thought they would be and those who tested negative were not as elated. Knowing these reactions can lead to better public policy. For example, people can be counseled to have an HIV test and reassured that they will be counseled after finding out the results of the test to help them cope or deal with the diagnosis. Similarly, those who are afraid of going to the doctor or the dentist can be reassured that the treatment will not be as bad as they imagine.

6.3.6 *Productivity and well-being*

There is a considerable amount of research suggesting that both job satisfaction and a positive attitude contribute to raising worker productivity. Experiencing more positive emotions at work is also associated with higher levels of interaction with others in the organization as well as better performance. There are also lower turnover rates, lower rates of absenteeism and more punctual attendance and cooperative behavior when workers are satisfied with their job and have a strong sense of accomplishment, ownership and well-being (Spector, 1997; Miner, 2001; Diener and Seligman, 2004). Thus, happy workers are not only more productive themselves; they also contribute to raising productivity for others and the firm. Higher levels of well-being of employees also result in higher levels of consumer satisfaction (Harter *et al.*, 2002), resulting in higher levels of profits for the firm. On the other hand, poor customer relations can cause large losses if customers are dissatisfied and take their business elsewhere. Srinivasan and Pugliese (2000) estimated that lack of consumer loyalty cost a large bank chain $44 million in a year because customers closed accounts.

Greater involvement of workers in decision making also raises productivity (Black and Lynch, 2004; Hamilton *et al.*, 2003). It is also likely that this involvement in decision making contributes to a greater feeling of well-being as workers become more involved in management and in group interaction. Graham *et al.* (2003) suggest that the usual demographic factors such as health, marital status, gender, race and position in the lifecycle influence happiness. Combining these factors with positive expectations correlated with higher income for the future provide strong evidence that positive psychological factors related to happiness such as self-esteem, self-control and optimism are also important factors in enhancing earnings and general labor market performance.

It is well-known that paying workers a higher salary than industry norms — the so-called efficiency wage argument — can be a contributing factor in raising productivity (see Campbell, 1993, for example). It is also possible that efficiency wages may also increase workers' feeling of well-being as a result of workers feeling more appreciated and valuable to the firm.

The above research does not consider the possibility that happy workers are simply happy and would be so no matter what, and that workplace characteristics have nothing to do with their state of mind. However, other studies suggest that there may be a two-way causality between worker well-being and workplace conditions. Most of these studies suggest that:

> the positive effects of well-being at work on performance go beyond the effects of personality. The well-being of workers results in positive organizational citizenship, customer satisfaction and perhaps even greater productivity. Because specific workplace variables are known to enhance well-being at work, organizational policies can raise workers' well-being and thereby enhance organizational citizenship and possibly profitability (Diener and Seligman, 2004, p. 12).

6.3.7 Health and well-being

In general, positive physical states of well-being are positively correlated with good health. People in poor health are generally not happy.
This may seem obvious, but it is an important result that has implications for health policy as it influences productivity and government
initiatives. Another aspect of this relationship is that feelings of well-
being are also positively correlated with longer life expectancy and
people's subjective view of their own health. Happy people think they
are healthy and there may be positive feedback loops that make this a
self-fulfilling prophesy.

Conversely, the intensity of physical pain can be magnified by feelings of unhappiness or low self-image. In addition, longevity is greater
in nations where well-being is high, even after controlling statistically
for the level of income and the size of infant mortality (Vazquez et al.,
2004). Also, other research suggests that optimistic patients live
longer than pessimistic patients, happy people recover faster, and
some diseases can be cured or treated more effectively when the
patient has a happy and upbeat attitude (see Diener and Seligman,
2004, p. 14, for details). As a corollary to this, a pleasant mood seems
to lower blood pressure, whereas stress results in a decrease in the
ability of the immune system to fight off disease.

The incidence of mental disease in industrial countries has been
rising steadily over the past fifty or sixty years, even as per capita
income has been increasing (Cross-National Collaborative Group,
1992). In a sample of over 40,000 adults from several different countries, results showed a dramatic increase in mental illness over the
20th century. The cost to society and to the individual is high.
Depression and anxiety, two major forms of mental illness, lead to significant declines in well-being (Spitzer et al., 1995; Packer et al.,
1997). On the other hand, there is evidence that happy people show
fewer signs of mental illness (Diener and Seligman, 2002).

While many with psychological disorders still fail to seek or receive
help, treatment for many kinds of mental illness is effective.
Sometimes these therapies are more effective when patients are
encouraged and allowed to interact with others in social settings
(McCrady et al., 1991, on alcoholism is an example).

Despite these negative relationships between health and well-being, it should also be noted that people have a strong *coping mechanism* that enhances their capacity to overcome adversity and unexpected negative events. For example, paraplegics initially suffer from a huge drop in well-being. However, many are able to recover and adapt to their disabilities. As people age, they lose some of their ability to actively participate in sports or other activities they enjoyed when they were younger; yet this does not seem to significantly affect their feeling of well-being in a negative way (see Frey and Stutzer, 2002b).

6.3.8 *Happiness and social relationships*

There are various social settings which are associated with greater levels of well-being. Conversely, other states are associated with low levels. Interpersonal problems including difficult family relationships, stressful work environment and ostracism from social groups can all cause strong negative feelings and low self-esteem. Loneliness stems from a lack of a confidant and friends, which in turn increases the risk of psychological problems and low life satisfaction (Argyle, 1987; Baumeister, 1991). Social developments which cause disruption to life, including moving, dissolution of marriage and death of a partner can have a devastating impact on well-being. Others, such as moving, can be addressed either by the business community or the government. Disruptions caused to employees by movement to different locations can be minimized by tax incentives and reorientation of business human relations departments to focus on keeping families together in one location for longer periods of time.

Besides counseling and support of friends and relatives, some of these negative impacts can be dealt with by society. There are also several techniques that have been successful in experiments conducted by Sonja Lyubomirsky (1994). For one, Lyubomirsky argues that unhappiness is related to negative thinking and "dwelling on bad moments" unnecessarily. She suggests going through "self-reflection", rather like counting your blessings, practicing kindness and altruism, and keeping a diary of happy moments on a regular basis. For example, doing five acts of kindness in a single day boosted the spirits of her subjects. Along the same lines, Martin Seligman (2002) has experimented with writing down three things that went well at the end of the day. This exercise seemed to have a long-term beneficial impact on perceived well-being (*Time*, 2005). Being alert to the opportunities of the present moment is another way to move from an unhappy state to a happy one. By being in the present moment all the time, we can stop the trends of negative thinking.

6.3.9 *Happiness and social capital*

Social capital will be discussed comprehensively in the next chapter. There is evidence that well-being is positively correlated with the level of social capital in the society (Helliwell, 2005). Here we can note that in situations where there is an abundant supply of social capital, suicide rates are low (the extreme of unhappiness), trust in others is high and there is also a high level of membership in organizations outside of work. See Helliwell (2003, 2005) for further details. Where there is a breakdown in social connectedness, the level of well-being tends to decline (Twenge *et al.*, 2002). In the US, there seems to be a trend toward a lower level of social connectedness and a rise in mental illness even as incomes per capita are rising. Graham and Pettinato (2002) find that different objectives underlying civic participation have different effects on labor mobility and on perceived well-being.

6.3.10 *Happiness and governance*

As noted previously, there is a concave relationship between income and happiness across a variety of countries as reflected in Figure 6.2. Examination of Figure 6.7 shows that many of the countries showing low happiness levels were those with authoritarian states without much economic or political freedom. This could mean that other factors, including democracy but also better health and more personal freedoms, could account for the positive relationship between income and happiness. It also exhibits the weakness of depending too much on simple correlations and two-dimensional graphical schematics to

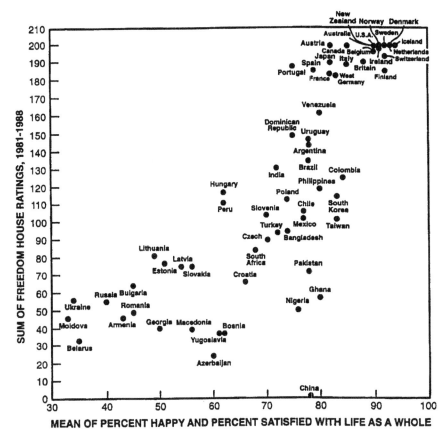

Figure 6.7 Governance and Happiness Across Nations, 1981–1988

Source: Inglehart and Klingemann (2000, p. 178, Figure 7.5).

prove a point. If we expand our range of variables that could be correlated with happiness, we observe that political and personal freedoms are also closely correlated with happiness (see Figure 6.8).

Frey and Stutzer (2002b) explored the relationship between direct democratic participation and indices of subjective well-being in Switzerland. They found a highly significant relationship between life satisfaction and direct democratic rights and participation using data from 1992–1994 for Swiss cantons. They also found that a stronger democratic environment raised the well-being coefficients across the

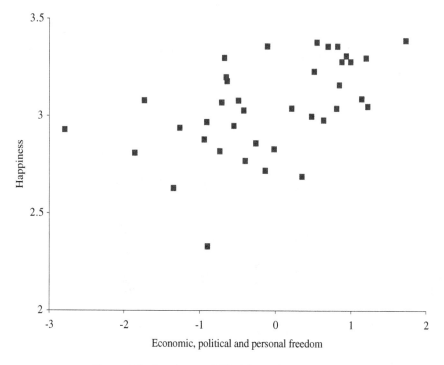

Figure 6.8 Freedom and Happiness Across Nations
Source: Frey and Stutzer (2002b, p. 58).

board for a wide range of individuals in the entire society, not just a selected few.

6.3.11 *Happiness, freedom, trust, stability and corruption*

More broadly, Helliwell (2003, 2005) concludes that people with the highest feeling of well-being are those who live in societies where social and political institutions are effective, with a high degree of mutual trust and where the level of corruption is low. Other studies including those of Inglehart and Klingemann (2000) and Veenhoven (2000) also found that economic freedom was positively related to happiness, particularly in poorer countries. Diener *et al.* (1995) suggest that human rights and individual freedom are also correlated with well-being. Repressive regimes reduce the sense of well-being. Stability in society is an important component in establishing a feeling of well-being. This is reflected by low well-being indicators in the former Soviet Union in the unstable years following liberation from Soviet oppression (Helliwell, 2003; Inglehart and Klingemann, 2000; Veenhoven, 2000).

6.3.12 *Happiness and leisure*

We know from Section 6.3.2 that relative income is a more reliable index of well-being than is absolute income. We also know that leisure is an important component of happiness, at least from the survey results displayed in Table 6.4. Working is very low on the happiness

Table 6.4 Happiness and Time

	Happiness Index	Average Hours (per day)
Sex	4.7	0.2
Socializing after work	4.1	1.1
Dinner	3.9	0.8
Relaxing	3.9	2.2
Lunch	3.8	0.6
Exercising	3.8	0.2
Praying	3.8	0.5
Socializing at work	3.8	1.1
Watching TV	3.6	2.2
Phone at home	3.5	0.9
Napping	3.3	0.9
Cooking	3.2	1.1
Shopping	3.2	0.4
Computer at home	3.1	0.5
Housework	3.0	1.1
Childcare	3.0	1.1
Evening commute	2.8	0.6
Working	2.7	6.9
Morning commute	2.0	0.4

Source: Kahneman *et al.* (2004b).
Note: Average happiness is the net effect.

scale and leisure activities including sex, socializing, eating and relaxing are high up on the happiness scale.

We can ask the question, "How are relative income and leisure related to happiness?" A good example of these two relationships is demonstrated by some questions that were asked of Harvard University students:

1. Participants were asked whether they would prefer (a) $50,000 a year while others got half, or (b) $100,000 a year while others got twice as much. The majority chose (a).
2. Harvard students were asked to choose between (c) two weeks' vacation while others had one week, or (d) four weeks' holiday while others got eight. The majority chose (d).

The conclusion we can draw from these results is that people have strong rivalry over income, and this rivalry over income does not extend to leisure. As a result, developed societies tend to work too hard to consume more material goods and seem to consume too little leisure (see Konow, 2003, for further details). Although it seems that more leisure makes people happy, there are as yet no definitive studies of this relationship for large samples.

Indirect evidence seems to suggest that when leisure time is spent in enjoyable and fulfilling activities like being with the family, traveling, pursuing hobbies or exercise, then leisure does indeed increase well-being. If leisure time is spent as a couch potato, the chances that leisure enhances well-being are reduced. However, as far as we know, there is no good study of this tradeoff using large sample outcomes and the Day Reconstruction Survey (Kahneman *et al.*, 2004b) finds that watching TV is relatively high up on the scale of happiness.

6.3.13 *Are the happiness results independent of social context?*

Some psychologists have argued that happiness is strongly conditioned by a collective outlook, which can be captured by measuring the impact of different cultures on happiness. If this is true, then different cultures will show different happiness coefficients, other things being equal. For example, Calvinist influences in Europe could lead to a lower level of happiness because of its religious influence on society. Another observation by Inglehart (1990) suggests that relatively low happiness in the Mediterranean countries in Europe could be the result of a cynical attitude which is rooted in historical experience. This would be reflected not only in lower happiness coefficients, but also in a lack of trust in society. Veenhoven (1994) studied these relationships using World Values Survey data and found little support for the argument that Calvinist countries are less happy, other things equal. With respect to the relationship between trust and happiness, we refer to the discussion in Section 6.3.11. The role of trust in economic growth and subjective well-being is also explored further in Chapter 7.

Recent work comparing the US with European countries by Alesina *et al.* (2001) suggests that the social context has important impacts on well-being, particularly to those in the lower levels of the income distribution. Alesina and his colleagues found a large and significant negative effect of income inequality on happiness in Europe, but not in the US. They suggest two possible explanations. First, Europeans prefer more equal societies and secondly, the US allows for more social mobility. Looking at different social groups, they find that only rich "leftists" in the US show evidence of inequality-generated unhappiness, whereas in Europe, inequality makes the poor unhappy just as much as the "leftists". The results suggest that there is greater popular demand for governments to fight inequality in Europe than in the US. Put another way, the greater the belief among the poor that they can improve their economic status, the less is their commitment to achieving wealth redistribution through social policy. The "dole" is something to move away from in the US, while it is more socially acceptable in Europe.

There are few studies that compare Asian cultures with others; Ng's (2002a) study is an exception. Ng follows the standard argument presented elsewhere that after a certain threshold, increasing income does not lead to greater happiness. He argues that this is true in Asia. He goes on to contend that East Asian economies have lower happiness coefficients than industrial economies, even though living standards are nearly comparable. Also, he notes that measures of life satisfaction are lower in Asia than in many countries with lower standards of living. These conclusions are reinforced by Table 6.5 below.

Ng's arguments for Asia's lower life satisfaction coefficients are similar to those of other researchers summarized and surveyed previously. He argues that other factors are important in determining happiness like being married or having a partner, being employed and having friends. He stresses the importance of having some religious connection. More importantly, he relates the lower coefficient of well-being in Asia to the competitiveness of the Asian economies. They vigorously strive for higher standards of living and take less leisure time than their European or North American counterparts. Furthermore, high levels of population concentration and pollution contribute to stress and reduced levels of well-being. He argues that the emphasis on scholarly attainment and doing well in exams may be detrimental to real creativity and personal and social happiness:

> East-Asian culture is over-emphatic on conformity, order and the collective interest to the detriment of individualism, freedom and hence happiness (Ng, 2002a, p. 57).

Table 6.5 Index of Life Satisfaction for Selected Countries

Country	Index of Life Satisfaction
China	4.00
Korea	4.98
Hong Kong	5.07
Japan	5.14
Singapore	5.72
Nigeria	5.11
India	5.15
Pakistan	5.49
Peru	5.77
Eygpt	6.14
Colombia	6.20
Australia	6.23

Source: Diener and Suh (1999, p. 444).
Note: Higher numbers reflect greater satisfaction.

Furthermore, Ng notes that in Confucian culture the ideal level of life satisfaction is considered to be a neutral stance — neither satisfied nor dissatisfied. Ng asserts that there is also an abstinence factor in Confucianism. Hedonic striving for happiness is regarded as unworthy or shameful. He then asks the question, how can one enjoy life happily if one is brought up to be opposed to pleasant feelings (Ng, 2002a, p. 58)? Finally, Ng argues that East Asian culture is too preoccupied with appearance, on not losing face and less on the real content and true feelings. East Asians place more value on reputation and appearances, and emphasize family history and other objective factors, while western cultures emphasize happiness. He goes on to mention that societies may be better off by shifting resources to spending on public goods such as better education, pollution reduction and other environmental protective measures. He also thinks that all societies should put more emphasis on health, social relationships and spiritual fulfillment since these are the factors that lead to lasting happiness.

The views of Ng receive some support by Swinyard *et al.* (2001). Using probability samples of adults in the US and Singapore, they find that adults in Singapore are less happy and more materialistic than those in the US. The assumption that Asians in general work longer hours than their counterparts in other regions, particularly the US and Europe, is supported by evidence compiled for hours worked as displayed in Table 6.6.

However, this relationship between hours worked and happiness has not been thoroughly studied and it remains to be proven whether more hours worked and less leisure time do have a significant negative impact on well-being. Also, it is yet to be determined whether the structural relationships between well-being and other variables differ from culture to culture, or whether the observations of Ng and others simply relate to choices made between work and leisure. These choices could be a reflection of the work ethic of the Asian region. Well-being in other regions could be negatively impacted in the same way if their residents chose to work as hard and put in such long hours. On the other hand, it is also possible that the length of the work week has little impact on overall happiness, particularly if everyone in the

Table 6.6 Percentage Change in Hours Worked per Person, 1973–1996

Country	Average Growth	Country	Average Growth
Austria	−2.15	Switzerland	−10.99
Belgium	−17.36	UK	−11.26
Denmark	−5.34	West Germany	−19.09
Finland	−18.67	Hong Kong	11.80
France	−23.37	Indonesia	19.76
Greece	−11.46	Japan	−8.35
Ireland	−18.47	Korea	37.71
Italy	−17.92	Philippines	−12.5
Netherlands	−14.45	Singapore	36.81
Norway	−5.76	Taiwan	6.23
Portugal	11.06	Thailand	13.14

Source: Crafts (1996, Table 5.9).

society follows the same patterns of behavior. The answers to these questions remain unanswered and are subjects for further research.

6.3.14 Happiness and regret

We have seen in the last few sections that behavior is varied and responds to different stimuli. Some people act on baser instincts that might make them happy for the moment. Most people regret their actions sometime later. We will look into this aspect of behavior further in the next chapter. For now, it is important to recognize that the problem for social scientists is to develop theories that hold generally and are simple enough that they are useful for making generalizations.

6.3.15 Is the lack of happiness a matter of ignorance?

Adults often counsel their children to avoid actions and activities that they will regret later on. Children usually ignore this advice. Life's experiences teach us some things to avoid and others to seek out. Logically, however, ignorance is somewhat related to age and experience. If you burn your hand at the stove as a child, you will be wary in the future. For those who reflect upon their experiences, the lessons they have learned can lead them to a more fruitful and fulfilling life. For those who forget, they may have to learn and relearn. Ignorance also plays a role in decisions that are regretted or reevaluated once more information becomes available. Despite the ability to benefit from experience, much of the research on happiness suggests that human nature has an in-built general inability to make choices that would increase their level of happiness.

6.3.16 *Are we hard wired for happiness?*

In the debate between nature and nurture as determinants of character and psychological makeup, it is often asserted that many of our personality characteristics and tendencies are determined at birth, and so there is little that can be done to change or modify individual attitudes. This could include subjective well-being and happiness. If the role of nature is quite large, then the scope for generating greater happiness is limited. That being the case, should we give up on achieving greater levels of subjective well-being and happiness? Certainly not!! If nurture is at all important, then we can increase well-being by understanding what makes people respond in ways that increase happiness. The magnitude of the response may depend upon the natural hard wiring of the individual. Nevertheless, the direction will surely be to increase well-being and happiness.

Some of our happiness and well-being is relatively invariant with respect to demographic variables. Happiness varies somewhat with age although the details of the relationship are subject to question. Alesina *et al.* (2001) and Easterlin (2001b) found that happiness increases with age up until between 40 and 45, after which happiness begins to decrease (an inverse "U" relationship). Results reported by other researchers show a different pattern of well-being over the lifecycle, with a low point in the mid-forties to early-fifties age groups for both men and women (Helliwell, 2005; Frey and Stutzer, 2002a, b; Blanchflower and Oswald, 2004b). This could reflect what is commonly referred to as the mid-life crisis.

The explanation given by Easterlin for differences between his result and the U-shaped pattern reported by Helliwell, Blanchflower and Oswald and others is that these other studies included lifecycle variables such as work, marital and economic status. Easterlin (2001b) suggests that the inverse U shape is a result of not including control for these changing life circumstances. However, this explanation does not apply to the analysis presented by Dowling and Yap (2005), who also included controls for changing life circumstances and also found an inverse U pattern which is strikingly similar to the Easterlin result. It seems that the inverse U shape is a more robust description of the relationship between well-being and age than Easterlin imagined. In any event, whatever the shape of the relationship between age and well-being, the overall impact on well-being is small in comparison with the impact of other variables.

Looking at gender influences, women are generally a bit happier than men but the differences are small. Minorities tend to be somewhat less happy than others, probably as a result of discrimination.

Recent research by psychologists and neuroscientists has explored the relationship between the brain and subjective well-being (Urry et al., 2004; Davidson et al., 2003). One of the findings from this work is that people who report higher levels of either psychological well-being or subjective well-being or both, exhibit greater brain activity in the left prefrontal cortex as opposed to the right prefrontal cortex.

Other work in the field of neuroscience demonstrates that the brain adjusts to changes in circumstances and in the environment, and there is additional research which suggests that meditation contributes to well-being by developing the left side of the prefrontal cortex and other related areas in the left side of the brain (Davidson et al., 2003). Meditation activates the middle frontal gyrus, an area of the brain associated with joy and enthusiasm, and tends to decrease anxiety in a number of different experiments. A transcendental meditation practice is the most noteworthy.

Davidson et al. (2003) conclude from their study of meditators that individuals with more left anterior activity were more likely to recover quickly from emotional shocks and to achieve a state of equanimity faster. Studies involving monks with thousands of hours of meditation experience show that they have developed better pathways to coordinate different brain functions as a result of changes in the baseline state of their brains. James Austin (1998) argues that the reduction in respiration observed in veteran meditators reduces neuronal firing in the medulla. This stimulates higher order functioning of the brain. Furthermore, meditation seems to stimulate the flow of blood to the amygdala, a part of the brain associated with relaxation (see also the discussion of altruistic reciprocity or social reciprocity in Chapter 7 and the discussion of altruism in Chapter 5).

Comparisons of the brain waves of monks that meditate and those that do not meditate also show dramatic differences in the amount of activity in the brain. For most people, brain activity was a mixture of positive and negative emotions as reflected by activity in the left pre-frontal cortex (positive) and right prefrontal cortex (negative). However, meditating monks show a much greater tendency of brain waves that focus in the left prefrontal cortex, and this is reflected in their behavior in the world as well. They are less emotionally volatile, less judgmental and more even-tempered (see Barasch, 2005).

6.3.17 *Intuition, "flow" and happiness*

This section turns to another aspect of happiness — namely the role intuition or what has been called flow. Flow or being in the zone is the total immersion in something — usually a task, sports activity, leisure activity like reading an engrossing book, playing a game or playing/enjoying music. It requires being in the moment and focusing completely on what you are doing. On a scale of one to four — one being complete immersion and four being zero immersion — the experience of people seems to be surprisingly uniform when large samples are taken. Experiencing flow requires engagement and is usually easier to experience when "doing something" rather than just relaxing. As noted above, this "doing something" could be playing a game, mountain climbing, enjoying music or playing a sport. It can also be work-related activities such as architectural design or computer programming. In a German survey, 23 percent of respondents said they often "get involved so deeply in something that nothing else matters and you lose track of time", while 12 percent said they never "got involved …." The rest of the respondents said they "got involved …" sometimes. The extreme percentages are fairly similar in other samples according to Csikszentmihalyi (1997). He notes that flow is harder to experience at play than at work.

People sometimes do not organize their lives to maximize flow. For example, Csikszentmihalyi says that US teens experience flow 13 percent of the time when they watch television but 44 percent of the time when involved in sports. Yet teens spend much more time watching TV than participating in sports. This could be because each of the flow producing activities requires an initial investment of attention before it begins to become enjoyable. If a person is too tired, too anxious or lacks the discipline to overcome the initial obstacle to focus or learn, he or she will have to settle for something that may be less accessible but perhaps not as enjoyable. "Only lack of imagination or lack of energy, stand in the way of each of us becoming a poet or a musician, an inventor or an explorer, an amateur scholar, scientist, artist or collector" (Csikszentmihalyi, 1997, p. 47).

Csikszentmihalyi also says that being with people is better than being alone, which could be a possible contradiction. Flow is solitary or can be solitary. Happiness is being with people. We are encouraged to husband time carefully in order to enjoy life in the here and now. Be in the present moment and everything will be enjoyable. This is the key to the experience of flow and an acute awareness of a deeper level of experience.

Zen Buddhists have this idea paramount in their minds when they explore complete focus on different activities. This approach to experience is expounded further in a number of Buddhist texts and also by westerners who have studied Zen Buddhism. Cult favorites Eugen Herrigel (1953) or Robert Pirsig (1974) are well-known examples. Even mundane tasks like household chores can open a doorway to flow experience if we concentrate on them completely. Do the dishes the best way possible, make the bed the best way possible, focus completely on eating a meal. Savor the food — the taste, the aroma, the texture, the way you lift your fork, the way the jaws open and close and the way you swallow. If we are immersed in the present moment, then we will be able to experience flow in everything we do.

This concept of flow is very similar to spiritual experiences that the sages talk about (see Tolle, 1999). The idea is to make life more enjoyable by focusing on the present moment completely. You can reorganize your time to start doing more of the things you enjoy and spending less time on things you do not enjoy. By refocusing your attention to the present moment and nothing else, worry and anxiety will disappear. They are both constructs of thinking about the future or the past.

Being in the zone leads to decisions that flow from consciousness and not from the mind. This process makes use of intuition as an integral part of decision making. Expanding on this idea, John E. Young (2002) argues that CEOs can make better decisions if they operate from an expanded space that goes beyond the ego. Decisions taken from the space of inner consciousness based on intuition would be less ego-driven and could result in better decision making.

Thinking outside the box could result more frequently if a CEO is less influenced by the views of others and the conventional way to do things. FEDEX adopting a central hub distribution system; DELL selling directly over the web; Southwest airlines' no reservations, no meals policy to cut costs; and AVON's direct sales to home were all new ideas that flaunted traditional ways of doing business. They were the result of lateral thinking which went beyond conventional approaches to business management. Using this kind of approach, the CEO can also direct his workers to expand their level of consciousness as well. To quote:

> Comprehensive programs could be initiated at the workplace to aid subordinates' progress along the spectrum. For example, the CEO can make both space and time available for engaging in transformational practices such as meditation, yoga, qigong, and/or contemplative prayer. The CEO could encourage the organization's participation in health plans that include service in mind-body therapies, body work, bioenergetics analysis, traditional Chinese or Indian medicine and so forth (Young, 2002, p. 46).

The bottom line is that we are all capable of tuning into our intuition and rising above the pettiness and ego-based decision making that often lead to poor decisions. Furthermore, by adopting policies that foster a congenial work environment conducive to a higher level of subjective well-being or happiness, businesses can increase productivity, foster innovation and improve the bottom line. We focus on the self-reported states of flow and happiness and what aspects of respondents' lives were important in achieving these states of flow and happiness.

These states of consciousness where we become completely focused on something leads to a kind of joy or peace or ecstasy. How does this relate to happiness? Csikszentmihalyi (1997) says it is not happiness. In earlier work, Csikszentmihalyi (1975) makes comparisons between flow and happiness. There are a number of different ways to achieve happiness and well-being. Happiness could be enjoying other people's company in a social setting. Flow, by definition, tends to be a more solitary experience. It is possible that since most people cannot find flow, they are happier when with others.

6.3.18 *Happiness and the role of emotions*

Another aspect of happiness which has been the subject of several articles by behavioral scientists is the role of emotions on well-being. Loewenstein (2004) emphasized that cravings and addictions as well as other visceral/emotional influences have the capacity to "drive a wedge between self-interest and behavior" (p. 269). He argues that self-interest in a rational model diverges significantly from actual behavior when visceral factors are strong. When we follow our impulses, we often neglect to consider the longer-term consequences of these immediate and impulsive actions. These impulsive behaviors include using addictive substances that are harmful to our health and have adverse effects on our economic and social life, displaying fits of anger that cause emotional and possibly physical harm to others, gambling large sums of money, undercutting business associates to gain the bosses' favor and so on.

Loewenstein also demonstrated that vividness of memories often leads to biases in predictions. Publicity following spectacular air disasters makes travelers averse to flying, terrorist attacks in distant locations cause widespread fear locally and cause governments to introduce various preventive measures against future terrorist attacks.

Tourists shied away from Bali and Madrid after the terrorist bombings when those places were probably safer after the terrorist attacks because of added security and, as the saying goes, "lightning doesn't strike twice". However, the second bombing in Bali brings that popular aphorism into question.

Many of these actions that take place because of emotional feelings or whims result in negative outcomes and a reduction in well-being. If we can control these visceral impulses, it is likely that we can move to a higher level of happiness. These visceral factors also lead people to believe that they are behaving in an irresponsible and irrational way. In fact, they are responding to a set of instructions from the emotional part of the brain which overrides their logical and cognitive instincts. They are responding to their behavioral conditioning.

Experiencing happiness can result in the repetition of activities that promote happiness. It can be as simple as eating a chocolate. It has also been established that dwelling on negativities results in a downward spiral of negativities and further depression. On the other hand, replacing a negative thought with a positive thought can uplift and reverse the downward spiral of emotions.

Actions that reinforce positive feelings and emotions such as trust, altruism and cooperation contribute to individual happiness and also to the well-being of society through greater efficiency, less corruption and general externalities that promote well-being of others. Zak (2004) shows a positive relationship between trust and stock market returns in OECD countries. There are several other studies that show the importance of trust in increasing well-being (see Helliwell, 2003; Zak and Knack, 2001; Zak, 2004).

6.3.19 *Happiness and time allocation*

Some aspects of happiness research suggest we do not value things that make us happy as much as we should — at least according to the utilitarian calculus. We strive for goods which are measurable in levels such as time and money that do not make us happy. In interviews, people say they value friends, family, good company, sex and hobbies more than work and that a higher level of income does not necessarily make them happier (see Tables 6.4 and 6.7). Yet they continue to work harder, spending more time at the office and less time doing what they say they value most. People are more stressed as reflected by higher rates of mental illness, suicide, obesity and other addictions in many industrialized countries (Layard, 2005b, Chapter 3). More time is spent on activities which are the least satisfying, such as work. After work, watching television occupies the most time along with relaxing, rather than the preferred leisure time activities that are mentioned by respondents in the Day Reconstruction Survey.[2] Oddly enough, we know a lot about what makes us unhappy — unemployment, divorce, death of loved ones, illness, social disruption, feeling of powerlessness, low self-worth, discrimination and inability to influence governmental decision making. But researchers have neglected to look at the other side of the coin — what makes us happy? Perhaps these research findings about unhappiness are simply a reflection of concern with the causes of large negative displacement from the homeostatic equilibrium.

Table 6.7 Happiness While Spending Time with Different People

Interaction With	Average Happiness
Friends	3.3
Parents/relatives	3.0
Spouse	2.8
My children	2.7
Co-workers	2.6
Clients/customers	2.4
Alone	2.2
Boss	2.0

Source: Based on Day Reconstruction Survey.

---

[2]The Day Reconstruction Method (DRM) was used to survey experiences of women in Texas. The DRM is designed to collect data describing the experiences of a person on a given day, through a systematic reconstruction conducted on the following day. For more on the DRM survey instrument and method, see Kahneman *et al.* (2004b).

6.3.20 *Happiness, frustration and competition*

Frank (1999) notes that competition among consumers does not necessarily result in an increase in happiness. He presents a simple comparison of a situation where the average house size is 1,250 square feet. Consumers who have houses larger than 1,250 square feet are happier simply because they are above the average. If the average house size doubles to 2,500 square feet, then those same home owners who were above the average before will now be unhappy and strive to increase their earning capacity so they can qualify to buy a house larger than 2,500 square feet. In the new equilibrium, there is no increase in happiness, despite the considerable expenditure of resources to build houses twice as big.

What is the relationship between happiness and competition? Should policies be adopted to temper the competitive nature of western societies in order to increase well-being? It seems logical that there might be some relationship between the degree of competition in a society and the amount of happiness. Societies that are more competitive probably have more stress and therefore a lower index of well-being. Societies that are more cooperative and "laid back" might be expected to have a higher level of subjective well-being. Ian Thorpe, the highly competitive Australian swimming champion, when asked about his experience in his second Olympics, commented, "It's not about winning medals. It's about sharing your experience with your friends". Even the most highly competitive athletes like Thorpe are moved more by cooperation and comradeship than competition.

Surprisingly, there is very little evidence of a negative relationship between competition and well-being, other things equal. It is definitely an area for further research. We noted in Section 6.3.13 that Asians may be less happy than their counterparts in Europe because they are under more pressure and work longer hours. More importantly, Ng (2002b) relates the lower coefficient of well-being to the competitiveness of the Asian economies. However, it is not clear whether the relationship that Ng finds for Singapore relates to the competitive nature of the economic system or the position of business firms and the government to promote work versus leisure. As Table 6.6

demonstrates, other competitive societies have reduced the work week over the past 20 years.

6.3.21   *Unemployment and happiness*

The accumulated research evidence on the impact of unemployment on happiness suggests that being unemployed has a very strong negative impact on well-being and happiness. Studies of British workers by Clark and Oswald (1994, p. 65) note that:

> joblessness depressed well-being more than any other single characteristic, including important negative ones such as divorce and separation.

Similar results have been observed in Germany, Australia and the US, and these are reviewed in more detail in Frey and Stutzer (2002a, b). They argue that the costs of unemployment are both psychological and social. The psychological costs are loss of self-esteem and self-worth, which can lead to depression and hopelessness, particularly if unemployment is prolonged. Social position and status is often defined by people's work. Loss of work has a strong negative impact on social status. Furthermore, an increase in unemployment can cause distress and anxiety among the employed who begin to fear for their jobs. It also has a negative impact on the families of those who have become unemployed. Finally, unemployment is a heavier burden in societies where having a job is an important social norm. This is the case in most industrial countries, while having a job is a goal in many developing countries.

While it could be argued that the causation runs from unhappiness to unemployed — those who are unhappy are less productive workers and are therefore more subject to retrenchment — there is no evidence to support this position. Indeed, there is significant evidence to support the conclusion that the unemployed are unhappier and have higher incidence of mental illness, depression, alcohol and drug abuse (see Box 6.1 for evidence that these difficulties are not confined to the middle-classes and the poor). High rates of youth unemployment in industrial countries are also associated with a higher incidence of sociopath behavior, more gangs and higher crime rates.

Box 6.1 Depression, a Frequent Visitor to Wall St.

EARLY one afternoon in July, Dennis J. Bertrum, a former top broker-age executive at Prudential Securities, leapt out of the bedroom window of his 26th-floor apartment on the Upper West Side of Manhattan.

No note was found, but the police said the death was a suicide.

In and out of work since 1996, Mr. Bertrum, a pioneer in the man-aged account business who was described by friends as a bon vivant, had been on a persistent quest to return to the brokerage business that he had loved since his days selling stocks for E. F. Hutton in the 1970s, col-leagues say. But for Mr. Bertrum, an unemployed 55–year-old who friends say had a history of Jekyll-and-Hyde-type mood swings, few doors were opening.

Just weeks before he took his own life, he had been interviewing for a senior job in the private wealth management division of Merrill Lynch but he and the firm could not come to terms, friends said, adding that they do not blame the firm for what ultimately happened. Merrill declined to comment.

Instead, his friends and family described a man who for years had been in therapy for a bipolar condition and who had quit taking his med-ication, Wellbutrin, just three weeks before his death. Mr. Bertrum was twice divorced and in the process of ending a relationship, and family members say that with no income, he was feeling financial pressure. His brother, Carl A. Butrum, who called him a week before he died, said he was on a down swing.

For a man who had achieved financial and professional success in the 1990s, the letdown of not securing the Merrill job could have been bru-tal, his friends and family said.

"It's pretty traumatic when you are in your 50s, you are skilled and can operate at a high level but your expectations don't pan out," said Stephen C. Winks, a financial consultant and a former colleague of Mr. Bertrum's at Prudential. "I think it weighed heavily on him."

Suicides in the brokerage industry are rare, and those that can be documented have been linked in the public mind to wiped-out portfolios and plummeting markets like those of 1929, 1987 and even 2000. But the chronic depression associated with suicides is not rare on Wall Street.

(Continued)

Box 6.1 (*Continued*)

A survey conducted in 2000 — the only known study of its kind — concluded that 23 percent of a small sampling of male brokers and traders at seven of the largest firms on Wall Street suffered from clinical depression, a rate far above what was then the national average of 7 percent for men. And that was before the market fell by one-third from its record high, before Wall Street firms shed 30,000 jobs and before an explosion of investor lawsuits and arbitration cases.

All of this has led some experts to conclude that the rate of depression among brokers and traders is related more to the grinding pressures of a rapidly changing industry than to the vicissitudes of the markets.

"Brokers have little control over their jobs or the outcomes of their trades," said Alden M. Cass, a licensed clinical psychologist who wrote the study and now coaches Wall Street traders and brokers on coping with the psychological travails of their professions. "These frustrations can lead to a form of 'learned helplessness,' or a feeling that you are in a prison with no way out. Such feelings have been linked to levels of clinical depression."

Relatively few brokers and bankers appear to be seeking professional help to cope with the pressure, according to data collected by insurance companies. Experts say many brokers fear that doing so would be seen by their employers as a sign of weakness in a high-testosterone industry like finance. So brokers bottle up their feelings and soldier on — until they crack, health professionals say.

"I would have predicted higher rates of behavioral health claims for stock brokers because of the high stress," said Dr. Ronald S. Leopold, the national director for group disability at MetLife, who collected the data. "But what we see in jobs where there is a combination of tremendous stress and opportunity is the work-until-you-drop phenomenon. There is no question in my mind that these people have high rates of depression, and it is no wonder that we are seeing some of them crash."

Source: Thomas (2004).

In addition, there is some evidence that an increase in the general level of unemployment makes the rest of society feel worse (Di Tella *et al.*, 2001, 2003). Looking at 12 European countries, the authors find that a small rise in unemployment is consistent with a downward shift from one life satisfaction category to another (e.g., from "satisfied" to "not very satisfied") on an average basis. However, these effects are not linear since, when unemployment is high, there are more unemployed around to make the individual feel as if he is not alone (Di Tella *et al.*, 2001).

The old adage "misery loves company" does something to assuage the social disruption and pain of unemployment. Nevertheless, this does not discount the real and significant impact on job loss on happiness and subjective well-being of job loss. Di Tella *et al.* argue:

> the economist's standard method of judging the disutility of being laid off focuses on pecuniary loss. According to our calculations this is a mistake, because it understates the full well-being costs, which ... appear to be non-pecuniary (2003, p. 819).

The sting also appears to be more painful to those who have lost the most in terms of status, self-esteem and income. Losing one low-paying entry level job is not particularly painful, particularly if you can find another. It is another matter to be ousted as CEO of a big company with bleak future prospects. The fall from a much greater height is more painful.

This result is supported by the work of Helliwell (2003), who found that unemployment had a greater negative impact on well-being in rich nations than in poor nations. The psychological impact of loss of self-esteem was greater where there was greater emphasis on material success. This result is also consistent with the finding that unemployment has a larger deleterious effect on men than on women.

The general evidence on the deleterious impact of unemployment on well-being for developing countries is similar to the evidence reported for industrial countries. For example, in South Africa, Kingdon and Knight (2000) found that well-being was adversely affected by unemployment. They further discovered that even those in the labor force that were not actively seeking employment were as adversely affected as those who were actively seeking work. These results suggest that the "discouraged worker effect" tends to reduce the perceived negative impact of unemployment on well-being. To capture this underestimation phenomenon, some adjustments should be made to the official unemployment rate to reflect labor force dropouts and those who are underemployed. Both of these groups of individuals are also negatively impacted by not being fully employed, and their well-being and happiness are reduced.

6.4 Summary

Layard (2005b) sums up much of the research on happiness. First, he lists five variables that have a negligible impact on well-being and happiness. They are age, gender, looks, education and IQ, although education and IQ might have an indirect and positive impact on happiness by raising income and relative income. He then lists seven factors that stand out in his mind as determinants of well-being and happiness. He lists five that have been quantified by statistical analysis — family relationships; financial situation; work; community and friends; and health. He adds two others — personal freedom and personal values — which are difficult to quantify but which appear to be important in different surveys.

John Helliwell (2003) has developed an index based on survey responses for over 90,000 people in 46 countries that show how happiness is negatively impacted by changes in these variables. His work is summarized in Table 6.8. While the responses for personal freedom are dependent on the specifics of two countries, the results for the other variables are easy to understand. The impact of the level of income is reflected by a large reduction in income of 33 percent, a very unusual and large displacement. Yet, even this dramatic fall is responsible for a relatively small reduction in happiness of two points.

Aside from personal freedom, divorce and separation along with health and unemployment have the most devastating impact on happiness. These results are consistent with much of the review of the literature on happiness discussed in the previous sections of this chapter. The discussion of the social context, of leisure, intuition and the role of social capital and trust reflect the importance of family and community on happiness.

Table 6.8 Effect on Happiness

Variables	Fall in Happiness in Points
Financial situation (family income down by a third)	2
Family relationships	
Divorced rather than married	5
Separated rather than married	8
Widowed rather than married	4
Never married rather than married	4.5
Cohabiting rather than married	2
Work	
Unemployed rather than employed	6
Job insecure rather than secure	3
Unemployment rate up 10 percentage points	3
Community and friends	
"In general people can be trusted". Percentage of citizens saying yes in response to this question down 50 percentage points	1.5
Health	
Subjective health down 1 point on a five-point scale	6
Personal freedom	
Quality of government measured by Belarus (1995) rather than Hungary (1995)	5
Personal values	
"God is important in my life". Answer is no rather than yes.	3.5

Source: Layard (2005b, p. 64).

6.5 Policy Implications

Are there policy implications that can be drawn from the happiness research we just reviewed in Section 6.4? In the discussion that follows, we explore both macroeconomic and microeconomic policies that should be considered if well-being and happiness are to be supported and enhanced by government policy.

6.5.1 *Tax policies*

Layard, Frank and Lane all make persuasive arguments for reorienting general tax and expenditure policy for governments to raise subjective well-being. They argue that we must recognize many of the things that bring happiness are outside the market economy. There are a number of policy adjustments that could be made to increase the supply of these goods and stimulate the appreciation of them. These would make happiness more responsive to choices made in the market. Greater public spending on public goods such as better education, parks and recreational facilities, pollution reduction and other environmental protective measures would be beneficial.

Frank (1999) has gone so far to suggest a shift from income tax to consumption taxes or, alternatively, exempting savings from taxation. This would reduce the level of consumption of conspicuous goods and the money saved could be spent on public goods that raise the spirit of society.

> Milton Friedman and many other free marketers will object to higher taxes in any form, saying that no government bureaucrat ever spends people's money with the same care as they themselves spend it. The best society, in this view, is one in which the largest possible proportion of spending decisions are made at the individual level. We have little reason to doubt Friedman's claim that most people know what pleases them better than bureaucrats do. But this claim simply does not imply that market incentives lead individuals to make choices that are best for all. Indeed, even Friedman concedes that at least some decisions are **not** best left in the hands of individuals — again the most commonly cited examples being those with respect to activities that generate pollution. Yet ordinary consumption is often precisely analogous to activities that generate pollution.... And we have no reason to believe that the stresses people experience in trying to keep up with escalating community consumption standards are any less damaging to their health and longevity than the soot and ozone in the air they breathe (Frank, 1999, pp. 270–271).

Frank, Lane and Layard suggest that taxes on consumption goods should be raised, particularly on luxury items, to cut off such conspicuous consumption. The additional tax revenue generated could be used to provide more parks, better health care, better education, protecting the environment and on more research and development. This shift in the tax burden would be accompanied by a system of incentives to invest in social and physical infrastructure that would support the development of recreation and social interactions that would contribute to greater well-being.

Whether these proposals will be favorably supported by voters is another matter. It stretches the credibility of the argument in some people's view that the nub of the problem and "the real source of our skewed consumption pattern is the gap between individual and group incentives" (Frank, 1999, p. 273).

In assessing this potential shift in resources, it is important to note that the provision of more public goods would not necessarily be subject to diminishing returns. Happiness and well-being may be subject to increasing returns rather than decreasing returns, particularly if we are talking about maintaining an environment where families can enjoy public goods like clean water, parks and forest reserves, clean air and a noise-free setting, to enjoy leisure time together. Since taxes on consumption will close the gap between individual and group preferences, we can therefore be assured, using this line of reasoning, that a consumption tax will make the society better off as a result.

6.5.2 *Happiness and the unemployment–inflation tradeoff*

Macroeconomic policy tends to concentrate on maintaining a balance between the level of unemployment and the rate of inflation. Layard (2005b) discusses the implications of creating a happier society by putting greater emphasis on job security. Since unemployment reduces happiness a lot, more resources should be devoted to maintaining low levels of unemployment.

What are the effects of inflation on happiness? Di Tella *et al.* (2001) cite evidence that suggests inflation has a considerably smaller and less onerous effect on happiness than unemployment. The "misery index", which simply adds the two together, puts too much weight on inflation and too little weight on unemployment. While inflation has a negative impact on well-being, it is not as severe as a corresponding increase in unemployment.

Macroeconomists are fond of using this "misery index" to describe the converse of happiness as it relates to the macroeconomy. Research on happiness suggests that the misery index is quite misleading. This is because unemployment and inflation affect people's happiness levels in different ways. Unemployment has a far greater negative effect on consumers and society in general than inflation. The social stigma of being out of work and the negative effect on feelings of self-worth are quite high when a worker is laid off. This suggests that obtaining unemployment compensations does little to reduce these feelings and increase happiness. The negative impact on social well-being (SWB) is also related to the social norms of the society. The stronger the social norm to be self-sufficient and live from one's own income rather than relying on public assistance, the greater is the negative impact on satisfaction with life (see Stutzer and Lalive, 2001).

Di Tella *et al.* (2001) measure the tradeoff between unemployment and inflation on feelings of SWB and suggest that the weight of unemployment is nearly two times as much as inflation. The implication is that the inflation rate would have to decrease by two percentage points to offset a one percent rise in unemployment.

Others such as Frank (1988) suggest that the tradeoff is even more lopsided, although he does not present any evidence to support this claim. Frank argues that while high levels of inflation can be very unsettling and reduce happiness, the evidence suggests that the adverse impact on happiness is not very large when inflation is low.

These results suggest that macroeconomic policy makers should take a more aggressive stance in reducing unemployment — *perhaps adopting an "unemployment target" rather than an "inflation target" for macroeconomic policy.*

6.5.3 *Raising economic growth by raising well-being*

If happy people are more productive, then raising happiness should also raise productivity and income. Charles Kenny (1999) suggests that happiness does cause growth to accelerate. His theory is supported by time series data on happiness and GDP growth for a series of OECD countries. One powerful argument that supports this inference is that happiness and trust (see more on trust in Chapter 7) are correlated, and that greater trust and happiness leads to social cohesiveness and more rapid growth. Another argument states that many of the costs, including moral hazard, cut throat competition, free riders, high transactions costs, corruption, principal/agent problems and crime that arise in an unhappy society lacking trust will be ameliorated and lead to stronger and more efficient growth if members of a society are happy and trust each other. If these arguments are true, then policies that increase the general level of well-being will also increase the rate of income growth. Notice that similar arguments were made in Chapter 5 with respect to cooperation and altruism, and their impact on economic growth.

6.5.4 *Improved governance*

It is logical to think that people living under a repressive and controlling authoritarian regime are less likely to be happy than in a democracy and there is some evidence to support this statement. Open and transparent economic systems are correlated with greater happiness (see Frey and Stutzer, 2002a, b; Veenhoven, 2000). Graphs that plot well-being against measures of democracy and freedom show very strong positive correlations and these correlations are stronger than plots of well-being and income. There is a possibility, however, that the strength of this relationship may depend to some extent upon extreme values. There is a very large middle ground where it may be difficult to say whether the form and nature of government has a very strong effect on happiness or subjective well-being.

Certainly there is evidence that Russian citizens were unhappy under the repressive Soviet system. The repressive regimes of Idi Amin and Pol Pot also created a large measure of unhappiness. In more benign cases, the positive relationship between happiness and freedom is strong although not overwhelming. Happiness levels are around 3.5 (out of a possible 4) in the most open and democratic societies and around 3 in those that are less free and more authoritarian (Veenhoven, 2000).

6.5.5 *Lifestyle*

Someone once suggested a hedonistic paradox — those seeking happiness never find it, while a person who helps others attains happiness right away. If goods do not make us happy, what does? Or perhaps the natural hard wiring makes it difficult or not possible to achieve happiness through our action. This existentialist view was very popular in Europe in the 1920s and 1930s, in the works of Sartre and Camus. These are the characteristics of people we found in the fatalistic group in Figure 1.1 in Chapter 1. However, there is evidence that some things do bring lasting happiness and subjective well-being to many people.

Layard (2005b) and Lane (2000) both talk about the importance of developing a sound philosophy of life, reducing stress, enjoying leisure, friends and family, and nature. They also talk about developing a moral sense of values and about being cooperative and friendly to others. There is, however, very little hard evidence to suggest that these attitudes and practices lead to happiness. The difficulty is in quantifying what "a sound philosophy of life" might be and also how to measure "enjoyment of leisure, friends and family". Nevertheless, it is true that happiness research shows that enjoying friends and family are ranked high in promoting a higher level of SWB by those interviewed. Furthermore, the material in Section 6.3.17 suggests that cultivating intuition and getting in touch with the process of flow can increase decision making efficiency as well as raise levels of well-being.

Lane's (2000) analysis is convincing and backed by a number of studies. His argument is simple. Most of the responses to questionnaires about whether people are happy or what gives them pleasure revolved around congenial and pleasurable relationships with family, workmates and friends. Satisfaction with the experience of work — the environment, the challenge and other subjective characteristics also figured high on the list. From this, Lane infers that subjective well-being is not primarily a result of the utilitarian calculus of goods. It is more related to what Frank calls *"inconspicuous" consumption — "freedom from traffic congestion, time with family and friends, vacation time and a variety of favorable job characteristics"* (Frank, 1999, p. 90). One study found that the number of friends recorded on a questionnaire was the best indicator of subjective well-being. Evidence from similar studies suggests that interactions with people, usually outside work, provides the most satisfaction and increases SWB (see Tables 6.4 and 6.7).

Both Lane and Frank argue that society should put more resources into those kinds of goods and services that support the ability of citizens to interact with others to enjoy a rich social life and to reduce their striving to compete with others to accumulate more consumer goods. Frank argues that by spending less on conspicuous consumption — big houses, expensive cars, lots of appliances — and more on these "inconspicuous" items such as better air quality, more urban parks, cleaner water, reduction in crime and medical research to extend life, happiness will be enhanced (Frank, 1999, p. 90).

This analysis by Frank and Lane is based on a compilation of results and averages for large numbers of respondents to questionnaires. When we ask the question "Are people the best judges of their own well-being?", the answer is more complex. Certainly, this analysis would lead us to believe that if people generally knew what made them happy, they would get off the money making treadmill and work fewer hours in less stressful jobs. Yet most people continue to run on the money treadmill. The most time spent is on activities such as work which are the least satisfying. After work, time spent watching television occupies the most time, along with relaxing, yet it offers less pleasure than spending time with friends and relatives (recall Tables 6.4 and 6.7).

David Niven (2000) reviewed over a thousand studies written by psychologists and other social scientists in the 1990s that explored the characteristics and beliefs of happy people. He distilled these into 100 aphorisms. Nearly 40 percent of these aphorisms had to do with the importance of relationships (friends and family) and leisure. The pursuit of higher income figured as a negative impact on happiness. Some of the keys to happiness headings, not necessarily mutually exclusive, were: Don't confuse "stuff" with success; Keep your family close; Be socially supportive; Join a group; Share with others how important they are to you; Cultivate friendships.

There are other studies that have explored individual social characteristics that contribute most strongly to a happy outlook on life.

Chris Peterson (2003) has devised tests to measure a person's personality strengths. His preliminary analysis suggests that curiosity, zest, gratitude, hope and love are more highly correlated with life satisfaction than some of the other qualities. Seligman (2002) uses visualization and other positive feedback techniques to emphasize the positive aspects of experience and also stresses replacing negative thoughts with positive thoughts. Myers and Diener (1995) found that feeling in control of life's circumstances is strongly related to a positive feeling of well-being. Other characteristics such as strongly positive feelings of self-worth, optimism and extroverted personalities are also highly correlated with happiness.

Fordyce (1988) suggests 14 fundamentals of happiness — be active and keep busy; spend more time socializing; be productive and meaningful at work; get better organized and plan things out; stop worrying; lower your expectations and aspirations; develop positive and optimistic thinking; focus on the present moment; work on a healthy personality; develop an outgoing social personality; be yourself; eliminate negative feelings; develop close interpersonal relationships; and put happiness as your number one goal.

Putting all of these studies together, we observe that while there are some differences in emphasis, subjective well-being is highly correlated with a few basically universal characteristics such as:

- being engaged in life;
- having a positive attitude toward life's experiences;
- putting less focus on possessions;
- bringing focus on the here and now;
- developing a rich social life; and
- attaining some measure of spiritual/religious commitment and faith.

A full analysis to answer the question of how people become attuned to their own well-being and adjust their action accordingly is beyond the scope of this chapter. One thing which is clear is that the answer is not the same for everyone. Introspection may work for some people, while others are naturally good-natured and might be better off just winging it and using their intuition. In some cases it may also be true that goods substitute for emotional needs which have not been met, and reducing them could exacerbate unhappiness.

An approach that would have merit for most people contains several components. First, periodic contemplation and reflection are proven to be useful practices to get in better touch with what is valuable in our lives. These periods of quiet thought are ways to get off the daily treadmill and competitive routine that has become the "normal" way of life for most of us.

Second, it is important to consider the relationship between happiness and the broad idea of "right action" or the virtues. In the tradition of Socrates, people seeking wisdom, contentment and happiness should reflect and deliberate how to develop and refine desirable character traits such as compassion, understanding, friendliness and steadiness of mind. These virtues contribute to well-being and feelings of happiness. When cultivated over a lifetime, these virtues support us and help us make the kinds of economic choices that will contribute rather than subtract from our "happiness coefficient".

You may be one of those people for whom happiness and consumption are closely related. If this is the case, perhaps you can just go on the way you have been and enjoy life as it unfolds — buying all the new consumption goods that come on the market each year.

Lastly, it is important to consider the social context. Social capital and private capital can be accumulated and developed. We can move to a community where the level of social capital is higher and through our own efforts we can build up and sustain our own levels of personal capital. The sense of individual accomplishment and social cohesion that comes from attaining a modicum of emotional stability, feeling of belonging to a community and a deep sense of job satisfaction can go a long way in raising the level of subjective well-being and happiness.

In concluding this section, we might offer a series of suggestions for leading a happy life both for a society and for individuals living in that society:

- Live in a democratic and stable political environment where income per capita is high enough to meet basic needs and social policy protects against poverty.
- Live in an environment where the social network supports the ability to form social bonds and friendships and where family values are supported.

- Live in a society where the work environment is supportive and not confrontational and where work is interesting, challenging and income adequate.
- Live in a society with good medical benefits, including mental as well as physical health.
- Have important goals related to your own values.
- Adopt a philosophy or religion that provides intention, guidelines, purpose and meaning in your life.

6.5.6 *Development of happiness indicators*

Many of the impacts of economic and social change on happiness are not captured by the current array of social and economic indicators. The usual economic indicators that stress GNP/GDP, unemployment and inflation, exchange rates, monetary growth and budget and international deficits have been recently supplemented by measures of social progress, as exemplified by the human development report of the United Nations, which puts emphasis on education, life expectancy, infant mortality, poverty, women's issues and discrimination.

However, these measures fall short of directly reflecting the subjective measures of well-being of individuals in society. Health expenditures, particularly mental health expenditures, are going up and this is reflected in a growing GDP. Expenditures on prisons, crime prevention and the justice system, consumption of alcohol, cigarettes and illegal substances are going up and this is reflected in growing GDP. Defense spending is going up and this is also reflected in a growing GDP. Environmental protection expenditures are going up and this is reflected in a growing GDP. Yet in all of these cases, growing expenditures could reflect a diminution in the perceived well-being of society.

We have seen time and time again in our review of the literature on psychology and sociology that social relationships are a key ingredient in having a happy life. Family and friends are important in achieving a feeling of well-being. Yet students are likely to be unable to obtain any information about the social environment that they are likely to encounter when looking for a job. There are oodles of material on wages and benefits, but

> very little information about how meaningful or engaging particular jobs will be. Indeed, because of the lack of systematic well-being indicators, young adults might not systematically compare professions and consider how engaging the work is or how much stress is involved. If they do consider how engaging, meaningful or stressful the work is, they are likely to have garnered this information from a favorite television drama series rather than from systematic research findings (Diener and Seligman, 2004, p. 22).

Consider for example the kinds of questions that are stimulated by alternative economic and well-being approaches that are suggested in Table 6.9. We know that economic models are constructed on the assumption that actions arise from this approach. Individuals choose among alternatives to maximize their well-being. However, if individuals are not aware of the alternatives and, in some cases, do not realize what would enhance their well-being because of a lack of data or inefficient use of data they have, then a more useful set of data on the benefits and drawbacks of different alternatives based on well-being indicators might be useful. A set of well-being indicators would make it easier for people to make choices that increase well-being. These choices might not necessarily yield the largest salary or the highest level of savings.

Having well-being indicators would also allow researchers to look at well-being and consumption patterns to see how they are related. In this way, more concrete statements could be made about some of the questions raised earlier concerning prisons, defense spending, and consumption of alcohol, cigarettes, banned substances and environmental abuse.

It could be that societies that have put so much emphasis on worker productivity and ways to increase it have lost their focus on what a society should be aiming to do. By developing a series of indicators of well-being, we can at least give people alternative choices to focus on. As we have noted above, people who are happy and well-adjusted and who have a high level of well-being are generally more

Table 6.9 Types of Questions Stimulated by Economic versus Well-Being Approaches

Domain	Economic Approach	Well-Being Approach
Society	How can government stimulate economic growth? How does central bank policy affect unemployment and inflation?	How does economic growth influence well-being?
Income	How does income inequality affect economic growth? How do tax rates influence economic growth?	Does income inequality influence well-being?
Work	How does pay influence productivity? What are the causes of unemployment?	How does unemployment influence well-being? What makes a job enjoyable and engaging? Are happy workers more or less productive than unhappy workers?
Physical health	How much is productivity reduced by illness? What are the monetary costs and benefits of various treatments for diseases?	Do individuals who report high well-being have better health than those who report low well-being? What illness most interferes with health?
Mental disorders	How do mental disorders interfere with productivity? How costly are mental disorders to society?	How much misery do mental disorders cause? Does therapy enhance the well-being of persons with mental disorders?
Social relationships	How do couples jointly determine their participation in the labor market? How are resources distributed within a household?	Why are married people on average happier than unmarried people? How does geographic mobility influence well-being?
*Defense	How does defense spending influence income and government budgets?	What are the social consequences of war and war preparedness?

Source: Diener and Seligman (2004, Table 2) and *augmented with authors' comments.

productive at work and in society than those who are unhappy and maladjusted.

Basically, the index of economic well-being has four basic components — consumption flows, wealth stocks, income distribution and economic security. These are then broken down into different sub-components which are aggregated to give a time series for each of the components.

Looking at these variables over time for the US, Canada and other OECD countries, Osberg and Sharpe (2003) show that while income per capita has been increasing rapidly for the past 25 years or so, other variables pertinent for well-being have not been increasing. In some cases, variables like economic security and measure of inequality have been declining. When these variables are aggregated into an index along with income per capita, there have been only slight increases between 1980 and 2001 for the US and Great Britain. Where this index grows slowly, measures of subjective well-being have also grown slowly or stagnated.

This evidence suggests that perhaps we are looking at the wrong income series when investigating whether income and subjective well-being are related. Maybe we should be incorporating more aspects of income distribution and security in addition to income per capita when devising measures of economic well-being. It is important to include them when devising policies to improve well-being, particularly issues such as economic inequality and insecurity. We have noted in our analysis of happiness that economic and social security and placement in the income distribution are matters that impact negatively on subjective well-being. So in this respect, happiness research and broad measures of economic well-being go hand in hand.

6.5.7 *A final note of caution*

In this chapter, we have noted that happiness and the consumption of goods are not highly correlated in large groups of individuals in high-income societies. From these general observations, we have made several points and policy suggestions regarding ways that the happiness quotient or social well-being (SWB) can be lifted.

To implement these recommendations, we have to be clear that by making these adjustments to public policy, the level of SWB will indeed be lifted. The evidence that this will happen is more tenuous and limited. Indeed, few societies have attempted to undertake adjustments in policies that make large adjustments in the mix of social and private goods. Comparing Europe with the US, we observe a distinctly higher level of government spending and provision of social services in Europe. Yet this is not reflected in a higher level of SWB as indicated by consumer surveys. It could be that lifting the index of SWB requires a concerted effort on a number of different fronts, not simply in the provision of more public goods. It is also possible that government policies are not the most effective method of raising SWB. Aside from providing better health facilities and redirecting data collection analysis efforts to providing better information on SWB and related variables, it may be prudent for individuals and the communities in which they live to take responsibility for other initiatives to raise SWB. These are points that must be debated and discussed within each country and community.

Appendix: Data Sources for Happiness Research

European data is collected by various research firms within the European Community under the direction of the European Commission. This data source has been used by the researchers conducting an analysis of happiness and subjective well-being including Di Tella *et al.* (2001, 2003), Blanchflower and Oswald (2002) and Frey and Stutzer (2002a, b). Di Tella *et al.* report results from a sample of 271,224 respondents from European countries from 1975 to 1992, while Blanchflower and Oswald (2000) report results for over 54,000 respondents in Great Britain between 1975 and 1998, also using Eurobarometer surveys. Clark and Oswald (1996) also report results for a sample of over 5,000 workers in Great Britain.

In the US, most researchers have relied upon information gathered by National Research Center at the University of Chicago.

Di Tella *et al.*'s report results for over 25,000 observations for the years 1972 to 1994. The regression results from these studies are typically obtained from ordered probit or logit models with a number of controls introduced for the impact of the independent variables such as income, marital status, race, age, employed or unemployed and models with a number of controls for other variables.

To study well-being on a world scale, the data set assembled by Inglehart *et al.* (2000) in the World Value Surveys and European Values Surveys 1981–1984, 1990–1993, 1995–1997 ICPSR version, Ann Arbor Michigan, Institute for Social Research and Inter-university Consortium for Political and Social Research, has been used by a number of researchers including Helliwell (2003).

There are also a number of articles on happiness in the *Journal of Happiness Studies*, and further references are available at http://www.eur.nl/fsw/research/happiness/. The various dimensions of happiness are explored and particular attention is paid to the measurement of happiness and subjective well-being. Veenhoven (2000) introduces four measures of happiness: livability of the environment, livability of the individual, external utility of life and internal utility of life. By breaking down happiness in this way, Veenhoven hopes to be able to isolate the different aspects of emotional, psychological and environmental factors that contribute to happiness.

Bibliography

Alesina, A.F., R. Di Tella and R. MacCulloch (2001) Inequality and Happiness: Are Europeans and Americans Different? Harvard University, Department of Economics, Harvard Business School-Business, Government and the International Economy Unit and Princeton University-Center for Health and Well-Being.

Andrews, F.M. and J.P. Robinson (1991) Measures of Subjective Well-Being. In J.P. Robinson, P.R. Shaver and L.S. Wrightsman (eds.), *Measures of Personality and Social Psychological Attitudes* (pp. 61–114). San Diego, CA: Academic Press.

Argyle, M. (1987) *The Psychology of Happiness*. London: Methuen.

Argyle, M. (1999) Causes and Correlates of Happiness. In D. Kahneman, E. Diener and N. Schwarz (eds.), *Well-Being: The Foundations of Hedonic Psychology* (pp. 353–373). New York: Russel Sage Foundation.

Austin, J.H. (1998) *Zen and the Brain: Toward an Understanding of Meditation and Consciousness*. Cambridge, MA: MIT Press.

Barasch, M.I. (2005) *Field Notes on the Compassionate Life: A Search for the Soul of Kindness.* Emmaus, PA: Rodale Press.

Baumeister, R.F. (1991) *Escaping the Self: Alcoholism, Spirituality, Masochism, and Other Flights from the Burden of Selfhood.* New York: Basic Books.

Baumeister, R.F. and D.M. Tice (1990) Anxiety and Social Exclusion. *Journal of Social and Clinical Psychology*, 9, 165–195.

Bentham, J. (1824/1987) An Introduction to the Principles of Morals and Legislation. In J.S. Mill and J. Bentham (eds.), *Utilitarianism and Other Essays.* Harmandsworth: Penguin.

Black, S.E. and L.M. Lynch (2004) What's Driving the New Economy? The Benefits of Workplace Innovation. *Economic Journal*, 114, 97–116.

Blanchflower, D.G. and A.J. Oswald (2000) Well-Being Over Time in Britain and the USA. NBER Working Paper No. 7487.

Blanchflower, D.G. and A.J. Oswald (2002) Unemployment, Well-Being and Wage Curves in Eastern Europe. *Journal of Japanese and International Economies*, 15, 364–402.

Blanchflower, D.G. and A.J. Oswald (2004a) Money, Sex and Happiness: An Empirical Study. *Scandinavian Journal of Economics*, 106(3), 393–415.

Blanchflower, D.G and A.J. Oswald (2004b) Well-Being Over Time in Britain and the USA. *Journal of Public Economics*, 88(7), 1359–1386.

Camerer, C., G. Loewenstein and D. Prelec (2005) Neuroeconomics: How Neuroscience Can Inform Economics. *Journal of Economic Literature*, XLII(March), 9–64.

Camerer, C., G. Loewenstein and M. Rabin (eds.) (2003) *Advances in Behavioral Economics.* Princeton, NJ: Princeton University Press.

Campbell, III, C. (1993) Do Firms Pay Efficiency Wages? Evidence with Data at the Firm Level. *Journal of Labor Economics*, 11, 442–470.

Clark, A.E. and A. Oswald (1994) Unhappiness and Unemployment. *Economic Journal*, 104, 648–659.

Clark, A.E. and A. Oswald (1996) Satisfaction and Comparison Income. *Journal of Public Economics*, 61, 359–381.

Crafts, N. (1996) East Asian Growth Before and After the Crisis. IMF Working Paper No. 98/137.

Cross-National Collaborative Group (1992) The Changing Rate of Major Depression: Cross-National Comparisons. *Journal of the American Medical Association*, 268(21), 3098–3114.

Csikszentmihalyi, M. (1975) *Beyond Boredom and Anxiety.* San Francisco: Jossey-Bass Publishers.

Csikszentmihalyi, M. (1997) *Finding Flow: The Psychology of Engagement with Everyday Life.* New York: Basic Books.

Csikszentmihalyi, M., B. Schneider, E. Steele and D.J. Shernoff (2003) Student Engagement in High School Classrooms from the Perspective of Flow Theory. *School Psychology Quarterly*, 18, 158–176.

Damasio, A. (1994) *Descartes' Error: Emotion, Reason, and the Human Brain.* New York: Putnam.

Damasio, A. (2000) *The Feeling of What Happens: Body and Emotion in the Making of Consciousness.* London: W. Heinemann.

Damasio, A. (2003) *Looking for Spinoza: Joy, Sorrow, and the Feeling Brain.* Orlando: Harcourt.

Davidson, R.J., J. Kabat-Zinn, J. Schumacher, M. Rosenkranz, D. Muller, S.F. Santorelli *et al.* (2003) Alterations in Brain and Immune Function Produced by Mindfulness Meditation. *Psychosomatic Medicine,* 65, 564–570.

Davis, J., T. Smith and P.V. Marsden (2001) *General Social Surveys, 1972–2000, Cumulative Codebook.* Storrs, CT: The Roper Center for Public Opinion Research.

Di Tella, R., R.J. MacCulloch and A.J. Oswald (2001) The Macroeconomics of Happiness. The Warwick Economics Research Paper Series (TWERPS). http://econpapers.repec.org/paper/wrkwarwec/615.htm [Retrieved 21 January 2006].

Di Tella, R., R.J. MacCulloch and A.J. Oswald (2003) The Macroeconomics of Happiness. *The Review of Economics and Statistics,* 85(4), 809–827.

Diener, E. and S. Oishi (2000) Money and Happiness: Income and Subjective Well-Being Across Nations. In E. Diener and E.M. Suh (eds.), *Culture and Subjective Well-Being* (pp. 185–218). Cambridge, MA: MIT Press.

Diener, E. and M.E.P. Seligman (2002) Very Happy People. *Psychological Science,* 13, 80–83.

Diener, E. and M.E.P. Seligman (2004) Beyond Money: Toward an Economy of Well-Being. *Psychological Science in the Public Interest,* 5(5), 1–30.

Diener, E. and E. Suh (1999) National Differences in Subjective Well-Being. In D. Kahneman, E. Diener and N. Schwarz (eds.), *Well-Being: The Foundations of Hedonic Psychology* (pp. 434–450). New York: Russell Sage Foundation.

Diener, E., M. Diener and C. Diener (1995) Factors Predicting the Subjective Well-Being of Nations. *Journal of Personality and Social Psychology,* 69, 851–864.

Diener, E., E.M. Suh, R.E. Lucas and H.L. Smith (1999) Subjective Well-Being: Three Decades of Progress. *Psychological Bulletin,* 125(2), 276–303.

Dowling, J.M. and C.-F. Yap (2005) Determinants of Well-Being: Evidence from World Value Surveys. Singapore Management University Working Paper.

Duesenberry, J. (1949) *Income, Saving and the Theory of Consumer Behavior.* Cambridge: Harvard University Press.

Easterlin, R.A. (2001a) Income and Happiness: Towards a Unified Theory. *Economic Journal,* 111, 465–484.

Easterlin, R.A. (2001b) Life Cycle Welfare: Trends and Differences. *Journal of Happiness Studies,* 2, 1–12.

Easterlin, R.A. (2004) The Economics of Happiness. *Daedalus,* 133(2), 26–33.

Easterlin, R.A. (2005) Is There an Iron Law of Happiness? IEPR Working Paper 05.8, Institute of Policy Research, University of Southern California. http://www.usc.edu/iepr [Retrieved 20 June 2005].

Easterlin, R.A. (2006) Building a Better Theory of Well-Being. In L. Bruni and P.L. Porta (eds.), *Economics and Happiness: Framing the Analysis* (pp. 29–64). New York: Oxford University Press.

Elster, J. (1998) Emotions and Economic Theory. *Journal of Economic Literature*, 36(1), 47–74.

Eurobarometer Surveys. http://ec.europa.eu/public_opinion/index_en.htm [Retrieved 20 May 2005].

Ferrer-i-Carbonell, A. and P. Frojters (2004) How Important is Methodology for the Estimates of the Determinants of Happiness? *The Economic Journal*, 114, 641–659.

Fordyce, M. (1988) A Review of Research on Happiness Measures: A Sixty Second Index of Happiness and Mental Health. *Social Indicators Research*, 20, 355–381.

Frank, R.H. (1988) *Passions within Reason: The Strategic Role of the Emotions.* New York: W.W. Norton.

Frank, R.H. (1999) *Luxury Fever: Money and Happiness in an Era of Excess.* Princeton: Princeton University Press.

Frey, B.S. and A. Stutzer (2000) Happiness, Economy and Institutions. *The Economic Journal*, 110, 918–938.

Frey, B.S. and A. Stutzer (2001) *Happiness and Economics: How the Economy and Institutions Affect Well-Being.* Princeton: Princeton University Press.

Frey, B.S. and A. Stutzer (2002a) The Economics of Happiness. *World Economics*, 3(1), 25–41.

Frey, B.S. and A. Stutzer (2002b) What Can Economists Learn from Happiness Research? *Journal of Economic Literature*, 40(2), 402–435.

Friedman, M. (1957) *A Theory of the Consumption Function.* Chicago: University of Chicago Press.

Fukuyama, F. (1995) *Trust: The Social Virtues and the Creation of Prosperity.* New York: Free Press.

Gilbert, D.T. and T.D. Wilson (2000) Miswanting: Some Problems in the Forecasting of Future Affective States. In J. Forgas (ed.), *Thinking and Feeling: The Role of Affect in Social Cognition.* Cambridge: Cambridge University Press.

Gilovich, T. (1991) *How Do We Know What Isn't So: The Fallibility of Human Reason in Everyday Life.* New York: The Free Press.

Graham, C. and S. Pettinato (2002) *Happiness and Hardship: Opportunity and Insecurity in New Market Economies.* Washington, DC: Brookings Institution.

Graham, C., A. Eggers and S. Sukhtankar (2003) Does Happiness Pay? An Exploration Based on Panel Data from Russia. Paper presented at Brookings/Warwick Conference on Why Inequality Matters: Lessons for Policy from the Economics of Happiness.

Hagerty, M.R. (2000) Social Comparisons of Income in One's Community: National Surveys of Income and Happiness. *Journal of Personality and Social Psychology*, 78, 746–771.

Hamilton, B., J.A. Nickerson and H. Owan (2003) Diversity and Productivity. In Production Teams, Mimeo. Washington University, St. Louis.

Harter, J.K., F.L. Schmidt and T.L. Hayes (2002) Business-Unit-Level Relationship between Employee Satisfaction, Employee Engagement, and Business Outcomes: A Meta-Analysis Pro. *Journal of Applied Psychology*, 87(2), 268–279.

Helliwell, J.F. (2003) How's Life? Combining Individual and National Variables to Explain Subjective Well-Being. *Economic Modelling*, 20, 331–360.

Helliwell, J.F. (2005) Well-Being, Social Capital and Public Policy: What's New? NBER Working Paper No. 11807.

Herrigel, E. (1953) *Zen in the Art of Archery* (originally, *Zen in der Kunst des Bogenschiessens*, 1948). Translated by R.F.C. Hull with an introduction by D.T. Suzuki. New York: Pantheon Books.

Hirsch, F. (1976) *The Social Limits to Growth*. Cambridge, Mass: Harvard University Press.

Holmes, T.H. and R.H. Rahe (1967) The Social Readjustment Rating Scale. *Journal of Psycosomatic Research*, 11, 213–318.

Inglehart, R. (1990) *Culture Shift in Advanced Industrial Society*. Princeton: Princeton University Press.

Inglehart, R. and H. Klingemann (2000) Genes, Culture, Democracy, and Happiness. In E. Diener and E.M. Suh (eds.), *Culture and Subjective Well-Being*. Cambridge: MIT Press.

Inglehart, R. *et al.* (2000) World Value Surveys and European Values Surveys 1981–1984, 1990–1993, 1995–1997. ICPSR version. Ann Arbor Michigan, Institute for Social Research and Inter-university Consortium for Political and Social Research.

Kahneman, D. and A. Tversky (1979) Prospect Theory: An Analysis of Decision under Risk. *Econometrica*, 47, 263–291.

Kahneman, D., J. Knetsch and R. Thaler (1991) The Endowment Effect, Loss Aversion, and Status Quo Bias: Anomalies. *Journal of Economic Perspectives*, 5(1) 193–206.

Kahneman, D., P. Slovic and A. Tversky (eds.) (1982) *Judgment under Uncertainty: Heuristics and Biases*. Cambridge: Cambridge University Press.

Kahneman, D., A.B. Krueger, D. Schkade, N. Schwarz and A. Stone (2004a) Toward National Well-Being Accounts. *American Economic Review*, 94(2) 429–434.

Kahneman, D., A.B. Krueger, D. Schkade, N. Schwarz and A.A. Stone (2004b) A Survey Method for Characterizing Daily Life Experience: The Day Reconstruction Method (DRM). *Science*, 1776–1780.

Kasser, T. and A.D. Kanner (eds.) (2004) *Psychology and Consumer Culture: The Struggle for a Good Life in a Materialistic Culture*. Washington, DC: APA Books.

Kenny, C. (1999) Does Growth Cause Happiness, Or Does Happiness Cause Growth? *Kyklos*, 52(1), 3–26.

Kingdon, G. and J. Knight (2000) Are Searching and Non-Searching Unemployment Distinct States when Unemployment is High? The Case of South Africa. Working Paper Series 2002–2. Center for the Study of African Economies, Economics Department, University of Oxford.

Kirkcaldy, B.D., A. Furnham and T. Martin (1998) National Differences in Personality, Socio-Economic, and Work-Related Attitudinal Variables. *European Psychologist*, 3, 255–262.

Konow, J. (2003) Which Is the Fairest One of All? A Positive Analysis of Justice Theories. *Journal of Economic Literature*, 41(4), 1188–1239.

Lane, R.E. (2000) *The Loss of Happiness in Market Democracies*. New Haven: Yale University Press.

Layard, R. (2005a) Happiness and Public Policy. LSE Health and Social Care Discussion Paper No. 14. LSE Health and Social Care, The London School of Economics and Political Science.

Layard, R. (2005b) *Happiness: Lessons from a New Science*. New York: Penguin Press.

Loewenstein, G. (2004) Out of Control: Visceral Influences on Behavior. In C. Camerer, G. Loewenstein and M. Rabin (eds.), *Advances in Behavioral Economics*. Princeton, NJ: Princeton University Press.

Luthar, S.S. (2003) The Culture of Affluence: Psychological Costs of Material Wealth. *Child Development*, 74, 1581–1593.

Lykken, D.T. (2000) *Happiness: The Nature and Nurture of Joy and Contentment*. Golden Guides from St. Martin's Press.

Lyubomirsky, S. (1994) http://faculty.ucr.edu/~sonja/ [Retrieved 18 May 2005].

Lyubomirsky, S. (2001) Why are Some People Happier than Others? The Role of Cognitive and Motivational Processes in Well-Being. *American Psychologist*, 56, 239–249.

Maslow, A. (1968) *Toward a Psychology of Being*. Princeton, NJ: Van Nostrand.

McAdams, D.P. (1985) Motivation and Friendship. In S. Duck and D. Perlman (eds.), *Understanding Personal Relationships: An Interdisciplinary Approach*. Beverly Hills, CA: Sage.

McCabe, K., D. Houser, L. Ryan, V. Smith and T. Trouard (2001) A Functional Imaging Study of Cooperation in Two-Person Reciprocal Exchange. In *Proceedings of the National Academy of Sciences USA*, 98(20), 11832–11835. Interdisciplinary Center for Economic Science, George Mason University.

McCrady, B., R. Stout, N. Noel, D. Abrams and H. Nelson (1991) Comparative Effectiveness of Three Types of Spouse Involved Alcohol Treatment: Outcomes 18 Months After Treatment. *British Journal of Addiction*, 86, 1415–1424.

McEvily, B., R. Weber, C. Bicchiere and V. Ho (2003) Can Groups be Trusted? An Experimental Study of Collective Trust. CMU Working Paper. http://www.andrew.emu/user/rwe-ber/CollectiveTrust10.pdf [Retrieved 21 May 2005].

McEwen, B.S. and T. Seeman (1999) Protective and Damaging Effects of Mediators of Stress: Elaborating and Testing the Concept of Allostasis and Allostatic Load. *Annals of the New York Academy of Science*, 896, 30–47.

Mill, J.S. (1980) *On Liberty*. Indianapolis: Bobbs-Merrill.

Miner, A.G. (2001) Experience Sampling Events, Moods, Behavior and Performance at Work. Unpublished doctoral dissertation, University of Illinois, Urbana, IL.

Mullainathan, S. (1998) A Memory-Based Model of Bounded Rationality. *Quarterly Journal of Economics*, 117 (3), 735–774.

Myers, D.G. and E. Diener (1995) Who is Happy? *Psychological Science*, 6(1), 10–19.

Nettle, D. (2005) *Happiness: The Science behind your Smile.* Oxford: Oxford University Press.

Ng, Y.K. (2002a) The East-Asian Happiness Gap: Speculating on Causes and Implications. *Pacific Economic Review*, 7(1), 51–63.

Ng, Y.K. (2002b) Economic Policies in the Light of Happiness Studies with Reference to Singapore. *Singapore Economic Review*, 47(2), 199–212.

Ng, Y.K. (2003) From Preference to Happiness: Towards a More Complete Welfare Economics. *Social Choice and Welfare*, 20, 307–350.

Niven, D. (2000) *The 100 Simple Secrets of Happy People: What Scientists Have Learned and How You Can Use It.* San Francisco: Harper.

Osberg, L. and A. Sharpe (2003) Human Well-Being and Economic Well-Being: What Values are Implicit in Current Indices? Paper presented at WIDER Conference on Inequality, Poverty and Human Well-Being at the annual meeting of the Canadian Economic Association, Carleton University, Ottawa, Ontario, 30 May–1 June.

Oswald, A.J. (1997) Happiness and Economic Performance. *Economic Journal*, 107(445), 1815–1831.

Oswald, A., R. Di Tella and R. MacCulloch (2001) Preferences Over Inflation and Unemployment: Evidence from Surveys of Happiness. *American Economic Review*, 91, 335–341.

Packer, S., J. Husted, S. Cohen and G. Tomlinson (1997) Psychopathology and Quality of Life. *Journal of Psychiatry and Neuroscience*, 22, 231–234.

Palmore, E. (1969) Predicting Longevity: A Follow-Up Controlling for Age. *Journal of Gerontology*, 39, 109–116.

Pavot, W. and E. Diener (1993) The Affective and Cognitive Context of Self-Reported Measure of Subjective Well-Being. *Social Indicators Research*, 28(1), 1–20.

Peterson, C. (2003) Values in Action Structured Interview of Strengths. Mimeo, University of Michigan. http://www.viastrengths.org/pdfs/VIAStructuredInterview. pdf [Retrieved 1 January 2005].

Pirsig, R. (1974) *Zen and the Art of Motorcycle Maintenance: An Inquiry into Values*, 10th Ed. New York: William Morrow.

Price, S.J. and P.C. McKenry (1988) *Divorce.* Beverly Hills, CA: Sage.

Putnam, R.D. (1993) *Making Democracy Work: Civic Traditions in Modern Italy.* Princeton: Princeton University Press.

Putnam, R.D. (2001) *Bowling Alone: The Collapse and Revival of American Community.* New York: Simon & Schuster.

Ryff, C.D. (1995) Psychological Well-Being in Adult Life. *Current Directions in Psychological Science*, 4, 99–104.

Sanfey, A.G., J.K. Rilling, J.A. Aronson, L.E. Nystrom and J.D. Cohen (2003) The Neural Basis of Economic Decision Making in the Ultimatum Game. *Science*, 300(5626), 1755–1758.

Schwarz, N. Day Reconstruction Method. http://sitemaker.umich.edu/norbert.schwarz/day_reconstruction_method [Retrieved 1 January 2006].

Scitovsky, T. (1976) *The Joyless Economy: An Inquiry into Human Satisfaction and Consumer Dissatisfaction*, Revised edition (1992). Oxford: Oxford University Press.

Seligman, J.S. (1997) Social Security: A Regulatory History with Comparative Benefit Expense Measures. Paper presented at The All-UC Conference in Economic History, University of California, Davis.

Seligman, M.E.P. (2002) *Authentic Happiness: Using the New Positive Psychology to Realize Your Potential for Lasting Fulfillment.* New York: Free Press.

Shefrin, H. (2002) *Beyond Greed and Fear: Understanding Behavioral Finance and the Psychology of Investing.* Oxford: Oxford University Press.

Shefrin, H. and M. Statman (1985) The Disposition to Sell Winners Too Early and Ride Losers Too Long: Theory and Evidence. *Journal of Finance*, 40(3), 777–782.

Shepard, P. (1996) *Traces of an Omnivore.* Washington, DC: Island Press.

Slovic, P. (1984) Facts vs. Fears: Understanding Perceived Risks. Science and Public Policy Seminar, Federation of Behavioral, Psychological and Cognitive Sciences, Washington, DC.

Smith, A. (1776) In E. Cannan (ed.), *An Inquiry into the Nature and Causes of the Wealth of Nations*, 5th Ed. London: Methuen and Co. Ltd., 1904.

Spector, P.E. (1997) *Job Satisfaction: Application, Assessment, Cause and Consequences.* California: Sage Publications.

Spitzer, R.L., K. Kroenke, R. Linzer, S.R. Hahn, J.B. Williams, F.V. deGruy, D. Bridy and M. Davies (1995) Health-Related Quality of Life in Primary Care Patients with Mental Disorders. *Journal of the American Medical Association*, 274, 1511–1517.

Srinivasan, R. and A. Pugliese (2000) Customer Satisfaction, Loyalty and Behavior. *The Gallup Research Journal*, 3(1), 79–90.

Srivastava, A., E.A. Locke and K.M. Barto (2001) Money and Subjective Well-Being: It's Not the Money, It's the Motives. *Journal of Personality and Social Psychology*, 80(6), 959–971.

Sternberg, R.J. (1986) A Triangular Theory of Love. *Psychological Review*, 93, 119–135.

Stutzer, A. and R. Lalive (2001) The Role of Social Work Norms in Job Searching and Subjective Well-Being. IZA Discussion Papers 300, Institute for the Study of Labor (IZA).

Swinyard, W.R., A.-K. Kau and H.-Y. Phua (2001) Happiness, Materialism, and Religious Experience in the US and Singapore. *Journal of Happiness Studies*, 2, 13–32.

Thaler, R. (1988) Anomalies: The Ultimatum Game. *Journal of Economic Perspectives*, 2(4), 195–206.

Thaler, R.H. and E. Johnson (1990) Gambling with the House Money and Trying to Break Even: The Effect of Prior Outcomes in Risky Choice. *Management Science*, 36(6), 643–660.

Thomas, Jr., L. (2004) Depression, a Frequent Visitor to Wall St. *New York Times*, 12 September.

Time Magazine (2005) *The Science of Happiness*, 28 February 2005, p. 36.

Tolle, E. (1999) *The Power of Now: A Guide to Spiritual Enlightenment.* New California: World Library.

Triandis, H.C. (1994) *Culture and Social Behavior.* New York: McGraw-Hill.

Triandis, H.C. (1995) *Individualism and Collectivism.* Boulder, CO: Westview Press.

Triandis, H.C. (2000) Cultural Syndromes and Subjective Well-Being. In E. Diener and E.M. Suh (eds.), *Culture and Subjective Well-Being.* Cambridge: MIT Press.

Tversky, A. and D. Kahneman (1974) Judgment under Uncertainty: Heuristics and Biases. *Science*, 185, 1124–1131.

Twenge, J.M., K.R. Catanese and R.F. Baumeister (2002) Social Exclusion Causes Self-Defeating Behavior. *Journal of Personality and Social Psychology*, 83, 606–615.

Urry, H.L., J. Nitschke, I. Dolski, D. Jackson, K. Dalton, C. Mueller, M. Rosenkranz, C. Ryff, B. Singer and R. Davidson (2004) Making a Life Worth Living: Neural Correlates of Well-Being. *Psychological Science*, 15(6), 367–372.

Vazquez, C., L. Hernango'mez and G. Herva's (2004) Longevidad y Emociones Positivas [Longevity and Positive Emotions]. In L. Salvador, A. Cano and J.R. Cabo (eds.), *Longevidad: Tratado Integral Sobre Salud en la Segunda Mitad de la Vida* (pp. 752–761). Madrid, Spain: Panamericana.

Veblen, T. (1899) *The Theory of the Leisure Class.* Dover Third Edition, 1994.

Veenhoven, R. (1994) *Correlates of Happiness: 7837 Findings from 603 Studies in 69 Countries 1911–1994*, 3 Vols. Rotterdam: Erasmus University Press.

Veenhoven, R. (2000) Freedom and Happiness: A Comparative Study in Forty-Four Nations in the Early 1990s. In E. Diener and E.M. Suh (eds.), *Culture and Subjective Well-Being* (pp. 257–288). Cambridge, MA: MIT Press.

Veenhoven, R. (2001) Are the Russians as Unhappy as They Say They Are? Comparability of Self-Reports Across Nations. *Journal of Happiness Studies*, 2, 111–136.

Veenhoven, R. (2002) Average Happiness in 68 Nations in the 1990s: How Much People Enjoy Their Life-as-a-Whole. World Database of Happiness. http://www.eur.nl/fsw/research/happiness/hap_nat/nat_fp.htm [Retrieved 12 April 2004].

Weiss, R.S. (1973) *Loneliness: The Experience of Emotional and Social Isolation.* Cambridge, MA: MIT Press.

Weiss, R.S. (1979) The Emotional Impact of Marital Separation. In G. Levinson and O.C. Moles (eds.), *Divorce and Separation: Context, Causes and Consequences*. New York: Basic Books.

Wilson, T. and D. Gilbert (2003) Affective Forecasting. *Advances in Experimental Social Psychology*, 35, 345–411.

World Values Study Group (1994) *World Values Survey 1981–1984 and 1990–1993*. Inter-University Consortium for Political and Social Research, Ann Arbor: Institute for Social Research, University of Michigan.

Young, J.E. (2002) A Spectrum of Consciousness for CEOs: A Business Application of Ken Wilber's Spectrum of Consciousness. *The International Journal of Organizational Analysis*, 10(1), 30–54.

Zak, P.J. (2004) Neuroeconomics. *Philosophical Transactions of the Royal Society B*, 359, 1737–1748.

Zak, P. and S. Knack (2001) Trust and Growth. *The Economic Journal*, 111(4), 295–321.

Chapter 7

Social Capital, Personal Capital and Fairness

7.1 Social Conditioning and Consumption Patterns

Lane (2000) and others argue that the social milieu we grow up in is an important conditioner of spending. He makes several points: first, tastes are determined to a large extent by the tastes and spending patterns of those in our social group; second, one of the benefits of buying is to show our purchases to others which serves as a socialization device as well as a display of income and purchasing power [for example, see Heffetz's (2004) study of visibility of individual consumption to others in Figure 7.1 — housing and the automobile take center stage]; third, advertising affects the shared ideals of a society and does not change individuals so much as the social world in which they operate. As a particular technology gets adopted by more and more people, it becomes increasingly difficult to resist, whether it is TV, SUVs, the Internet, DVDs, CDs, computers or cell phones (Lane, 2000, p. 187). Fads in music, dress, hair styles, skirt length and so on are good examples of how trends can be influential to a large group of people.

Economists have long ignored the social setting within which economic actions take place. By viewing each economic agent as a utility maximizing individual, it ignores choices of others. Economic theory has put a premium on logical maximization of utility and ignored the process of economic life which is imbedded in the social fabric of a society. Social capital attempts to fill this gap by introducing social interactions and the social network.

Furthermore, because of interactions with others in the social milieu, the individual may not always behave in his or her self-interest only. He may be swayed by standards of his reference group. If he is

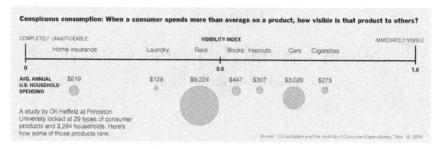

Figure 7.1 Conspicuous Consumption

Source: *New York Times* (2005, 1 January).

in a gang, he is forced to act like his fellow gang members. If he wears a suit and works in a big office, he adopts the values and behavior of the business community. As part of this reference group, he may experience cooperation or competition. He may be treated fairly or be discriminated against. All of these experiences help to form the decision making environment and they are all important elements that need to be considered when we investigate the individual's decision making process.

7.2 Social Capital

One reason why economists have shied away from discussing the social setting is that it is hard to define and quantify. To begin with, social capital may not be capital at all. If it is created, who owns it and who pays for its creation? Can it be bought and sold and its rate of return calculated? Nobel Prize winners Kenneth Arrow (2000) and Robert Solow (2000) argue that social capital fails to satisfy several fundamental characteristics of capital. Arrow argues that to be called capital, a variable must have a time dimension, that it requires current sacrifice for future benefit and its ownership can be transferred. Social capital does not require any material sacrifice to be created and ownership of social capital is difficult to transfer.

Furthermore, social capital is not an individual asset. Rather, it arises through the interaction of individuals within the society. Investment by one person depends upon the investment by others (see, for example, Field *et al.*, 2000). Therefore, it is difficult to treat social capital as having the characteristics of physical or human capital. We do not invest in social capital up to the point where marginal returns are equal to marginal cost.

This suggests that social capital is entirely different from other kinds of physical capital and it is also quite distinct from human capital. Social capital resembles a generalized social externality that exists as part of the background conditions that characterize an economy. There are likely to be considerable positive externalities related to the formation of social capital, particularly when we consider the kinds of social capital that have been discussed recently by the World Bank in its development assistance programs. In these programs, there are efforts made to establish an institutional environment that develops a responsive government and the promotion of grassroots networks (see Holm, 2004). Nevertheless, even though it is not really capital as such in the conventional sense of the common usage of economists, we shall continue to use this label in the ensuing discussion.

As a preamble to further discussion of this elusive concept, we begin with an investigation of recent attempts to summarize and systematize the definition of social capital. Some have characterized social capital as the individual's ability to take advantage of social networks to increase opportunity. Loury (2000, p. 233) argues that "Each individual is socially situated and one's location within the network of social affiliations substantially affects one's access to various resources. Opportunity travels along these social networks." Or, quoting Glaeser *et al.* (2002), "social capital as a person's social characteristics — including social skills, charisma and the size of his Rolodex — which enables him to reap market and nonmarket return from interactions with others" (p. 439).

On the other hand, others view social capital as a characteristic of the society. Features of social organization such as networks, norms and social trust that facilitate coordination and cooperation for mutual benefit (Putnam, 1995, p. 67) see social capital as "norms, values, attitudes and beliefs that predispose people to cooperate". Uphoff and Wijayaratna (2000, p. 1876) believe social capital to be "the normal and social relations embedded in the social structure of societies that enable people to coordinate action to achieve desired goals".

James Coleman (1988) is credited with coining the term "social capital" and has done much to popularize the idea of social capital. However, his definition sometimes includes what Quibria (2003) calls both the mechanism that generates social capital such as reciprocity and group enforcement of norms, as well as the benefits accruing from the possession of social capital such as access to group resources or the ability to network effectively.

Putnam gives us a key to interrelating these two ideas — of a network of cooperating individuals sensitive to the need for reciprocity operating within a social framework where such cooperation is energized, enforced and encouraged. He says, "Social capital is closely related to what some have called "civic virtue" .... (which is) embedded in a network of reciprocal social relations. A society of many virtuous but isolated individuals is not necessarily rich in social capital" (Putnam, 2000, p. 19). Adler and Kwon (1998) suggest that these two factors can be characterized as internal and external aspects of social capital. They list a number of definitions that they then categorize which encompass both internal and external definitions (see Table 7.1).

By looking at the various definitions, we observe that a key feature of this network, however it is defined, is trust and honesty. Fukuyama (1995) puts it nicely: "Trust acts like a lubricant that makes any group or organization run more effectively" (p. 16). With trust comes the responsibility of upholding the norms established by the social network. Bowles and Gintis (2002) define social capital as "trust, concern for one's associates, a willingness to live by the norm's of one's community and to punish those who do not" (p. 419).

It is possible that a particular society has a series of groups possessing a stock of social capital defined in what Hayami (2001, p. 291) calls a "community" that generates a number of positive social externalities. Such a community contains possible aspects of trust, tolerance and honesty, as well as other social virtues such as adherence to law and a willingness to contribute to public projects without free riding.

Table 7.1　Definitions of Social Capital

Author	Definition	Category
Fukuyama	"the ability of people to work together for some common purposes in groups and organizations" (1995, p. 10). "Social capital can be defined simply as the existence of a certain set of informal values or norms shared among members of a group that permits cooperation among them" (1997).	internal
Inglehart	"a culture of trust and tolerance, in which extensive networks of voluntary associations emerge" (1997, p. 188).	internal
Thomas	"those voluntary means and processes developed within civil society which promotes development for the collective whole" (1996, p. 11).	internal
Portes and Sensenbrenner	"those expectations for action within a collectivity that affect the economic goals and goal-seeking behavior of its members, even if these expectations are not oriented towards the economic sphere" (1993, p. 1323).	internal
Putnam	"features of social organization such as networks, norms, and social trust that facilitates coordination and cooperation for mutual benefit" (1995, p. 67).	internal
Loury	"naturally occurring social relationships among persons which promote or assist the acquisition of skills and traits valued in the marketplace... an asset which may be as significant as financial bequests in accounting for the maintenance of inequality in our society" (1992, p. 100).	both
Nahapiet and Ghosal	"the sum of the actual and potential resources embedded within, available through, and derived from the network of relationships possessed by an individual or social unit. Social capital thus comprises both the network and the assets that may be mobilized through the network" (1997, p. 154).	both

(*Continued*)

Table 7.1 (*Continued*)

Author	Definition	Category
Pennar	"the web of social relationships that influences individual behavior and thereby affects economic growth" (1997, p. 154).	both
Schiff	"the set of elements of the social structure that affects relationships among people and are inputs or arguments of the production among people and are inputs or arguments of the production and/or utility function" (1992, p. 160).	both
Woolcock	"the information, trust, and norms of reciprocity inhering in one's social networks" (1998, p. 153).	both

Source: Adler and Kwon (1998).

Shared values, common interests and similar beliefs can also characterize such a "community".

To take advantage of an effective social capital network that has already been developed, the individual must be able to plug into it. He must have a sufficiently large "Rolodex" and social skills to take advantage of the network and to internalize the social externalities that the social capital provides.

The network must also be welcoming to him and a wide range of other individuals with varied skills, ethnic, economic and social backgrounds. This requires a certain amount of sympathy and empathy among those members of the network. In a more general context, Robison and Flora (2003) suggest that social capital networks also contain socio-emotional goods. The exchange of these socio-emotional goods is, in their view, the primary means of investing in social capital. These socio-emotional goods also serve to cement relationships within the social capital network. The mutual respect and recognition that comes from members within the network can help to establish a deeper bond and foster greater self-esteem among the members. Membership in sports teams, fraternity or sorority membership, and membership in social and business clubs can establish social and emotional ties that create mutual reinforcing interdependence and increase feelings of self-worth and happiness.

To summarize, social capital requires a number of individuals who are willing to cooperate and trust others, as well as be trustworthy and virtuous themselves. To generate social capital, these individuals have to be linked together in a social network that also encourages and embodies trust and stimulates social interaction.

7.2.1 *Measures of social capital*

As social capital has so many different possible definitions, researchers have adopted a number of different ways to measure the concept. Putnam (1995, 2000) has suggested a number of different measures that reflect social cohesion and the tendencies of groups to gather together for recreation, religious, social or civic purposes. Temple and Johnson (1998) suggest translating these into numbers by recording the number of bowling centers, public golf courses per 10,000 residents as well as membership in sports and recreation clubs, civic and social associations and religious organizations.

Another aspect of social capital has been suggested by Mancur Olson (1996, p. 19) and Douglas North (1998, p. 494). They argue that social capital is embodied in the quality and efficiency of social and governmental institutions. In places where institutions are trustworthy (see Section 7.2.7 for more on this) and effective, economic growth is strong and vibrant. Where social trust is low, then government is ineffective, corruption increases and growth is adversely affected.

To measure and quantify the effectiveness of institutions, Temple and Johnson (1998) suggest a series of measures of citizen involvement, again measured as the number of these institutions per 10,000 residents. They are: the number of labor organizations, number of business associations, number of professional organizations and the number of political organizations.

Clearly, numbers alone cannot tell us the quality of social institutions. We should note that the Olson/North type measures suggested by Temple and Johnson are also sometimes reflective of measures of rent seeking by individual interest groups that are trying to influence the thrust of public policy. This points us to one of the anomalies of social capital in a pluralistic and open society. Interest groups will follow their own self-interest. When interest groups do this and feel free to express their views openly, this helps to ensure that the society is responsive to a ensemble of different points of view and is not guided by a few powerful interests that can extract exorbitant rents from the system. In this way, competition among interest groups helps to make the society responsive to the changing pattern of social agendas.

7.2.2 Benefits from social capital

How does social capital work in everyday practice? Putnam (2000) makes a series of arguments. First, social capital reduces transaction costs because of reduced agency costs — i.e., additional costs by principals to monitor agents. Secondly, a social capital network allows people to resolve collective issues more easily. This applies in any number of mundane situations like keeping public rest rooms clean, abiding by the law, paying appropriate taxes and reporting corrupt or illegal practices. Third, a well-developed social capital network results in a win/win situation. Those growing up in an environment of mutual respect, trust and confidence develop similar feelings towards others. Fourth, networks help to channel information and help those in the network to take advantage of new opportunities. Finally, Putnam argues that social capital also improves attitudes and contributes to greater happiness and feelings of well-being. The development of social capital can be an important factor in helping to mitigate conflict between neighbors, particularly in rural settings where land use is often an issue (see Libby and Sharp, 2003).

Social capital and the development of social networks such as local crime watch groups can also provide a way to increase social cohesiveness in poor urban areas where social stability is threatened by drug rings, crime and gang terror. Such community action has been instrumental in bringing crime rates down in Boston (see, for example, Hurley, 2004). Concentrated poverty and the lack of "collective efficacy", defined as a shared belief system or social cohesion in urban neighborhoods, are the most important determinant of high crime rates in the central city (see Sampson et al., 1997).

7.2.3 *Social capital and trust*

"It's a vice to trust all, and equally a vice to trust none."

Sennaca's Letters to Lucilius
(quoted in Bohnet, 2004, p. 1)

As noted above, trust is an important and indispensable component of social capital. Trust provides a strong basis for doing business, reduces the cost of doing business and increases both social well-being (SWB) and economic efficiency. Trust is primarily related to social and cultural bonds that bind people into groups. These bonds are many and varied, ranging from small community-based charitable groups to professional associations, to the Mafia. The more wide-spread the level of mutual trust, the greater the external benefit to society. Trust also reduces transaction costs by reducing costs of monitoring and enforcement, and helps curb corruption and bribery (see Chapter 9). Etzioni (1988) argues that an economic system will be more cost efficient if there is enough trust, but competition will tend to reduce the level of trust. To some extent, then, he views trust and competition as mutually exclusive. However, this may need not be the case, if all businesses agree to act ethically.

Francis Fukuyama (1995) details the relationship between trust, economic growth and industrial organization in a number of high income economies in North America, Europe and Asia. He explains how the presence of or lack of trust plays a critical role in how industries evolved in these economies. In China, trust is firmly embedded within the family while there is less trust outside the family. Because of this characteristic of trust, businesses evolved with the family as the core organizational unit. Even in the communist era, the return of power and economic authority to the family helped to fuel rapid growth. The communist regime tried to kill off the strength of the family by establishing communes, but it was not completely successful and productivity fell as a result. The communes did not work because they were not based on the extended family structure. As the communist system began to liberalize, the strength of the family reasserted itself. In countries such as Taiwan,

Hong Kong and Singapore where overseas Chinese have been operating within a capitalist framework for many years, the pattern of industrial organization still relies to a large extent upon family firms or firms which have grown through an extended family apparatus. Fukuyama argues that this is because there is less trust of outsiders than of family members, even distant relations (see Box 7.1 for an empirical cross-country study of trust in China and the US). Interlocking family businesses, therefore, have spread through the Chinese communities in these three economies and also with families in the PRC.

Box 7.1 Trust Game in China and US

Fukuyama's provocative hypothesis that there is more trust of nonkin members in the US than China has been tried in two empirical studies, one by the World Value Survey and another by Buchan and Croson (2004). The empirical evidence appears to be mixed. World Value Survey (WVS) data in Figure 1 is supportive of Fukuyama's claim that the boundary of trust in the US appears to be wider than that of China. Trust within the latter appears to fall sharply for noncitizens to less than 10 percent. On the other hand, critics such as Buchan and Croson comment that Inglehart *et al.*'s (2000) WVS data is too generalized, which merely asks participants for the amount of individual trust in other members to confirm the significance of trust in the countries.

Instead they make use of the investment game to investigate the significance of trust and trustworthiness of participants in China and US, by surveying the actual amount of money the second party would return to the first party. The investment game is actually a version of the dictator game mentioned earlier in Chapter 4. The first party is given $10 and he has the option of giving some, all or none of the money to the second party. Any money that the second party receives is tripled and the second party has the option of giving back any amount of the money to the first party that gave him his money in the

(*Continued*)

Box 7.1 (*Continued*)

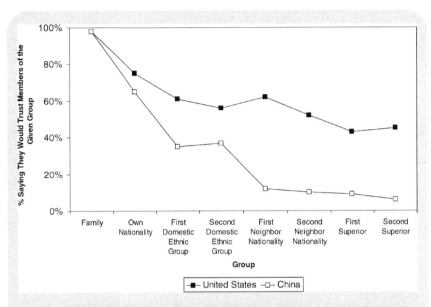

Figure 1. In Response to World Value Survey Questions: Percentage Saying that They Would Trust Members of Given Group

Note: Domestic ethnic groups referred to an important ethnic group within a given country; for example in the US, this question mentioned Hispanic Americans and African Americans. Neighbor nationality referred to people in neighboring countries. First superior and second superior referred to the Americans, Chinese or Russians, depending on surveyed country.
Source: Buchan and Croson (2004, Figure 1).

first place without any penalties in place. When the first party gives the money to the second party, it implicitly signifies that the first party has trust in his partner and it is expected that some money will be given back to him in the second round. If his partner's action complies with his expectation, it proves that the partner is trustworthy. However, the unique subgame perfect Nash equilibrium would be for the second party to return no money and thus for the first party to send no money in the very first place.

(*Continued*)

Box 7.1 (*Continued*)

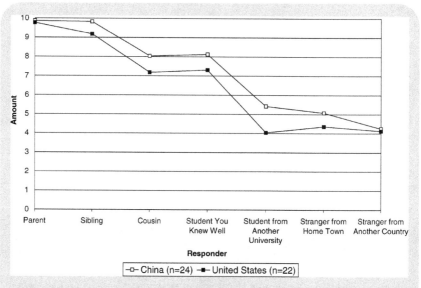

Figure 2. Amount Proposers Would Send Across Countries

Source: Buchan and Croson (2004, Figure 2).

Buchan and Croson's study showed that social distance mattered; indeed there was an expected drop in trust in both country surveys as difference in race and nationality of the participants widened. However, the boundaries of trust in China do not appear to be as restricted to kin members as Fukuyama proposed. The amount sent by Chinese first party participants exceeded those of the US for all the classified categories of members. Amount returned by second party Chinese participants also showed the same trend. Hence they concluded that there was no particular significant drop in trust among Chinese participants between kin and nonkin counterparts as seen for the American counterparts.

Making the decision to trust a stranger in a one-shot game can be a risky venture as the second party is not penalized for not sending back any money to the first party. Hence Bohnet (2004) comments that for

(*Continued*)

Box 7.1 (*Continued*)

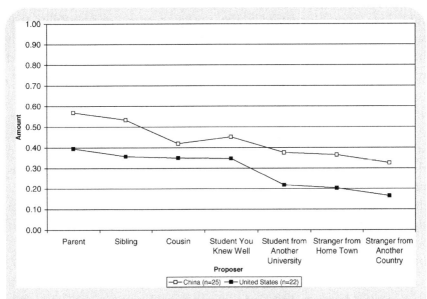

Figure 3. Proportion Responders Would Return Across Countries

Note: A survey done for 50 Chinese students and 44 US students.
Source: Buchan and Croson (2004, Figure 4).

the individual to take the risk to trust, he would have to be compensated a certain risk premium for possible betrayal costs which could be higher than mere monetary losses.

Source: Buchan and Croson (2004) and Bohnet (2004).

In Japan, on the other hand, loyalty and trust reside more clearly with the business firms where workers are employed. The lifetime employment system, close relationships between worker and supervisor that extend to drinking sessions after working hours, company songs, bottom-up management and a lack of a confrontational stance between workers and supervisors contribute to the development of a trustworthy and safe work environment. This pattern of behavior, where loyalty and trust within the context of the company may even supersede family ties, may have had its origins in the samurai mentality and the strong feudal system that still exists within Japanese culture. This is complemented by the mutual trust and responsibility that such a system built up and the rigid code of conduct that could result in ritual suicide by the owner/manager/samurai if trust, loyalty and responsibility somehow broke down. For example, some CEOs committed suicide when the Japanese growth bubble burst in the late 1980s and early 1990s.

Historically, the Japanese system did not have a strong family structural basis. Inheritance was based on primogeniture and even then, the eldest son could be easily forced out of the business if he was not competent. Efficiency and skill counted for much more than family relationship in Japan. As a result of this social setup, the extent of trust within Japan is extremely high. Crime rates are low and there are few problems of corruption except as it relates to politicians raising money from supporters.

There is an elaborate system of interlocking directorates in Japan that extends between firms and financial institutions as well as a well-developed subcontracting system where suppliers work closely with the principal. Principal-agent problems and free riding are, consequently, minimal. At the same time, this system makes it hard to establish direct responsibility for mistakes, and a system which is highly cooperative finds it difficult to make dramatic changes such as might be needed when a financial crisis arises. No single individual is willing to institute needed changes. These difficulties are one reason why Japan has had so much trouble getting untracked from the problems that it encountered when the financial bubble burst in the late 1980s and early 1990s. As a result, the 1990s was a decade of very low growth. Only recently has there been some acceleration in economic growth.

Fukuyama discusses the experience of trust in a number of other countries. Several interesting conclusions can be drawn from this analysis. First, social capital, in the form of trust and other social virtues, is important in improving the efficiency of economic systems. It is also important in enriching social and political life. Many studies have shown that "workers are happier in group oriented organizations than in more individualistic ones. Thus, even if productivity was equal between low- and high-trust factories and offices, the latter are humanly satisfying places in which to work" (Fukuyama, 1995, p. 356). Furthermore, trust is important in establishing a durable and effective political system. If there is not sufficient trust in the political system and "if individuals are not tolerant and respectful of each other or do not abide by the laws they set for themselves, they will require a strong and coercive state to keep each other in line" (Fukuyama, 1995, p. 357). He also argues that "economic life is pursued not simply for the sake of accumulating the greatest number of material goods possible but also for the sake of recognition....." (Fukuyama, 1995, p. 359).

This search for recognition, Fukuyama argues, is what drives capitalists to innovate, to take over other companies, to build industrial empires and to enhance overall economic well-being and produce and accumulate wealth. To do this requires enough trust in the economic system to allow entrepreneurship to flourish and innovation to take place. Without sufficient social capital and trust, this process could not have taken place. We need look only to the former Soviet Union and to extremely repressive authoritarian regimes like Burma to recognize this fundamental fact. To a lesser extent, a low degree of trust has led to overcentralized political authority.

Societies with strong family roots with a low degree of generalized trust in the PRC and to a lesser extent in France and southern Italy were products of centralized monarchies in the past that undercut the autonomy of many social institutions and therefore reduced trust. Consequently, this resulted in the need to develop a political process that substituted political authority and regimen for trust and natural social capital. Fukuyama concludes that the preservation and accumulation of social capital will play a central role in the future of capitalistic societies.

Other researchers have also concluded that there is a relationship between trust and the rate of economic growth. For example, Zak and Knack (2001) show that low rates of trust, as measured by responses to questions about whether the social environment is trustworthy, are associated with a lower rate of investment. Douglas North (1998) says that the inability of societies to develop effective low-cost enforcement of contracts is the most important source of both historical stagnation and contemporary underdevelopment in the third world. Zak and Knack argue that the high transaction costs that result from a lack of trust lead to economic inefficiency. They also present econometric evidence for this relationship which shows that trust and economic growth are positively correlated over a cross-section of many developing and developed countries. There are many ways that trust contributes to economic growth including less need for law enforcement, less corruption, greater economic efficiency, less rent seeking and so on. Bowles *et al.* (2001, pp. 1137–1176) argue that a series of traits like truthfulness and loyalty to the firm as well as high marginal utility of income and willingness to work hard are important in reducing tendencies for free riding and agency problems (recall also the discussion in Chapter 4).

7.2.4 *Enforcement, reciprocity and social capital*

Trust is an indispensable component in the societal dynamic that results in a high level of social capital. How does this process work? Bo Rothstein (2003) follows Bowles and Gintis quoted earlier as saying that social capital involves "trust, concern for one's associates, a willingness to live by the norms of one's community and to punish those who do not" (p. 419). Rothstein argues that generalized trust in a society is developed from the trust in particular institutions, particularly the police and the judicial system. He argues that it is only when these institutions are trusted that universal trust can manifest within the society as a whole.

Rothstein points to Scandinavian societies that are high in both social trust and social capital. He also refers to other studies that show that the quality of the bureaucracy, the low level of corruption and confidence in government contribute to a high level of trust. A virtuous upward spiral is created whereby: "Social trust (builds) effective social and political institutions which can help governments perform effectively, and this in turn encourages confidence in civic institutions" (Newton, 1999). As a consequence Rothstein argues that "generalized trust runs from trust in the universalism and impartiality of government to trust in 'most people' .... It makes no sense to trust 'most people' if they are generally known to bribe, threaten or in other ways corrupt the impartiality of government institutions in order to extract favors" (2003, p. 69). We will come back to these issues once again when we deal with the issue of crime and corruption in the next chapter.

Group loyalty and trust are extremely important in very stressful situations such as war. Costa and Kahn (2003a) demonstrate that creating social capital promotes group loyalty and this was of paramount importance in the US Civil War. It helped to cement cohesiveness in both armies. Costa and Kahn found that individual and regimental socioeconomic and demographic characteristics, ideology and morale were important predictors of group loyalty in the Union Army. Soldiers in companies that were more homogeneous in ethnicity, occupation and age were less likely to shirk. They also found that these characteristics were more important factors in determining loyalty than either ideology or morale.

Trust and loyalty involve an understanding of reciprocity. Putnam puts it this way: "Networks involve mutual obligations; they are not interesting as mere 'contacts'. Networks of community engagement foster sturdy norms of reciprocity. I'll do this for you now, in the expectation that you (or perhaps someone else) will return the favor" (2000, p. 20). Notice that this social network is not based on altruistic motives alone, but rather a social contract of mutually cooperative and reinforcing behavior. Coleman (1988) differentiates between specific and generalized reciprocity, where the former is very much like a market exchange. Coleman sites the jewelry market in New York City as a good example of specific reciprocity. In this closed system of mutual trust, bags of gems worth thousands of dollars are often passed from one merchant to another for private inspection without any formal insurance, receipt or other legal agreement. An ironclad environment of trust is necessary for this to take place and the trust, in turn, reduces transaction costs dramatically.

7.2.5 *Strong and weak linkages in social capital networks*

A distinction can be drawn between individual "insider" strength of social networks and the interaction between different networks. Diamond traders in New York City are a group with a very strong internal code of trust and mutual reciprocity. It is also characterized by a bounded structure in the sense that the rules are strong and enforced. Typically, such relationships are characterized by frequent and varied interactions combined with some kind of well-recognized structural characteristics and rules that are strong and inviolable.

When members of such communities interacted with other groups and/or society as a whole, the social links are likely to be more open-ended. Granovetter (1973, 1985) and Burt (1992) stress the importance of these networks. Granovetter notes that often, new employment opportunities come to those outside the "inner circle" through so-called "friends of friends". Burt stresses the importance of such contacts, which can be even more beneficial than well-established social ties. This is because the information content of a new contact is much greater than a continuation of old and established contacts. If learning and innovation is to increase, then it is important to develop such new contacts. This is the lesson that various investigations into network relationships within and between firms has taught us. By establishing contacts that span such "structural holes", individuals and groups can learn from one another and businesses can improve their economic efficiency.

Both forms of networking and social capital formation ("bonds" and "bridges" in Putnam's terminology) are important and serve different purposes for the individual, business firms and society as a whole. Each serves different purposes at different points of time. Family businesses that could depend for support exclusively among family members require more diverse contacts as they expand. Generally, those moving from simple family and social relationships such as borrowing from friends and family come to rely more on social institutions that involve more bridging than bonding. Sometimes, institutions can build on bonding relationships to build more durable and broader bridging relationship such as the Grameen Bank in Bangladesh. This Bank uses the bonding of women's social networks to ensure loan repayment while at the same time allowing these women to borrow and begin small businesses, something they could not afford when they were stuck in pure bonding relationships which provided security and safety. As a general matter, it does seem that as societies evolve and become more sophisticated, more bridging relationships evolve to supplement traditional bonding ones. The difficulty that some developing countries face is in developing a trusting relationship with the new and modern institutions that allows people to relate to the institutions themselves rather than as "friend of friends" that work in these institutions.

7.2.6 *Social capital paradox*

One of the paradoxes of social trust is that societies that have sharply defined "insiders" and "outsiders" such as Japan, Germany and the Mormons tend to be somewhat hostile to outsiders, however outsider is defined. In the past, the Japanese and German elitism and racial arrogance contributed to the development of war machines that led to geographic expansion which culminated in World War II. The Mormons, while expanding their base of operations to many developing countries in recent years, are still narrowly WASP (white Anglo-Saxon Protestant) in their home base of Utah. There are few openly gay, feminist, black or other minority members. Japan and Germany are now two of the most successful industrial countries because they have taken advantage of the large stock of social capital that has been developed over the years prior to WWII and built upon it to recover from the ravages of war. Japan is still ethnically homogeneous to a considerable extent and discourages permanent immigration. For example, Koreans who have been living in Japan for many years still have difficulty in obtaining citizenship. Germany has encouraged some migration into low skilled occupations although it is still very difficult for immigrants to obtain German citizenship. Those that have successfully migrated sometimes feel socially isolated (see Box 7.2).

Box 7.2 Adolescent Violence in Germany

A storeroom became a torture chamber for Marcus O. For months, the eighteen-year-old was kicked, hit and mistreated by fellow pupils in a room next to the classroom. The public prosecutor stated that Marcus had to strip naked and "carry out humiliating sexual acts on himself." His tormentors videoed the incident and dispatched the pictures via e-mail. Eleven pupils are now in jail for grievous bodily harm, unlawful compulsion, damage to property and extortionate robbery.

Is this a new dimension in brutality? The ordeal of Marcus O. at a vocational school in Hildesheim, a town in lower Saxony, which came to light in February 2004, heated up the discussion on youth violence, particularly since it led to other cases coming to light in which abuse had taken place in schools, including in Bremen and Hanover. It is the existence of despairing young people, many of them immigrants or the children of immigrants, who are not doing well in school, feel alienated and unwanted in Germany and are resentful of their German classmates.… [T]his school-age subculture feeds on a steady diet of horror films and extremely violent video games that encourages them to be hard and pitiless themselves. Here, perhaps, is the hidden secret of prosperous, smoothly functioning, highly pacifist, even moralistic Germany — a sadistic youth subculture born out of a wider failure to provide opportunities for young immigrants. All but 2 of the 11 boys who tortured their classmate in Hildesheim came from Turkey or from the republics of the former Soviet Union. The boys implicated in the Hildesheim case were all students at a hauptschule, or vocational school, the lower tier of the German secondary school system that channels young people into the blue collar jobs.

According to Christian Pfeiffer, head of the Criminological Research Institute in Lower Saxony, nearly two-thirds of school violence in Germany is committed by boys like the ones at Hildesheim, immigrant children who feel they have no future in Germany and take their anger out on nonimmigrant Germans. Pfeiffer has established that the risk of juvenile violence increases drastically when three factors coincide: a) violence has been experienced within the family; b) the family is socially deprived; and c) the future outlook is bleak due to a low level of education. This was the case in Hildesheim, where the violence took place in a so-called vocational preparatory class, where students have

(*Continued*)

Box 7.2 (*Continued*)

poor academic records and are unlikely to easily find a job. Mr. Pfeiffer cited another case of school torture in Lower Saxony a couple of years ago in which mostly German-born boys were beaten up on their birthdays by mostly immigrant classmates. "The beatings went on for four months," Mr. Pfeiffer said, "and nobody said a thing."

What makes these cases of violence particularly disturbing is the seemingly irrational cause: not money or revenge or a barroom quarrel run amok, but a sort of free-floating cruelty, an unmodulated will to inflict suffering.

Sources: Kilgannon (2004) and Goethe Institute website (2006).
Note: This box is a compilation of edited news reports in the *New York Times* and the Goethe Institute website. It bears an eerie resemblance to the story of the violent murder of Kitty Genovese in New York which was described in Box 5.1.

The Mormons have diversified somewhat by expanding their missionary activities. Yet they remain a highly successful and cohesive organization, demanding large sacrifices of money and time to the church, which, in turn, bears a heavy responsibility for taking care of its members.

Successful countries or organizations take advantage of the large stock of social capital that exists within cohesive and trusting networks, while ensuring that they do not alienate themselves from the larger communities to which they belong.

When splinter groups feel isolated, discriminated against and otherwise dominated by the majority in national or geopolitical situations, they may resort to terrorism. Historically, there is a tradition of anarchism in European society. In the Middle East there has also been a history of armed conflict and antipathy toward European conquest that began hundreds of years ago in the Middle Ages.

Lately, the conflict between some Islamic states and industrial economies has led to the spread of terrorism. Small terrorist cells, such as the group of Al-Qaeda fanatics that attacked the World Trade Center in New York City, were able to infiltrate the US and make elaborate preparations to hijack four jetliners. These preparations involved learning how to fly and to get on board these aircrafts carrying weapons in a coordinated way. Coming mostly from poor family backgrounds in

Saudi Arabia, it appears that at no time were any of the members influenced by the opulent US standard of living or friendly atmosphere that they lived in for a period of a year or more. The trust within the groups was unshakable and their distrust of the rest of the society they were living in was absolute.

The Al-Qaeda case is an extreme example of cohesive trust that led to a terrible antisocial act that resulted in widespread death and destruction. On a less cataclysmic level, corruption, drugs and other criminal and other antisocial subcultures foster a feeling of trust among members. They survive based on the development and nurture of "antisocial capital" that is highly detrimental to the rest of society, yet persists based on shared values and strong interaction and common purposes among the members.

There are also a number of historical examples of genocide throughout history including the Pol Pot massacres in Cambodia, the WWII holocaust, various ethic cleansings in Africa and the ongoing conflicts in the Middle East between Israel and the Palestinians and the war in Iraq. See, for example, the experience of two survivors, one from the holocaust in WWII and another from genocide in Rwanda in 1994, described in Box 7.3.

Box 7.3 Fighting Hate, Across Cultures and Generations

David Gewirtzman and Jacqueline Murekatete stood before a restless group of students at Great Neck North High School, waiting to tell their stories. They seemed to be an unlikely pair speaking on what seemed an unlikely topic — genocide — for a group of teenagers munching on sandwiches and rustling snack wrappers. By the time they had finished, however, the only sound that could be heard in the room was the faint hum of a radiator. Mr. Gewirtzman, a 75-year-old retired pharmacist who lives in Great Neck, Long Island, New York survived the Holocaust by spending almost two years burrowed with other members of his family under a pigsty on a Polish farm. Now, he visits local schools, hoping that by telling of his experiences, he can educate

(*Continued*)

Box 7.3 (*Continued*)

students and help to prevent a killing like the Holocaust from happening again.

When he spoke at a high school in Queens two years ago, Ms. Murekatete, then a student, was in the audience. She said his story had made her burst into tears. She wrote him a note relating her own horrible story, which took place in Rwanda, in central Africa, in 1994. She narrowly escaped being hacked to death by a rival tribe. Her family — both parents and all six siblings — did not.

"I finally found someone who understood what I went through because he went through the same thing," said Ms. Murekatete, now 19 and a freshman at the State University at Stony Brook. Mr. Gewirtzman met the teenager, heard her story and suggested she begin speaking to groups with him. It would not bring her family back, he said, but it might save other families from potential genocide. It would also help to heal her own pain.

"We are as different as can be," he told the students. "She's black, I'm white; she's young, I'm old; she's African and Christian and I'm a Jew from Poland. Yet we're like brother and sister, because we're bound by the common trauma of our experience and a common history of pain and suffering and persecution." Now they appear regularly together, hoping that they can bring experience and relevance to a harsh subject. But neither expected the impression they would have on each other, and how deep their friendship would grow with the only apparent bond being death. Elaine Weiss, a history teacher at the high school who directs its social science research center, said she asked them to speak because "the kids can identify with an 18-year-old girl better than they can with a 75-year-old man." She said, "Our kids read theories about racism and genocide in books. But when they hear similar real-life stories from a white European man and a black African teenager 55 years apart in age, who lived through events 50 years apart in history, it's not a theory anymore. It's alive."

Mr. Gewirtzman grew up in a small village in Poland and in November 1942, the family persuaded a local farmer to hide them and some relatives — eight people in all — for 20 months in a small trench below a pigsty strewn with mud and pig waste. Day after day in the hole, they would argue whether to surrender to the Nazis, he recalled.

(*Continued*)

Box 7.3 (*Continued*)

"At times my father would yell at me, 'Why did you lead us here? We should have gone to Treblinka and gotten it over with,'" Mr. Gewirtzman said. "I'd tell him, 'You may want to die, but don't you want your children to live?' Then he would snap out of it."

"We thought there wasn't a Jew in Europe still alive, but for some reason, I never once doubted we would survive," he said. "Maybe I was too young and naïve, but I never lost hope."

They did not escape until July 31, 1944, when the Nazis retreated. Mr. Gewirtzman and his family lived in Europe for several years, then came to the United States in 1948. He served in the United States Army in Germany. He and his wife have two grown sons and he also volunteers at the Nassau Holocaust Memorial Center, in Glen Cove, Long Island.

As Mr. Gewirtzman spoke, the students became spellbound. Some still held back tears as Ms. Murekatete began telling how she grew up as the second oldest of seven children on a family farm in Rwanda. She and her family were members of a Tutsi tribe. In April 1994, when she was 9, the news came over the radio that the Hutu president had been killed. Groups of Hutu men and boys wielding guns, machetes and clubs began descending upon villages, killing Tutsis.

The day they reached her village, Ms. Murekatete was visiting her grandmother Magdalene Mukasharangabo in a nearby village. Her grandmother saved her by taking her to an orphanage. After two months, she learned from surviving cousins that her family — her mother, father, two sisters, and four brothers — had been tortured and hacked to pieces with machetes. Most of her other relatives were also killed, including her grandmother.

She was brought to New York in October 1995, by an uncle who legally adopted her and applied for political asylum for her. She spoke only Kinyarwanda, but was placed in a fifth-grade class and soon learned English and began excelling in school. She said she still sees her family in her dreams. Other times, though, she is chased by the men with machetes.

(*Continued*)

Box 7.3 (*Continued*)

"I've never gone to a counselor or a therapist," she said. "At first, I guess I hoped it might just go away." She said, "Some of my friends are afraid to ask me about it and I'm not a person who talks about my problems."

Ms. Murekatete is currently writing a book about her recollections of the genocide in Rwanda. She also said that last September, she met the human rights advocate Elie Wiesel at an International Day of Peace ceremony at the United Nations. After hearing her story, he hugged her and said he would help her publish it.

With many cousins, aunts and uncles killed and only a few relatives left, Ms. Murekatete has grown close to Mr. Gewirtzman and his wife, Lillian, a Polish Jew, who had been sent with her family to Siberia for six years while Russia occupied Poland. Ms. Murekatete visits their home in Great Neck and has been to their summer home in the Hamptons. The Gewirtzmans went to her high school graduation, and she had tears in her eyes.

"I didn't know what to do with my experience and he showed me," she said when asked about that day.

Mr. Gewirtzman said, "In a way, we've become sort of parents to her. We both went through a traumatic experience," he said, "but instead of remaining bitter and angry and seeking revenge, we both resolved to spend the anger in a positive manner, to prevent this from ever happening again."

Ms. Murekatete shows listeners that racial hatred has outlived the Holocaust, and that genocide was not just something that happened to an old Jewish man from Poland, he said. "When I go to an inner-city school, the kids might think they have nothing in common with some Jews 60 years ago, or me with slavery," he said. "But when they see both of us, they see the problem is the same," he said. "It transcends race and ethnicity. People are still being taught hatred and it is hatred that we are fighting."

Ms. Murekatete said, "Sometimes, students ask if they can help, and I say, The best thing you can do for me is to educate yourselves so this doesn't continue to happen."

Source: Kilgannon (2004).

These are the most extreme examples of negative social capital, where feelings of antipathy and hatred were so strong that then led to genocide on a horrific scale. They represent a complete breakdown in trust and other positive reinforcing emotions, and the triumph of distrust and hatred.

Another possible negative aspect of social capital is that it may inhibit free thinking and initiative: "...it often enforces strict conformity, infringes on individual freedoms and creates pressure for submission to mediocrity....(and) can have a similar dampening effect on the dynamics of economic development" (Quibria, 2002, p. 30). Schumpeter (1934) emphasized the importance of moving out of traditional behavioral models to what he calls rational capitalism, which thrives on the impersonal force of the market. Social capital that has developed within traditional societies stressing the importance of family, clan and village norms and customs, may inhibit the transition to a modern industrial state.

Certain kinds of social capital can be detrimental to growth and development. Interest groups that have developed a strong network can collude within the group to restrict trade, develop monopoly power or otherwise subvert the market. Similarly, political interest groups can collude to restrict entry, strengthen rent seeking and support other practices that reduce competition and promote economic inefficiency (see Olson, 1982).

7.2.7 Institutional issues

How can society as a whole combat such tendencies? Particularly worrisome is the tendency for small disenfranchised groups to isolate themselves from the mainstream of society. How can society work to moderate the behavior of groups that harbor extreme antisocial motives? There are no easy answers to these questions. Strict enforcement of laws is one approach, but this treats the symptom rather than the cause. Longer-term strategies include integration of these groups into the economic and social mainstream through a reduction in all kinds of discrimination (racial, sex, ethnic and cultural), as well as the provision of better education and health facilities for disenfranchised groups. It also requires a law enforcement and judicial system that is trustworthy and impartial. A lack of trust in these fundamental institutions reinforces the isolationist and antisocial tendencies within the society. If individuals cannot "plug into" the social capital network because of discrimination, then these tendencies are reinforced. The extent of corruption and discrimination within the governmental apparatus will either reinforce or discourage corruption, bribery and other divisive and detrimental characteristics (see also Chapter 9).

A society that is characterized by internal segmentation and "alienation" is a society where the social capital network can create strong negative externalities. Breaking down these barriers by increasing trust in the honesty of public officials, reducing discrimination and allowing social capital to develop reduces the impediments to the development of a more universal social capital network and creates the opportunity for more to share in its potential. This in turn creates more social capital and more opportunities, creating an upward spiraling virtuous cycle of greater flexibility and greater social cohesion. If the social capital network is bounded and excludes groups for any reason, there is a risk of conflict and the creation of negative externalities. In addition, the formation of community groups as suggested by Sampson *et al.* (1997) can contribute to the development of a sense of a wider community that allows dissident groups to be neutralized and even brought under the community umbrella. The objective would be to transform societies where strong bonds have developed within closely knit ethnic, racial or social groups, into societies where more broadly based social institutions welcome these groups into becoming part of wider networks characterized by both bonding and bridging behavior.

This is not an easy job. It requires the recognition of the rights of other "interest groups" and the willingness to adjudicate disputes within the legal, political and governmental apparatus. Olson (1996) and North (1998) have written extensively about the need to develop what they call "efficient institutions". They believe that the lack of such institutions goes a long way toward explaining why some countries remain poor while others have been able to prosper. While many neoclassical economists would dispute this conclusion, there is much to be said for the need to establish an effective, fair, impartial and incorruptible institutional, governmental and legal environment in order to sustain and nurture economic development and increase the opportunities for leading a happy and fulfilling life.

The United Nations and the World Bank are dedicated to developing and nurturing social capital on a global basis for the betterment of all mankind. Diplomacy to solve disputes that spill over national borders has worked in some cases, but not in others. Resort to force, in the case of Kosovo, seems to have worked. In Vietnam and now in Afghanistan and Iraq, the record seems less successful. Can we apply the lessons of game theory and cooperation to these problems? What are the stakes in terms of lives and economic development potential? Whose responsibility is it to depose tyrants? These are not easy questions and serve as a focus for each of us to contemplate as informed citizens and economics and business students.

7.2.8 *Personal capital and emotional intelligence*

Some people follow patterns of action that are the converse of creating a happy situation. For example, by always expecting more through the process of increasing expectations, consumers create a cycle of dissatisfaction leading to more purchases in an ever-expanding upward cycle of consumption without increasing SWB or happiness. If this cycle is accompanied by disenfranchisement and isolation from others, it can result in antisocial or binge behavior, such as overeating, drinking, credit card debt buildup or other behavior that shows frustration with life rather than pleasure in consumption (see also Chapter 6).

A more general approach to analyzing individual social skills and emotional factors has been suggested as a component of personal capital and emotional intelligence. Tomer (2003) and Goleman (1998) have argued that emotional factors play an extremely important role in determining the productivity of workers. They distinguish such personal capital from human capital, which relates to skills acquisition through education, experience and on-the-job training, and social capital, which we have discussed in the previous section. The starting point for such an analysis of personal capital can begin with a study of individual differences in productivity. Research by Goleman (1998) and Hunter *et al.* (1990) find that the variability in output valued in dollar terms increases dramatically with the complexity of the job (see Table 7.2).

Table 7.2 Variability in Output by Occupational Class

Occupational Class	Ratio of Value Added by Top One Percent to the Mean of the Occupational Class
Clerical and blue collar	1.5
Jobs of medium complexity	1.85
Jobs of high complexity such as lawyers, physicians, account managers	2.27

Source: Hunter *et al.* (1990).

Table 7.3 Aspects of Personal Capital

Personal Competence	Social Competence
Self-awareness: emotional awareness, accurate self-assessment and self-confidence	*Empathy*: understanding others, developing others, service orientation, political awareness
Self-regulation: self-control, trustworthiness, conscientiousness, adaptability, innovation	*Social Skills*: influence, communication, conflict management, leadership, catalyst for change, building bonds, cooperation and collaboration, team capabilities
Motivation: achievement drive, commitment, initiative, optimism	

Source: Goleman (1998, pp. 26–27).

When most employees do the same kind of work, the range of worker compensation is small. When there are complex tasks which require extensive training, then it is likely that some will be outstanding and their pay will be much above the average.

As an explanation for these differences, McClelland (1975) suggests that they are not determined by differences in academic performance or intelligence. Rather, he suggests that they are a result of moderate goal setting, patience, ability to communicate emotions, initiative, ability to respond in unclear situations and moral development.

In a similar vein, Goleman (1998) suggests that personal capital can be broken down into personal and social competence. He develops a table to reflect these two aspects of personal capital which is reproduced in Table 7.3.

Notice that several characteristics such as conflict management, empathy, collaboration, understanding others and service orientation are what we have been stressing in the previous discussions of cooperation and competition in Chapters 4 and 5. These are complements to the usual attributes of successful, highly competitive and career-driven people like initiative, leadership and innovation.

7.2.9 Interaction between social capital and personal capital

Social and personal capital are interrelated. Tomer (2003) argues that sometimes they are complements and sometimes they are substitutes. Often, social capital and personal capital will be complementary. Gregarious and highly motivated individuals with good social skills who are emotionally stable and who are trustworthy, optimistic and conscientious often make useful contributions to the formation and sustenance of social capital networks. When there is a strong and supportive social capital network, it can sometimes substitute for the shortcomings of individual members by calming people's negative emotions. Similarly, strong individuals with well-developed and strong personal capital characteristics can be compensative for a weak social capital base. The cases of successful African-Americans coming out of the ghetto are a good example of this kind of substitution.

7.2.10 Social capital, personal capital and economic growth

Temple and Johnson (1998), Helliwell and Putnam (1995), Rapushinga et al. (2002a, b) and Knack and Keefer (1997) all found evidence that economic growth and social capital are positively related using data from the counties of the US, regions of Italy as well as a cross-section of countries. A variety of different variables were used to measure social capital. Rapushinga et al. and Knack and Keefer use two sets of variables — what they call Putnam (1995) and Olson (1982)-type variables, for the authors who popularized this terminology.

Putnam-type of social capital variables include the number of bowling centers, and public golf courses and membership in sports or recreation clubs, civic and social associations and religious organizations. These variables reflect the depth of the social organizations that exist within each county of the US. The Olson variables such as the number of labor organizations, business associations, professional and political organizations reflect the strength of coalitions in the county. Helliwell and Putnam (1995) use indices of civic community, effectiveness of regional governments and citizens' satisfaction with regional governments to reflect social capital.

The variety in the ways that researchers interpret the meaning of social capital and the innate fuzziness of the term make it difficult to draw strong conclusions from these results. Nevertheless, the evidence does show the significant impact of social capital is registered for a variety of different data sets and variable definitions.

One final point made by Irene van Staveren (2000) is relevant here: social capital research has not paid sufficient attention to the impact of social capital formation on the poor. Econometric evidence suggests that the stock of social capital is smaller in regions or countries that are growing more slowly than others. Therefore, it would seem logical to spend additional resources building up the social capital of the poorest regions and countries. This involves the development of social organizations that are open to many different social classes and promote greater social bonding. Such a program would serve the dual purposes of enhancing the prospects for economic growth and also contributing to the uplifting of society by developing a sense of community and belonging.

7.3 Fairness and Decision Making

In dealings with other individuals, there are many reasons why individuals might choose to follow a fairness strategy even when this is not in line with pure self-interest. For example, Alvi (1998) analyzes three reasons for fairness — altruistic or moral motives, conventional practice and reciprocity. The first involves some kind of moral imperative, while the second is based strictly on custom. Reciprocity, on the other hand, is driven by psychological beliefs and is related to self-interest in the sense that a fair response is "expected" from others.

It is also partly moral because players feel obligated to reciprocate. Hence, an individual's decisions are affected by his reference group and the overall social context in which he operates. We can see the importance of these different motives in the following discussion (and also if we look back at game theory situations discussed in Chapter 4).

Wade (2003) argues that genetic factors may be responsible for fairness, morality and trust. Hunters shared with others and this behavior may be traced to our primate ancestors. Wade argues that more selfish behavior is learned, while virtuous sharing behavior is innate. If this is true, then it would be simpler to unlearn the selfish behavior that has been taught to us and revert to our natural inclinations to be cooperative, trusting and fair with others. This is consistent with religious and spiritual traditions that assert that each person is fundamentally good and caring.

In a more general approach, Sashkin and Williams (1990) identifies nine aspects of fairness — trust, consistency, truthfulness, integrity, expectations, equity, influence, justice and respect. When fairness is violated, productivity can be adversely affected. They suggest stressing different aspects of fairness depending on the context. For example, they believe that it would be more effective for managers to focus on involvement and job expectations when speaking with supervisory personnel, and on relational factors such as trust, integrity and justice when speaking with nonmanagerial or workshop floor personnel.

7.3.1 Reservation price and fairness

One area where fairness comes into play is when cost and demand curves interact in markets. Relative costs and incomes may bring the concept of fairness into play. In a transaction that takes place in a conventional market, the demand schedule is downward sloping and the supply curve is upward sloping. At the equilibrium price where supply equals demand, both consumers and suppliers will experience a surplus. Some consumers get a surplus because they would only be willing to buy fewer items at a higher price. Some suppliers get a surplus because they would only be willing to sell fewer items at a lower price (the consumer surplus is the triangular area *abd* in Figure 7.2

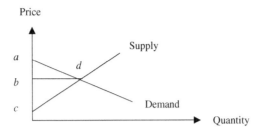

Figure 7.2 Interaction of Supply and Demand

and the producer surplus is the triangular area *bcd*). Figure 7.2 shows a conventional supply and demand curve with consumer surplus and producer surplus shown as the two subject triangles.

Put another way, and abstracting from demand and supply curve, both the consumer and the supplier have "reservation prices" that set limits on what price they are willing to either buy or sell the item. A transaction will take place only if the buyer's reservation price is at least higher or equal to the reservation price of the seller. Depending on the shapes of the demand and supply curves, a transaction takes place at equilibrium. The total surplus will be split between them.

This "split of the surplus" can help us to define fairness. When one party gets much more than the other, the transaction may seem unfair, even in a competitive market. You can see by looking at the shape of demand and supply curves that the surpluses will depend upon the shapes of the curves. When the demand curve is very steep (inelastic), the consumer surplus is very large because the consumer will be willing to pay a very high price. Similarly, when the consumer is pretty much willing to forgo the purchase if the price rises by even a little bit, the demand curve is flat (elastic) and there is very little consumer surplus.

In circumstances where the demand curve is quite inelastic, suppliers may be tempted to raise prices above the equilibrium, knowing that most consumers are willing to pay more than the competitive price that would be determined by the interaction of supply and demand. What stops this from happening is either competition from other suppliers or the pressure to maintain a "fair" price so that suppliers do not extract the full amount of the consumer surplus.

Markets can also change quickly with circumstances. Perishable goods are discounted heavily toward the end of the day because if the goods are not sold today, they cannot be sold tomorrow. What may have been a "fair" price early in the day may be "unfair" near the end of the day.

7.3.2 *Price gouging and fairness*

In many other situations, the concept of "price gouging" comes into play. We all know that prices are higher at expensive locations than at inexpensive locations. If you are lying on the beach and want to order a beer from a store or a luxury hotel that is situated nearby, you will be willing to pay more for the beer at the luxury hotel. The luxury hotel has to cover overheads. If the cheap beer garden charged the same price, you might feel indignant because you know that he could sell it for much less and still make a profit (see Frank, 1988; Thaler, 1988; Kahneman *et al.*, 1986). A "fair price" at the luxury hotel is higher than a "fair price" at the beer garden.

Concepts of fairness also apply to products and services that are provided for a substantial part (or all) of the year but where demand spikes during a particular time or season. Ski facilities and sports stadiums are two examples. During the peak part of the skiing season in Europe and North America (first quarter of the year and Christmas), demand is very high. However, ski operators do not (usually) charge as much as they could in order to extract the full consumer surplus, because it would appear to be excessive and they would lose customers during the rest of the skiing season. The same holds for tickets to sporting events that are in high demand. As a result, scalpers are able to sell all the tickets they can buy at very high prices. Yet fairness suggests that the ticket vendor at the site location does not raise ticket prices. Similarly, tickets for popular shows on Broadway and in the London theater district are rationed and sold out months in advance. Surely the box office could charge higher prices and reduce the queue. Ticket prices are higher for some shows, but not enough to eliminate the queue. Why? It is probably because of fairness consider-ations including alienating the majority of theater goers who would be outraged by such prices, even though it would clear the market and get rid of scalpers.

One example where gouging does occur and causes public out-rage is the high pay that US business executives receive relative to similar executives in Europe and Japan. The outrage has nothing to do with whether these executives are "worth" these high salaries or not in terms of their contribution to the company. It is all about fair-ness. The same outrage is not evident for sports figures, perhaps because their playing life is short and they are unlikely to maintain such high incomes once they retire. Their level of skill and effort is also more visible to the public. Furthermore, audience participation is largely related to these salaries — the public "sees" what it is paying for by way of the entertainment value of the competitions in which the sports figures are participating. This is not the case with most highly paid executives.

There are instances where some conflicting results have been observed. Kahneman *et al.* (1986) show that cost plus pricing was rejected by many people in an experiment who said that when costs fall, the seller need not pass on the savings to the customer! They also point out surveys which show that survey participants believe it is unfair for a firm to exploit an increase in market power to alter the terms of contract or transaction at the direct expense to a customer, tenant or employee. However, according to those surveyed, it is acceptable for a firm to maintain profit at a reference level by raising prices or cutting wages.

7.3.3 *Fairness and framing of transactions*

Fairness issues generally arise when one party gets a lion's share of the perceived surplus from the transaction. In such situations, a person may reject a transaction even though the price is below his reservation price (see Frank, 1988, p. 167). If the consumer were operating from the point of view of his own self-interest and maximization principles, such a situation could never arise. We saw that the same sort of fairness judgment occurred in the dictator or ultimate bargaining game in Chapter 4. However, in that situation one party could penalize the other. If the dictator offered an amount that was deemed too low or unfair, then the transaction was rejected by the other player and both parties would lose out. Sigmund *et al.* (2002) discuss the dictator/ultimatum game, whereby one person offers another a share of a prize. In the version of the game discussed in their article, the second person offered a share by the dictator can either refuse or accept. If he accepts, then they share the prize according to the offer made by the first person (the dictator). If the second person refuses, neither person gets anything. The rational decision on the part of the second person is to accept any offer and the rational decision for the first person is to offer a minimal amount. Based on their study of the results of different games, Sigmund *et al.* found that many low offers are refused and most accepted offers are in the range of 40 to 50 percent of the total.

In operation, here is the concept of "fairness", which is not rational in the economic textbook sense. An explanation for the rejection of small offers looking through the eyes of the recipient of the offer is the idea that "if others know that I am content with a small share, they will make me low offers in the future. If, on the other hand, I show anger and reject a low offer, they will have to make me higher offers in the future". In games where the second person cannot punish the dictator — that is, where there is no "penalty", "blackmail" or "revenge" potential — payoffs to the second person by the dictator are substantially lower. This is because in this version of the game, there is no risk to the dictator when offers are rejected.

Revenge and penalties are also reviewed by Sigmund *et al.* in public goods games. These games include elements of fairness in the strategy of players. Every player gets $20 and they have to decide independently whether to invest (and how much) in a common pool. The common pool is doubled and distributed equally to all players. The article discusses the selfish scenario — no one contributes hoping that others will and the selfish player will get his original $20 plus something more. If everyone follows that strategy, no one is able to increase his initial stake — this is a lose/lose strategy. If everyone contributes their entire stake to the common pool, then everyone doubles their money. But each person cannot be sure of the cooperation of the others. If only one person decides to free ride, he gets to keep his money plus a share of the contributions of the others to the common pool.

This is a good example of the free rider problem. In reality, only some people contribute some portion of their money to the common pool. Any contribution to the common pool is not in the individual's self-interest, which is a puzzle to those believing that self-interest is the prevailing force for all market participants. However, if punishment is allowed, meaning those who do not contribute anything are taxed/penalized by others playing the game, the amount of cooperation increases dramatically. This kind of behavior is supported by the sociobiology argument that societies become cohesive by taxing free riders and maintaining internal discipline.

In a comprehensive (and highly technical) review of different game setups, Fehr and Schmidt (1999) analyze the ultimatum game, the public goods game with punishment and a "gift exchange" game. In these games, the vast majority of subjects behaved with fairness and not according to the self-interest model.

In other games, such as the public goods game without punishment or the market game, people behaved in a self-interested way, as predicted by economic theory. In the market game, there are many individual agents and any one agent cannot affect the outcome, so cooperation or fairness does not have an impact on the competitive outcome. The market games have many sellers who want to sell to one buyer who demands only one unit of the good. Of course there is competition and a bid at the lowest prices.

Fairness plays a bigger role in markets for labor primarily because in labor markets, workers can loiter and reduce productivity if they do not believe the wage offers are fair. So morale and fairness play a much stronger role in markets where participants have some control over the supply of effort. If wage offers are not high enough, workers are less productive. This is one argument in favor of the efficiency wage hypothesis where productive firms pay rates above the market wage.

7.3.4 *Workers consider relative wages and salaries as well as the absolute level*

Say a worker refuses a job that pays more, and elects to stay in his present occupation even when other factors like commuting distance, work environment and job satisfaction suggest a move would be favorable and increase utility. Why? Workers consider the relative as well as the absolute salary level in evaluating job opportunities. Being at the high end of the salary scale in one job may be preferable to being at the low end of the salary scale in another, even though the new job pays more than the previous one. Within a particular company, the concept of fairness will tend to reduce the variation in the distribution of income within the company. The salary compression will depend on the relative productivity differentials between the most highly and the least productive employee.

However, above and beyond these variations, salaries will be compressed in relationship to the degree to which co-workers work closely together. Where the degree of cooperation is high, then salary compression will be high. The military and research laboratories are good examples. For occupations where there is more individual effort and little interaction with co-workers like door-to-door sales or real estate and less of the increment in productivity is shared, there is less salary compression. Frank (1988, p. 182) found that in the US, on average about 70 cents of every dollar of extra productivity is passed on to the individual in the real estate industry, whereas only nine cents is passed on to research chemists (see Table 7.4).

Table 7.4 Pay versus Productivity for Three Occupations

Occupation	Actual Earnings per Extra Dollar of Production	Extra Earnings per Extra Dollar of Production Predicted by Self-Interest Model
Real Estate Sales	$0.70	$1.00
Automobile Sales	$0.24	$1.00
Research Chemists	$0.09	$1.00

Source: Frank (1988, Chapter 4).

Nevertheless, in public goods games repeated a number of times, two alternatives can arise. More people contribute, which reduces the free rider problem and results in a win/win situation, or we see greater defection as the self-interest model suggests. There is not enough evidence accumulated yet to say which result tends to prevail.

We do have more evidence of cases of privately provided public goods being negatively framed as having no external benefits as compared with the cost of investing in the private good. In these cases, where the framing of the problem has been changed without any modification of the payoffs, several researchers have found that there is less free riding and more cooperation in the game where the outcomes are viewed as positive advantages versus a framing where investment in the public good yields no external benefit. James Andreoni (1995) calls these two alternatives the "warm glow" and the "cold prickle".

The "cold prickle" framing could explain why common property and free rider problems such as the tragedy of the commons, where the externality is posed in a negative frame, elicit less cooperation than other free rider issues where the framing is more positive. Andreoni concludes that:

> People are significantly more willing to cooperate in a public goods experiment when the problem is posed as a positive externality rather than as a negative externality.... This suggests that cooperation in public goods experiments cannot be explained by pure altruism.... Instead, there must be some asymmetry in the way people feel personally about doing good for others versus not doing bad: the warm glow must be stronger than the cold-prickle (1995, p. 13).

In Chapter 9, we delve further into the framing effect on agents' behavior, this time involving a change in attitude toward taking risk.

7.3.5 *Efficiency wages and fairness*

Yet another case of fairness presents itself when firms that are more profitable pay higher wages than those firms that are less profitable, even if workers have the same skill and qualifications. We mentioned this possibility in Section 7.3.3. Why should this be the case? The highly profitable firms could pay the same wages as less profitable firms and make even more profit. The efficiency wage argument was created to explain this phenomenon. It is argued that by paying higher wages, firms retain the best workers and maintain harmony in the work force, which in turn raises productivity. However, this argument is not completely persuasive, particularly when labor market conditions in the two firms are very similar. An alternative reason for the existence of wage differentials is suggested. If the profitable firms were to pay the same as less profitable firms, it would be earning disproportionally higher profits and that would be deemed "unfair". It is implied that the profitable firm is willing to share profits with its employees, even when profit sharing is not part of the contract negotiations.

7.3.6 *Gender and fairness*

In one experiment, Dickinson and Tiefenthaler (2002) looked at how a third person allocates resources between two people with different status and work input. There were significant variations in outcomes. However, the authors were able to draw several possible conclusions. Men were less likely than women to choose equal outcomes, but more likely to pick the most efficient outcome. Women were more likely to divide resources in an effort to equalize outcomes or results. If individuals did not seem to have earned their favored outcome or result, it was often judged to be not fair by the participants in the game. Becker and Miles (1978) studied the difference in gender response in fairness and cooperation experiments. They conducted an experiment with nearly 300 college students in two introductory psychology courses. From the results of these experiments, they concluded that men were more likely to compete rather than cooperate and it did not matter whether the counterpart was male or female. Females were more likely to cooperate with other females and compete with males.

The tentative conclusion from these studies is that women are more likely to allocate resources to achieve an equitable result, while men are more likely to focus on efficiency — giving rewards to the most deserving.

7.3.7 *Fairness and distributive justice in Asia*

A number of studies have focused on the Asian experience of income distribution. Different studies have compared the use of the *equity rule* that allocates according to individual merit with the *equality rule* that allocates equally to all members of a group. Kashima *et al.* (1988) look at different allocations of income in Japan and Australia. They conclude that Asian children and workers tend to favor the equality rule *vis-à-vis* the equity rule. Equity was preferred to equality by Australians as a measure of fairness and the converse was true for the Japanese worker.

Chiu (1990) studied Hong Kong students and looked at how they evaluated ways that grades are allocated to students doing a group project. The authors looked at how small groups of students doing a project assessed the fairness of giving the same grade to all members of the group. The author concluded that group cohesiveness was the best predictor of participants' endorsement of equal allocation of the same grade to all students in the group. Groups that were not cohesive were less comfortable with giving out the same grade for every student.

What general conclusions can we draw from these few studies of Asian culture? Firstly, it is more likely that Asian students will consider group factors such as equal allocation than their Western counterparts. Secondly, the cohesion or cohesiveness of the group is an important factor in determining whether equity is preferred over efficiency as an allocating mechanism. However, it is unclear whether this is an Asian characteristic or whether it is a more general conclusion about group dynamics for many societies.

7.3.8 *Fairness and distributive justice*

Many writers have studied the concept of fairness and justice in the distribution of income. We postpone a full discussion of this topic until a later chapter. However, we note here that some writers have linked the concept of fairness with justice. For example, Berliant *et al.* (2000) deal with fairness as it relates to income distribution. They relate fairness to Rawlsian justice (see Chapters 1 and 10 for more on Rawls) and note that Rawls himself also equated justice with fairness. They also discuss what they call a "no envy" solution, whereby no one envies anyone else or prefers another's bundle of goods to his own. This could qualify as a fair distribution of income. They also discuss other developments in the fairness literature as it relates to income distribution. In a slightly different context, Phelan (2002) argues that using Rawl's fairness criterion, inequality and fairness are compatible. There is more discussion on this issue in Chapter 10.

7.4 Conclusion

This chapter has attempted to discuss on a broader scale how societies create virtuous social networks where formation of social capital can take place. Some of the questions discussed in this chapter are: What is social capital? What are the social externalities that can arise from social capital? How can social capital be nurtured to attain desired social outcomes, assuming it can be nurtured in the very place? Economists are still investigating these questions.

To get additional insights regarding social group interaction, maybe we can take a leaf out of the insect world. In ant and bee colonies, complex social structures arise from initial simple interactions between members. According to behavioral ecology, bees share labor and specialize in tasks to coordinate efforts to build a colony that can support up to a million individuals. The behavior of individual insects is directly affected by interaction with other insects. The role of the individual bee is often affected by other bees in the colony such as whether to gather pollen for the colony, be part of the food production process or be involved in the building of the colony. There is a complex communication system which relays information regarding needs for specific tasks, and each specific individual contributes to each association, as each association contributes to the productivity of the hive.

Similarly, social capital emphasizes the importance of the individual's social milieu — the economic stage upon which his decisions affect others and are being affected by others in his reference group — and its impact on the individual level, firm level and society. According to new studies of biology networks, when behavior of the social group of bees changes, the fitness level of the bees also changes and has a profound effect on the community (refer to Booker, 2004, for more details).

This is similarly so for human beings and their accumulated level of social capital. We have learned about the benefits of social capital and how it opens up opportunities to the individual, contributes to the social cohesion of society, while allowing for social stability, economic development and poverty alleviation As noted in Chapter 6, higher levels of social capital also contribute to greater happiness and well-being (Helliwell, 2005).

According to the simplest aphorism of social network, "it is not what you know but rather who you know" that influences the critical flow of social interaction in the community. If you belong to a small clique, you have a certain circle of close friends with whom you share similar associated characteristics. From "knowing" the individuals in the clique, you become part of the group, an insider, and the desire to cooperate for the betterment of the group becomes greater. The level of trust within the reference group is higher. Of course, there will always be the loner, the nonconformist and the minority groups. But unlike the ant or bee colonies, where the insects are all part of the society with the same overriding aim of survival, humans are more complex creatures with our own agenda and selfish desires. We may appear to be within a group, yet we can camouflage our self-interest to get what we want.

Whether it is due to reciprocity, custom or moral altruistic reasons, or a combination of all three, we find that the decision to cooperate rather than compete affects social cohesion and economic stability. Reciprocity, trust and fairness are important "lubricants" to the smooth working of a society. The "warm glow" factors that we get from helping others may be stronger in some societies or social settings than in others. Certain societies could have cultural factors that naturally make them more inclined towards cooperation rather than competition. To delve into these specific factors, we look at instances of how certain organizations have successfully fostered collective action and how they have accomplished the goal of developing cohesive organizations.

To understand further how these groups function, we introduce in Chapter 8 the concept of a club and developments in what is now known as club theory. The actions and motives of clubs are often complex and have implications for aspects of market failure, including the provision of public goods and corruption (Chapter 9) and justice (Chapter 10).

Bibliography

Adler, P. and S.-W. Kwon (1998) Social Capital: The Good, the Bad and the Ugly. In E.L. Sesser (ed.), *Knowledge and Social Capital: Foundations and Applications.* Boston, MA: Butterworth Heineman.

Alvi, E. (1998) Fairness and Self-Interest: An Assessment. *Journal of Socio-Economics,* 27(2), 245–261.

Andreoni, J. (1995) Warm Glow versus Cold Prickle: The Effects of Positive and Negative Framing on Cooperation in Experiments. *Quarterly Journal of Economics,* 110, 1–21.

Aoki, M. and Y. Hayami (eds.) (2001) *Communities and Markets in Economic Development.* Oxford: Oxford University Press.

Arrow, K.J. (1971) Political and Economic Evaluation of Social Effects of Externalities. In M.D. Intriligator (ed.), *Frontiers of Quantitative Economics.* Amsterdam: North Holland.

Arrow, K.J. (2000) Observations on Social Capital. In P. Dasgupta and I. Serageldin (eds.), *Social Capital: A Multifaceted Perspective.* Washington, DC: World Bank.

Becker, M.W. and C. Miles (1978) Interpersonal Competition and Cooperation as a Function of Sex of Subject and Sex of Counterpart. *The Journal of Social Psychology,* 104, 303–304.

Berliant, M., K. Dunz and W. Thomson (2000) On the Fairness Literature: Comment. *Southern Economic Journal,* 67(2), 479–485.

Bertrand, M. and S. Mullainathan (2001) Do People Mean What They Say? Implications for Subjective Survey Data. *American Economic Review,* 91(2), 67–72.

Bertrand, M., E.F.P. Luttmer and S. Mullainathan (2000) Network Effects and Welfare Culture. *Quarterly Journal of Economics,* 115(August), 1019–1055.

Bohnet, I. (2004) The Payoff of Trust. *Negotiation,* 9–11 July.

Booker, R. (2004) For Social Insight, Look to the Insects. http://www.stnews.org/News-897.htm [Retrieved 2 September 2006].

Bourdieu, P. (1986) Forms of Capital. In J. Richardson (ed.), *Handbook of Theory and Research for the Sociology of Education*. Westport, CT: Greenwood Press.

Bowles, S. and H. Gintis (2002) Social Capital and Community Governance. *Economic Journal*, 112(487), F419–436.

Bowles, S., H. Gintis and M. Osborne (2001) The Determinants of Earnings: A Behavioural Approach. *Journal of Economic Literature*, 39, 1137–1176.

Bruni, L. and R. Sugden (2000) Moral Canals: Trust and Social Capital in the Work of Hume, Smith and Genovesi. *Economics and Philosophy*, 16(Spring), 21–45.

Buchan, N. and R. Croson (2004) The Boundaries of Trust: Own and Others' Actions in the US and China. *Journal of Economic Behavior and Organization*, 55(4), 485–504.

Burt, R.S. (1992) *Structural Holes: The Social Structure of Competition*. Cambridge: Harvard University Press.

Chiu, C.-Y. (1990) Distributive Justice among Hong Kong Chinese College Students. *The Journal of Social Psychology*, 130, 649–656.

Coleman, J.S. (1988) Social Capital in the Creation of Human Capital. *American Journal of Sociology*, 94, S95–S120. Reprinted in Dasgupta, P. and I. Serageldin (eds.), *Social Capital: A Multifaceted Perspective*. Washington, DC: World Bank.

Coleman, J.S. (1990) *Foundations of Social Theory*. Cambridge: Harvard University Press.

Costa, D. and M.E. Kahn (2003a) Forging a New Identity: The Costs and Benefits of Diversity in Civil War Combat Units for Black Slaves and Freemen. NBER Discussion Paper No.11013.

Costa, D. and M.E. Kahn (2003b) Civic Engagement and Community Heterogeneity: An Economist's Perspective. *Perspectives on Politics*, 1(1), 103–111.

Dasgupta, P. (2000) Economic Progress and the Idea of Social Capital. In P. Dasgupta and I. Serageldin (eds.), *Social Capital: A Multifaceted Perspective*. Washington, DC: World Bank.

Dickinson, D.L. and J. Tiefenthaler (2002) What is Fair? Experimental Evidence. *Southern Economic Journal*, 69(2), 414–428.

Etzioni, A. (1988) *The Moral Dimension: Toward a New Economics*. New York: The Free Press.

Fafchamps, M. and S. Lund (2003) Risk-Sharing Networks in Rural Philippines. *Journal of Development Economics*, 71, 261–287.

Fehr, E. and K.M. Schmidt (1999) A Theory of Fairness, Competition, and Cooperation. *The Quarterly Journal of Economics*, 114(3), 817–868.

Field, J. (2003) *Social Capital*. London: Routledge.

Field, J. (2005) *Social Capital and Lifelong Learning*. Bristol: Policy Press.

Field, J., T. Schuller and S. Baron (2000) Social Capital and Human Capital Revisited. In S. Baron, J. Field and T. Schuller (eds.) *Social Capital: Critical Perspectives* (pp. 243–263). Oxford: Oxford University Press.

Fischer, C.S. (2001) Bowling Alone: What's the Score? Paper presented at the meetings of the American Sociological Association, Anaheim, California, August 2001.

Frank, R.H. (1988) *Passions within Reason: The Strategic Role of the Emotions.* New York: Norton.

Fukuyama, F. (1995) *Trust.* New York: Free Press.

Fukuyama, F. (1997) Social Capital and the Modern Capitalist Economy: Creating a High Trust Workplace. *Stern Business Magazine,* 4(1).

Fukuyama, F. (1999) *The Great Disruption.* New York: Simon and Schuster.

Furstenberg, F. and M. Hughes (1995) Social Capital and Successful Development among At-Risk Youth. *Journal of Marriage and the Family,* 57, 580–592.

Glaeser, E., D. Laibson and B. Sacerdote (2002) The Economic Approach to Social Capital. *Economic Journal,* 112(483), F437–458.

Glaeser, E., D. Laibson, J. Scheinkman and C. Soutter (2000) Measuring Trust. *Quarterly Journal of Economics,* 115, 811–841.

Goethe Institute website (2006) http://www.goethe.de/kug/ges/soz/thm/en113172.htm [Retrieved 25 January 2006].

Goldstein, M., A. DeJanvry and E. Sadoulet (2001) Is a Friend in Need a Friend Indeed? Inclusion and Exclusion in Mutual Insurance Networks in Southern Ghana. Mimeo paper. University of California, Berkeley, Department of Agriculture and Resource Economics.

Goleman, D. (1998) *Working with Emotional Intelligence.* New York: Bantam.

Granovetter, M. (1973) The Strength of Weak Ties. *American Journal of Sociology,* 78, 1360–1380.

Granovetter, M. (1985) Economic Action and Social Structure: The Problem of Embeddedness. *American Journal of Sociology,* 91, 481–510.

Hayami, Y. (2001) *Development Economics.* Oxford: Oxford University Press.

Heffetz, O. (2004) Conspicuous Consumption and the Visibility of Consumer Expenditures. Mimeo. Cornell University, Johnson School of Management.

Helliwell, J.F. (2005) Well-Being, Social Capital and Public Policy: What's New? NBER Working Paper No. 11807.

Helliwell, J.F. and R.D. Putnam (1995) Economic Growth and Social Capital in Italy. *Eastern Economic Journal,* 21(3), 295–307.

Holm, A. (2004) A Social Capital Idea: Making Development Work. *Harvard International Review,* Winter.

Hume, D. (1740, 1978) *A Treatise on Human Nature.* Oxford: Oxford University Press.

Hunter, J.E., F.L. Schmidt and M.K. Judiesch (1990) Individual Differences in Output Variability as a Function of Job Complexity. *Journal of Applied Psychology,* 75, 28–42.

Hurley, D. (2004) On Crime as Science (a Neighbor at a Time). *New York Times,* 6 January.

Inglehart, R. (1997) *Modernization and Post-Modernization: Cultural, Economic, and Political Change in 43 Societies.* Princeton, NJ: Princeton University Press.

Inglehart, R., *et al.* (2000) World Value Surveys and European Values Surveys 1981–1984, 1990–1993, 1995–1997. ICPSR version. Ann Arbor, Michigan, Institute for Social Research and Inter-University Consortium for Political and Social Research.

Kahneman, D., J.L. Knetsch and R.H. Thaler (1986) Fairness and the Assumptions of Economics. *Journal of Business*, 59(4), S285–S300.

Kandori, M. (1992) Social Norms and Community Enforcement. *Review of Economic Studies*, 59, 63–80.

Karlan, D. (2003) Social Capital and Group Banking. Mimeo. Princeton University, Woodrow Wilson School.

Kashima, Y., K. Tanaka, M. Siegal and H. Isaka (1988) Universalism in Lay Concepts of Distributive Justice: A Cross-Cultural Examination. *International Journal of Psychology*, 23, 51–64.

Kennedy, B., I. Kawachi and E. Brainward (1998) The Role of Social Capital in the Russian Mortality Crisis. *World Development*, 26(11), 2029–2043.

Kikuchi, M., M. Fujita and Y. Hayami (2001) State, Community and Market in the Determination of a National Irrigation System in the Philippines. In M. Aoki and Y. Hayami (eds.), *Communities and Markets in Economic Development*. Oxford: Oxford University Press.

Kilgannon, C. (2004) Fighting Hate, Across Cultures and Generations. *New York Times*, 14 January.

Knack, S. and P. Keefer (1997) Does Social Capital Have an Economic Payoff? *Quarterly Journal of Economics*, 112, 1251–1288.

Ladd, E.C. (1996) The Data Just Don't Show Erosion of America's Social Capital. *Public Perspective*, 7, 1–30.

Lane, R.E. (2000) *The Loss of Happiness in Market Democracies*. New Haven: Yale University Press.

Libby, L. and J. Sharp (2003) Land Use Compatibility, Change, and Policy at the Rural-Urban Fringe: Insights from Social Capital. *American Journal of Agricultural Economics*, 85, 1194–1200.

Loury, G. (1992) The Economics of Discrimination: Getting to the Core of the Problem. *Harvard Journal for African American Public Policy*, 1, 91–110.

Loury, G. (2000) Social Exclusion and Ethnic Group: The Challenge to Development Economics 1999. In B. Pleskovic and J. Stiglitz (eds.), *Annual World Bank Conference on Development Economics 1999*. Oxford: Oxford University Press.

McClelland, D.C. (1975) *Power: The Inner Experience*. New York: Irving.

Nahapiet, J. and S. Ghoshal (1998) Social Capital, Intellectual Capital, and the Organizational Advantage. *Academy of Management Review*, 23(2), 242–266.

New York Times (2005, 1 January) Doctoral Thesis Says Rich People Spend More on Conspicuous Things.

Newton, K. (1999) Social Capital in Modern Europe. In J.W. van Deth (ed.), *Social Capital and European Democracy*. London: Routledge.

North, D. (1998) Where Have We Been and Where Are We Going. In A. Ben-Nur and L. Putterman (eds.), *Economics, Values and Organizations*. Cambridge: Cambridge University Press.

Olson, M. (1982) *The Rise and Decline of Nations*. New Haven: Yale University Press.

Olson, M. (1996) Big Bills Left on the Sidewalk: Why Some Nations are Rich and Others Poor? *Journal of Economic Perspectives*, Spring, 3–24.

Ostrom, E. (2000) Social Capital: A Fad or a Fundamental Concept. In P. Dasgupta and I. Serageldin (eds.), *Social Capital: A Multifaceted Perspective*. Washington, DC: World Bank.

Ostrom, E., R. Gardner and J. Walker (1994) *Rules, Games and Common Pool Resources*. Ann Arbor: University of Michigan Press.

Paxton, P. (1999) Is Social Capital Declining in the United States? A Multiple Indicator Assessment. *American Journal of Sociology*, 105(1), 88–127.

Pennar, K. (1997) The Ties that Lead to Prosperity: The Economic Value of Social Bonds is Only Beginning to be Measured. *Business Week*, 15 December, pp. 153–155.

Phelan, C. (2002) Inequality and Fairness. *Federal Reserve Bank of Minneaopolis Quarterly Review*, 26(2), 2–11.

Portes, A. (1998) Social Capital: Its Origins and Applications in Modern Sociology. *Annual Review of Sociology*, 24, 1–24.

Portes, A. and P. Landolt (1996) The Downside of Social Capital. *The American Prospects*, 26(May–June), 18–21.

Portes, A. and J. Sensenbrenner (1993) Embeddedness and Immigration: Notes on the Social Determinants of Economic Action. *American Journal of Sociology*, 98, 1320–1350.

Putnam, R. (1995) Bowling Alone: America's Declining Social Capital. *Journal of Democracy*, 6, 65–78.

Putnam, R. (2000) *Bowling Alone: The Collapse and Revival of American Community*. New York: Simon and Schuster.

Quibria, M.G. (2002) Growth and Poverty: Lessons from the East Asian Miracle Revisited. ADB Institute Research Paper No. 33. Tokyo, Japan: ADB.

Quibria, M.G. (2003) The Puzzle of Social Capital: A Critical Review. *Asian Development Review*, 20(2), 9–39.

Rapushinga, A., S.J. Goetz and D. Freshwater (2002a) Social Capital and Economic Growth: A Country-Level Analysis. *Journal of Agricultural and Applied Economics*, 32(3), 565–572.

Rapushinga, A., S.J. Goetz and D. Freshwater (2002b) Social and Institutional Factors as Determinants of Economic Growth: Evidence from the United States Counties *Papers in Regional Science*, 81(2), 139–155.

Robison, L.J. and J.L. Flora (2003) The Social Capital Paradigm: Bridging Across Disciplines. *American Journal of Agricultural Economics*, 85(5), 1187–1193.

Rodrik, D. (1998) Where Did All the Growth Go? External Shocks, Social Conflict and Growth Collapses. NBER Working Paper No. 6350.

Rothstein, B. (2003) Social Capital, Economic Growth and the Quality of Government: The Causal Mechanism. *New Political Economy*, 8(1), 49–71.

Sampson, R.J., S.W. Raudenbush and F. Earls (1997) Neighborhoods and Violent Crime: A Multilevel Study of Collective Efficacy. *Science*, 277, 918–924.

Sashkin, M. and R.L. Williams (1990) Does Fairness Make a Difference? *Organizational Dynamics*, 19(2), 56–72.

Schiff, M. (1992) Social Capital, Labor Mobility, and Welfare: The Impact of Uniting States. *Rationality and Society*, 4, 157–175.

Schumpeter, J.A. (1934) *The Theory of Economic Development*. Cambridge: Harvard University Press.

Schumpeter, J.A. (1950) *Capitalism, Socialism, and Democracy*, 2nd Ed. New York: Harper and Brothers.

Sigmund, K., E. Fehr and M.A. Nowak (2002) The Economics of Fair Play. *Scientific American*, 83(January), 83–87.

Sobel, J. (2002) Can We Trust Social Capital? *Journal of Economic Literature*, 40(March), 139–154.

Solow, R.M. (2000) Notes on Social Capital and Economic Performance. In P. Dasgupta and I. Serageldin (eds.), *Social Capital: A Multifaceted Perspective*. Washington, DC: World Bank.

Songtag, D. (2003) In a Homeland Far from Home. *New York Times*, 16 November. http://www.nytimes.com/2003/11/16/magazine/16CAMBODIA.html [Retrieved 28 January 2004].

Temple, J. and P.A. Johnson (1998) Social Capital and Economic Growth. *Quarterly Journal of Economics*, 113, 965–990.

Thaler, R.H. (1988) Anomalies: The Ultimatum Game. *The Journal of Economic Perspectives*, 2(4), 195–206.

Thomas, C.Y. (1996) Capital Markets, Financial Markets and Social Capital. *Social and Economic Studies*, 45(2&3), 1–23.

Tomer, J. (2003) Personal Capital and Emotional Intelligence: An Increasingly Important Intangible Source of Economic Growth. *Eastern Economic Journal*, 29 (3), 453–470.

Uphoff, N. and C.M. Wijayaratna (2000) Demonstrated Benefits from Social Capital: The Productivity of Farmer Organizations in Gal Oya, Sri Lanka. *World Development*, 28(11), 1875–1890.

van Bastelaer, T. (2000) Imperfect Information, Social Capital and the Poor's Access to Credit. Working Paper No. 234, Center for Institutional Reform and Informal Sector, University of Maryland.

van Staveren, I. (2000) A Conceptualization of Social Capital in Economics: Commitments and Spillover Effects. Working Paper No. 324, Institute of Social Studies, The Hague.

Wade, N. (2003) Play Fair: Your Life May Depend on It. *New York Times*, 21 September.

Waldinger, R. (1996) *Still the Promised City? African Americans and New Immigrants in Post-Industrial New York*. Cambridge, MA: Harvard University Press.

Weitzman, M. and C. Xu (1994) Chinese Township Village Enterprises as Vaguely Defined Cooperatives. *Journal of Comparative Economics*, 18(2), 121–145.

Williamson, O.E. (1993) Calculativeness, Trust, and Economic Organization. *Journal of Law and Economics*, 36, 453–486.

Woolcock, M. (1998) Social Capital and Economic Development: Toward a Theoretical Synthesis and Policy Framework. *Theory and Society*, 27(2), 151–208.

Zak, P.J. and S. Knack (2001) Trust and Growth. *Economic Journal*, 111, 295–321.

Zhang, Z. and C.-F. Yang (1998) Beyond Distributive Justice: The Reasonableness Norm in Chinese Reward Allocation. *Asian Journal of Social Psychology*, 1(3), 253–269.

Chapter 8

Collective Action

"How do populations of flashing fireflies and chirping crickets manage to synchronize their rhythms without the aid of a central conductor? How do small outbreaks of disease become epidemics, or a new idea become the latest craze?" These are some of the questions posed by sociologist Duncan Watts (2003) in an attempt to answer that most fundamental question of all — how does individual behavior aggregate to collective action? This brings forth more questions like how is this spontaneous coordination accomplished? Man is a complex creature with emotions, perceptions and memory. Why might people work together to provide goods and services that are not provided by the government? What are the reasons for collective action? When might it occur? What can collective action accomplish? Does some sort of man-made central conductor have to be in place to stimulate collective action? What are some of the institutions that have effectively fostered collective action?

From the viewpoint of classical economists, it was always assumed that when the rational and self-interested individual maximizes his utility, collective well-being in the economy will also eventually be maximized, given a perfectly competitive market. However, this assumption does not always hold true. In most cases, it is violated. Recall the case of the Prisoner's Dilemma illustrated in Chapter 4. Self-interested individualistic choice may not always promote the collective well-being of the party or on a broader scope, society. Examples abound in the real world — from international issues of global warming and terrorism, to domestic issues such as traffic congestion, public and merit goods provision, and personal issues such as posting and visiting pornographic websites on the Internet.

Adam Smith proposed that the pursuit of self-interest of the individual would lead to the operation of the free market and maximization of societal welfare. However, self-interest in its utmost sense could be destructive to the free market if firms develop into collusive cartels and monopolies with purposeful intent. The free market also breaks down in the case of externalities, public goods and merit goods. The individual could pursue his self-interest in the form of rent seeking activities which damages the efficient functioning of the economy. This chapter serves to introduce some of the interesting issues that arise when collective action is taken. These issues are further discussed in the final two chapters of this book, Chapters 9 and 10.

Individual rationality is not a sufficient condition for collective rationality (Olson, 1965). Collective rationality is only achieved when two or more individuals are able to coordinate their actions to further their common purposes. Collective action can be viewed in terms of group action within a certain number of individuals, or, on a larger viewpoint, from the transnational country's perspective. This coordination is thus of utmost importance. Trust and fairness, touched on in the earlier chapters, is an important and required element for the successful interactions between the group members. Individual incentives and the factors influencing the group's capacity to cooperate greatly affect the effectiveness of collective action.

This chapter will introduce the reader to the concept of club theory (which was developed specifically in the 1950s by Buchanan and Tiebout to explain the observed interactions among group members). Next, we will look at the factors influencing the group's capacity to collaborate. The later parts of the chapter focus on how collective action may or may not work in the best interest of the public, with examples on local and international levels. We also see how collective action or the lack of it can result in economic stagnation and environmental depletion.

8.1 Games and Collective Action

8.1.1 *Collective action in clubs*

Why do some people work together to provide goods and services not provided by the government, while others do not? Why is it that some public goods are provided more than others in some communities?

Our answer may come from club theory. Preliminary work on club theory was first done by American economists James Buchanan (1965) and Charles Tiebout (1956), and later developed by economists such as Olson (1965) and Sandler (1993).

Clubs are defined as voluntary groups of individuals who derive mutual benefit from sharing the costs of production, other members' company or some aspects of a public good that is provided by the club to its members. Clubs provide a nongovernment alternative to the provision of wanted goods and services. With fees willingly paid by group members, the club provides members with the desired goods and services that group members share, thereby increasing their overall welfare. Clubs provide an interesting solution to the allocation of public goods, which are generally nonrival and nonexcludable, and merit goods that are commonly overly demanded within the society. Clubs can also be formed to reduce negative externalities. If clubs could provide the same services as the public sector at lower transaction costs, clubs are generally deemed to be a more efficient alternative. Instances of possible club goods include highways, parks, private education, private housing, Internet, etc. The list goes on. Later extensions of club theory by Scotchmer (2005) have also allowed for the sharing of private goods in clubs, and where members also share the "externalities" conferred by characteristics or activities of members. Such externalities could include membership in exclusive clubs where some other members are widely known in the community.

8.1.2 *Revisit of game theory and clubs*

Club theory by Olson (1965) and Sandler (1993) and its game theory context has been mentioned earlier in Chapter 4. To briefly summarize, the individual's willingness to participate is affected by his individual incentive payout. Collective action takes place when individuals coordinate their actions within a group context so as to further their collective well-being. However, it may not be easy to coordinate the actions of the members in a group to further collective well-being. For instance, the media furors over scandals like the Clinton impeachment or Michael Jackson's child molestation charges are instances of collective action problems. When every major network is covering the same particular story, audiences are quickly saturated with information. News media persist in showing the scandal, reasoning that it is in their best interest to keep up with other TV stations. Yet when all the networks adopt the same strategy, they are stuck in a suboptimal equilibrium which becomes collectively self-defeating (Heath, 2000). To solve the problem, someone has to change his behavior and also believe that others will make similar changes. But other people's actions are often exogenous and beyond the control of any individual, which is a reason why collective action problems often persist the way they do.

According to Olson (1965), the formation of a club depends on two related factors: (i) privilege (when at least one individual derives sufficient net benefits from the collective action to go it alone); and (ii) the size and design of the payoff matrix. Recall from Chapter 4 how a collective good is provided once the game changes from a Prisoner's Dilemma to an assurance game, where there is a strong incentive to cooperate and a big penalty if one defects. This incentive structure is applicable to costly infrastructure investment, like highways or bridges, where it would benefit the group if all members contributed. Members have to assure each other that there would be no free riding. In an evolutionary setting where the equilibrium is evolutionarily stable, a club might emerge where each individual helps other individuals.

Another classic instance of collective action is when demonstrators simultaneously call for the resignation of a political leader or organize a mass rally for change in a certain government policy. One example is the 1989 Leipzig Monday Demonstration where there was (at least initially) little political leadership or explicit coordination, the people power rallies in the Philippines to protest against the Marcos or Estrada regimes, or the demonstrations in Thailand to protest the Thaksin regime. Protestors collectively benefit from the mass rally if they win, but incur individual costs of time, resources and possible risk of arrest, injury and/or loss of life. Such mass protests are infrequent and of short duration.

Sociologists such as Granovetter (1978) and Oliver and Marwell (1988) use "tipping" or threshold models to study and analyze the phenomenon of collective action. They argue that individuals vary in their willingness to participate in collective action. Therefore, such actions will only occur if there is a sufficiently large critical mass of participants who are willing to take the first step to trigger off the collective action. The tipping point or threshold level will depend on the distribution of individual participation thresholds in the population. These participation thresholds are volatile and can easy be swayed by mass psychology as people get swept up in the energy of the moment.

8.1.3 *General principles of collective action*[1]

Olson (1965) sets forth three general principles for collective action. Of course, these principles are not universal truths, but they serve to highlight some of the important conditions for the success of collective action. First, the smaller the club, the more efficient its outcome and the higher the probability of group cooperation manifesting. Secondly, if we are talking about countries, the more heterogeneity within group members' endowments, the more likely that richer countries will shoulder the burden for collective action for the collective welfare of smaller members. Lastly, collective action can be fostered through selective incentives and changes in institutional rules.

Extension of the theory by Sandler (1993) and Little (2002) are also incorporated in the discussion that follows:

• *Size of the club*

A small club would incur lower organizational costs than a large club and the amount of organizational costs could hinder collective action from taking place. A larger club with more group members could also imply that share of benefits going to any individual group member shrinks if absolute amount of benefits are fixed.

Sandler (2001, p. 71) disagrees with the first principle of smallness and states that the principle is valid only if costs are not shared among group members. In the case of cost-sharing among group

---

[1]See Sandler (2001, Chapter 4).

members, the hypothesized shrinking of individual benefits would not occur. However, it is possible that once costs have exceeded a certain threshold that the group cannot afford, then collective action could be impeded. There is also the constraint of introducing new group members since clubs often stress exclusivity and there has to be consensus among existing members to allow new entrants. For instance, note the ongoing and often heated debate in the European Union over the admission of Turkey.

Club theory is interesting in that it appears to resolve a number of puzzling economic policies in the real world and sheds light onto the influence of small groups. For instance, in the wake of the 9/11 bombing, we have seen various countries providing assistance for ailing airlines. These bailouts seem to make little economic sense. However, Moffatt (2004) suggests the following rationale. Suppose there are four major airlines in the US and each are on the brink of bankruptcy. The CEO of one of the airlines realizes that they would be more successful at garnering government support if the four airlines could band together than going it alone. They hire a firm to lobby on their behalf for government support for their airlines, say $400 million. Each American pays $4 more in taxes in order to pay for the bailout. No opposing group is formed against the proposed bailout, other than from a few academic economists and think tanks.

The lobbying by the airlines is successful. Why? From the perspective of the tax paying individual, the cost of opposition (time, energy and financial resources spent on understanding the issue and garnering similarly like-minded individuals to lobby to congress) is much higher than the cost of a few dollars. So he feels it is not really worth his effort to oppose the bailout. Other individuals feel the same way, and the airlines get their way. From the perspective of the airlines, they have much more at stake than the large group of tax paying public, i.e., financial viability versus bankruptcy. It is a matter of "life and death" for them and they have much more to gain — $400 million.

Small groups can have more influential power than larger groups because they have more at stake and they are willing to pool their common resources to attain a common goal. That explains how many small groups in the form of special interest groups can outmaneuver larger groups of consumers and tax payers. There are many examples aside from our group of four hypothetical airlines including EU farmers protecting farm subsidies and gun lobbyists in the US. Larger groups are often unable to find a lobby to represent their common interests, or their interests could be conflicting in the first place.

Larger groups face difficulties of free riding unless enforcement measures are firmly in place. The resources pooled by an individual in a large group is also relatively less vital to the critical functioning of the group than in a small group, hence the entry of the individual into the club might be less compelling. Furthermore, as pointed out by Olson (1965), there are relatively fewer economic and social pressures in a large club favoring cooperative action than a small club. In a large club with many members, the action of a single member is not really a decisive factor affecting the outcome. For instance, in an industry where there is monopolistic competition or oligopoly, if a firm decides to raise its price above the market price, other firms would not follow suit (the kinked oligopoly model), and it would be to its own disadvantage since profits will fall when consumers turn to other firms. Also, in a large group, there are fewer obligations to meet social expectations since not all members will know each other.

Little (2002, p. 100) supports the argument for a small efficient club and adds that individuals must exhibit similar traits favoring cooperation. The ease of monitoring group members is generally greater in a smaller club as they could simply find out who failed to comply with club requirements. Little utilizes Gauthier's bargaining model between similar parties to illustrate his point. In this model there are two kinds of utility maximizers present: individuals who act in their own self-interest and individuals who realize the possibility of benefits from cooperation, i.e., constrained maximizers. An important feature of this model is that cooperators are able to recognize each other as such.

Hence, if individuals recognize similar altruistic and cooperative traits in each other, they would be able to cooperate together without the need for external intervention, i.e., the government. Critics might argue that the ability to discern between like and unlike individuals is not inherent and hence the model is not robust. However, it makes lots of sense. There are many examples where discernment is well-developed. Trustworthy people tend to interact with other trustworthy people more and it is highly likely that these powers of discernment are enhanced with age and experience, at least for some individuals.

The National Rifle Association (NRA) in the US is a good example of trust and a goal-oriented approach of an effective club. The NRA brings together people from a variety of occupations who are interested in keeping gun control legalization to a minimum. Over the years, they have been extremely effective in lobbying against legislation that restricts the freedom to "bear arms", a right they feel is enshrined on an individual basis by the constitution. The political structure in the US is sympathetic to these interests to the extent that individual legislators from states with powerful NRA lobbies feel great pressure to vote for legislation in keeping with NRA objectives. As a result, firearms ownership in the US is the highest in the world. The incidence of deaths from gunshot wounds in the US is also the highest in the world.

To demonstrate how cooperation between two individuals can result in the formation of a small club, consider the objective of repairing a road that serves two houses. Rowena would cooperate with the repair of the road if Colin does likewise, but would defect if he does not. Rowena could cooperate with Colin to jointly share the cost of repairing the road, or Rowena could choose to shoulder the entire cost of the road repair rather than endure the current muddy condition. Colin would be the free rider. Or Colin could adopt a similar strategy, and then Rowena becomes the free rider. The analogy can be extended to include other individuals who exhibit similar behavior to those of Rowena and Colin. Hence, if Rowena and Colin trusted each other and agreed to split the cost of the bill, it would resolve the public good problem. If either values the road repair enough to "go it alone", the club objective of building a new road would be achieved despite the presence of a free rider (Colin or Rowena as the case may be).

In this simple example, the limited number of club members allows the individual to ascertain the character of the other individual and hence, effective social cooperation is established. Little (2002) argues that once the number of individuals simultaneously desiring the public good becomes large, the government has to be present to enforce regulations preventing or minimizing the number of free riders. In the case of the NRA where legislation rather than provision of public goods and services is the objective, a large membership is advantageous in achieving legislative objectives.

- *Heterogeneity within clubs*

Generally, if members share similar characteristics such as social, economic and cultural circumstances, it is easier for them to communicate and come to mutually beneficial agreements, hence improving cooperation. On the other hand, diversity in group members' characteristics generally impedes cooperation and displaces collective action.

Secondly, the more heterogeneity within group members' endowments, the more likely it is that the richer members will shoulder the burden for collective action for the collective welfare of poorer members. In NATO, richer allies such as the US, UK and France bear the main organizational and administrative costs. Sandler (2001, p. 183) calls this phenomenon "free-riding aid". But this arrangement is dependent on the smaller member's preferences for collective action. If smaller countries face higher risks from not joining, it could alter the manner of group interaction. Sandler further lists the military club example of the US-Israeli alliance, where Israel devotes a larger proportion of its GDP for defense than the US. The threat is much more compelling for Israel owing to local hostile conditions.

- *Institutional rules and incentives for collective action*

Olson (1965) suggests some ways to foster collective action, which includes cost sharing, recognition of individual members' efforts and selective incentives. Institutional rules also mattered. For instance, in the initial start up of AOL, it had to deal with a government suspicious of the content of the Internet and its varying uses. Because of this, it took some time before AOL could realize its full potential as a network providing for the needs of its members.

Framing of treaties between countries also requires that the two countries or groups of countries find a common agenda and series of purposes that can bind them together. Mutual defense is the cornerstone of the NATO alliances, and alliances in other regions have built upon this intention. The small are protected by the large and, as a result, inequities in payment for membership are bound to arise as noted above. Nevertheless, all countries are willing to belong, in the same way that Athens and Sparta were willing to protect smaller provinces on the periphery of the Greek empire in exchange for the ability to be warned of invasions by the Persians and other predators from the east.

The success of treaties and contracts also depends on the number of players involved and the effectiveness of penalties imposed. For instance, in environmental studies, it has always been far easier to control pollution from specific production plants by imposing taxes on the firm level than pollution emitted from numerous individuals' car exhaust pipes. The Montreal Protocol to curb ozone-depleting substances in a few key polluting countries was easier to draw up than an international treaty dealing with global warming such as the Kyoto Protocol. Hence, size of the club plays a crucial part, not only in the amount of benefits each individual gets and the degree of cooperation, but also in the effectiveness of the drawn up agreement.

Other methods to induce collective action include recognition of individuals' efforts and selective incentives to alter institutional design. A classic case study would be charity fundraising. A possible strategic action to recognize individuals' effort would be to offer donor-specific benefits (ranging from a sticker to discounts at participating stores involved in the fundraising campaign, and so on). Some fundraising campaigns have gotten large pledge contributions before beginning the campaign drive so as to assure other would-be donors that the attainment of desired outcomes is plausible and to encourage them to support the campaign. Another example of collective action is antisoftware web-based centers such as Trend Virus Center, which successfully makes use of incentives to foster collective action. The center monitors the emergence of new computer viruses and hackers from computer users around the world. In return for the users status report, the center develops antivirus software to deal with the latest strains of viruses. The user's incentive to report his computer status is his guaranteed share in the benefits of collective action (in the form of free antivirus downloads if his computer does get infected). The cost of reporting is small and there is no gain to free riding.

Government policies can also affect collective action positively. One instance is the matching of funds raised by private organizers for charitable purposes with an equal contribution from the public coffers. This raises public awareness of the campaign, with the implicit government approval of the drive. It also promotes greater support from individuals and small groups since their support is publicly acknowledged. There is shared responsibility between the government and individual parties for the success of the campaign. It mitigates free riding problems since each individual effort counts towards raising overall level of contribution.

To briefly summarize, collective action is affected by: (i) individuals' incentive to cooperate with one another; and (ii) factors affecting the group's capacity to collaborate such as size and makeup of the club, trust among members, autonomy to impose enforcement measures, institutional rules, government policies and last but not least, the strength of the binding common agenda. After understanding the various factors influencing group interactions within the club, Section 8.2 shall attempt to introduce examples of collective action at the local level and discuss if collective action will always improve societal welfare and be beneficial to the public interest.

8.2 Clubs and the Public Interest

Olson (1965) has argued that strong clubs working to pass legislation in their self-interest often results in a suboptimal solution. With the unequal exercise of power by such clubs, the interests of those less well-organized and poorly funded segments of society are not being served. The NRA has successfully lobbied for legislation that allows private citizens to purchase a wide array of pistols, handguns, rifles and automatic weapons. It is estimated that there are more guns in the possession of private individuals than there are people living in the US. It is not surprising that many of these weapons have found their way into the hands of criminals. As a result, there are many more shooting fatalities in the US than there are in other countries during peacetime. Surveys show that the majority of US citizens would like to see legislation passed to further limit the sale of firearms and to adopt more stringent regulations to obtain permits to own firearms. The gun lobby has generally been able to successfully block such legislation.

Farm lobbies in many countries, including the US, Europe and Japan, have blocked the World Trade Organization from lowering tariffs on agricultural products from developing countries. Many economists believe that reducing tariffs on agricultural products is a win/win situation that would benefit industrial country consumers and developing country producers. However, such legislation has been effectively blocked by farm lobbies from industrial countries.

In recent years, the formation of violently religious groups has caused havoc and unrest around the world. According to Berman (2003), the Taliban terrorists in Afghanistan and the Hamas radicals in Palestinian territories operate in the form of strong clubs and provide religious members with club goods such as education, health and even law and order when the state government has been ineffective. There also appears to be a positive correlation between religious commitment and provision of public goods to their members. Commitment in a normal club would generally tend to pale in comparison with such religious groups whose members are required to show their devotion by studying holy texts for years or even committing extreme acts such as ritual suicide. With the ability to extract signals of high commitment by religious members, their formation can have potentially destructive results for the public interest. Berman points out the failure of a similar religious group, the Gush Emunim, an Orthodox Jewish group. In the late 1970s and early 1980s, they provided social services to their members. However, since the state was also providing these goods, their influence was undermined. Berman's prescription is simple and commonsensical. To undermine the influence of extremist elements over members of a sect, he advocates the provision of schools, medical care and old folks' home by the state.

Religious groups such as churches may be viewed as clubs that are dedicated to the collective production of religious services (Iannaccone, 1998). Members can derive utility from their inputs of time, goods, capital and other fellow church members' inputs. Screening of the behavior of members by others in the congregation mitigates free rider problems. Sectarian congregations which require members to self-sacrifice and behave unorthodoxly are often forced to remain small in size because of the need to maintain high levels of monitoring over individual members. Those outside the congregation may not be trusted. On the other hand, mainstream churches are often bigger as they impose less demanding requirements of their members. Figure 8.1

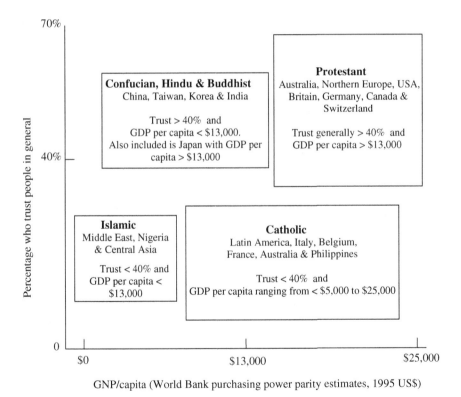

Figure 8.1 Trust versus GDP per Capita by Religious Affiliation
Source: Adapted from Inglehart and Klingemann (2000).

spells out the relationship between trust and income per capita for various religious groups. Islamic groups in countries such as Nigeria and Bangladesh are shown to be concentrated in the lower left corner. These groups are concentrated in low income countries and the general level of trust is low. Protestants in Norway, Denmark and Sweden occupy the upper right corner of the diagram with high interpersonal trust and high gross domestic per capita. Other groups such as Catholics have more disperse trust characteristics and per capita incomes.

8.2.1 *Collective action and property rights for sustainable development*

The tragedy of the commons is a classic case of how individuals focus on short-term self-interest goals and overuse common resources, resulting in a danger of depletion of natural environmental resources. The sustainability of common resources in developing countries and the circumstances of the rural poor are often decried by developed countries and intelligent think tanks. Collective action, in the form of community groups, has been suggested as a way of reducing poverty and giving the poor effective measures for resource conservation. However, this is often easier said than done. A lot depends on the individual incentives for collaborating and the factors affecting the community or groups' ability to collaborate. The absence of property rights is a common hindrance to collective action which retards the implementation of sustainable development.

Governments committed to following environmental friendly policies and promoting sustainable government often draw up community-driven development initiatives. These might include programs where local farmers are allowed to manage natural resources such as forests, fisheries, irrigation, watersheds and rangelands. These initiatives tend to fail unless corresponding property rights are well spelled out and enforced. Bromley (1991) defines property rights as "the capacity to call upon the collective to stand behind one's claim to a benefit stream", and not merely restricted to the narrow definition of full ownership and sole authority to manage.

Without established property rights for community farmers, the group's capacity to collaborate is not only impeded, but the individual's incentive to conserve or invest in the land is also sorely lacking. Meinzen-Dick and Gregorio (2004) conclude that property rights reinforce collective action: "Without recognized decision making rights; the groups lack the authority to manage the resource or to stop members or outsiders from breaking the rules. Recognized property rights not only reinforce collective action that is needed for collective management, but also provide security for individuals and households."

Property rights and collective action are often interdependent and especially important for most natural resource management schemes. As can be seen in Figure 8.2, over longer time periods and larger areas for agroforestry, both property rights and collective action appear to grow in importance. Instances of agroforestry collective action include large farms working together to jointly fence off lands to restore natural woody vegetation (in Australia), farmers establishing

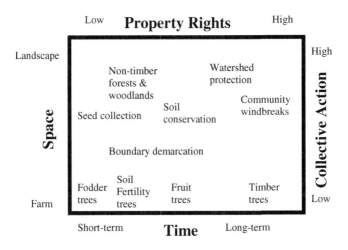

Figure 8.2 Relative Importance of Property Rights and Collective Action in Agroforestry
Source: Place *et al.* (2004).

windbreaks to protect coffee trees (in Costa Rica), or planting trees to decrease soil erosion in watersheds (Place *et al.*, 2004).

Ostrom (2004) recommends that governments supplement community groups' action through provision of reliable and up-to-date information about the natural resource systems such as groundwater replenishment rates and geological structure, provide guidelines and design principles upon which to model, and lastly, create institutional mechanisms for communication through forums, meetings and debates to resolve conflicting aims or interests.

8.2.2 Spatial clubs — an extended model

We now turn to see how geographical space can affect the formation of clubs and its sharing of impure public goods (Scotchmer, 2002). Recall public goods share two main characteristics, namely: (i) nonexcludability, and (ii) nonrivalry. Goods provided by clubs would violate the first condition of nonexcludability since nonmembers are effectively barred from enjoying the benefits of club membership, either through subscription fees or other nonprice exclusion mechanisms. In addition, the amount of club goods that can be provided for the individual is not only constrained by the number of club members but also the limited geographic space, further violating the second condition of nonrivalry. Overcrowding could occur due to the scarcity of land too. A dual price system could arise — for both the price of land and price of membership — for the joint sharing of impure public goods.

The case of spatial clubs in the context of housing reveals an interesting twist to the original club theory model advocated by Buchanan (1965), as it includes a geographical context for the club and has serious implications for social equality and economic development. Such spatial clubs have been termed gated communities: "Gated communities go further in several aspects than other means of exclusion. They create physical barriers to access. They also privatize community space, not just individual space" (Blakely and Snyder, 1997, p. 8).

Gated communities have been on the rise in different parts of the world for different reasons, including the US, Europe and China. In countries where the government plays a less interventionist role in the economy, they have been particularly prominent. In its simplest form, residential properties of citizens are simply enclosed, fencing in residents and excluding them from other neighbors. Residents get to enjoy amenities within the enclosed property; the former public spaces such as parks, traffic lights and streets have been demarcated exclusively for the use of residents. In the US, around one-tenth of citizens live in gated communities and numbers appear to be on the rise (Aalbers, 2003). Reasons for living in a gated community range from security reasons (fear of crime, violence and drugs), retirement, living among similarly like-minded individuals and families, or enjoying a luxurious lifestyle. See Box 8.1 for gated communities for the wealthy in Beijing, China.

Aalbers (2003) has termed this effect as dual closure — exclusion of residents in gated communities from the rest of society either voluntarily or involuntarily. There could be voluntary exclusion from individuals at the top income levels to live away from public institutions and services; there could also be involuntary exclusion of individuals at the bottom rung of the income ladder, who are cut off from the rest of society and from opportunities for upward income mobility (for instance, ghetto inhabitants in parts of Mexico). The exclusion of these two groups of individuals, the very rich and the very poor, could have dangerous repercussions for societal equality and development of the economy. The very rich may have the ability to exclude themselves spatially, though not economically or socially, but they are also depriving the rest of society of their economic, social and cultural capital. Critics have argued that gated communities promote a vicious circle of weakened social interactions among citizens, distorted work patterns and worsening of social inequality. It could also lead to a reduction of government services to the poor since former public provided goods are now provided by the members of clubs who can afford them.

Box 8.1   Spatial Clubs — Clubs within Clubs (e.g., Beijing)

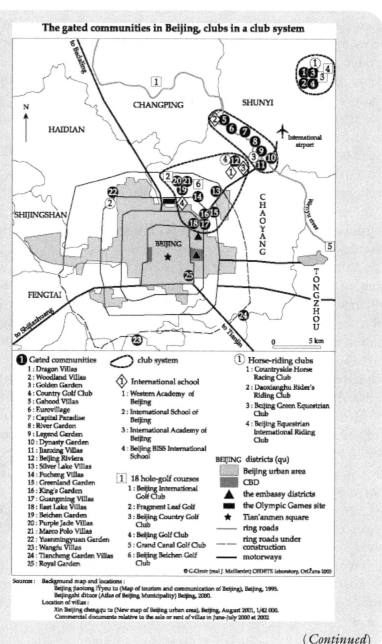

(*Continued*)

Box 8.1 (*Continued*)

The sharing of impure public goods is constrained by the geographical space on which Beijing's gated communities are constructed (Giroir, 2003). See how the clubs are enclosed within the black circles on the outskirts of Beijing in the map. The clubs are in fact many luxury villas (*bieshu qu*) set up for the rich and elite of China, with housing prices reaching astronomical highs and names such as Purple Jade Villa and Green River Manor. Citizens of luxury villas get to enjoy public property in the form of nice scenery and lakes provided by the community and inaccessible to the rest of the resident population. For instance, over 80 percent of land areas in Purple Jade Villas are lakeside spaces. They have significant control over the sculpturing of their environment and also influence the pattern of production of other forms of recreational and educational goods and services around them (namely, horse-riding clubs, golf courses, shopping malls and international schools). Citizens share common characteristics of wealth and/or power and are of a certain social status. Citizens include foreign expatriates working in China, heads of important organizations, the newly rich and retired politicians with powerful networks of influence. Such gated communities are strategically located along the expressway to the airport, the Wenyu River and Asian games village in the north-eastern part of Beijing. As can be seen in the map, the gated communities near the Wenyu River follow a more linear-type system with the Euroville, Capital Paradise and amenities such as Beijing Green Equestrian Club and International School of Beijing. The latter was set up to provide schooling for primary and secondary students from rapidly expanding neighboring luxury villas. To the right of Wenyu River, the gated community presents a circular form near the International Airport, whereas in the north of Bejing, a more polycentric type system emerges. Such gated communities exhibit club characteristics with exclusive membership and share the usage of club goods, both public and private, within their geographical territory. This extension of club theory has important implications for urban planners on city governance and structuring.

Source: Giroir (2003).

8.3 International Clubs

From an international perspective, club theory can also be applied to explain the stances of states with different preferences and the resulting degree of collective action taken on global issues such as greenhouse gases and intellectual property rights. As mentioned earlier, a club could contain heterogeneous members, and stronger members could actually influence the compliance of weaker members. This is very true in the international arena. Some countries are richer and more powerful than others such as G7 and OECD members, while some are less developed. Drezner (2003) illustrates the interesting variations in the constructed regulatory frameworks when preferences of great powers such as G7 and developing states and within the great powers themselves are not in total agreement (refer to Tables 8.1 and 8.2).

Table 8.1 shows that when there is low conflict between preferences of states, for instance on global product standards like ISO 9000 and Internet protocols, collective agreements can be easily reached. At the other extreme, when great powers are not in agreement and the preferences of great powers and developing states clash drastically, for instance on greenhouse gases and labor standards, collective action is difficult. The costs to the developing states to reduce greenhouse gases by cutting down fewer trees and slowing the pace of industrialization (in terms of foregone income and adjustment costs) are significantly higher than that of developed states, but the benefits are enjoyed by all members. In the case of control of CFC emissions and whaling, when the interests of the great powers are more at stake and developing states have less conflicting aims with these great powers, the resulting equilibrium may be highly unstable and rival standards could occur. The end result will depend on negotiation and consensus building, especially among stronger members.

On the other hand, when the great powers are in agreement and only the preferences of the developed countries are not in total accord with the great powers, for instance in the cases of intellectual property rights and money laundering, Drezner (2003, and Tables 8.1 and 8.2) claims that club standards will be easier to maintain. Club methods to influence the compliance of the members such as multilateral coercion and inducements are used. Intervention would be in the form of standard setting and monitoring of enforced standards.

Table 8.1 Divergence of Preferences

		Divergence of Preferences between Great Powers and Developing States	
		High Conflict	Low Conflict
Divergence of Preferences among Great Powers	High Conflict	Sham standards	Rival standards
	Low Conflict	Club standards	Harmonized standards

Source: Drezner (2003, p. 37, Table 1).

Table 8.2 Standards and Strategies

	Sham Standards or No Standards	Rival Standards	Club Standards	Harmonized Standards
State Strategies	Unilateral coercion and inducements	Competing standards	Great power concert	Functional optimization; delegation
Predicted Solution	Weakly enforced standards; repeated conflicts	Competing standards in multiple for great power opt outs; unstable equilbria	Core-created and core-imposed standards	Technical standards
IGO Role	Political cover	Competing arenas for bargaining	Coalition building; standard setting	Legitimization
NGO Role	Lobbyists; norm promoters	Consensus builders	Proselytizers; protestors	Standard setters
Empirical Examples	Greenhouse gases; labor standards	CFC emissions; whaling; GMO	Money laundering; intellectual property rights	Product standards; Internet protocol

Source: Drezner (2003, p. 37, Table 2).
Note: Sham standards are equivalent to no standards or very minimal standards.

8.3.1 *An application — the Asian financial crisis*

Drezner (2003) illustrates how the G7 have made use of club organizations to influence the pattern of international financial monitoring and its governance, especially in less developed countries, particularly after the Asian financial crisis. He splits international governmental organizations (IGOs) into three categories:

1. Universal IGOs such as the United Nations (UN), World Bank and International Monetary Fund (IMF) that try to maximize membership interests;
2. IGOs such as G7 and OECD that only admit like-minded states for collective action purposes;
3. Neighborhood IGOs such as ASEAN and Council of Europe based on geographical territories to form stronger positions with other allies.

Owing to the difficulty of reaching consensus in a universal IGO such as the UN or the IMF, where the large number of members made agreement difficult, it was difficult to get initiatives ratified. It is relative easy for developing states to block action since the decision making procedures require wide agreement. Within the IMF, the required tacit agreement of all members and in the UN, the members of the Security Council, has to reach agreement. "On complex issues there is generally an understanding that 'nothing will be decided until everything is agreed'" (Van Houtven, 2002, p. 24).

The G7 has fewer problems reaching agreement since its club only admits "like-minded" high income industrial countries, thereby promoting the same preferences and paving the way for collective actions. Transaction costs of decision making are also relatively less compared to the UN and the IMF.

Hence, Drezner argues that the focus of attention on international financial institutions have been overly concentrated on the IMF and World Bank, and have overlooked the ability of G7-empowered club organizations such as Financial Stability Forum (FSF), Bank of International Settlement (BIS), Basel Committee and Financial Action Task Force to make in line with their preferences. These organizations facilitate the formation of "coalitions of the willing" and enable them to bypass the IMF to a certain degree when drawing up the design of international financial standards.

For instance, the FSF was delegated with the responsibility of developing guidelines for global financial standards. The deliberate outnumbering of G7 members to non-G7 members within the FSF made it relatively easier to shift the balance of the vote towards the G7 agenda. Membership in the BIS is restricted to industrial countries and closed-door meetings were often held. The homogeneity of club members within the BIS members was regarded as an advantage since it allowed for speedy responses to policy changes. For this very reason, it was deliberately selected by G7 to establish global financial standards.

This is what Drezner (2003) termed "forum shopping". The intentional choice of G7 members to empower these "club" IGOs with certain powers, enabled the G7 to successfully influence the outcome of collective action in their favor. They were able to override the international IGOs (the IMF) which they also belonged to. If their forum shopping were less successful or if they had chosen a club IGO which did not exhibit the similar characteristics and preferences as desired, the outcome is likely to have been entirely different.

FSF is an example of a "club within a club". The very existence of such clubs in the first place affects the market payoffs to nonmembers. The ability of the FSF to draw up financial standards effectively preempted the establishment of any other alternative sets of standards, thereby in part ensuring the market payoffs that the G7 desired (Schelling, 1960; Garett and Weingast, 1993). Despite the voluntary submission of IMF reports on the observance of standards and codes by developing states, it still resulted in a high rate of submission by the end of 2002 since the very decision of a less developed state not to submit its IMF report was very much publicly noticed and would "raise eyebrows" regarding that particular country's financial observance. Such club IGOs ensured the compliance of other members and had the authority to penalize the violator with sanctions. FSF had to publicly identify countries that violated financial observance and other club IGOs such as the Financial Action Task Force (FATF) deals with uncovering tax havens and prosecuting violators.

Other instances of how clubs affect the outcomes of collective action can be found in the US telecommunication industry and global nuclear regulations. (Please see Krasner, 1991; Braithwaite and Drahos, 2000, for further details.)

8.4   Collective Decision Making

We have seen how the great powers manage to enforce their preferences through a combination of persuasion and coercion through the club IGOs. We now turn to an analysis of how certain members are able to manipulate the outcome of collective action.

8.4.1   *Aggregation of collective preferences*[2]

To improve the well-being of the group members, it is first necessary to identify the goal of the club. To know the goal of the club, we would need to know group preferences of club members. A simple method for aggregating the individual preferences of members of the clubs is through voting. Market transactions are regarded as efficient when there is voluntary consent by all members and each member benefits — there is movement towards Pareto optimality. In a similar vein, all members would have to be in unanimous agreement on club principles in order to derive efficient collective action. However, it is highly unlikely that all members have identical preferences. Unanimity rule appears to be highly unlikely and would register relatively high costs of decision making.

For instance, it would take a long time for all members to decide on the optimal type and size of the good they want. In many cases, clubs apply the majority rule principle instead of unanimity rule. If a majority of the members agree upon a decision, the club passes it. However, since majority rule confers a negative cost on the minority group who opposed the decision, they will be worse off if this policy is adopted. Hence, there is no movement towards Pareto optimality unless it can be guaranteed that the benefits received by the majority outweigh the losses of the minority, or unless all members have unanimously agreed beforehand to adopt a decision rule of "less than unanimity" for the group's future decisions. This result could arise because of the relatively lower decision making costs.

---

[2]Drawn from Holcombe (1996, Chapter 7).

In some cases, decision with less than majority vote could also take place. For example, making a pot of coffee within a coffee club of 20 members might only require the consent of three members — only 15 percent agreement is necessary. Conversely, more than 85 percent of the club would have to vote not to make a pot of coffee. The less than majority rule is also true for a case to be heard by the US Supreme Court. If four out of nine Supreme Court justices want the case to be heard, it will be heard.

The condition for club membership requires cost/benefit analysis. Regardless of the decision rule applied, a member of the group is better off as long as benefits outweigh the decision making costs and external costs on the minority. The most commonly used decision rule is simple majority rule, which is very often used in tandem with representative voting. Representative voting delegates the responsibility of voting to a few selected members within the club and allows for lower decision making costs since fewer people are directly involved.

In the case of the universal IGOs such as the IMF, there are representatives from each country when global negotiations take place. In coordinating negotiations on global financial monitoring in the aftermath of the Mexican and Asian financial crises, specific IGOs were deliberately selected for their member characteristics, so that representatives of G7 members would more than outnumber non-G7 members, and hence be able to influence the outcome of the collective action.

Some important decisions that the club would have to make collectively include the optimal club output, club size and the type of good or service provided. The size of the club would depend on the type of club good provided since different goods have different characteristics. For instance, the size of clubs for sport and recreation such as horse-riding clubs and golf courses would be smaller than that of national parks, highways or schools. Decisions at the national level would involve a much larger club such as a parliament or an executive branch of government, say for the provision of subsidized university education or national defense. If the problem of congestion arises (the tragedy of the commons, for example), the number of members would have to be limited in order to allow existing members to enjoy a certain level of satisfaction with the provided good.

To achieve the objectives of the club, Hotelling (1929) suggests that the outcome of the voting process will most likely lead to a result that is somewhere near the median or close to the views or choice of the most representative agent of the club. On the other hand, strategic voting could also come into play where club members deliberately vote for something they oppose in order to gain votes for something they desire elsewhere or at another time. For greater discussion on these, please refer to Sandler (2001, Chapter 5).

8.4.2 *Multiple interest groups, democracy and economic sclerosis*

Collective action can be taken in the form of clubs and governments. Admittedly, there is an important distinction between clubs and government regarding the nature of the entry and exit of members. Clubs allow members to voluntarily exit, whereas government does not allow its citizens to do so unless they give up citizenship and leave the country or migrate elsewhere (Holcombe, 1996). But there are interesting insights regarding club theory that can be gleaned from the experience of governments.

Olson (1965) has argued that multiple interest groups with conflicting aims could lead to economic sclerosis or slower economic growth. In the case of Japan, conflicts still exist between competing factions within the controlling party, the Liberal Democratic Party (LDP). Such competing factions have formed alliances with like-minded banks and companies. With the advent of the slowing down of the Japanese economy, there has been slow progress in economic and primarily financial restructuring due to the close links between the multiple interest groups and their financer backers. The interests of these clubs is not necessarily aligned with the national interest, which is one reason why progress on restructuring and a return to higher growth been so difficult in Japan, and also why Prime Minister Koizumi received high marks for creating a consensus for political and economic action in a number of areas. Hence, Olson (2000) deliberately stresses the importance of "secure democracy" for continued economic prosperity and growth.

Within Asia and Latin America, large groups or networks that play a critical role in economic development have emerged. In Korea there are the *chaebol*, in Japan the *keiretsu* and in Latin America the *grupos*. At times, the interests of such groups conflict with that of the society as a whole. Although theirs has weakened since the Asian financial crisis, Japan's economy is dominated by six traditional *keiretsu* who are responsible for approximately half the trade on the Japanese stock exchange. However, major relations between *keiretsu*, such as the vertical linkages between Toyota and Honda and the horizontal linkages of Toyota and Mitsui *keiretsu*, still exist. The debt-laden trading company Nissho Iwai is affiliated with the DKB and Sanwa *keiretsu* and this has made restructuring difficult. One well-known Latin American *grupo* is the Monterrey Group, which accounts for nearly one-fifth of Mexico's national GDP and holds sizeable stakes in the country's steel and soft drinks companies (Haley *et al.*, 2004).

Olson (1965) also inferred that there could be other substantial costs to the economy from dominance by a few clubs. They come in the form of lobbying costs and deadweight taxation losses. Lobbying costs are incurred when groups try to subvert the course of action in their favor, and resources and money are spent on nonproductive areas. The economy is generally worse off. Rent seeking activities and crony capitalism could also result from strong club influence, resulting in illegal profit making opportunities and corruption. Moreover, when the government gives handouts to favored small groups, this could create severe deadweight losses to the society in the long run if funded by additional taxation. Subsidies to inefficient state-owned industries in China and other developing countries have to be paid for by the rest of the tax paying public.

Schofield (2003) develops a detailed interpretation of the interplay between power, prosperity and social choice. On one hand, there could be total chaos with no veto groups. On the other hand, there could be stability with either multiple interest groups or autocracy but with differing degree of risk taking attitudes (see Figure 8.3). In the first scenario, power is distributed unevenly among various multiple interest groups in conflict with each other, like in the case of Japan. This is illustrated diagrammatically by the lower left hand corner of the triangle in Figure 8.3. Interest groups with multiple conflicting objectives have to face problems of time-consuming negotiations, lobbying and possible economic stalemate. Groups in this corner characterized by extreme stability also tend to be risk averse in undertaking reforms that could upset the existing power matrix. The other extreme scenario has power totally concentrated in the hands of the autocracy and is located in the lower right hand corner of the triangle of Figure 8.3. The Soviet Union under Stalin is a good example, as is Iraq under Saddam Hussein. There is political stability but no constraints on how to manage resources. Hence, there is also a high probability of facing economic slowdown and collapse in the case of failed leadership. Remember the quote "Power corrupts and absolute power corrupts absolutely". Schofield highlights the importance of democracy for collective action and continued economic prosperity in the country and stresses the importance of avoiding the extreme states of the power triangle.

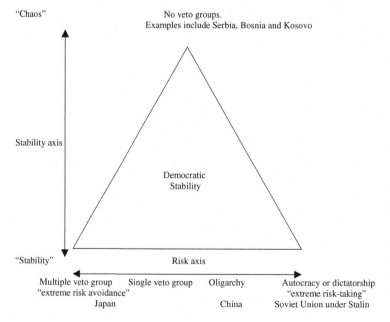

Figure 8.3 Interplay between Power and Social Choice
Source: Adapted from Schofield (2003, p. 102, Figure 2).

However, Schofield concludes that in the absence of democracy, economic growth could still be achieved, especially notable in the case of China's oligarchy state. It has to do with China's unique form of governance whereby provincial leaders have wide authority and an economic mandate to raise living standards.

Capitalism without democracy can be illustrated using a basic theorem of social contract. The theorem suggests that an individual enters into a "contract" with the state. Individuals comply with the law and the government in return agrees to protect the individual's rights of life, liberty and property. The rights of the individual serve to prohibit excessive interference by the government. If the government fails to keep up its end of the bargain, public rebellion would be justified. However, this theory has been criticized because of the fuzziness of the hypothesized contract between individuals and the government. There is no formal contract where actual obligations are spelled out.

In China, there is an apparent and lamentable lack of legal frameworks to sufficiently protect the rights of the individual, yet the economy still manages to achieve astonishing GDP growth each year. This is due to the Eastern nature of governance, which is not rule-based but rather relation-based. See Box 8.2 for more details on the Eastern style of governance and management which has often puzzled foreign investors.

8.4.3 *Institutions and the public interest*

Continuing with the train of thought from the previous section, assume the government and its citizens could operate as a club. The government has to decide on the optimal level of public goods provision that would maximize the welfare of its members. Collective action in the form of a club requires trust within members to function effectively. This condition also applies for collective action in the form of political institutions. We need to ask the question: do government institutions always act in the interest of the public?

The World Economic Forum (2003) reports a worrying trend that two-thirds of the surveyed population of 46 countries expressed

Box 8.2 Eastern Style of Governance and Management

Xiaotong Fei, one of China's leading sociologists, argued that the Chinese society emphasized egocentralism, with the family forming the basic network which extended through a series of bipolar relationships to lineages, localities, provinces and countries. Chinese society is based heavily on that of relationships and networks, unlike western individualism which follows a rule-based system. The Chinese owe their loyalty to people and networks, and not between people and the state. The legal system in the style of Western countries was almost nonexistent until very recently. The state laws were only used to supplement the network codes to force transgressors back into toeing the line. In ancient times, the emperor would use his network to put pressure on the transgressor's closest network, normally his family, who would, in turn, exert pressure on the individual, reminding him of his filial duty and obedience to society. Although there has been a shift towards property-rights legal codes, networks are still predominantly present in China, making personal loyalties in relationships very important.

Source: Haley *et al.* (2004).

little or no trust in their government agencies to act in their best interest. Listed below (see also Table 8.3) are some of the findings from their report based on ratings of 17 different institutions from different countries:

- The national legislative body (parliament or congress) is generally least trusted.
- Armed forces generally enjoy the highest level of trust worldwide, which could be due to the security role they play against terrorism.
- Nongovernment organizations (NGOs) and religious groups and churches also enjoy a fairly high level of trust.
- Trust in international organizations such as World Trade Organization (WTO), World Bank and International Monetary Fund (IMF) to operate in the interest of the society is mixed. About half agreed

Table 8.3 Trust in Institutions to Operate in Society's Best Interests

Column 1	Column 2	Column 3	Column 4 = 3–2
Institution	Little or No Trust (in percent)	A Lot or Some Trust (in percent)	Net Trust Rating
Armed Forces	26	69	43
NGOs	32	59	27
Educational System	35	62	26
UN	34	55	21
Religious Institutions	38	57	19
Police	40	57	17
Health Systems	40	57	17
WTO	39	44	5
Government	47	50	3
Press/Media	47	49	2
Trade Unions/Labor	45	47	2
World Bank	41	43	2
Legal System	49	47	–2
IMF	41	39	–2
Global Companies	48	39	–9
Large National Companies	52	42	–10
Parliament/Congress	51	38	–13

Source: Adapted from World Economic Forum (2003).

Note: Global ratings (n = 34,000 across 46 countries). Columns 2 and 3 do not necessarily add to 100 percent because of missing responses.

they act beneficially, whereas the other half disagreed. WTO has a slightly higher level of trust than the other two.

- Trust in media and trade unions are low.
- Corporate companies are generally ranked at the bottom of the rating next to government bodies due to the recent string of corporate scandals in 2002.

The current breakdown of trust reflects serious concerns over the effectiveness of government institutions and the quality of goods and services provided. Immediate questions to be resolved include: can trust in institutions be re-established successfully? If so, how do you go about doing so? What roles do leaders play? All these questions will need to be adequately answered in order to serve the various needs of society and to ensure optimal allocation of resources within the society.

8.5 Private-Public Sector Partnership in Asia

In recent years, there has been an increasing ratio of private-public participation in the provision of goods with positive spillovers like education and healthcare (Kikeri and Kolo, 2005). Such goods are not strictly private goods, but rather what economists call club goods. Instead of solely relying on government provision which tends to be inadequate at times, private-public partnership and voluntary welfare groups such as churches and charity groups have formed to provide social services like education and healthcare.

Participation from the private sector has also been on the rise in the past two decades, especially in areas of infrastructure like energy sector, telecommunication, transport, water and sewerage. Within the East Asian and Pacific region, Indonesia and Malaysia undertook major privatization efforts in the 1990s. In China, privatization has more than doubled, accounting for nearly 90 percent of the region's proceeds from privatization in 2000 up from 50 percent in the 1990s. For more data, please refer to the online World Bank Privatization Database.[3]

There are two possible roles for the private sector: it could either act as a supplement to publicly provided services or as an alternative to public provision if the individual is able to afford out-of-pocket expenses. According to club theory, members in the club enjoy mutual benefits from sharing an impure public good. For example, although the healthcare services enjoyed by the individual when he pays a visit to the clinic is his private benefit, he also lowers the risk of infecting others. Positive externalities are generated when there is a high level of healthcare, especially when there are infectious diseases. Positive externalities also arise with education.

---

[3]The online database provides information on privatization transactions in developing countries from 1998 to 2003. See http://rru.worldbank.org/Privatization/.

There is an underlying assumption that the private sector is likely to be more responsive to changes in demand and more efficient than the public sector. With the rising income levels in Asian countries, the role of the private sector in providing healthcare and higher education in Asia has been particularly rapid in the last two or three decades. GDP ratios of private-to-public sector spending has been on the rise. Figure 8.4 reports health expenditure in various Asian countries during the 1990s. The figures demonstrate the willingness of the people to pay for private sector goods and services in China, Indonesia, Philippines and especially Thailand. There were active calls for privatization of the healthcare industry within individual Asian countries during the later part of the 1990s. This trend came to a standstill with the Asian financial crisis. Recently, however, privatization and public-private partnerships have been on the rise again.

In addition to public-private partnerships in provisioning of public goods, the role of nonprofit organizations in the provision of social services has also attracted interest. NGOs combine altruism, charity and entrepreneurship in their bid to offer social services to society. The "warm glow" effect that members get from helping others somehow offsets the lack of or small size of monetary benefits. One prominent advantage of NGOs in comparison to the public sector is their relatively lower transaction costs in identifying needy groups. Unlike the public sector which requires some time and effort before resources can be mobilized for aid, NGOs find it easier to call on members for aid and to help needy individuals rather quickly. They are smaller in size and do not need to go through as much red tape. However, this strength can also be a limitation. Due to their small size, they often lack adequate resources to resolve the problem at hand and are unable to fully resolve free rider problems. They often display tendencies to channel aid towards specific subgroups, probably towards people of similar race or ethic group or religious belief. This results in gaps in the coverage of benefits to some needy groups, simply because they are not favored by particular NGOs. There could also be wasteful duplication of resources where the individual receives aid from both the public and NGOs (see Dollery and Wallis, 2001).

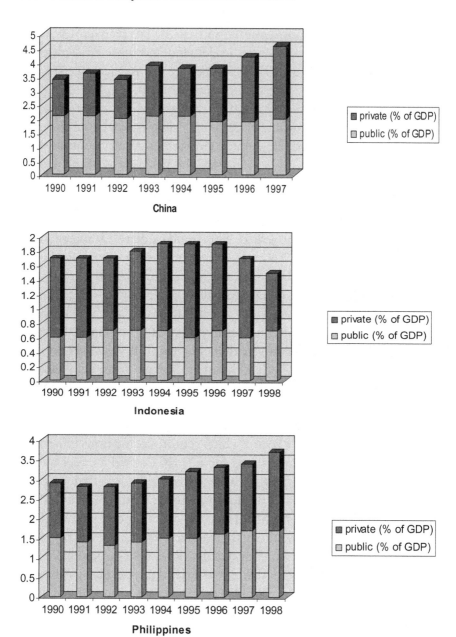

Figure 8.4 Health Expenditure in Selected Asian Countries, 1990s

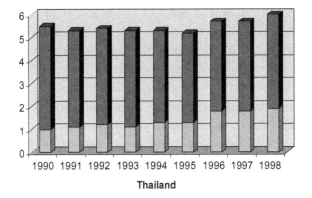

Thailand

Figure 8.4 (*Continued*)

Source: Data from World Bank (2001).

8.6 Conclusion

We conclude this chapter by attempting to address the factors affecting successful collective action. It builds upon the earlier chapter with emphasis on trust and social capital, and attempts to connect with Chapters 9 and 10 which analyze government intervention during market failure. On the micro level, we have discussed the provision of public goods through the collaboration of two or more individuals and the effect of externalities on group behavior.

As seen previously, the size of the group will affect the nature of cooperation and its efficiency. Olson (1965) explains why exploitation of the great by the small could exist. Interestingly, the same theory can be used to explain how small groups can actually "subvert" the original aims of the bigger groups through their collaboration, as in forum shopping. Policy suggestions aimed at minimizing collaborative failure include the formation of clubs to introduce exclusion mechanisms to turn a pure public good into an impure public good. At the macro level, we had a brief discussion on international club shopping, multiple interest groups, governance and economic sclerosis. This is a new and exciting field. Collective action has been used to analyze many new and exciting areas such as city planning (gated communities) and even terrorism.

Collective action demonstrates that unity of the whole is greater than the sum of its parts. However, there are delicate intricacies in individual decision making, not to mention collective decision making, which touches on aspects of trust and conflicts of interest that could easily displace collective action. As globalization and advances in information technology hasten the pace of communications and the growth of networking, collective action can only grow in importance over the decades. Collective action and group formation has valuable applications in various fields of economics such as environment studies, political economy and industrial organization.

In the next chapter, we shall continue with a greater discussion of public and merit goods and see how altruism and selfishness affect the provision of such goods. Charity and corruption are also explored to see how they enter the equation of individual decision making.

Bibliography

Aalbers, M.B. (2003) The Double Function of the Gate: Social Inclusion and Exclusion in Gated Communities and Security Zones. Paper presented at the conference on "Gated Communities: Building Social Division or Safer Communities?", 18–19 September 2003, University of Glasgow, UK.

Berman, E. (2003) Hamas, Taliban and the Jewish Underground: An Economist's View of Radical Religious Militias. NBER Working Paper No. 10004. http://www.nber.org/papers/w10004 [Retrieved 5 June 2005].

Blakely, E.J. and M.G. Snyder (1997) *Fortress America: Gated Communities in the United States.* Washington, DC and Cambridge: Brooking Institution Press/Lincoln Institute of Land Policy.

Braithwaite, J. and P. Drahos (2000) *Global Business Regulation.* Cambridge: Cambridge University Press.

Bromley, D. (1991) *Environment and Economy: Property Rights and Public Policy.* Cambridge, MA: Basil Blackwell.

Buchanan, J.M. (1965) An Economic Theory of Clubs. *Economica*, 32, 1–14.

Dollery, B. and J. Wallis (2001) Economic Approaches to the Voluntary Sector: A Note on Voluntary Failure and Human Service Delivery. Working Paper Series in Economics No. 2001-16, University of New England, School of Economics.

Drezner, D.W. (2003) Clubs, Neighbourhoods and Universes: The Governance of Global Finance. Paper prepared for presentation at 2003 Annual Meeting of the American Political Science Association, 28–31 August 2003.

Economist (2004, 15 September) Turkey and EU.

Garett, G. and B. Weingast (1993) Ideas, Interests and Institutions: Constructing the European Community's Common Market. In J. Goldstein and R. Keohane (eds.), *Ideas and Foreign Policy*. Ithaca: Cornell University Press.

Gauthier, D. (1986) *Morals by Agreement*. Oxford: Clarendon Press.

Giroir, G. (2003) Gated Communities, Clubs in a Club System: The Case of Beijing (China). http://www.neighbourhoodcenter.org.uk/gated.html [Retrieved 11 October 2004].

Granovetter, M. (1978) Threshold Models of Collective Action. *American Journal of Sociology*, 83, 1420–1443.

Haley, G., T. Haley, C.V. Usha and C.T. Tan (2004) *The Chinese Tao of Business: The Logic of Successful Business Strategy*. Singapore: John Wiley & Sons.

Heath, J. (2000) Ideology, Irrationality and Collectively Self-Defeating Behaviour. *Constellations*, 7(3), 363–371.

Holcombe, R.G. (1996) *Public Finance: Government Revenues and Expenditures in the US Economy*. St. Paul, MN: West Pub. Co.

Hotelling, H. (1929) Stability and Competition. *Economic Journal*, 39, 41–57.

Iannaccone, L.R. (1998) Introduction to the Economics of Religion. *Journal of Economic Literature*, XXXVI, 1465–1496.

Inglehart, R. and H. Klingemann (2000) Genes, Culture, Democracy, and Happiness. In E. Diener and E.M. Suh (eds.), *Culture and Subjective Well-Being*. Cambridge: MIT Press.

Kikeri, S. and A.F. Kolo (2005) Privatisation: Trends and Recent Developments. World Bank Working Paper Series No. 3765.

Krasner, S.D. (1991) Global Communication and National Power: Life on the Pareto Frontier. *World Politics*, 43(April), 336–366.

Little, I.M.D. (2002) *Ethics, Economics and Politics: Principles of Public Policy*. Oxford: Oxford University Press.

Meinzen-Dick, R.S. and M. Di Gregorio (eds.) (2004) *Collective Action and Property Rights for Sustainable Development*. IFPRI 2020 Vision Focus Brief 11, February. http://www.ifpri.org/pubs/catalog.htm#focus [Retrieved 5 June 2005].

Moffatt, M. (2004) The Logic of Collective Action. http://economics.about.com/cs/macroeconomics/a/logic_of_action.htm [Retrieved 11 October 2004].

Oliver, P.E. and G. Marwell (1988) The Paradox of Group Size in Collective Action: A Theory of Critical Mass II. *American Sociological Review*, 53(February), 1–8.

Olson, M. (1965) *The Logic of Collective Action*. Cambridge: Harvard University Press.

Olson, M. (2000) *Power and Prosperity: Outgrowing Communist and Capitalist Dictatorships*. New York: Basic.

Ostrom, E. (2004) Understanding Collective Action. In R.S. Meinzen-Dick and M. Di Gregorio (eds.), *Collective Action and Property Rights for Sustainable*

Development. IFPRI 2020 Vision Focus Brief 11, February. http://www.ifpri.org/pubs/catalog.htm#focus [Retrieved 5 June 2005].

Place, F., K. Otsuka and S. Scherr (2004) Property Rights, Collective Action, and Agroforestry. In R.S. Meinzen-Dick and M. Di Gregorio (eds.), *Collective Action and Property Rights for Sustainable Development*. IFPRI 2020 Vision Focus Brief 11, February. http://www.ifpri.org/pubs/catalog.htm#focus [Retrieved 5 June 2005].

Sandler, T. (1993) *Collective Action: Theory and Application*. Ann Arbor: University of Michigan Press.

Sandler, T. (2001) *Economic Concepts for the Social Sciences*. Cambridge: Cambridge University Press.

Schelling, T.C. (1960) *The Strategy of Conflict*. Cambridge, MA: Harvard University Press.

Schofield, N. (2003) Power, Prosperity and Social Choice: A Review. *Social Choice and Welfare*, 20, 85–118.

Scotchmer, S. (2002) Local Public Goods and Clubs. In A. Auerbach and M. Feinstein (eds.), *Handbook of Public Economics*, Vol. IV, Ch. 29. Amsterdam: North Holland.

Scotchmer, S. (2005) Consumption Externalities, Rental Markets and Purchase Clubs. *Economic Theory*, 25, 235–253.

Tiebout, C. (1956) A Pure Theory of Local Expenditures. *The Journal of Political Economy*, 64, 416–424.

Van Houtven, L. (2002) Governance of the IMF. IMF Pamphlet Series No. 53.

Watts, D. (2003) *Six Degrees: The Science of a Connected Age*. New York: W.W. Norton.

World Bank (2001) *World Development Indicators*. Washington, DC: World Bank.

World Bank Privatisation Database. http://rru.worldbank.org/Privatization/ [Retrieved 18 October 2006].

World Economic Forum (2003) Annual Meeting Theme: Trust and Values. http://www.weforum.org [Retrieved 5 June 2005].

Chapter 9

Public Goods, Charity and Corruption

Much of what we have discussed up to now has focused on the individual consumer or groups of consumers or workers. We learned how emotions played a role in altering economic decision making. We considered whether people are basically selfish or if they have altruistic tendencies or propensities. We also looked at the determinants of subjective well-being and examined aspects of trust and fairness.

We now turn to some wider issues relating to the overall workings of an economic system. In the narrow world of the classical economists, there is no room for anything other than hedonistic calculus. In this system, economic efficiency is the primary goal. All the conditions imposed by fundamental theorems of welfare economics such as no externalities are upheld and every agent pursues his or her self-interest. This leads to a Pareto optimal solution. In such a system, there is no reason to abandon self-interest. This is an artificial, yet very elegant theoretical construct, where everyone is paid the value of their marginal product, all decisions made by consumers are consistent with demand theory, all markets contain perfect information, markets are competitive and the government's role is limited, supplying some services and the courts.

Since economic efficiency, competitive markets and economic freedom are given such a high standing in such a system, it is difficult for economists to deal with other important values. Ordinarily other values are treated as exceptions to this theoretical construct. Notice that the neoclassical theory says nothing about income distribution. It arises from the marginal productivity conditions and the supply of labor to markets. Those with high marginal productivity get paid more than those with lower marginal productivity.

To go beyond the conventional analysis, we introduce the possibility that economic agents have noneconomic motives. We can move away from purely economic motives for action when we include other arguments in the utility function. Using the same framework for utility maximization, the arguments in this utility function will change as well as the outcomes, as seen in previous chapters. For this chapter, our broad focus will be on market failure and the provision of public goods. We will explore the relationship between the public at large and the government in its role as the agent that provides goods that are not efficiently provided by the private sector. The primary thrust of this chapter is a discussion of charity and corruption.

9.1 Corruption, Charity and the Provision of Public Goods

Market failure occurs when markets do not allocate resources effectively. Many of the standard economic arguments for allocating and pricing resources break down when we consider the provision of public goods. This is because the ownership of public goods does not reside with private parties who can charge each individual for the consumption of the good or service. Rather, public goods have the general characteristic of being provided to the public by the government or some other public agency, and its consumption by one individual does not preclude the enjoyment of anyone else. The "exclusion principle" cannot be applied for public goods. This means that when I consume a public good or avail myself of a public service, it does not have any measurable effect on the consumption of the public good or service by others.

Furthermore, public goods are "nonrival". This means that an individual cannot stop others from consuming or enjoying the public good. There are many examples of what some economists call "pure" public goods that we see every day, including defense, public safety, equal protection under the law, recreational facilities such as public beaches and parks as well as the benefits of nature such as a beautiful sunset, clear air and beautiful scenery. These pure public goods adhere completely to both the exclusion principle and the nonrival principle. Since they are not owned by private individuals or corporations, goods and services traded in these markets are not easy to understand and regulate using conventional economic principles.

Since the use of a public good cannot exclude anyone, there may be a tendency for citizens to *free ride*, which is using the public good without paying for it. "Quasi-public goods" are very similar to public goods, although in the case of a quasi-public good, use of the resource may slightly alter the enjoyment by others. These quasi-public goods are also not completely nonrival. A crowded beach on a hot summer day is an example of a quasi-public good; crowds have an impact on the enjoyment of others even though one person would not have a measurable effect. The use of the beach is also not completely "nonrival". The inclination of many people to come to the beach on the same day causes the overcrowding, which may reduce others' enjoyment to the extent that crowds create negative utility (although some people love crowds and the opportunity to intermingle with others and make new friends).

In some cases the quality of pure public goods such as beautiful sunsets, clear air and the natural beauty of nature can be degraded by pollution and other environmental degradation. In these instances, the damage to the environment has to be factored into the costs and benefits of private enterprise and the government's role in maintaining the quality of the environment.

It is also possible that society produces goods and services that may be considered "public bads". These include the flip side of "public goods", e.g., polluted air and water, social discord and crime, a lack of public areas and parks, garbage strewn on sidewalks and surly people who do not respect the rights of others. As part of our discussion in this chapter, we will focus on a few aspects of public goods as they relate to altruism, cooperation and self-interest. We begin with public goods and charity, and we will discuss some undesirable aspects of society such as bribery and corruption later in the chapter.

9.2 Charity

In this section, we deal with the relationship between the provision of public goods and private charity. Intuitively, it stands to reason that when more public goods are provided, there will be a lower level of charitable contributions. This will generally be true if individual utility is a function of the consumption of private goods as well as the total supply of public goods. In addition, people are assumed not to gain any special utility from their individual private charitable contribution aside from the increase in the level of service that his or her contribution entails. If charity is "purely altruistic", then the giver has no hidden motive for giving. When public charity goes up, a purely altruistic charitable person will reduce his charitable contributions.

In a large economy with few purely altruistic people, the average amount of giving tends to approach zero in the limit (see Warr, 1982, for example). Private giving has almost no impact on the total supply of the public good. Furthermore, a dollar more of public spending will (nearly) crowd out a dollar of private charity. This scenario is popularly known as *Ricardian equivalence* after David Ricardo, who first studied this relationship between public and private charity.

However interesting these results are, they do not square with reality. In actual fact, there is a substantial amount of private charity in many societies and these contributions are made for a wide array of public goods. This is because charities exist and charitable contributions are made for a number of reasons besides pure altruism. As a result, charities do not provide a pure public good. Furthermore, charities are able to negate the free rider problem by earmarking their contributions.

If the output of charitable activities produces benefits that are nonrival and can be consumed equally by both those who contribute and those who do not, and individuals are acting to maximize their utility, then a charity will be a pure public good. However, people may not maximize their own utility if they act to maximize others' utility as well or if they are acting out of Kantian duty.

A feeling of guilt or compassion may spark a charitable contribution to a particular organization, or an individual may seek recognition from the community or the general public for his or her contribution. An important reason for charitable giving could be a sense of ethical duty to help achieve a more equitable and fair distribution of income and wealth. Furthermore, some of the benefits from the charity may flow to those who donate — the benefits can be excluded. (Recall the arguments for altruistic behavior discussed in Chapter 5.) As a result, private charity is not a pure public good.

Posnet and Sandler (1995) show that for British charities, fees and subscriptions account for a sizable source of income. These charities depend on service fees for a substantial proportion of their income, while allowing tax benefits to accrue to private charities. Similar results hold for the US according to information reported by Andreoni (1988):

> Over 85% of all households in the United States make donations to charities. Over 50% of all tax returns include deductions for charitable giving. The United Way fund boasts millions of contributors. Second, both aggregate and individual gifts are large. In total, the charitable sector of the American economy accounts for about 2% of GNP. Average giving was over $200 per household in 1971, ranging from $70 for the lowest income quartile to $350 for the highest quartile. In addition, religious organizations collected about $10 billion in 1981, health organizations and hospitals raised over $7 billion, and civic orchestras received $150 million in donations.

Furthermore, Weisbrod (1988) reports that 4.4 percent of national income originated from productive activities in the nonprofit sector in 1985. More recent data from *BBC* and *New York Times* report that the level of charitable donations by US companies has gone up by 14 percent in 2005, and there is increased giving by the ultra rich tycoons. The Bill and Melinda Gates Foundation to support research in health started with billions from Microsoft; Warren Buffett's contribution of up to 85 percent of his fortune to the Gates' foundation; and Virgin group's Richard Branson's pledge of some $3 billion to nonfossil-based energy development are visible examples.

Charitable foundations and NGOs depend wholly or in part on substantial amounts of voluntary donations. When the government joins with the private sector in providing the public good, government donations do not necessarily crowd out private sector donations. Econometric studies indicate that a one dollar increase in government contributions to "charitable activities" is associated with a decrease of private giving of less than 25 cents (Andreoni, 1988). All of this evidence suggests that public charity need not crowd out private charity.

Since the level of charitable contributions in the US is so much larger than a model of pure altruism would predict, we have to look beyond simple altruism for a solution to the phenomena of private charity. In other countries, the amount of private charity varies. In Europe, for example, the amount of private charity is smaller than in the US, probably because of the partial "crowding out" effect that a large public sector has on private charity. Nevertheless, Posnet and

Sandler (1995) have indicated that private charity in Britain still makes a substantial contribution to the overall economy.

9.3 "Warm Glow", Public Goods and the Determinants of Charitable Contributions

If individuals gain some personal satisfaction from charitable giving over and above the overall provision of the public good, then the crowding out effect will be less than one and private contributions can complement the provision of public goods. Andreoni (1990) shows this by constructing a model where an individual's utility is a function both of the provision of the public good (to which he has made a contribution) and the size of his own contribution. Andreoni calls this impure altruism, characterized by what he calls a "warm glow" from giving.

In this model, Andreoni shows that crowding out will depend upon the amount of impure altruism. In general, as noted above, those who give with a purely altruistic motive will reduce the amount of their giving in direct proportion to the increase in public provision of the resource. As a result, when the public provision of these goods is increased, private giving will be reduced accordingly.

The impure altruist, on the other hand, receives utility from giving because he obtains utility by acknowledgment from others. His or her contributions can be publicized in various ways. Thus, the impure altruist will continue to give even when the provision of public goods is increased. Riber and Wilhelm (2002) show that private giving is not crowded out by increased provision of public services for the same good. They suggest that donations seem to be motivated by the joy of giving rather than for other "impure" reasons suggested by Andreoni such as motivation to be recognized by society for these contributions. In any event, whatever the motive, private and public charities are not close substitutes.

Riber and Wilhelm note that experimental evidence of free riding is at odds with this kind of econometric evidence. They question whether this may be due to the fact that the experiments did not have charities that attracted benefactors who give for the pure joy of giving and commitment to causes. Or, it could be that the pressure of society to be charitable overcomes self-interest. In game theory studies (see Chapter 4), we have seen that self-interest is often stronger than the urge to give or cooperate unless there are penalties imposed by other players.

So people contribute to charities for several reasons that fall into the "impure altruism" category. They contribute for the pure joy of helping someone else. They can contribute because they have a special interest in a particular charity, e.g., a relative died from a certain disease and they want to help eradicate it. They contribute because there is pressure from friends, family or "society" to make contributions. Finally, they contribute because they want to be recognized for their contributions either by the charity itself or by the general public.

It is difficult to distinguish the individual motivations for charitable contributions, although the research we have reviewed above does suggest that all of these motives are supported to some extent by empirical observations. Dziko and Oki (2001) interviewed three different sets of people. The results of these interviews show that income and philanthropy may be related in a nonlinear manner. As some people become very rich, they become more philanthropic while they may not have been so charitable on their way to becoming rich. The interviews conducted by Dziko and Oki also demonstrated the powerful influence of the "warm glow" of giving along with the importance of donor interest in the projects being funded with their charitable contributions. A similar point is made by David Collard (1983). He notes that the tendency to free ride is very strong. To offset the free rider problem, a degree of sympathy, a "warm glow", altruistic or other caring behavior of some kind has to be cultivated in the society. This point is consistent with earlier references to the importance of "warm glow" and the importance of "ownership" of charitable projects. As we know from Chapter 4, the incentive to defect in a Prisoner's Dilemma game is high and as a result, it is hard to get people not to defect in the provision of public services.

Two other econometric studies (Yen, 2002; Chua and Wong, 1999) find that age, education and income are important determinants of giving, although the underlying motives for giving are not explored in these studies. Chua and Wong also find that tax breaks on giving increases giving by more than a proportional amount, since the price elasticity of giving is greater than one with respect to a reduction in taxes. It is possible for society to increase the amount of charitable giving by increasing tax breaks for such gifts. This also provides motivation for businesses to make charitable contributions. In some cases, company donations are tied to employees' donations in a matching scheme. The amount of taxes foregone will be more than offset by increases in private charity. This is an advisable strategy only if the government is willing to surrender its own charitable agenda to the private sector.

Establishing a tradition of charity is also a factor. The Mormons tithe and the children of Mormons also usually tithe. Other traditions encouraging contributions to the church or other charities motivate succeeding generations to make charitable donations. This tradition of charity can also extend to businesses and their employees.

Charitable behavior is probably strongest toward close relatives and weakens as social and genetic ties weaken. Such behavior can be explained in terms of Darwinian genetic fitness. We are more closely allied with those who share our gene pool than with strangers, and are therefore more willing to help close relatives. Richard Dawkins (1990) calls this the "selfish" gene and Peter Singer (2006) argues that this behavioral characteristic explains why rich countries are reluctant to devote a larger proportion of their GDP to poor countries. He goes on to argue that such behavior is ethically misplaced — isn't it better to save ten starving African babies than to keep your 95-year-old uncle on life support?

9.4 Charity and the Lottery

The question has been raised as to whether lotteries will increase or reduce the amount of private charity. Peacock (2000) argues that the lottery raises money for charity in England, but it has eroded "real/genuine" charity that is purely altruistic. He argues that the poor contribute to the lottery and not for charitable reasons, but rather with the hope of winning. He raises the question of whether true charity will die because of the lottery. Certainly the introduction of a lottery changes the ground rules for charity because it makes profit possible. Many economists would say that the lottery is regressive because many people buy lottery tickets knowing the odds are stacked against their winning. Recalling the discussion of prospect theory, buyers of lottery tickets may act from the same motivational mindset as gamblers at the race track who bet a small amount on a long shot near the end of the day, hoping to recover their losses (see Chapter 3, Section 3.3).

9.5 Gender, Race and Charity

9.5.1 *Gender differences in charity*

We discussed gender differences in Chapter 7 when we were looking at fairness. There we concluded that women tend to be more egalitarian when judging fairness issues in the workplace, whereas men tend to be more focused on efficiency. How do gender differences manifest when it comes to charity? Andreoni and Vesterlund (2001) conclude that the tendencies toward equality that have been reviewed in the fairness discussion carry over into the investigation of charity. However, the overall relationship between charity and income is somewhat more complicated. Men's giving behavior is more sensitive to price (such as the amount of tax relief for charitable contributions) than that of women. The demand curves for altruistic and charitable acts of men and women cross, with men being more responsive to price changes. These conclusions are based on evidence from experiments at the University of Wisconsin and Iowa State University. The results are supported by studies of differences in tipping behavior in Texas. These experiments and the fairness discussion in Chapter 7 suggest that gender differences can be important sources of variation in behavior when it comes to issues involving altruism and fairness. Fundraisers would do well to investigate such differences in developing their campaigns to raise money.

9.5.2 *African American schooling and private philanthropy*

As noted previously, the literature on charity stresses the importance of donor identification with those who are being helped. Such identification provides a strong impetus for giving and introduces incentives for developing meaningful and well-focused programs. In some cases, charity is directed toward redressing imbalances in income, social status or quality of healthcare. An interesting example of such philanthropy based on racial differences is discussed by Donohue *et al.* (2002). They present the activities of three foundations that were instrumental in stimulating local participation in improving black schools in the early years of the 20th century in the US. These organizations focused their activities on providing resources that were not easy to divert to other uses such as physical capital and teacher training, and they also directed resources to those states that needed them most. Their contributions increased access to schools by African Americans and improved the quality of education when there were few alternatives for improving educational facilities for African Americans through the political process. This case study demonstrates the capability of private charitable organizations to bring additionality of resources and, when focused properly, to have a significant impact on the mobilization of resources and outcomes for a large segment of the population. The charitable work of private foundations was complemented by legal steps to increase teacher pay, the establishment of guidelines for standardizing the length of the school year for blacks and increased social activism in the latter part of the 20th century.

9.6 Corruption and Bribery

We turn now to a different subject on the other side of the public goods coin — corruption and bribery. While corruption and bribery may be looked at from the point of view of "public bads", we do not pursue this line of argument in this section. This is simply because these topics have been analyzed by economists, for the most part within the market framework. Corruption and bribery are used to pursue self-interest outside of the legal framework. An altruistic person would refrain from these behaviors because these actions could hurt others in the society. Generally, those who are less altruistically motivated and perhaps lacking a strong ethical compass may find it easy to enter into corrupt relationships. Considerable research suggests that corruption and bribery are substantial and have detrimental impacts on economic growth, economic efficiency, income distribution and poverty. It is sufficiently important that we have devoted a separate section to it.

We touched on the topic of corruption briefly when we were discussing social capital and the formation of interest groups that feel isolated from the rest of society. However, corruption and bribery are more pervasive and widespread and need not involve well-defined interest groups. For our purposes, corruption is defined as the use of power and authority by government officials to subvert the use of resources for personal gain.

Corruption and bribery exist throughout the world in all societies, rich and poor alike. It has been around as long as humans have been organized into social groups where the possibility of corruption can exist. Some believe it is worse now in developing countries and in many of these countries it is often associated with the government. Officials are bribed to avoid paying taxes on income, output, exports or imports. Officials are bribed to avoid taking a driving test, register a car, get your children into the right school, win a contract to build a road, bridge or some other public work, get a permit for a new building, open a restaurant or sell liquor. The list goes on.

Corruption and other illegal practices impose considerable costs on society in terms of the misallocation of resources that result from corrupt practices, drawing resources away from productive work, risks to health from sale of illegal substances, human rights violations from illegal immigration and the dangers that arise from substandard roads, buildings, factories and infrastructure built by corrupt contractors. As much as $1.5 trillion is paid in bribes each year, according to ongoing research at the World Bank Institute (WBI) on a worldwide basis in both developing and developed countries. This is about five percent of world GDP, which is estimated at $30 trillion. This figure, as large as it may seem, could also be underestimated since it may miss embezzlement of public funds. (For further details, see: http://go. worldbank.org/LJA29GHA80.)

We can use the principal-agent framework to give us some insights into the motivations and the general economic analysis of corruption. In this context, the one who is seeking a favor through bribery is the principal and the official who is being bribed is the agent. The agent who is in public office awards contracts to the principal who offers the largest bribe. In this scenario, the contract is awarded openly, although the bribe may be given privately. There are other instances where the transaction between principal and agent is kept secret. These cases of corruption and bribery could include the importation and illegal sale of contraband goods, tax evasion and lax enforcement of quality control standards and legal regulations.

Legislative corruption exists when those running for public office buy votes or have legislation enacted that benefits only the legislators and their constituents. Bureaucratic corruption, on the other hand, involves the use of power to extract bribes or "grease money" to speed up granting of licenses or release of goods from customs.

There are also various other sorts of corruption and bribery in the private sector such as ticket scalping, hoarding of scarce goods and then auctioning them to the highest bidder, and also more general corruption where favors are granted to large political campaign contributors.

Most economic analysis deals with the case of bribing of public officials for private gain. In the following sections, we will deal with several aspects of corruption including how to measure it; its effect on economic efficiency and economic growth; the relationship between competition, openness and corruption; the relationship between corruption, income inequality and poverty; and the dynamics of corruption. Dealing with corruption is discussed in Section 9.11.

9.7 Bribery, Corruption and Economic Efficiency

As noted in Chapter 7, corruption is one of the forces that can impede the development of social capital. In a corrupt society, there are few incentives to develop a trusting, impartial and cooperative environment where social capital development can flourish. In general, the overall level of bribery and corruption can only be estimated for any society simply because it is kept secret by both parties. Anecdotal evidence suggests that in developing countries, most people pay bribes as part of everyday life and that as much as half of total income goes unreported for income tax. Tax collectors and auditors accept bribes as a matter of course.

Murder, kidnapping and extortion are the more sinister forms of corruption. Moreover, the manifest corruption and bribery results in a loss of revenue to the government. When the violation involves those with a punitive role in the system (e.g., judges, policemen, etc.), corruption reduces the effectiveness of the legal justice system. Other aspects of corruption can be more subtle. For example, in order to discourage corruption there are elaborate rules and regulations and a lot of red tape — leaving a paper trail, as it is called. In cases where countries are trying to attract foreign investors, the bribery requirement can be a significant deterrent, not only because of the ethical overtones but also because of the potential for blackmail and additional bribes and extortion.

In terms of the impact on efficiency and allocation of resources, there are two lines of argument. The first asserts that corruption speeds up efficiency by bypassing bureaucratic procedures and a centralized corruption network improves efficiency. Research tends to discount that line of argument. There is a lot of evidence that bureaucratic procedures that are bypassed are themselves a source of economic inefficiency. Furthermore, when bribes are made, there is also the chance that the agent will renege and the principal does not have any recourse. In economic and political systems where there are many different political constituencies, overlapping jurisdictions and areas of political responsibility, it is more difficult to make corruption effective, since more people need to be bribed.

Generally, research seems to support the second line of argument, that corruption and bribery reduce economic efficiency. Bribery and corruption distort the allocation of resources by diverting funds to large investment projects where bidders for the contract can be bribed, and discourage spending on other kinds of projects, often smaller in nature and less capital intensive such as education, health, and repair and maintenance. When these aspects of human capital formation are neglected, economic efficiency is adversely affected. This neglect then results in lower rates of economic growth.

Jain's (2001) extensive review of the literature suggests that corruption can have pervasive effects on economic efficiency. This is particularly relevant to the way public resources are spent. If the level of corruption is high, then misallocation and waste of resources will overwhelm the good intentions to spend for useful projects. Furthermore, research suggests that the adverse effects of corruption on the social fabric of society are significant. Theft, assault and other crimes against property and people tend to increase in corrupt societies as law enforcement becomes lax and the lack of trust in the legal system increases.

9.8 How to Measure Corruption

Several agencies such as Business International, Political Risk Services and Transparency International generate indices of corruption (see websites in Bibliography). Mocan (2004) has also conducted a survey in 40 countries. These indices are based on the perceptions of the level of corruption by international observers, members of the local and foreign business communities, risk analysts and private citizens. These indices are generally highly correlated. They suggest that the level of corruption is considerably higher in developing countries than in industrial countries. The results of some of these corruption studies are displayed in Tables 9.2–9.4 and discussed further for selected Asian economies in Section 9.12.

9.9 Determinants of Corruption

The nature and scope of corruption depend on various factors. Generally, there are two critical determinants — the power to control the allocation of or access to resources, and the value of the economic rents that can be gained from the exercise of that power. Rent seeking and the ability to obtain rents is a major incentive for corruption. Where contracts are awarded without impartially monitored competitive bidding, there is likely to be very strong incentives for corrupt practices to arise. When markets become more globally competitive and there is a level playing field, the opportunities for rent seeking and corruption go down. In the financial sector, US banks have reduced their contributions to legislators as financial services have become more globalized. Ades and Di Tella (1997) show that when governments pursue active industrial policies, rents are transferred to favored industries and bribery is more likely to occur. This is particularly true when contract bidding is restricted.

There have been a number of empirical studies of corruption using cross-section information from a wide array of industrial and developing countries. These studies are based on a number of hypothetical relationships between corruption and a variety of explanatory variables. There are several economic, political, judicial and social variables that are important determinants of corruption (see Treisman, 2000; Ades and Di Tella, 1997; Kaufmann, 1997; Seldadyo and di Haan, 2005; Serra, 2004).

9.9.1 *Economic variables*

Economic variables include the level of per capita income, the relative level of pay for government officials, the openness to international trade and a high level of oligopoly and economic rents in the domestic economy. Income is the most powerful economic determinant of corruption. Generally, richer countries are much less corrupt than poor countries, other things equal.

Table 9.1 shows the result of a simple regression between corruption and per capita income for 26 Asian economies in 2002. Income per capita is highly related to the level of corruption. Nearly 90 percent in the variation in corruption is explained by the best fitting regression. The elasticity at the mean shows that a change in income reduces corruption between 0.21 and 0.27 standard deviations, depending on whether PPP or atlas income series are used.[1]

Economic theory also suggests that corruption could be reduced by increasing wages of government officials. This theoretical result is supported by evidence assembled by Van Rijckeghem and Weder (2001). They show that the level of corruption declines as the ratio of government officials' salaries relative to wages of manufacturing workers increased. In general, higher pay serves as an incentive for government officials to eschew corruption. However, it is also possible and even likely that corrupt regimes pay their civil servants well, resulting in problems in determining cause and effect.

---

[1]Kaufmann measures corruption as a standard normal variable with mean zero and variance one.

Table 9.1 Regression Results — Income per Capita and Level of Corruption

Dependent Variable	Income — PPP	Income — Atlas Method	R^2 Adjusted
.TI		0.00018 (9.94)	0.802
WB		0.00076 (7.82)	0.707
TI	0.0000157 (13.16)		0.882
WB	0.0000086 (8.92)		0.773

Note: Regression coefficient — *t* values in parentheses.
Sources: TI — Transparency International Corruption Index (2004), WB — Kauffman *et al.* corruption index (2002). Atlas method income is obtained using local exchange rate to US$, while PPP is purchasing power parity level of income.

Openness is important because it reduces rents and introduces competition, both of which reduce corruption. The same holds true for domestic monopoly power, which is reflected by the positive relationship between corruption and the size of the mining (including oil and natural gas) sector. Mining leases and contracts for extraction of mineral resources are controlled by the government and are often subject to bribery and corruption.

9.9.2 *Social, political and judicial variables*

Whether a country had a long period of British rule is the one social variable that has a significant negative impact on corruption. The impact of this British tradition, in Britain itself and on its former colonies including North America, Australia, India and many other countries in Asia and Africa, resulted in a system of justice that held corruption down. Anglican and other Protestant religious traditions also show a lower level of corruption than Catholic, Moslem, Hindu, Buddhist or other religious traditions. It is speculated that Protestantism instills a distrust of state institutions which is helpful in exposing corruption. Other religious traditions have a hierarchical structure that often works in concert with the state.

Countries whose legal framework is similar to the British legal tradition are likely, other things equal, to have a lower level of corruption than countries such as Sweden, France and Germany. This is because civil law in these countries was designed as instruments of the state to sustain and expand its power, whereas in the British tradition, civil law is intended to limit the role of the state (see La Porta *et al.*, 1998).

From another point of view, British rule is also correlated with the common law judicial tradition that prevailed in these countries and offered protection against official abuse of power. However, the importance of common law in reducing corruption has an impact over and above British heritage. Countries that have adopted the common law tradition, where law evolves based on precedents rather than codes drawn up by central governments, seem to have less corruption. As a result, common law is more flexible and arguably more in tune with the will of the people and emphasizes procedures rather than fixed codes. Consequently, residents of countries with common law traditions are more likely to see corrupt procedures as violations of the legal system. Democratic institutions tend to reduce corruption, but only when such institutions have been in place for many decades.

9.9.3 *Governmental variables*

The economic analysis of Becker and Stigler (1974) and others working in this field suggests that corruption is a positive function of incentives such as higher pay and better chances for promotion, as well as being a negative function of the risk of being caught and punished. We saw that countries observing common law traditions probably provide a more credible threat of punishment and this threat seems to deter corruption. Economic logic would suggest that higher salaries for government officials would reduce corruption; officials would not risk getting caught and lose their high paying government jobs.

Husted (1999) conducted a cross-cultural study of corruption using regression analysis. He concluded that there were several factors related to corruption including the size of government. The larger the size of government as a proportion of GNP, the greater is the intensity of corruption. Governments grant privileges and licenses that allow many opportunities for corruption. Opportunities for corruption are also increased if the government is involved in many sectors of the economy and there is more government interference. Thus, when the government's role in the economy is reduced, there is more competition and potentially less corruption.

In terms of governmental structure, federal governmental structures tend to be more corrupt than those run by a central administration, although the evidence is not overwhelming. This is probably because corruption becomes more diffused with the devolution of power from the central government. High level corruption gives way to more petty corruption and bribery. Local officials that have more autonomy are able to develop their own network of corruption over which the central authorities have little control.

9.10 Corruption, Economic Growth and Investment

Why are economic development and corruption negatively related? Richer countries can usually afford to pay public officials well, which helps cut down on the amount of corruption. Of course, there are other reasons, including stiff penalties imposed on those found guilty of bribery and corruption, and fewer opportunities for corruption.

Free and open economies seem to have less corruption because openness and economic freedom seem to be highly correlated with economic development. Table 9.2 shows that the degree of economic freedom is correlated with the level of per capita income, while Table 9.3 demonstrates this relationship for some Asian countries. In Asia, the Newly Industrialized Economies (NIEs) score high, while South Asia's economies score low. Southeast Asia is somewhere in between.

Table 9.2 Index of Economic Freedom and Average per Capita Income in US Dollars, 2001

Free	$21,000
Mostly free	$11,000
Mostly unfree	$2,800
Repressed	$2,900

Source: Holmes *et al.* (2001).

Table 9.3 Index of Economic Freedom 2001 — One is Most Free

Bangladesh	132
Myanmar	145
China	114
Hong Kong	1
India	133
Indonesia	114
Japan	14
Korea	20
Malaysia	75
Nepal	110
Pakistan	106
Philippines	81
Singapore	2
Sri Lanka	48
Taiwan	20
Thailand	27
Vietnam	144
United States	5
United Kingdom	7
Australia	9

Source: Holmes *et al.* (2001).

Table 9.4 shows a strong relationship between corruption and per capita income. The more competitive and open economies have lower indices of corruption. Ades and Di Tella (1997) found that corruption is higher in countries where domestic firms are sheltered from foreign competition. This suggests that corruption is high when rent seeking is high. Furthermore, Graeff and Mehlkop (2003) found that economic freedom is inversely related to the level of corruption.

9.10.1 *Other economic relationships with corruption*

Husted (1999) found that cultural factors identified by Hofstede (1997) are also important determinants and positively related to the level of corruption. These cultural factors include the willingness of the less powerful members of society to accept the unequal distribution of power

Table 9.4 Corruption Indices

Economy	Business International	Transparency International	Global Competitiveness Report
Singapore	1	2.34	1.77
Hong Kong	3	3.72	2.17
Japan	2.25	4.43	2.96
Taiwan	4.25	5.58	4.60
Malaysia	5	5.99	5.67
South Korea	5.25	6.71	6.20
Thailand	9.5	7.94	7.93
Philippines	6.5	7.98	7.94
China	na	8.12	5.86
India	5.75	8.25	7.30
Indonesia	9.5	8.28	7.94
Pakistan	7	8.97	Na
Bangladesh	7	9.20	Na

Source: Wei (1999).

Note: The Global Competitiveness is prepared by Political Risk Services, the transparency index by Transparency International and the Business International index by Business International. Wei has made some transformations of the original data to make the indices comparable.

(called power distance) and high levels of uncertainty. Hofstede also notes two different groups of countries, one consisting of rich, individualistic countries with low power distance, and a second comprised of poor countries with high power distance. The poor countries with high power distance tend to have high levels of corruption. Mocan's (2004) results tend to reinforce these arguments as they show that the size of government is positively related to the level of corruption.

Further, if the income distribution is skewed toward the wealthy, the chances for corruption are also greater and unlikely to be sanctioned by the rest of the society. There is some evidence that income inequality is positively correlated with corruption as the elites try to increase their share of rents through bribery and other corrupt practices (Gupta *et al.*, 2002). Similarly, egalitarian cultures discourage corruption as opposed to cultures which are more hierarchical. These results are reinforced by the work of Gupta *et al.* (2002) who provide evidence that high and rising corruption are associated with income inequality and poverty. An increase of one standard deviation in the index of corruption is associated with an increase in the Gini coefficient of income inequality by about 11 points and reduces income growth of the poor by about 5 percent points per year. Gupta *et al.* (2002) suggest that policies to reduce corruption will most likely also reduce poverty and income inequality. Andrei Schleifer and Robert W. Vishny (1993) argue that the structure of the political process and government institutions has a direct bearing on the level of corruption. More democratic governments in which government officials are elected and subject to voter recall are less likely to be corrupt.

Roumasset (1997) argues that a free press and a high degree of investigative reporting is also a good way to control corruption. This echoes the result reported by Brunetti and Weder (2003), who found that freedom of the press is negatively correlated with the level of corruption; corruption is high when the press is more controlled.

Empirical evidence and economic theory both suggest that corruption reduces incentives to invest in new businesses and innovations. This is because all of these new activities need government approval and are therefore subject to potential bribery and corruption. There is also a corollary reduction in the pace of economic growth and innovation as a result of lower investment and capital formation. Conversely, economic growth seems to eventually reduce corruption since the rewards to entrepreneurship rise as incomes grow rapidly, thereby reducing the need for rent seeking.

Investment as well as the aggregate level of economic activity is also related to the level of corruption. Mauro (1995) presents information from a cross-section of countries for the period of the early 1980s. This evidence suggests that, other things equal, a one standard deviation reduction in the corruption index (he uses the Business International Index) will increase the investment rate by nearly three percent of GDP. He also finds that a one standard deviation fall in corruption results in about a one percent increase in the GDP per capita. While these results are subject to sampling error, they do suggest that the effect of corruption on aggregate economic activity can be substantial.

In a cross-cultural study of growth in about 100 countries from 1960 to 1993 containing a number of other explanatory variables such as the initial levels of GDP and human capital, government spending, fertility, inflation and the terms of trade, Barro and Sala-i-Martin (1995) found that a variable identified as the "rule of law" was an important determinant of the rate of growth of income. This variable serves as a catch all for a variety of different attributes of government and society including the quality of bureaucracy, political corruption, risk of government expropriation and repudiation of contracts. An improvement of one rank in the index is estimated to raise the growth rate by 0.5 percentage points, other factors being held equal.

Mocan (2004) reports the results of interviews with over 90,000 individuals in 49 countries pertaining to their experience with corruption. The probability of being asked for a bribe is related to a series of personal characteristics as well as country variables. Males are more likely to be asked for a bribe as are wealthier, highly educated individuals and those that are employed. The young and the old do not have a high probability of being asked for a bribe.

In many developing countries, the lower and lower middle classes are also often preyed upon by the police, such as jeepney drivers in the Philippines. In summary, Mocan's results suggest that the probability of being asked for a bribe depends on certain personality characteristics. He also shows that the strength of the legal system is a deterrent to corruption.

9.10.2 *The importance of institutions*

The work of Mocan (2004), the research of Barro and Sala-i-Martin (1995) and Schleifer and Vishny (1993) highlight the importance of institutions in lowering the level of corruption. Hall and Jones (1997) also emphasize the diversion of resources away from productive activities toward corruption. Mocan (2004) uses the risk of expropriation as an instrument for the strength of national institutions and shows that stronger institutions foster economic growth. Furthermore, when the quality of institutions is taken into account, corruption does not have a direct impact on growth.

These results suggest that there is a strong correlation between corruption and the strength of institutions. Stronger institutions are able to reduce the level of corruption. The importance of institutions on growth is sustained even when the level of corruption, geographic locations, legal heritage, religious composition, presence of war, governmental status, educational level and income are taken into account. Mocan's results suggest that a one-half standard deviation increase in the quality of institutions generates an additional 0.7 percent increase in the average annual rate of per capita income growth. For a developing country with a per capita income level of $2,500 in 1975, this translates into an additional $500 per capita by 1995, a 20 percent increase.

These results are only indicative, since the study comprises only a few developing economies (16 of the 49 countries were in Africa, Latin America and Asia). Nevertheless, Mocan's results reemphasize the importance of establishing a strong institutional framework that promotes honesty, integrity and transparency, and discourages corruption.

9.11 Dynamics of Corruption and Its Remedies

Game theory has been used to analyze corruption. In some models, each time a principal tries to bribe an agent, the agent runs the risk of being arrested or fired by an honest official. The chances of being fired from accepting bribes goes down as the number of corrupt officials goes up. In due time, the level of corruption is bound to increase. This causes principals to revise their probabilities of meeting corrupt officials, which results in even more bribery. Furthermore, news that corruption is rampant tends to encourage more corruption. Due to these dynamics, it is possible to have similar economies with different levels of corruption because of a shock that sent them in one direction or the other. Northern and southern Italy are used as examples of this possibility of multiple equilibria. There is more corruption in the south than in the north.

Bardhan (1997) suggests that the equilibrium will depend upon the number of corrupt officials. Marginal benefits from corruption follow an inverted U curve. As the number of corrupt officials increases, marginal benefits for honest officials decrease. There are two stable equilibriums, the first where every official is honest and the second where every official is dishonest. An unstable situation exists somewhere in the middle where there is a rough balance between the number of corrupt and honest officials. In such cases, a campaign to reduce corruption by raising salaries and increasing penalties can lead to a dramatic reduction in corruption.

Corruption requires cooperation between the conspirators who are involved in the corrupt activities. Some ways to break down corruption conspiracies are: imposing penalties for joining conspiracies, encouraging defection from conspiracies and destabilizing trust among conspirators. N. Katyal (2003) discusses legal means for accomplishing these ends and also ways to use defectors to break up conspiracies.

A number of other suggestions have been offered to deal with corruption. The most obvious is to reduce the amount of bureaucracy and red tape that led to this kind of rent seeking in the first place. Another suggestion is to increase the number of overlapping bureaucracies, or have two bureaucrats working together. In the latter case, both officials will need to be bribed, where there is a higher risk that one of them is honest and will report the other. A greater risk here is that the level of red tape will escalate without reducing corruption. However, this system seems to have worked well in Singapore where officials who might be bribed are forced to work in pairs.

Another suggestion that has been widely applied with considerable success is to increase the pay of government bureaucrats while strengthening anticorruption efforts. The results of Husted (1999), Mocan (2004) and Van Rijckeghem and Weder (2001) noted in Section 9.10.1 show that raising salaries can be a powerful way to reduce corruption. By working both sides of the risk/reward nexus, corruption can be reduced. If we think of bribery as another choice to be made, the reward must be balanced against the cost of being caught. If penalties are stiff and the chances of getting caught are high, the cost of corruption goes up and the return goes down. As a result there will be less corruption, particularly if individuals can make a decent living without resorting to corruption. Evidence compiled by C. Van Rijckeghem and B. Weder (2001) suggests that this is indeed the case — returns from corruption are balanced against the threat of being caught.

Would a greater degree of altruism reduce the amount of corruption and bribery? Theoretically, it probably would. However, when the beneficiaries of reduced corruption or increased tax collections are in question, then altruistic actions may be less clear cut. A person living overseas avoids tax because he is not benefiting from the expenditures made possible by higher tax revenues. He may feel a moral obligation to avoid rather than to pay taxes.

In the remainder of this section, a number of suggestions are presented to increase the costs of corruption through enforcement and other measures, reduce the benefits of corruption by raising salaries and provide performance inducements for good performance.

9.11.1 *Financial rewards and penalties*

There has been a real decline in government salary levels in many countries. This is particularly true in Africa, where the interaction between corruption and revenue intake has put many countries on a downward spiral of lower salaries and more corruption.

Evidence from Asia suggests that the comparison of government salaries with the next best alternative employment opportunity, given education and experience, is what is important. Higher salaries relative to manufacturing wages helped the schools in Korea and Taiwan to attract better and more qualified teachers. The same principles apply when recruiting government officials in areas where corruption is a threat. A policy of paying higher salaries for government officials is supported by the work of Van Rijckeghem and Weder (1997, 2001), who show that when government officials are paid well relative to those working in the private sector, then the level of corruption is lower. The impact of higher wages on corruption has secondary impacts as well. This is because civil service pay is also highly correlated with the effectiveness of the legal system and the quality of the bureaucracy.

Mookherjee and Png (1995) also show that stiff penalties reduce the incidence of bribery. Rewards for those who report corruption can also be introduced along with guaranteed protection from reprisal. In China, execution of corrupt officials is not uncommon. However, it is unclear how much of a deterrent this has been. Transparency International's index of corruption for China has not changed much in recent years.

9.11.2 *Better record keeping*

A systematic and secure system of record keeping would make it easier to supervise and control corruption, particularly if there are secondary checks on the transactions involved. It requires many honest officials to be effective, otherwise the pressure to collude is enormous. It helps to have periodic unannounced spot checks and have teams of workers tasking together. It is also important to develop systems so that greater competition can be introduced which serves to control against rents being accumulated through collusion and "cooking the books".

9.11.3 *Better quality bureaucrats and judges*

A small core of incorruptible officials at the top and sprinkled throughout the system will make it easier to enforce regulations, prosecute wrongdoers and get rid of those who are corrupt. But this will only work if those doing the hiring are not corrupt. There are successes: the customs services in Thailand, Philippines and Indonesia have been cleaned up and customs procedures have been streamlined and improved. It must begin at the top, because if the reputation of the bureaucracy is one of corruption, it is difficult to attract honest workers.

9.11.4 *Promotion based on performance, not on nepotism*

If civil service pays well and is managed on a meritorious basis, then the opportunities for crony relationships will be minimized. It will also permit more flexible hiring and firing policies so that corrupt officials can be fired and perhaps prosecuted. This can only be accomplished if the bureaucracy is free of political intervention and headed by honest officials.

9.11.5 *Reduce discretion*

There is opportunity for corruption when officials have discretion to make exceptions and exclusions when enforcing laws and regulations. Establishing flat tax rates on all goods imported, as Chile has done, would reduce corruption. It would most certainly raise more tax revenues. However, there is great reluctance to undertake this process of simplification because of vested interests, not only in corrupt bureaucracies, but also among businessmen who get exemptions through bribery or the "old boy" network. A thorough "housecleaning" can only be achieved with strong political support.

9.11.6 *Reduce the scope for corruption*

In general, reducing the scope for corruption by government officials involves cutting down the amount of bureaucratic red tape. This can be done by rationing procedures where licenses and permits are needed. Avoiding situations where individual officials have discretionary authority to make decisions that have wide financial implications is paramount. The authority to grant licenses and contracts is one area where there is significant abuse in many developing countries. It often results in shoddy work with substandard materials which may result in the collapse of buildings, roadways and other civil works.

9.11.7 *Introduce anticorruption campaigns and agencies, free press and mobilize international pressure*

There are various other ways to put pressure on the government to reduce corruption, including media coverage of corrupt practices and the formation of a watch dog agency to monitor reports on corruption and take action to stop it. Pressure by international agencies such as the United Nations, World Bank, the Asian Development Bank, the InterAmerican Development Bank and bilateral agencies like USAID can also help to galvanize public opinion and government intent. Pressure can be financial as well as verbal. Contracts can be voided and extension of loans and other development assistance can be tied to reforms of agencies with corrupt practices.

9.11.8 *Tax farming — a radical proposal*

With corruption so widespread and few successes in reducing it in developing countries, legalizing corruption has been proposed. The government sets the tax rates for various categories of tax payers and then sells/auctions the right to collect taxes for a fixed sum of money. The tax collector winning the bid would then be responsible for determining the liabilities of individual tax payers as well as collecting money from them. Tax payers could file an appeal in a tax court that would be set up by the government. To simplify procedures, losers pay court costs and a fine. This system would allow for the tax collector to work in an honest way to assess taxes correctly. It would not require as much honesty as a regular tax collection system, since only the judge would have to be honest and incorruptible.

Due to the nature of this system, the incentive to cheat the government is replaced by the possibility of extorting money from tax payers. This is where the tax court comes in. If the sources of income are unknown to the tax collector and to the government and if tax payers lie, then this system will yield more revenue than the current system where everyone bribes and some collectors accept the bribes. The tax collector will try to get as much income as possible because he has paid for the right to collect. Hidden income will be revealed. However, each tax payer has the option of going to tax court. There will be intense scrutiny of his income, but if he has nothing to worry about he will be vindicated. There is always the risk that after intensive investigation by the tax court, he will be asked to pay an even higher tax bill as his taxes are raised further. The success of the system would depend critically on the tax courts. Can honest judges who are incorruptible in the face of what would be significant bribes and pressure from influential businessmen be found? Honest judges are key to the success of such a system and if they are dishonest, the entire system would fail. Despite these risks, it may be a viable solution in situations where the present system has broken down and tax collections are low.

9.12 Regional Analysis: Corruption in Asia

S.-J. Wei (1999) has surveyed evidence from a number of studies in Asia. The determinants of corruption are comparable to the general factors discussed earlier in this chapter. These studies show that, other things being equal, corruption tends to reduce the amount of investment, increase the level of poverty, reduce tax revenue and divert money away from health, education and maintenance to construction projects where bribes are possible. It also tends to reduce growth and foreign direct investment from overseas lenders.

In Asia, corruption is highly correlated with the level of income and the rate of growth in income. This is evident from Table 9.4, which displays three measures of corruption for several Asian countries. Singapore and Hong Kong rate at the top in terms of honesty, while India, Indonesia, Pakistan and Bangladesh rank near the bottom. These results are consistent with the results reported in Tables 9.2 and 9.3. This information, which is based on subjective measures of corruption, is compiled based on surveys of international business firms, risk analysts, expatriates and local residents.

Hofstede (1997) and Husted (1999) also emphasize Confucian dynamics, where a premium is placed on honoring relationships by status and also emphasizing truth and virtue. However, Husted concludes that Confucian values do not have any clear *prima facia* impact on corruption. The continuation of corrupt practices in China despite rapid increases in income suggests that the impact of Confucian values in the current Chinese regime need to be reconsidered.

Systematic surveys of time series data on corruption is available from the files of Transparency International since the early 1980s, a period of 25 years or so. Looking at this evidence reported in Figure 9.1, where high values reflect less corruption and more honesty, there does

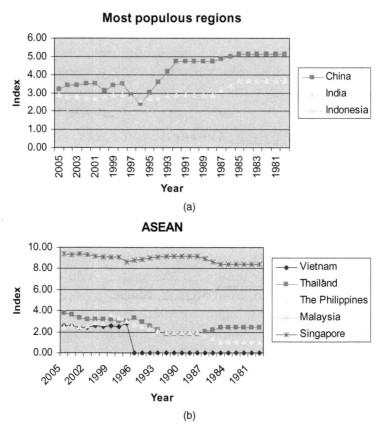

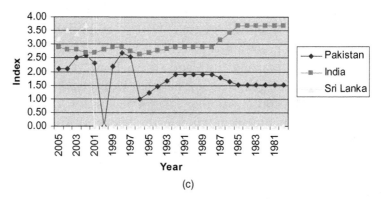

Figure 9.1 Corruption 1980–2005 — Transparency International

The 4 Asian Tigers

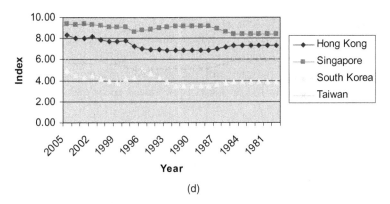

(d)

Figure 9.1 (*Continued*)

Source: Transparency International.

not seem to be a downward trend in indices of measures of corruption for many countries.

Among the three largest economies, corruption has been trending upward in India and China and downward in Indonesia. Among the NIEs, Singapore has an exemplary record of low corruption and this record has improved slightly from high to very high levels of honesty. Corruption has been low in the other NIEs as well, remaining rather flat in Taiwan and Hong Kong with a slight dip in the late 1980s and early 1990s and improving slowly in South Korea up until the Asian financial crisis.

In Southeast Asia, Thailand has seen a reduction in corruption in the last decade compared with the 1980s and early 1990s. Corruption in the Philippines has increased since the Asian crisis after falling for nearly two decades, while there has been a slight increase in Malaysia. There are not enough data to draw conclusions for Vietnam. In South Asia, aside from the increase in India, the experience in Pakistan and Sri Lanka is hard to interpret because of a lack of a continuous time series.

We conclude this section by referring to Box 9.1 containing further information about corruptive practices in three Asian countries — Indonesia, Korea and Thailand.

Box 9.1 Corruption in Indonesia, Korea and Thailand

Corrupt practices in Indonesia and Korea have been particularly widespread during the 1990s even as both countries made attempts to reduce corruption after the Asian financial crisis. Box Figure 9.1 displays the Corruption Perception Index[2] for the two countries from 1995, 1997 and 2002. Corruption in Indonesia is perceived to be twice as great as that in Korea.

Indonesia

While President Suharto was in power, massive public funds were siphoned from charitable organizations (*yayasans*) and joint ventures to his friends and family who received preferential treatment including lucrative contracts, exclusive licenses and loans at favorable terms. Major industries in the telecommunications, electronics, construction and minerals sectors were under the direct control of the Suharto family. These state-owned enterprises were poorly managed and often sustained financial losses that had to be funded from government revenue. Furthermore, low salaries created strong rent seeking incentives. Corruption pervaded many aspects

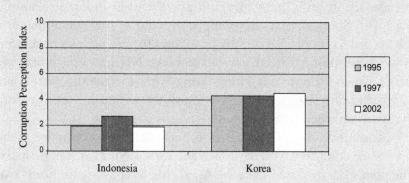

Box Figure 9.1 Corruption Perception Index in Indonesia and Korea

Source: Transparency International.

(*Continued*)

---

[2]The CPI index indicates the perception of businessmen, academics and risk analysts regarding the degree of corruption. The higher the CPI, the more "clean" an economy is perceived to be. A value of 10 is regarded as very clean whereas 0 is highly corrupt.

Box 9.1 (*Continued*)

of everyday life and bribes were considered standard operating procedure for getting a job, obtaining a business licence or a driver's license. College graduates looking for jobs paid bribes to personnel managers, construction companies paid bribes to government bureaucrats to get contracts and drivers paid bribes to policemen to avoid traffic court. Furthermore, high profile public officials, military officers and cronies of the leaders of the country often borrowed from banks with a letter from the Suharto family and were given loans without any credit checks and often without any plan to repay. This kind of "memo lending" is largely responsible for the high level of nonperforming loans in Indonesia. Since the Asian financial crisis, Indonesia has enacted new anticorruption legislations and passed a rule requiring civil servants to declare their assets to an independent auditing agency. The recently established government of Susilo Bambang Yudhoyono has taken a number of steps to deal with corruption. Initial implementation of these anticorruption measures has been mixed (see Rosser, 2003). Recent surveys by Transparency International (TI) and the Political and Economic Risk Consultancy (PERC) suggest that these measures are having some impact on corruption, particularly public perception of corruption. The TI scores recorded in Box Figure 9.1 show that Indonesia made steady upward progress in reducing corruption until the Asian crisis. Thereafter the index dipped for a few years and is now improving again, although it still remains low. This trend in corruption has dovetailed with devolution of responsibility from the central government to the provincial authorities. Even greater autonomy is possible in the future as Aceh has become more independent. Other provinces, particularly in the eastern region, are also gaining greater control over budgets. However, experiences of other countries suggest that the opportunities for corruption multiply as power devolves from the center to the periphery, and this will present an ongoing challenge for the government. The most probable outcome is that there will be a period of consolidation of gains in fighting corruption as the newly elected regime gains more confidence in dealing with various forms of corruption. Recent changes in the management of Pertamina and the signing of new oil exploration contracts with overseas partners is a good sign.

(*Continued*)

Box 9.1 (*Continued*)

Korea

Historically, there was widespread corruption in Korea. Legal sanctions were weak until 1974 when major corruption scandals involving civil servants were exposed and there was increasing public dissatisfaction with bureaucratic corruption. Korean suppliers subverted the US army policy of competitive bidding by colluding to overcharge the US army by 30 percent or more. Firms also bribed Korean accountants and contractors working for the US army to increase cost estimates. At the political level, vote buying was commonplace. Estimates made by M. Lee (1990) estimated that the ruling Democratic Justice Party spent between US$300 million and $1 billion to buy votes in the 1987 presidential election. Polls conducted in Korea show that politicians are considered much more corrupt than any other group in society — over 70 percent of respondents named politicians as the most corrupt group in South Korea, compared with less than 10 for businessmen and government officials (see Quah, 2003, p. 158 for further details and references). Low salaries for civil servants, the gift giving culture and other cultural variables have been offered as explanations for corruption in Korea. It was mired with financial scandals and illegal collusion between politicians and local big businesses (*chaebols*) during its transition from an authoritarian rule to democracy in 1993. The chaebols supported the ruling party in return for special favors because the government had strong political control over commercial legislation and developments. In return for the *chaebols'* continued financial support of the ruling party, the government would grant them special licenses or loans. Blechinger (2000) reported that the top four donors to former President General Roh Tae-Woo in the "Slush Fund Scandal" in 1995 were Hyundai and Samsung Group ($32.7 million each), Daewoo Group ($31.4 million) and Lucky Goldstar ($27.5 million). Also, the lack of accountability and clear guidelines in the governance of government operations as well as low wages of civil servants contributed to the high level of corruption in the public sector. High corruption-prone areas within the public sector included those of tax administration, law enforcement, construction, education, procurement, budget and policy funds (Korean Information

(*Continued*)

Box 9.1 (*Continued*)

Service, 2000). For instance, the tax system in the past allowed officials to have control over the selection of tax payers to be audited, thereby leading to opportunities for *chonji* practices (money given for favors granted). Corruption often arose in the education sector because school officers did not have to account for their financial operations to the government. Furthermore, the assignment of an official to one place for an extended time period often allowed cozy relationships with local business interests to develop.

In order to qualify for the aid assistance offered by the IMF and World Bank in the aftermath of the Asian financial crisis, Korea established stronger anticorruption reforms in 1998. First, it introduced an anticorruption index of each government agency by means of a public poll, so as to diagnose and combat corruption in the public sector. Then in order to combat the lack of accountability and clear guidelines in the governance of government operations, Korea has employed the use of ICT in its government administration. It introduced the OPEN system, which allowed the public to monitor the progress of various government applications using the Internet. Income tax related records have since been computerized, eradicating the meetings between tax officers and payers. Government procurement procedures have been simplified and made available online via the Electronic Data Interchange system. Efforts have also been made to raise civil service salary rates on a scale comparable to the private sector, so that government officers will not be easily tempted into corrupt practices. Codes of conduct are established for civil servants and state-run enterprises' employees. The Korean police have set up a "conscience room" in each police station for police officers to return "gifts" to their respective senders. Lastly, new criminal legislations with heavy penalties including confiscation and freezing of bank assets have been set in place to deal with political bribery. There has been a decrease in the level of perceived corruption in Korea over the years, although progress has been slow (see Box Figure 9.1).

Sources: Transparency International, Rosser (2003), Blechinger (2000) and Korean Information Service (2000).

(*Continued*)

Box 9.1 (*Continued*)

Thailand

Thailand has a long historical tradition of presenting gifts to high officials as an acknowledgement of their service to the individual and the community. This patron/client relationship flourished from the 16th to the 19th century and persists today in the form of *sin nam jai* or a "gift of goodwill". This has become a fertile area for corruption of government officials when the gift has a *quid pro quo* attached. The purist would say that any gift, no matter how small, qualifies as a potential bribe. In most circumstances, small gifts at auspicious times of the year probably do not carry a significant corruption risk. However, large gifts have become routine and grease the bureaucratic wheels for many businessmen. As a result, the level of corruption in Thailand is large and has spread to a number of different areas including drug trafficking, illegal arms sales, diesel oil smuggling, prostitution, gambling and illegal immigration. These six activities account for somewhere between 8 and 13 percent of GNP. Gambling was the biggest contributor (about half of the total level of estimated corruption), followed by prostitution (about one-fourth) and the rest. "… we … uncovered a regular pattern of lineages to powerful figures in the bureaucracy, military, police and politics who provided protection to businessmen engaged across the whole range of the illegal economy" (Phongpaichit *et al.*, 1988, p. 9). Academic research has popularized the topic of corruption in Thailand in recent years and has helped to create a backlash from the public that is working to expose corrupt practices. Measures have been undertaken to introduce political, administrative and public controls to deal with corruption across the board. Recommendations have also been made to raise the salaries of low-income bureaucrats and other government officials as well as requiring high officials and military officers to disclose assets. The corruption index has also been improving since the Asian financial crisis. The combined efforts of anticorruption forces along with the academic community and journalists have exerted significant pressure to reduce the level of corruption and bribery. The works of Pasuk Phongpaichit and Sungsidh Piriyarangsan, whose two books (1988 and 1996) have helped to publicize the nature and extent of corruption, are good examples of

(*Continued*)

Box 9.1 (*Continued*)

how journalistic and academic expertise have come together to pressure the government to take action against corruption. Recent public demonstrations which overthrew the prime minister accused of corruption in the sale of company assets are additional evidence that anticorruption drives have taken root in the awareness of the middle class in Bangkok. Nevertheless, high level corruption continues in Thailand. Anticorruption forces in Thailand have to marshal enough public opinion to increase enforcement of anticorruption laws to reduce corruption further. Key to this drive will be the continued participation of the middle class, the journalistic community and vocal academics to continue to expose corrupt officials. Nevertheless, the culture of corruption is firmly entrenched historically, culturally and administratively. Many people still think that a small amount of bribery is necessary and indeed beneficial in order to grease the wheels of bureaucracy.

Sources: Phongpaichit and Piriyarangsan (1996); Phongpaichit *et al.* (1988).

9.13 Summary

In this chapter, we have learned about the determinants of charity and corruption. Many of the incentives for charity reside in emotional or psychological incentives that are not particularly amenable to economic analysis. The warm glow of giving and inclinations toward charity that are nonlinear with respect to income are examples where motives for charity are difficult to understand without a broad perspective of the determinants of decision making and the motivations of charitable individuals and foundations.

Corruption, on the other hand, is more tractable using the tools of economic analysis. There are a number of approaches that seem to bear fruit in slowing down and even reversing the spread of corruptive practices. Reduction in the opportunities to bribe, penalties for breaching laws against corruption and bribery, higher pay for public officials and closing loopholes that afford opportunities for government officials to accept bribes and grant favors all help to reduce the level of corruption. Raising the general level of income, introducing more competition and reducing the overall size of government can also work as incentives for establishing a more open and honest society.

Bibliography

Ades, A. and R. Di Tella (1997) National Champions and Corruption: Some Unpleasant Interventionist Arithmetic. *Economic Journal*, 108, 1381–1403.

Andreoni, J. (1988) Privately Provided Public Goods in a Large Economy: The Limits of Altruism. *Journal of Public Economics*, 35, 57–73.

Andreoni, J. (1990) Impure Altruism and Donations to Public Goods: A Theory of the Warm Glow of Giving. *Economic Journal*, 100, 464–477.

Andreoni, J. and L. Vesterlund (2001) Which is the Fair Sex? Gender Differences in Altruism. *Quarterly Journal of Economics*, 116(1), 293–313.

Bardhan, P. (1997) Corruption and Development: A Review of Issues. *Journal of Economic Literature*, 35, 1320–1346.

Barro, R.J. and X. Sala-i-Martin (1995) *Economic Growth*. Singapore: McGraw-Hill.

BBC (2006, 6 June) US Firms Raise Charity Donations. http://news.bbc.co.uk/1/hi/business/5051544.stm [Retrieved 5 October 2006].

Becker, G. and G. Stigler (1974) Law Enforcement, Malfeasance and the Compensation of Enforcers. *Journal of Legal Studies*, 3(1), 1–19.

Blechinger, V. (2000) Working Paper: Report on Recent Bribery Scandals, 1996–2000. Paper presented at a TI workshop on corruption and political party funding, La Pietra, Italy. http://www.transparency.org/working_papers/country/s_korea_paper.html [Retrieved 7 March 2003].

Brunetti, A. and B. Weder (2003) A Free Press is Bad News for Corruption. *Journal of Public Economics*, 87, 1801–1824.

Business International Corruption Index. http://www.transparency.org/cpi/index.html and www.gwdg.de/~uwvw/ [Retrieved 15 March 2005].

Chua, V.C.H. and C.M. Wong (1999) Tax Incentive, Individual Characteristics and Charitable Giving in Singapore. *International Journal of Social Economics*, 26(12), 1492–1504.

Collard, D.A. (1983) Economics of Philanthropy: A Comment. *Economic Journal*, 93, 637–638.

Dawkins, R. (1990) *The Selfish Gene*. Oxford University Press.

Donohue, III, J.J., J.J. Heckman and P.E. Todd (2002) The Schooling of Southern Blacks: The Roles of Legal Activism and Private Philanthropy, 1910–1960. *Quarterly Journal of Economics*, 117, 225–268.

Dziko, T. and S. Oki (2001) Sharing the Wealth: Charitable Giving in Prosperous Times. *Fund Raising Management*, 32(1), 29–35.

Graeff, P. and G. Mehlkop (2003) The Impact of Economic Freedom on Corruption: Different Patterns for Rich and Poor Countries. *European Journal of Political Economy*, 19(3), 605–620.

Gupta, S., H. Davoodi and R. Alonso-Terme (2002) Does Corruption Affect Income Inequality and Poverty? *Economics of Governance*, 3, 23–45.

Hall, R.E. and C.I. Jones (1997) Levels of Economic Activity Across Countries. *American Economic Review*, 87(2), 173–177.

Hofstede, G. (1997) *Cultures and Organizations: Software of the Mind*. New York: McGraw-Hill.

Holmes, K.R., M. Kirkpatrick and G.P. O'Driscoll, Jr. (2001) The 2001 Index of Economic Freedom. The Heritage Foundation and Dow Jones & Company. http://www.heritage.org/research/features/index/2001/ [Retrieved 15 February 2003].

Husted, B.W. (1999) Wealth, Culture and Corruption. *Journal of International Business Studies*, 30(2), 339–360.

Jain, A.K. (2001) Corruption: A Review. *Journal of Economic Surveys*, 15(1), 71–121.

Katyal, N. (2003) Conspiracy Theory. *Yale Law Journal*, 112(6), 1307–1398.

Kaufmann, D. (1997) Corruption: The Facts. *Foreign Policy*, 107(Summer), 114–131.

Korean Information Service (2000) Korea's Second-Phase Fighting against Corruption in the New Millennium. *Policy Series*. http://www.korea.net/learnaboutkorea/library/publication/corruption_200006.htm [Retrieved 3 April 2003].

La Porta, R., F. Lopez-de-Silanes and R. Vishny (1998) The Quality of Government. NBER Working Paper No. 6727.

Lee, M. (1990) *The Odyssey of Korean Democracy: Korean Politics, 1987–1990*. New York: Praeger.

Mauro, P. (1995) Corruption and Growth. *Quarterly Journal of Economics*, 110(2), 681–712.

Mocan, N. (2004) What Determines Corruption? International Evidence from Micro Data. NBER Working Paper No. 10460.

Mookherjee, D. and I.P.L. Png (1995) Corruptible Law Enforcers: How Should They be Compensated? *Economic Journal*, 105(January), 145–159.

New York Times (2006, 2 July) The Ultra-Rich Give Differently From You and Me. http://www.nytimes.com [Retrieved 2 July 2006].

Peacock, M. (2000) Charity Ends with the Lottery. *New Economy*, 7(2), 120–124.

Phongpaichit, P. and S. Piriyarangsan (1996) *Corruption and Democracy in Thailand*. Chiang Mai, Thailand: Silkworm Books.

Phongpaichit, P., S. Piriyarangsan and N. Treerat (1988) *Guns, Girls, Gambling and Ganja: Thailand's Illegal Economy and Public Policy*. Chiang Mai, Thailand: Silkworm Books.

Political Risk Services website. http://www.prsonline.com [Retrieved 15 May 2005].

Posnet, J. and T. Sandler (1995) Charity Donations in the UK: New Evidence Based on Panel Data. *Journal of Public Economics*, 56(2), 257–272.

Quah, J.S.T. (2003) *Curbing Corruption in Asia: A Comparative Study of Six Countries*. Manila, Philippines: Eastern Universities Press.

Riber, D.C. and M.O. Wilhelm (2002) Altruistic and Joy-of-Giving Motivations in Charitable Behavior. *Journal of Political Economy*, 110(21), 425–457.

Rosser, A. (2003) What Paradigm Shift? Public Sector Reforms in Indonesia since the Asian Crisis. In A.B.L. Cheung and I. Scott (eds.), *Governance and Public Sector Reform in Asia: Paradigm Shifts or Business as Usual?* London and New York: Routledge Curzon.

Roumasset, J. (1997) The Political Economy of Corruption. University of Hawaii, Department of Economics Working Paper No. 97–10.

Schleifer, A. and R.W. Vishny (1993) Corruption. *Quarterly Journal of Economics*, 108, 599–617.

Seldadyo, H. and J. di Haan (2005) The Determinants of Corruption: A Reivestigation. Paper prepared for EPCS-2005 Conference, Durham, England, 31 March–3 April.

Serra, D. (2004) Empirical Determinants of Corruption: A Sensitivity Analysis. Discussion paper, Global Poverty Research Group, Economic and Social Research Council, UK.

Singer, P. (2006) What Should a Billionaire Give and What Should You? *New York Times*, 17 December.

Transparency International website. http://www.transparency.org [Retrieved 15 May 2005].

Treisman, D. (2000) The Causes of Corruption: A Cross-National Study. *Journal of Public Economics*, 76, 399–457.

Van Rijckeghem, C. and B. Weder (1997) Bureaucratic Corruption and the Rate of Temptation: Do Low Wages in the Civil Service Cause Corruption? IMF Working Paper No. 97/73.

Van Rijckeghem, C. and B. Weder (2001) Bureaucratic Corruption and the Rate of Temptation: Do Wages in the Civil Service Affect Corruption, and by How Much? *Journal of Development Economics*, 65(2), 307–331.

Warr, P.G. (1982) Pareto Optimal Redistribution and Private Charity. *Journal of Public Economics*, 19, 131–138.

Wei, S.-J. (1999) Corruption in Economic Development: Beneficial Grease, Minor Annoyance, or Major Obstacle? Policy Research Working Paper No. 2048 (February). Washington, DC: World Bank.

Weisbred, B.A. (1988) *The Non-Profit Economy*. Cambridge, Mass.: Harvard University Press.

World Bank website. http://go.worldbank.org/LJA29GHA80.

Yen, S.T. (2002) An Econometric Analysis of Household Donations in the USA. *Applied Economic Letters*, 9, 837–841.

Chapter 10

Ethics and Government

In this final chapter, we turn to some of the most difficult issues confronting decision makers, economists and society. We have been able to establish in previous chapters the importance of subjective well-being and happiness, of trust, fairness and charity. We have also learned that cooperative and altruistic behavior can mitigate some of the unattractive aspects of competitive behavior. We have also learned that crime and corruption can be dealt with using both economic tools and social pressure. Many of the arguments that we have been making in previous chapters have to do with the benefits of a society that values consumption and material goods less and other people, community, friends and nature more. We have demonstrated a number of examples where economic models that assume economic agents are altruistic or cooperative have greater predictive power than competitive models. There is also some evidence that altruistic or cooperative behavior leads to more preferable outcomes for society in many cases. It could cut down on the problems inherent in behavior motivated by self-interest alone — principal-agent behavior, corruption and other dishonest behavior, crime and unethical business practices. Aspects of an ethical stance may also play a role in accelerating and raising economic living standards. Are these values taught in school? Should more time be spent on ethics, moral behavior and spiritual aspects of life? From what we have learned so far, the answer to these questions should be a resounding "Yes!"

Furthermore, we have reviewed a large body of evidence that suggests that people are generally not able to tell what increases utility and happiness. A number of suggestions have been made that indicate that a shift in emphasis away from consumption and toward leisure, particularly time spent with loved ones and friends, would increase the overall level of happiness, contentment and subjective well-being. It has also been shown that as consumers, emotions and the thrust of advertising often buffet us. Choices made under these circumstances can be welfare reducing, particularly when viewed over a lifetime profile.

It has also been suggested that a degree of inner reflection and contemplation of choices to be made can result in a more satisfactory set of consumer choices, when measured against a yardstick of subjective well-being or happiness rather than a yardstick of goods accumulated. Given these conclusions, it seems, in our view, that it is time to reconsider how we view the role of the government and the provision of welfare goods.

Earlier evidence presented in the previous chapters suggests that greater public spending on education, research and the protection of the natural environment generally will enhance subjective well-being. Furthermore, the psychic loss from unemployment, poverty and discrimination is such that even greater efforts need to be made to address these issues in order for there to be a significant improvement in happiness. The thrust of the arguments made also suggest that "inner work", time spent quietly in reflection and contemplation and a serious attempt to shift one's awareness away from narrow self-interest ("me") to greater concern and attention to others ("us") can also result in a greater degree of both economic and social satisfaction.

Many of the conclusions that have been drawn are based on surveys and objective evidence. Yet there is still a measure of judgment and normative analysis. Consequently, there is bound to be disagreement and discussion about the scope and extent of the redirection of resources required to address the goal of raising subjective well-being and happiness as opposed to raising gross domestic product (GDP). For this reason, what we have presented here is meant to spark discussion rather than serve as a set of prescriptions to be followed.

Given this background, we now turn to a discussion of how choices are made in pluralistic and complicated modern political systems and its relation to welfare.

10.1 The Role for Government Intervention

Earlier chapters (particularly Chapter 4) have primarily introduced the attainment of equilibrium outcomes in game theoretic situations

Table 10.1 Assurance Game

		Colin	
		Cooperate	Defect
Rowena	Cooperate	3, 3	0, 2
	Defect	2, 0	1, 1

Source: Little (2002, p. 94, Figure 9.4).

without intervention by any outside agents such as the government. In this chapter, we begin by showing the critical importance of external intervention in games without a dominant strategy, whereby the best possible outcome would only occur with the presence of external factors such as government intervention.

This particular kind of situation could arise in the case of negative externalities such as traffic congestion. In a Prisoner's Dilemma situation, it would be beneficial for Rowena to cooperate when Colin cooperates in resolving the traffic situation problem (see Table 10.1). However, aside from an accident, it is unlikely that either party will cooperate first unless there is some external mechanism in place to persuade or coerce the parties into believing that they will benefit from doing so. There has to be some form of assurance that the parties will indeed cooperate, possibly the existence of a legal system to penalize parties who fail to follow pre-determined rules. This increases the reward for cooperation and reduces the benefit of defection. This insight brings us to the crux of the chapter.

10.2 Nature of the State and Distributive Justice

Provision of public goods, the justice system and protection under the law depends upon the wishes of those who are governed. How does government arise? The nature of the state has been likened by philosophers and economists such as Robert Nozick (1974) and James Buchanan (1975) to a social contract drawn between the government and the public, where in return for the individual's compliance with the law, the government would agree to protect his rights of life, liberty and property. Others such as John Rawls (1971) and Amartya Sen (1983, 1995) maintain a similar position regarding protection of rights of life, liberty and property. However, they differ with Nozick and Buchanan on how government makes decisions. They place a high emphasis on normative judgments that the government makes regarding ethical and moral issues. To fix ideas further, we consider these two philosophical positions in more depth.

10.2.1 *The libertarian position*

We begin by looking at a minimalist view of the state as propounded by Nozick (1974) and Buchanan (1975). Earlier in the 17th century, Thomas Hobbes (1651) and John Locke (1690) began with an economy without government, which they dubbed the state of nature or pure anarchy. Nozick, for example, argues that in this state of anarchy, "The mutual recognition of rights in the state of nature is not sufficient to produce a peaceful society" (Gordon, 1976, p. 578). Locke and Nozick argue that alliances will spring up to protect members against other groups. However, bickering and fighting will erupt and protective agencies will be created to protect each of these groups from the others. This scenario describes well the relationships that exist even today in Africa and in feudal times when several different fiefdoms fought with each other over land and tribute.

Only when the concept of a nation state became widespread did the idea of a single monopolistic "protective agency" come into being. Nozick argues that the state arises from the voluntary contracting with those under its protection because of the economies of scale of having a government which operates as a protective shield against outsiders. As this process becomes entrenched, the government exacts its own tribute from the governed in the form of taxes. This is the Nozick concept of the minimal state — defense and taxation — and perhaps a legal system to decide disputes between members under its protection. In the Nozick minimalist system, there is virtually no concern with the distribution of income or how that distribution is derived or changes. Furthermore, Nozick does not discuss the public goods problem. Rather, Nozick is interested in the *process* by which a state comes into being and focuses only on the minimal set of services needed to run such a state. Like Nozick, Buchanan is concerned with the process and the contractionary obligations needed to sustain such a state:

> My natural proclivity as an economist is to place ultimate value on process or procedure, and by implication to define as "good" that which emerges from agreement among free men, independently of intrinsic evaluation of the outcome itself (Buchanan, 1975, p. 167).

Both Buchanan and Nozick deal with the concept of freedom within such a minimalist governmental framework. Some degree of freedom is surrendered to this newly established government. Then the question arises, "How do those under the protection of the government act in such a system?" Buchanan does not put a moral constraint on these actions. Predatory activities continue and those that are weak will fail. Protection against predators also arises and a natural balance will be struck where the cost of protection and gains from predation are in equilibrium, i.e., marginal cost (MC) = marginal revenue (MR). Resources in such a state with a minimalist government are devoted both to predatory behavior and to defensive measures against such behavior. The role of the state to stipulate a legal system of contracts and justice is missing. Nozick, on the other hand, operates from a position of moral rectitude. Therefore, there is less infighting within the Nozick system once a legal framework has been constructed. History seems to come down on Nozick's side. When there is a breakdown in the rule of law, then states tend to dissolve and reemerge again in a different form. Examples are many including post-Tito Yugoslavia and the breakdown of the Roman Empire.

Both Buchanan and Nozick focus on the process of how contracts are negotiated between actors in the economy. They are concerned with the process by which government emerges from anarchy, not with the end state. Neither Nozick nor Buchanan, but particularly Buchanan, puts much normative spin on the end product that results from this process. Buchanan does not accept freedom as a value as Nozick does. Rather, Buchanan recognizes it "much more simply as a necessary consequence of an individualistic-democratic methodology" (Buchanan, 1975, p. 2).

As philosophical constructs, the contractarian models of Buchanan and Nozick are interesting because they attempt to divorce themselves from normative judgments, relying rather on positive descriptions of processes of events. These writers are not particularly concerned about the establishment of private property, the distribution of income or the level of poverty. In their view, these are matters of normative interest and not the subject of the formation of government as a process of contract formation and negotiation between the ruler and those ruled. To summarize: "the market will be just, not as a means to some pattern, but insofar as the exchanges permitted in the market satisfy the conditions of just exchange described by the principles" (Lamont, 2006).

The difficulty with this libertarian/contractarian position is that the existing state of the world including the holdings of assets and other forms of wealth does not necessarily satisfy the theory of entitlement proposed by this manner of justice system. There is no level playing field at the start and no obvious way to make adjustments once the libertarian approach is implemented. While Nozick recognizes this and notes that some rectification for past injustices has to be made, as a practical matter it will be difficult to implement in his libertarian system.

10.2.2 The difference principle and distributive justice

Amartya Sen (1995) and John Rawls (1971) also adopt a contract theory of government. However, they are more concerned with the end result than the process. Thus, their approach is more normative. Rawls assumes that mankind is composed of prudent and rational and also self-interested individuals. In such a world, he introduces a thought experiment which is designed to tell us what kind of justice system would arise if all men had the same economic and social advantages. He does this by assuming there is a "veil of ignorance" erected so that no one knows what his state is. In such a condition, men are still full of self-interest and they want the justice system to serve these interests. However, all are ignorant of their endowments of these advantages such as intelligence, wealth, strength, charisma, political savvy and so on. This is a situation where everyone is lined up at the start of the race on the same starting line, yet no one knows where they will wind up at the end of the race.

Rawls characterizes such a position "justice as fairness". No bargaining is profitable since everyone is equally in the dark. Rawls argues that any rational, self-interested individual operating behind this veil of ignorance would arrive at two basic principles of justice. The first is that everyone should be granted certain basic liberties. The second, which is called the "difference principle", states that inequality of actual status is permissible to the degree that it improves the well-being of the least advantaged member of society.

The question that arises is whether the derivation of these two principles is free of normative judgment on the part of Rawls. Since there is no process by which we are assured that these outcomes will indeed arise, can we be sure that individuals have preferences that are identical enough to lead to this conclusion? For example, there may be some that are identical in every other characteristic except that some are risk takers and others are risk averse; or we could envision two societies with different time preferences that could lead to different intergenerational choices.

This is not an issue that is specific to Rawls alone. Wherever there is a social contract that is assumed to have universal validity, whatever conflicts that exist within the society are assumed away. This is the difference between the normative system of Rawls and the process theories of Nozick and Buchanan, where conflict is part of the process. Sen, on the other hand, stresses the importance of making a distinction between process and outcome and also stresses the importance of the process for social choice theory. However, his frame of reference focuses on the rights of the disadvantaged to participate in the process as opposed to Nozick's greater emphasis on freedom of choice.

As a theory of distributive justice, the Rawlsian/Sen position is motivated by the notion of justice as equality. Since earning more income will call forth more effort, this will result in a higher level of wealth even though it brings some inequality. The difference principle, however, insures that the poorest also benefit from this increase in wealth.

Resource-Based Principles of Distributive Justice. This theory, whose main proponent is Ronald Dworkin (1981), argues that natural endowments of health, talent or physical handicap should be compensated for by the social system. Circumstances which are beyond the control of individuals should be the basis for this compensation. It would be difficult to implement such a system as an overreaching set of social objectives since the level of compensation in a complex economic system is hard to gauge. Nevertheless, elements of such a theory are recognizable in social safety nets (e.g., unemployment benefits) that have been developed in industrial countries.

Utilitarianism and Distributive Justice. In its simplest form, utilitarianism, dating from John Stuart Mill, requires maximizing the utility of society, where this utility is the sum of all individual utilities. It is difficult to see how the general ideas of maximizing utility for a society can be adopted in any tangible way. First of all, it requires interpersonal comparison of utility. Secondly, the presence of prejudice could mean that overall utility is increased by greater discrimination, for example against women or different races or minorities. Finally, some utilitarian solutions are consistent with a big government, while others are compatible with a small government. Nevertheless, the concept of utilitarianism is embodied in the Pareto principle, whereby an optimum is reached if no one can be made better off without making someone else worse off. Because the Pareto principle does not require a comparison of utilities — only a departure from equilibrium — it is a powerful concept that is widely used by economists to value different alternative policies and outcomes in a variety of economic, political and social situations.

Just Deserts Principle of Distributive Justice. Just deserts principles of justice stress the importance of people's actions in determining economic benefits. This approach views work as a contribution to the social products (Miller, 1976, 1992) or as the effort people expend in work. In addition, people should be compensated for the costs they incur in their work activity (Lamont, 1994, 1997). In many instances, payoffs in the just deserts theory are rewards for raising the social product as opposed to private product. However, how society determines what is socially uplifting is subject to interpretation. While such a principle of just deserts is difficult to envision as a comprehensive system of distributive justice, it is something that can be applied selectively in particular situations where the value of particular actions can be measured and evaluated.

Strict Egalitarianism as Distributive Justice. The most radical proposal for implementing distributive justice is to give each member of society the same level of goods and services. There are several objections to this principle. The first is that it is difficult to apply the principle given that people have different objective functions and preferences. These are difficult to reconcile. Secondly, there are work effort effects that suggest that an unequal distribution of income could make everyone better off. Also, absolute equality could restrict freedom and such a result could be in conflict with what people "deserve". There will also be many free rider problems with such a system. Yet the thrust of income distribution toward greater equality cannot be denied. Honoring egalitarian motives is one of the underlying principles for the difference principle and just deserts.

10.2.3 *Ethics, rationality and public choice*

In Chapter 3, we dealt with situations where agents make decisions based on bounded rationality. Public choice is also subject to the same constraints of bounded rationality since there is incomplete information available to the government and lack of perfect foresight as a basis for implemented policies.

At the level of the individual, in some cases, these decisions were deemed to be irrational using the rational calculus set down by economists. In other cases, people were seen to be acting spontaneously without careful consideration of various alternatives. Much of this behavior could come from human instinctual imperatives based on our biological heritage. Fight or flight is one of these instincts and it is strongly imprinted on our psyche. We often respond, as a result, in ways that may be detrimental to ourselves and to others. As a point of public policy, it is important that individuals try to take decisions that are beneficial to themselves and to those around them. Sutherland (1994) suggests a thoughtful way to consider this problem. He says:

> How can we act spontaneously in good ways and not in bad ways? The difficulty is that it seems impossible to select without careful consideration

which actions to perform spontaneously and which to repress; but it is impossible both to ponder and to be spontaneous. ..... Aristotle believed that the truly good man did well naturally: he did not have to force himself to do it. One, of course, can take the opposite line and reason that the truly good man is one who succeeds in fighting his evil inclinations — if you are good by nature, behaving well is easy and, so the argument goes, you can't expect much credit for it. But regardless of this issue it is certainly true that the man for whom good comes naturally is better company than one who is always agonizing over it, even if he succeeds in quenching his doubts. There is still a dilemma — few of us if any are born naturally good. To this Aristotle has a partial answer. He believed that people form their own characters. Every time we resist a bad action it becomes easier to resist, and every time we do something good it becomes easier to do something good. By assiduous practice people can turn themselves into beings who spontaneously do the right thing and spontaneously avoid the wrong. ..... Aristotle's advice could only be taken by the rational man, by someone whose end was to form his character in a certain way and who accepted by careful selection of what he did was the best means to that end. To put oneself in a position where one does the right thing without thought, that is without considering what is rational, one has to undergo a period of deliberately acting in the ways that mould one's character to one's desires: that is rationally indeed (p. 328).

Aside from general moral principles that we can all agree upon, what is good and what is bad is not cast in stone. Put another way, what is desirable or good for one person may not be desirable or good for another. If we agree with the position of Aristotle, a position that is echoed by the "Scottish Enlightenment" view of justice which stresses the role of emotion, we can say that ethics and justice are determined in large part by the morally-based emotions that are part of human kind's basic mental structure.

One way to take a more detached view of what is good and what is bad for the society as a whole is to adopt the Rawlsian view of detachment and the "initial position" behind a veil of ignorance, as discussed previously. If we make decisions as to the nature of income distribution and social justice from this standpoint, we may be better able to cast off our own individual agenda for social action, helping us to adopt a more universal view of justice and fairness. From this stance, it becomes clearer that the well-being of the poorest is of more pressing concern to society than that of the well-to-do. Thus, a more equitable distribution of income and opportunity becomes a more pressing agenda than our own narrow personal agenda. We can also see more clearly that it is important for society to evolve in such a way that all members of the society have the chance to lead a happy and fulfilling life free of discrimination and prejudice.

10.2.4 *Altruism, cooperation and public choice*

The next question is how does the government come to its decision? How important is the role of altruism in public choice? In various parts of this book, we have stressed the beneficial aspects of altruistic behavior. Among other benefits, free riding, principal-agent problems and moral hazards are likely to be reduced. In this section, we ask the question whether a world inhabited by altruists would enable society to come to better grips with the challenges presented by public choice. In dealing with this issue in previous chapters, we have assumed that people are rational (or bounded rational) and that to achieve a unique solution to the public choice problem, we have to make some normative judgments regarding utility. This allows society and agents within the society to trade benefits and costs through the political process so that a politically acceptable equilibrium is reached.

Do the major results of this discussion change if we assume the world is populated by altruists rather than competitors? To begin to understand how this might work, consider the case of a cake that has to be divided. There are three people who "own" the cake and they have to decide, by majority rule, how to apportion it. You can perform a thought experiment as to how this would evolve. Suppose that two people decide they will split the cake between them and offer the third person nothing. What would happen? The third person could bribe one of the other two with a bigger share than half. So in the next round, the third person and the other person he bribed would split the cake, excluding the "new" third person; and so this cycle would continue *ad infinitum*. No stable solution would be reached, assuming that these three people do not somehow reach an agreement where they would each get equal shares.

How would this competitive game change if there was a panel of three judges to decide the distribution of the cake? See Widerquist (2003) where this example is suggested and further discussed. Imagine that the three people involved are the three stooges, Moe, Larry and Curly. Moe, Larry and Curly are in dispute over a cake. However, let us change the rules slightly — now the judges must decide by majority vote.

Moe arrives first and declares that the kitchen and all its ingredients belong to him. Then he steps out to buy a lock. While he is gone, Larry arrives and bakes a cake with the ingredients he finds in the kitchen. Finally, Curly arrives after being lost in the desert for a few days. He is on the verge of starvation and sees the cake.

Enter the three judges — Judge Judy, Judge Amy and Judge Hilary. They all believe in fairness and are all altruistic. Judge Judy believes in pure property rights based on the principle of first-come-first-served. She votes to give the cake to Moe. Judge Amy believes that a worker is entitled to the entire product of his labor and votes to give the cake to Larry. Judge Hilary believes in the principle "from each according to their abilities, to each according to their needs". Since Moe and Larry are a bit overweight and not too hungry while Curly is thin and starving, she votes to give the cake to Curly.

What is the solution? All judges believe in a fairness principle and in altruism, yet they cannot reach an agreement without trading because they have different standards for fairness and equity using altruistic principles. The obvious solution is trading and this is the solution that usually arises in the exercise of parliamentary democracy. Log rolling has become the term for this trading behavior and is widely employed in the US and elsewhere. So we see that altruism, despite its numerous beneficial attributes, does not necessarily provide a satisfactory solution to the problem of public choice in democratic societies. See the next section for a greater discussion of collective decision making in society.

10.3 Societal Decision Making and Justice

How does a society decide what is just and fair? How should income be distributed or redistributed? Since judgments on these kinds of issues are normative in nature, it is difficult to arrive at a single conclusion through a process of logical deduction. Much will depend upon the normative judgments that society makes. As we saw in Section 10.2, there is no shortage of theories of distributive justice.

To get a handle on how these judgments are passed down, we can look at evidence that has been accumulated from a variety of sources. These studies are positive in nature in the sense that they are designed to register what people do in particular circumstances, often under laboratory conditions. By studying these actions, we can get a better understanding on how judgments of fairness and justice are manifest in the decision making process. Some of these studies have already been discussed in the chapters dealing with game theory and fairness. The results will be discussed in this chapter as they pertain to the ideas of justice and fairness in the wider context of the distribution of income.

Generally, we are assuming that the decisions of individuals with respect to fairness and justice are communicated through a voting process within a political system. In an autocratic system they will be considered by the ruler or ruling committee, and in a democracy by majority or plurality rule. In this chapter, we are not particularly concerned with how this political process takes place. That is, we are not concerned with the justice system, but rather with the process by which individuals conclude that an action is just or not.

The position of the society on issues will depend to a significant extent upon the altruistic nature of the populous and also the tendency of the populous to engage in free riding or not, to vote for equity rather than efficiency and how the poorest members of the society are treated. How this works will depend in turn on the social contract that is established between the government and those governed. For example, in Europe, the social contract seems to call for a wider social security network and greater emphasis on unemployment compensation and income redistribution than in the US. Attitudes toward foreign relations and trade will also differ as well as a variety of social issues. From our previous study in Chapters 3 and 5, we can say that free riding will probably fall where there is a greater cooperative and altruistic sense in society, other things being equal. There are a number of other inferences we can make about the nature of the decisions that individuals make in specific circumstances. Much of this research has taken place under laboratory conditions and observations of behavior in different countries. Therefore, much of the work is cross-cultural. One of the strong conclusions that arise from this work is that, with a few exceptions, attitudes are quite stable across different cultural settings.

To move further in the discussion of fairness and justice, we consider several principles which are discussed separately. The narrative concludes with a summing up of how tradeoff takes place between the different principles as they operate in different situations. We depend on a number of different sources and research results. The overall organization is based on the approach followed by Konow (2003).

We look at four categories of justice: equality and need; utilitarianism and welfare economics; equity; and context and justice. These four categories are closely related to the public finance principles of the ability to pay and the benefit principle. They are also related to the principles of distributive justice discussed earlier. The benefit principle is akin to equality and need, while the ability to pay relates closely to economic efficiency and welfare economics.

Context and equity do not have a direct parallel in the traditional public finance literature. Context is a relatively new theory relating to the way in which decisions are framed and is closely aligned with what we have come to know as prospect theory in Chapter 3. It does not generate a theory of or principles for distribution. However, it does relate directly to fairness and justice and also has the benefit of tying these issues to other material we discussed earlier. Equity has to do with assigning benefits based on an equal basis or based on individual effort or responsibility. We discussed this earlier under the heading of just deserts.

In the traditional public finance literature, the distribution of income is determined by the way in which the benefit and ability to pay principles are applied to problems of collecting taxes and distributing expenditures. As we will see, distributive justice is a bit more complicated. It often involves groups of people making decisions about how to assign shares in a "just" way, and so it involves not only macroeconomic issues of overall income distribution, but also micro issues of fairness and justice in particular situations.

10.3.1 *Equality and need*

The needs approach to justice focuses on the poorest members of society and ways to raise their income. Redistribution of income is at the heart of this needs approach. Basic needs are the focus of many international agencies and the idea of progressive taxation based on the ability to pay and diminishing marginal utility of money is one of the foundations of such a basic needs view of justice. Beginning from a position of equal distribution of income or egalitarianism principle (see Section 10.2), equality gives us an extreme compass point against which to measure equal income as a principle of justice.

Most surveys of individuals in the general public show a lack of support for equality in the extreme form of "equality of income for everyone" and indeed, we saw that there are a number of negative side effects to a system of absolute equality (see Section 10.2). For example, Jasso (1999) reports results from a sample of nearly 9,000 individuals in 13 countries which concludes that if people received a "just" income by their own reckoning, then the distribution of income would deteriorate, not become more equal. Nevertheless, despite rejection of extreme solutions to inequality, the thought that there should be equal treatment of equals is a powerful idea among the general public and among economists.

As we reviewed previously, Rawls' (1971) second principle, the "difference principle", requires that greater inequality is only permissible so long as it improves the well-being of the least advantaged member of society. Some observers have noted that such a principle is by no means assured even if all individuals believe in some measure of help to the poorest. Binmore (1994) uses game theory to see whether justice emerges through cooperation in a game theoretic context. Others including Kolm (1985) suggest that justice can be arrived at through a social contract when people are motivated by cooperative and altruistic tendencies, even though they are not operating behind a veil of ignorance. Empirical tests of the Rawlsian justice system show that most people do not agree with its crucial assumption.

Many students tested in laboratory experiments do not pick the difference principle when allowed to choose among several options. The vast majority select a rule to maximize the minimum outcome rather than any other goal. This makes a lot of sense given our discussion of risk aversion in a loss making situation in Chapter 3. Subjects choose to maximize the probability that they will not be caught below a minimum value by maximizing that value. However, the thought experiment envisioned by Rawls does induce participants to consider the world as it might be and therefore to think "outside the box" and to put themselves in the position of others.

A Marxian approach is another way of viewing the principle of equality. However, when looking through Marx's writings, it is hard to find a strict adherence to absolute equality. Rather, he seems to vote for some kind of a needs approach such as the familiar "from each according to his ability, to each according to his needs" (Marx, 1875, p. 531).

Certainly, needs are supported by several dictator and ultimatum games' results where the subjects are arrayed as needy versus not so needy individuals or charities (Eckel and Grossman, 1996) and other studies summarized by Konow (2003, p. 1199). Nevertheless, when it comes to choosing between how hard people work and their needs, most Americans surveyed by Kleugel and Smith (1986) chose work. Only 13 percent of around 1,000 respondents thought family income should be based on needs rather than skills. However, this still does not resolve the question of whether this decision in favor of more or less equity is made because of "fairness" or other considerations.

10.3.2 *Utilitarianism and efficiency*

Utilitarianism relates primarily to the principle of economic efficiency. Basically, this principle stems from the belief that the consequences of actions are the most important outcomes. The implications for fairness and justice are then derived from these consequences. Using this kind of logic, the Pareto principle and the various assumptions about

Table 10.2 Fair Division of Pies

A. Two pies to Anne and four to Betty	40 percent voted for this option
B. Four pies to Anne and two to Betty	4 percent voted for this option
C. Three pies to each	56 percent voted for this option

Source: Konow (2003, p. 1200).

the way the economy works is sufficient to guarantee that an economic system achieves the most efficient way of production, given its natural and human resource endowments. Resources are allocated to those who derive the greatest marginal utility, and welfare comparisons and justice are to be made on the basis of these comparisons.

There is some empirical support for this form of utilitarianism as exhibited by the experiment outlined as in Table 10.2. Jane has baked six pies to give to her two friends, Anne and Betty, who do not know each other. Betty enjoys pies twice as much as Anne. In distributing the pies, which option is fairer? In the table, utilitarian considerations ran a close second to equality.

Another utility consideration would be to maximize the total utility of the recipients rather than allocating along marginal utility lines. Yaari and Bar-Hillel (1984) found that over 80 percent of respondents picked unequal quantities of food to be given to recipients (from a menu of five choices) that equalized the total derived health benefit to them.

A refinement of the utility approach is the Pareto principle, which does not require any cardinal measures of utility. The Pareto principle states that a movement in allocation of benefits is fine so long as someone is made better off while no one else is made worse off. The principle has been modified to say that any change in allocation is acceptable so long as the gains of some are more than sufficient to compensate any losers, even if compensation does not occur. We saw in Chapter 3 that one has to be careful in using this principle of compensation. This principle could be violated in cases where loss is felt more strongly than a gain. Nevertheless, when all gains and losses are treated equally, this principle comes down to one of economic efficiency and maximizing wealth or surplus.

In Chapter 4, we investigated various forms of the Prisoner's Dilemma, dictator games and the free rider problem. How do the results of these games relate to the Pareto principle and economic efficiency? In the Prisoner's Dilemma, the win/win solution is Pareto efficient and self-interested strategies are not. Strategies like Tit for Tat were successful in moving to an efficient outcome in many cases. Furthermore, in dictator games, there are some situations where the pie can be split more evenly than the typical case we explored in which the dictator has complete control and offers a small share of the pie. Hoffman and Spitzer (1985) develop a two person dictator-type game when one of the subjects, called the controller, enters into negotiation with the other player. These negotiations usually led to agreements that maximized the joint surplus. Often, this was achieved at some sacrifice to the controller. In this game, the controller has the authority to decide payments to both parties and in this sense he has the same power as the dictator in a dictator game. However, the introduction of the possibility of negotiation changes the outcome rather dramatically.

In public goods experiments, the efficient outcome is obtained if all players contribute to the public good and there are no free riders. In reviewing the results of a number of public goods experiments, Ledyard (1995) finds that total contributions lie typically between 40 and 60 percent of the group optimum. So free riding exists, yet there is also substantial contribution to the public good which exhibits a commitment toward an efficient outcome that increases the total pay-off to all participants. Other papers that show willingness to sacrifice individual payoff to achieve a higher total reward are reviewed by Konow (2003, p. 1203). A particularly interesting result obtained by James Andreoni and J.H. Miller (2002) demonstrates that while dictators in a dictator game allocate more to themselves, they also tend to give their opponent a larger payoff when giving increases the total.

A further test of whether the efficiency is judged to be fair is reflected by the results of experiments reported by Konow (2003, p. 1204), which show that efficiency is often weighed against other criteria for fairness. However, a broader study of general principles of efficiency shows that people with more ability should earn higher salaries and that giving everyone the same salary regardless of the type of work would destroy the desire to work hard and do a better job (see McClosky and Zaller, 1984).

The results of these studies and other work suggest that efficient outcomes are not only judged as fair outcomes, but are also judged against criteria of whether the decisions made are just. Konow (2003) concludes that efficiency alone is too narrow a criterion to serve as a general definition of justice. He argues that we also need to look at the process by which outcomes are obtained in order to get a fuller understanding of a just society. This leads us to equity, which we consider in the next section.

10.3.3   *Equity*

Equity considerations deviate from efficiency criteria in several ways. Those who consider equity seem to be more directly concerned with issues of justice and fairness. Efficiency results in justice as a byproduct of the process of allocative efficiency. Equity is more concerned with the process itself. In this sense, we can think of Rawls and Sen being associated with equity, and Nozick and Buchanan being associated with efficiency. Nozick is more interested in individually-based fairness and justice rather than the systems such as the Rawlsian veil of ignorance which supports redistribution of income based on an end result. Nozick and others studying equity are more interested in the process rather than the end result. To fix ideas, we can consider the famous Nozick example of inequality created when a "star" exacts payments from "fans", which results in a very high income for the star. Nozick finds this perfectly justifiable because it came about as a result of the process of redistribution of income. Konow (2003, pp. 1206–1207) reconsiders this case.

Suppose you are able to change the wealth of everyone in the world to the levels that you consider most fair. Let us say that you do. Now suppose Michael Jordan being greatly in demand signs the following contract with a team: in each home game, $25 from the price of each admission ticket goes to him. By the end of the season, Jordan has raked in $25 million. Please rate Jordan's earnings as fair or unfair.

59 percent said unfair ($N = 137$). Now suppose that you are able to change the wealth of everyone in the world to the levels you consider most fair. Would Jordan still earn \$25 million? Here, the "no" responses jumped to 76 percent. These results suggest that Nozick's criteria, though consistent with free choice, is not considered fair. Other evidence reviewed by Konow also supports this general conclusion. A simple criterion of equity which says that individuals are allowed to keep their possessions so long as they are not obtained by theft, fraud, enslavement or exercise of monopoly power is not widely accepted as a complete theory of fairness or justice.

To augment the Nozick theory, equity theorists consider just deserts. As we saw in Section 10.2.2, this is a catch all term for the contribution of other factors such as effort, choice, luck and birth that went into the acquisition of goods or into the decision to allocate resources. Buchanan (1975), although aligned with Nozick in emphasizing the importance of acquisition of goods, makes more explicit the situations that are allowable under a general theory of justice or fairness. Buchanan believes that only birth should be excluded, as does much research on fairness which suggests that only effort should be rewarded. Note that even under these criteria, Michael Jordan should be allowed to keep the \$25 million.

Studies of luck and effort come to similar conclusions regarding relative rewards. For example, in games where potential recipients were determined by a coin toss or performance on a test of skill and general knowledge, the dictator gave more to the latter group. Ruffle (1998), Burrows and Loomes (1994) and Hoffman and Spitzer (1985) suggest that giving is motivated by concern for fairness that is based on *effort* and not on *luck* or by *accident of birth*.

How do observers react to choice as a just and fair reason for obtaining a greater share of the pie? Choices to forgo consumption and undertake more education or save and invest to start a new business are often viewed as being fair and just. For example, a study by Schokkaert and Lagrou (1983) showed that subjects believed that occupations requiring greater skill and training should receive higher incomes. Some of these rankings may relate to higher productivity. However, another study by Kleugel and Smith (1986) suggests that greater effort should be rewarded over and above the level of education. Generally, rewards based on luck and birth rights are not thought to be fair and just rewards for effort and good choices are "just deserts". However, in the Michael Jordan example, public outcry over high CEO salaries and the compression observed between actual and fair incomes suggests that rewards which are too far out of line are not fair, even if they are based on effort and good choice.[1]

Going a bit further, some observers feel that equity and fairness can fit into a theory called *attribution theory* (see Konow, 2003, pp. 1210–1211), where agents are responsible for their own actions but not for circumstances outside their control. This kind of approach, which bears a close resemblance to just deserts, allows those who are born into adverse circumstances to receive a subsidy to get them started since they were not responsible for these life circumstances. However, if they do not take advantage of these transfers by way of effort and appropriate choices, then it is fair to remove these subsidies. One interesting study points out that fair judgment of behavior depends on effort by considering respondents' reactions to various comparative scenarios. These include poor class performance because of low effort versus low aptitude, spilling a drink because of being bumped or because of gesturing carelessly, and getting AIDS because of promiscuous sex or from a blood transfusion. Respondents' outcomes that were the result of irresponsibility-based actions (low effort, careless gesture, promiscuous sex) were judged differently from those actions considered to be bad luck and unfair, despite effort and responsible action.

How should assignments of income or adjustments in income be made to reflect views on equity? One method, which dates from Aristotle, is to calculate the outcome and input of different people and to equate these ratios for those involved. This is reminiscent of simple marginal productivity theory, where agents are rewarded in proportion (to the value of) their marginal product. The difference is that the outcomes discussed may be couched in different terms than

---

[1]The continued existence of royal families in several European and Asian countries serves as an interesting counter example.

the marginal product and its value in dollars per hour. Generally, it has to do with the proportionality between contribution and reward as it relates to different participants.

In summary, there are many studies that find the proportionality rule to hold and a few that do not. Partly, this reflects difficulty in establishing the value of inputs and outputs when we are not talking about a firm and its workers, but rather more difficult variables or situations such as marriage and race relations. What has emerged is a theory which says that agents should be rewarded in proportion to the discretionary inputs that they make. When there is a surplus, for example, this translates into a statement such as a fair distribution of the surplus is in proportion to their discretionary input into the transaction (Frank, 1988).

10.3.4 *Context*

We learned in Chapter 3 that many decisions are made in view of design, outcomes, attitudes toward risk and how alternatives are framed in terms of this risk. This prospect theory approach also has relevance for the study of fairness, justice and welfare provision. In this section, we summarize a series of these observations, drawing on material from Chapters 3 and 6, focusing on how these observations impact on justice, fairness and welfare provision. In Section 3.1, we noted that agents often make decisions with reference to others' actions. We followed this up in Chapter 6, where it was indicated that people's feelings of happiness and well-being are often related to their position in the income distribution. We take these ideas further here, focusing on the importance of "reference transactions" in determination of fairness and justice.

What Kahneman *et al.* (1986) suggest is that fair transactions are judged with reference to some established level. For example, to be fair, a firm should not raise profits above some acceptable level given the historical levels of wages, rents and other costs. This implicit contract is couched in terms of entitlements of each of the factors. These relationships between the different factor inputs and profits are determined by historical precedent. They are not necessarily based on justice

Table 10.3 What is a Fair Transaction?

---

1. A house painter employs two assistants and pays them $9 per hour. The painter decides to quit house painting and goes into the business of providing *landscape services, where the going wage is lower. He reduces* the workers' wages to $7 per hour for the landscaping work.

Judgment of action: Fair — 63 percent   Unfair — 37 percent   N = 94

2. ...... *landscape services. With about the same time and effort, the former house painter's profits fall significantly in his new business. In landscape services the going wage is lower so he reduces* .....

Judgment of action: Fair — 67 percent   Unfair — 33 percent   N = 220

3. ... *landscape services. With about the same time and effort, the former house painter's profits rise significantly in his new business. Nevertheless, in landscape the going wage is lower and so he reduces* ...

Judgment of action: Fair — 34 percent   Unfair — 66 percent   N = 213

Source: Kahneman *et al.* (1986).

or fairness. It is departures from this equilibrium that are judged to be fair or unfair. This is because psychologists have established that any well-maintained relationship is judged to be fair and acceptable, simply because it has survived for some time. Kahneman *et al.* have conducted some experiments that demonstrate these ideas in a more concrete way. Consider the three questions and responses displayed in Table 10.3.

The responses to these questions reflect an attitude that profit increases should be shared with employees, despite the fact that the going wage is lower in the new and more profitable business. The context which allows the reader to know that profits have increased and that the employer is working with the same people results in the predominant unfair judgment.

Another example shows that stability or normality does not necessarily equate with fairness and is again demonstrated by a case study. It was noted that a fast food restaurant where prices were relatively stable faces significant competition and the respondent is asked whether the prices in this restaurant are fair. 91 percent said yes. When the location of the restaurant was changed to an airport and everything else (aside from the lack of competition) remained unchanged, 71 percent thought prices would be unfair. So the level of competition is also important. Monopoly pricing is unfair. Responses to other questions suggest that a just price produces a fair division of the surplus from the transaction. For example, it is fair to lower wages to market levels if firms are not making a profit, but it is unfair if profits have gone up. If markets are competitive, most respondents believe that prices will be fairly determined. Furthermore, and this relates to the conclusions from prospect theory, losses are treated more heavily than gains and so framing effects result in different views of fairness. The endowment effect discussed in Chapter 3 serves as a fairness explanation in many cases. This accounts for the widespread use of "grandfather" clauses which maintain certain privileges for those with already established relationships, while new entrants play by different rules.

Context can also change people's attitudes depending on the information set available to those judging justice and fairness. When a CEO's high salary is compared to other CEOs and found to be about the same, this elicits a response that it is fair. When compared to the rank and file who are earning far less, the response is different. By putting a certain spin on the question, it is easy to change respondents' views of fairness.

Similarly, by putting a certain spin on default rules and the framing of the context, it is easy to change the public's views towards welfare policies. Choi *et al.* (2005) showed that people instinctively had a preference to follow the default option. Say if the default option was changed to from letting people opt-in to the 401(k) retirement pension scheme to letting them opt-out, the majority of employees would stay with the current course (default option of remaining). Since people tend to choose the path of least resistance, it was suggested that the government could frame welfare enhancing policies towards the default option of letting them join the welfare schemes. Sunstein and Thaler (2003) termed this "paternalist liberalism". They argued that since individuals had a choice on whether to join or not to join the pension schemes or be it any other welfare enhancing policies (such as medical insurance and motorist insurance), it was soft paternalism. The rationale was that people did not have complete knowledge and might not always act in their best interest; hence, it was up to the government to ensure that they are taking some steps to protect themselves from their baser instincts. The design of the context was subtly done and individuals (minority) who felt that they did not benefit from the default option had the chance to withdraw from the scheme. It would not "cost" those individuals much by withdrawing simply through writing in to inform the authorities, unlike the majority who would suffer a lot if they did not sign up for default retirement schemes, medical insurance schemes and gambling prohibition. An instance of where paternalism appears to be beneficial relates to the contrast between how Hong Kong and Singapore are dealing with pollution. Singapore has a more hands-on "paternalistic" approach and as a result, many expatriates have moved from Hong Kong to Singapore to escape escalating levels of air pollution (*Financial Times*, 2006, 3 April).

The state of Missouri has introduced a gambling scheme whereby 10,000 gamblers who know themselves to be compulsive gamblers can sign up on a list with the government to bar themselves entry from gambling in the casino ships that ply the river. If they violate the ban, the Missouri government can bring charges of trespassing against them and confiscate their winnings (*Economist*, 2006, 6 April). This is an interesting case of paternalist liberalism at work.

Similarly, retirement schemes (sometimes mandatory) such as social security and other private social insurance schemes impose financial discipline on those who might not otherwise have accumulated any nest egg for retirement. The *New York Times* (2006, 17 September) reports that even the rich do not appear to be insusceptible to going broke — they waste their fortunes, overspend and get exploited through fraud and injudicious deals. Bankruptcy is also commonplace in the middle class as credit card overspending, excessive stock market leverage and other risky financial speculation sometimes results in financial ruin.

Sunstein and Thaler (2003) remind us that it is sometimes difficult to distinguish between "good" paternalism and the abuse of power. Since the majority of the public would opt for the opt-in option, it would be easy for a corrupt but clever government to frame policies in their own self-interest. Further steps are needed to regulate the regulators in order to minimize repeats of the Enron, Hewlett-Packard and other cases of ethical misconduct.

10.3.5   Cross-cultural similarities

Surveys of attitudes toward justice in different countries are often remarkably similar, particularly when respondents do not have a personal stake in the outcome. Konow (2003, pp. 1227–1229) reports a number of these results drawn from different sources. Nearly an identical percentage of respondents in Switzerland, Germany and Canada (82–83 percent) thought it was unfair for the price of snow shovels to be raised after a snow storm. Around two-thirds of Russians and Americans thought it was unfair to raise the price of cut flowers because of a holiday or to raise the price of staples without an increase in costs. A majority of respondents in several European countries, Japan and the US believe that equal shares of income and wealth are not fair; rather, those who work harder deserve to earn more. Offers in the ultimatum game also tend to fall in a narrow range across several countries where similar experiments were conducted. These and other similar results "lend credence to the view that whatever variation in generosity one observes in experiments is due more to differences across cultures in the willingness to act on justice than to differences in the concept of justice itself" (Konow, 2003, p. 1228).

10.3.6   Balancing objectives

Several writers have attempted to bring together the various elements of justice into a general theory which Konow calls "pluralistic justice". The elements of such a theory are deceptively simple. Basically, they combine different combinations of *equality, equity, efficiency and need*. The equality principle establishes fairness and justice when individuals are treated in the same way based on the other features of justice — need, efficiency and equity. Most of the research suggests that the different objectives of fairness and justice weigh these objectives against one another depending upon the context. In one sense, fair refers only to equity, and in another sense it means good and includes the ideas of need and efficiency. Fair can be interpreted as relating to general moral criteria, while justice has a narrower meaning relating to the distribution of resources. Investigation of the tradeoffs between these different objectives is unable to put any empirical weight or value to these tradeoffs. Frohlick and Oppenheimer (1992) conclude that "distributive justice involves the competing claims of entitlements, need and the desirability of maintaining incentives" (p. 176).

An interesting hierarchy of preferences is suggested by Elster (1992). First, maximize total welfare. Second, deviate from maximizing welfare to ensure a minimum level of welfare (Rawls' suggestion). Third, deviate from the second criteria if people fall below the minimum level because of their own choices. Fourth, deviate from the third if failed choices are due to conditions beyond their control. Elster's first proposition is an efficiency criterion. The second is a statement of basic needs. The third and fourth are justice as just deserts "....whereby individuals are rewarded or punished for the choices they control but not for the ones they can't" (Konow, 2003, p. 1229).

An interesting application of this set of criteria applies to the selection of kidney donors and the allocation of kidneys. These include the likelihood the transplant will be a success, need or the lack of an alternative such as dialysis, and finally compensation for having a kidney that is difficult to match. These three criteria align closely with: (1) efficiency — a higher expected benefit if the kidney match is good; (2) need; and (3) the just desert norm which says that those with difficult to match kidneys should not be penalized.

10.3.7 *Process and fairness*

Recalling the distinction between process and outcome noted in the beginning of this chapter as a way to distinguish between theoretical notions of fairness, we can ask the question whether fairness is enhanced if the process of reaching decisions is more open, transparent and inclusive of various members of the society. Recall the results of the happiness research which concluded that more open and democratic societies were likely to have a higher level of well-being. Often, this level of well-being is also associated with greater fairness. The work of Frey and Stutzer (2001), whose work was noted in the happiness chapter, and also of P. Anand (2001) suggest that people view procedures that encourage greater participation and freedom and which provide more information as being fair and just, irrespective of the outcome.

Returning to the principles of public finance introduced at the beginning of this chapter, we see that these principles of pluralistic justice relate closely to the benefit and ability to pay principles. Efficiency and equity relate more to the benefit principle, while need and equality relate more to ability to pay.

How societies decide on the weights they attach to the different aspects of distributive justice depend upon their historical traditions, the workings of the political process and the intellectual resonance with writers stressing different objectives. Those stressing need and equity side with writers like Rawls, Marx and Sen. Those with a more free market and libertarian persuasion have views that resonate more with Nozick and Buchanan.

10.4 What are Alternatives for Governing?

10.4.1 *Hobbes' sovereign*

We begin our search for an appropriate (and viable) system of government by looking at some of the solutions suggested by the great philosophers of the English and German traditions. These philosophers were fond of starting from a starting point that they described as the "state of nature". Hobbes begins with and assumes that we are in a world where everyone is a defector in a Prisoner's Dilemma. The state of nature in such a world is one that is without morality or conscience. The natural equilibrium in such a world is chaos and anarchy. To deal with mankind in such a world, Hobbes suggests a solution that invokes the notion of a sovereign. The only way to insure a social

contract in such a world is to have rules and regulations that are created and enforced by a sovereign (read dictator). When the rules are
enforced by the sovereign through his own judicial system, it is
ensured that all contracting parties abide by the social contract established under this system. So in the language of game theory, we are
now in a cooperative game and not a competitive game. There is pre-
play communication (between the ruler and the ruled) and binding
agreements. These agreements are then enforced by the sovereign.

Anyone familiar with feudal systems around the world would
understand that these rules established by the sovereign were often
arbitrary and also changed to fit circumstances. There may have been
codes established that governed these arrangements between the sovereign and his subjects. They were not necessarily just, nor would they
seem particularly progressive in a modern setting. Slavery was widespread, the proletarian masses had few rights and the aristocracy was
often corrupt and decadent. Nevertheless, despite its shortcomings,
such a system was probably preferable to the near anarchy that existed
when small tribes attacked each other periodically, each trying to
achieve hegemony over some part of the countryside.

10.4.2 *Democracy and clubs*

Democracy is an alternative to rule of the sovereign that evolved grad-
ually in England as the sovereign's power was eroded by different
groups of lords. From our study of clubs in Chapter 8, we note that
in certain circumstances the interaction of different clubs in the political area may leave the views of some groups underrepresented. Often
these are minorities that do not have the financial resources to lobby
for their own agenda items. In these circumstances, rule by club may
not truly reflect democratic principles. The concept of rule by aristo-
cratic elite is a kind of club democracy that still survives with the
House of Lords in England and the Electoral College in the US. In
the Electoral College, it is possible for electors to vote for candidates
other than those selected by the popular election process. This has
happened occasionally in the past but not often enough to result in a
change in the system. In England, the House of Lords has much less

power than the House of Commons, where legislators are elected by popular vote. Keeping these factors in mind and the fact that majority or plurality rule is followed in many countries, we can safely assert that one man–one vote seems to be the most popular form of democracy now.

If we think in game theoretic terms, the entire voting process takes on a cyclical flavor. Voting in a democracy risks a cycle of "conjectural variation", where an individual thinks that he should not vote because one vote does not mean very much in the grand scheme of things (unless you happen to be the sovereign). Then he might think that if everyone thinks that way, maybe he should vote because not many others will. Then the thought cycle reverses and he begins to think that everyone will vote, and so on. In some countries like Australia, they force the issue by making people pay a fine if they do not vote.

Aside from this problem of conjectural variation, which in practical terms does not seem to be much of a problem because voting rates are high in many democracies, we have the difficulty that the one man–one vote theory is often not true in practice. There are many interest groups that wield power far beyond their absolute numbers. Small groups hold strategic power in the democratic process in many countries. Evidence is widespread. Just look at the swing votes of the farmers in Europe, the US, Japan and Korea; the power of small third parties in Germany and the UK; or the power of the National Rifle Association in the US. Olson (1965) also shows that a political system run by such power groups or clubs leads to a suboptimal solution as they pursue a more narrow agenda than that of the majority. Be that as it may, a democratic system is one method for seeing that the will of the public is enforced through a voting system that makes sure that win/win solutions are obtained wherever possible.

10.4.3 Planning, utilitarianism and "socialism"

The widespread use of planning is a method that democratic societies with a large public sector have developed to allocate resources and organize economic activity. Planning is popular in some parts of Europe and in many developing countries. Plans are made to fulfill growth objectives, achieve a tradeoff between inflation and unemployment, reduce poverty, allocate resources through cost-benefit analysis, and so on. The folly of widespread and pervasive planning is evident in the crash of the Soviet system and the misallocation of resources that exists wherever state-owned enterprises dominate the economic landscape, whether it be in China, Vietnam or Brazil. In the name of social justice, a fully operational socialist system aims at distributing income in a just way. This is based on the principle of diminishing marginal utility of money and is designed to shift income from the rich to the poor. In its extreme form, this practice robs people of the will to work by taking away any fruits of labor earned in excess of the average. In so doing it destroys incentives and work effort, reduces the productivity of the most efficient and subsidizes those who are least productive. However, when used judiciously and in moderation, it can provide an effective social policy as evidenced by the economic success of several European countries.

10.4.4 *Mutual advantage*

The idea of mutual advantage is closely related to the Hobbsian idea of the sovereign. However, instead of people working out mutual advantage in line with the rules established by the sovereign, these rules and codes of conduct are established through a process of mutual advantage and dialogue. The rules that are derived are similar to win/win situations in game theory. In many cases, they are quite simple and easily agreed upon like "drive on the left" and rules establishing ownership of goods. Others such as labor laws to ensure the rights of workers, voting for women and minorities and well-established property rights may take longer to establish. Mutual advantage may also include more fundamental human rights such as the right to hold property, the right to a fair trial, the right to be free from want and the consent of the governed to be governed.

10.5   General Aspects of Social Choice and Welfare Economics

How do we bring together the elements of governance described in Section 10.4 along with the different aspects of justice and fairness covered in Section 10.3? We address this question in this section. If we begin the discussion of social choice and welfare economics from the stance of the classical economist and the classical economic assumptions, we are immediately put in some jeopardy. If we assume the broad list of classical assumptions including diminishing marginal utility, rationality of individual preferences (transitivity and convexity), inability to make interpersonal comparisons of utility, competition and utility maximization by individuals, we are unable to reach a unique Pareto optimum for society as a whole. Arrow (1951) showed this in a very elegant way many years ago. Here we simply note that in the case of three people with a set of preferences for three goods, a unique equilibrium is not possible and that we are led around in an endless circle, much like the children's game of paper, rock and scissors.

For three individuals, suppose that $x > y > z$ for individual 1, that is x is preferred to y and y is preferred to z. For individual 2 we have $z > x > y$ and for individual 3 $y > z > x$. If we substitute, we find that $x > y > z > x$, which is an inconsistency. A social optimum is not possible under general conditions.

10.5.1   Is there a role for ethics?

How do ethics and moral aspects of life come into economic decision making at the aggregate level? There are several approaches to this question taken by different writers. We can begin with the utilitarian solution discussed above. Using utilitarian calculus to make some simple decisions based on the concept of decreasing marginal utility, this theory argues that since marginal utility is decreasing for nearly everything, the marginal utility of money must be declining too. Therefore, if we want to redistribute money from the rich to the poor, we can take money from the rich by way of progressive taxation and redistribute it to the poor. This should bring about an increase in welfare because the money transferred has more utility to the poor than it does to the rich.

As welfare economics evolved, the economics profession decided that this was not such a good criterion since it required making judgments on an interpersonal basis about the marginal utility of money. It also had detrimental effects on leisure. Economists decided that they did not like making these interpersonal comparisons of utility because it requires making a value judgment about the utility of one person and how it relates to the utility of another person. They were very concerned about this, as they thought that economics should be scientific and value free (normative and not positive, to use more familiar terms). As a result, they were able to devise other methods for deciding whether there was an increase in welfare without having to make such value judgments required in interpersonal comparisons.

Pareto came up with a very useful proposition that we could move from one situation or equilibrium to another, and there would be an increase in welfare if at least one person was made better off and no one was worse off. Economists led by Samuelson (1937) also hit upon the idea of *revealed preference* which allowed them to say that if one good or combination of goods was preferred in the market to another, then it gave a higher utility because it was "revealed to be preferred". Therefore, preferences did not have to be determined *a priori*. That would be a very difficult job. Instead, preferences could be determined from the market through revealed preference and this would not require any explicit interpersonal comparisons.

After a lot of theorizing of the use of the Pareto principle and revealed preferences, the analysis was left with the conclusion that, leaving aside the Arrow impossibility theorem, there were usually a lot of equilibrium points on a so-called "Pareto path". However, in order to find one unique equilibrium value, you had to know how to make interpersonal comparisons of utility in order to reach that unique solution (see Box 10.1 for a simple explanation of an Edgeworth box and how this Pareto path is generated).

Box 10.1 Edgeworth Box and Paretian Optimum

In Figure 1 below, A and B represent two individuals who are set about to exchange goods X and Y between them. Suppose we can draw indifference curves for each of them, A starting at the lower left hand corner and B at the upper right hand corner. The curves are convex from below. A move toward the upper right represents more of both goods for A and a move toward the lower left hand corner means more of both goods for B. You can see the situation from B's point of view by turning the chart around so that the upper right corner is in the lower left corner.

Suppose we start with an initial distribution of goods between A and B at W_1. W_1 is a legitimate combination of goods X and Y, whose value are shown on the two axes, because it is on the indifference curve of A as well as the indifference curve of B. Now consider what happens when we allow for A and B to trade goods. What happens? They can be better off if they trade so that the new equilibrium is a or b or c or d. If we draw a line through all of the possible points where the indifference curves of A and B are tangent to each other, then we have what is called the contract curve. However, since we cannot make interpersonal comparisons of utility, we cannot say which of these points is optimal. So we are left in a position of indeterminacy.

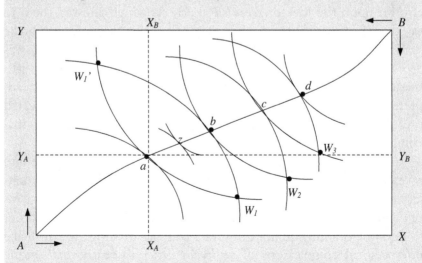

Figure 1. Edgeworth Box and Pareto Optimality

It is not that the analysis is back at square one, but it looks as if in order to make any reasonable kinds of welfare judgment, some form of interpersonal comparisons of utility have to be made and we are back in the realm of normative economics.

Once we are back in the world of value judgments, and recognizing that we are interested in the intersection of ethics and economics, a whole Pandora's box of possibilities is introduced when we consider what the income distribution should look like. K.W. Rothschild (1993) has listed some of them, which are listed below in Table 10.4.

In any event, the entire field of income distribution and how incomes can be reallocated through public choice is subject to considerable discussion both within the economics profession and as a matter of public policy. In addition, the question of how much of a role the government should play in the economy is also open to

Table 10.4 A List of Proposals on How to Handle Income Distribution

- The question of income distribution is unimportant.
- Incomes should be derived only from work (implying all other income taxed away).
- Complete equality of income modified by age, family size, etc.
- The highest incomes (say the top 10 percent) are too high.
- The lowest incomes (say the lowest 10 percent) are too low.
- High and medium incomes are immoral as long as poverty exists.
- Wage income should comprise a "just" share of total income.
- Progressive taxes.
- Easily earned income (windfalls) should be taxed at higher rates.
- The income distribution should be "fair" and should be based on a wide social consensus.
- The income distribution should be allowed to develop from equal opportunity and in the absence of any discrimination.
- To each according to his needs.
- Priority for family needs.
- Moral qualities of the services rendered should be reflected in income levels (priests and other clerics receive more income?).
- Leave the income distribution to market forces.

Source: Rothschild (1993).

discussion. Generally, these issues are settled through the ballot box as different politicians propose different solutions to the various issues facing society. Economists make suggestions for policy based on cost-benefit analysis and provide inferences based on econometric models of the economy. However, there are many different models and a range of possibilities depending upon different assumptions. Therefore, politicians and the general public have to make choices based on the limited information available to them.

Consider a problem in public choice where there are only two individuals and they have to make a choice about a public good that has to be provided by taxes on the two individuals. They can arrive at a solution if a series of success voting and revoting takes place. Consider the Edgeworth-Bowley Box and a public good where there are two consumers who share in the tax bill, as shown in Figure 10.1. If F falls within the "eye" formed by A_1 and B_1, then it will be preferred to a world without a public good. Through a process of recontracting, we would eventually go to a point G, which is on the contract curves and also within a series of smaller and smaller "eyes".

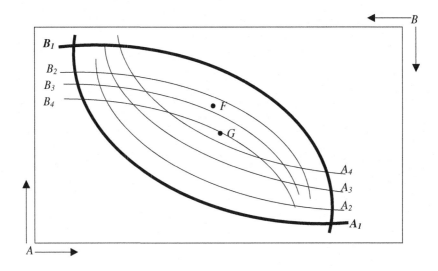

Figure 10.1 Edgeworth-Bowley Box and Public Good Provision

10.5.2 *Ethics, altruism and income distribution*

Returning to the question of income distribution, we are left with a potpourri of suggestions on how to redistribute income. To be honest, even those research studies that are undertaken with a view to being nonjudgmental also have implicit values attached; simply choosing one research topic over another is a value judgment that the research is more "important". Furthermore, the economists' seeming preoccupation with economic efficiency is in itself a value judgment. Where do we begin, once we accept that we are in a world of value judgments? How do ethical principles come into play? What do philosophers have to say about these issues?

One method that is very popular and familiar to economists is to set up a situation where there are two choices — one ethical and one unethical. How would decisions be made in such situations?

Using conventional economic principles, some simple inferences can be made, some of which were discussed in Chapter 9. The higher the cost of corruption, the less corruption will be observed. Pay higher wages and there will be less corruption. Melvin Reder (1975) suggests a simple code rule — "Meet your obligations without cheating" — and measure people's behavior relative to that code. If the adherence to that moral code is high, there is little cheating. Nevertheless, there will be some temptation to cheat, particularly if things are going bad and the rewards are high. However, in some Japanese companies, the adherence to this kind of code has been so high in the past that some CEOs of firms which have gone bankrupt have committed suicide.

Sociologists like to think of the ethical principles as being embodied in how society views the actions of individuals, whether they be economic decisions or other kinds of decisions. Therefore, they believe that there are social norms that influence people's behavior in addition to pure self-interest. In their view, action is taken as a result of interaction between self-interest and social norms. If someone lives in a lawless society with few adhering to ethical principles, then most actions will pay little cognizance to these ethical principles, whatever they may be.

Once we consider how all of this unfolds in the determination of how ethical standards are applied and enforced in a society, we have to look at the role of the state. The state is critical because it is the mechanism by which ethical principles are applied and enforced. The role of the state can be light on interference with market principles ala Friedman (1968) and Hayek (1944), or very heavy as in a highly socialist or communist system.

- *Rawls' suggestions*

Without getting into all this, there are certain principles that economists have found very attractive as extensions of the idea of "Pareto optimality", particularly the Rawlsian suggestion discussed in Section 10.2 to maximize the income of the least advantaged member of society. While Rawls considers a large number of ethical propositions, the one that is most attractive is this proposition, which puts great weight on being risk averse, a trait that economists believe is characteristic of many economic decisions.[2] To reiterate, Rawls says that a just solution or incremental movement from one equilibrium is just if it is characterized by a change in the income structure so that the income of the least advantaged (poorest) is improved or maximized. His views can be summarized by two sentences: "Each person is to have an equal right to the most extensive basic liberty compatible with a similar liberty for others" (p. 60) and "Social and economic inequalities are to be arranged so that they are to the greatest benefit to the least advantaged" (p. 83).

Many comparisons with a Rawls solution and a Pareto optimum are possible and it can be shown that Rawls solution and a Pareto solution are consistent. However, Rawls pays particular attention to the poorest elements of society and so this decision tool would often lead to a situation where the poor are made better off while others are not made worse off.

---

[2]This is consistent with our analysis of prospect theory and the work of Kahneman, Tversky and others in Chapter 3.

- *Progressive taxes and work effort*

One aspect of the discussion of ethics and improving income distribution through such government policies as progressive taxation is the impact that such policies, which stress equity, have on work effort. There is a large body of research that has investigated these impacts and has found them not to be minimal, particularly at high rates of marginal taxation. In formulating public policy, these adverse impacts have to be taken into account, along with the shift in preferences between work and leisure that occur as a result of higher rates of taxation. If we recall the discussion of happiness in Chapter 6, we also note the beneficial aspects that higher rates of taxation would have on the mix of consumption between public and privately purchased goods. More public goods would become available and individuals would be discouraged, to some extent, from increasing consumption of luxury goods.

Another aspect of income distribution involves the interaction of altruists and those who are primarily selfish and follow self-interest. We know from our discussion of these two motives and our discussion of fairness that altruists would be in favor of a more equal income distribution and would put greater emphasis on the "fairness" of such an income distribution. Some writers (McNutt, 1993) argue that a society occupied primarily by altruists would be a less envious and fairer society. Such a society would find cooperative and win/win solutions to a host of issues where cooperation seems a better strategy than confrontation. These include labor disputes, environmental cleanup, energy use in peak periods, management consensus on company policy issues, principal-agent and free rider problems and issues of corruption, fraud and extortion. However, recall the discussion in Section 10.2.4, which suggests that even altruists can disagree as to the most desirable outcome.

Those with extreme views would say that economists do not have a firm ethical foundation. However, most societies reach some sort of balance between the extreme position of the two groups — the cooperators and the defectors — so that even those who are self-interested will cooperate on occasions. For example, consider theft. There is always a small group that will steal or free ride. However, when this behavior threatens anarchy, even the self-interested cooperate to reduce theft by supporting law enforcement and being "good citizens". Even so, the altruist will likely be attracted to public programs that address the needs of the underprivileged and the poorer segments of society.

However, it must be kept in mind that the distribution of income and the problem of poverty are essentially different problems. The first relates to the entire populous and how each individual's income relates to others. The distribution of income is dynamic, although its essential features change only slowly over time. As we saw in the discussion of fairness and happiness, individuals are particularly interested in where they stand relative to others inside the income distribution. They are interested in how they stand relative to their friends, work associates and family members. They are less interested in those who are remote, except perhaps when they become indignant over an unfair situation such as huge bonuses for CEOs of companies or huge payments to movie and sports stars.

Poverty, on the other hand, is an absolute condition that can be dealt with without affecting the income distribution of others in the community (see Bronfenbrenner, 1985), except to the extent that raising those at the lowest end reduces the spread of the distribution.

10.5.3 *Application of ethical principles of justice and greater income equality — the experience of developing countries in Asia*

To focus on an application of ethical principles, consider the income distribution in Asian economies. Using the Gini coefficient as an index, there have been only very gradual changes in the overall income distribution in Asia over the past few decades. We also know that it is generally very difficult to make significant changes in the overall distribution of income short of a revolution or war or other cataclysmic event that rearranges the entire social order. Nevertheless, the evidence does support the conclusion that a society with a better income distribution to begin with is more likely to grow more rapidly in the future (see Persson and Tabellini, 1994). Societies where income is relatively equitably distributed such as Korea and Taiwan had higher rates of income growth than those societies where income was less equitably distributed at the beginning of the post-war period such as the Philippines and Indonesia. However, the fit is loose and these results are only indicative of a generally better initial starting point in Korea and Taiwan, probably as a result of land and asset redistribution following the social disruption of the 1940s and 1950s.

Given that it is very hard to change the distribution of income, which is relatively stable over long periods of time, how can the social order be rearranged quickly? Furthermore, from the material we looked at in Chapter 6 on happiness, it is not clear that improving the distribution of income is going to increase overall happiness. The richer members of society often get some satisfaction from seeing that they are superior to those in the lower echelons of the income distribution.

Therefore, if we are to investigate how to change the distribution of income in keeping with principles of justice as laid down by Rawls (1971) or based on one of the other methods described in Table 10.4 earlier, we have to rely on other ways than changing the entire income distribution. This involves microeconomic analysis and particular attention to the needs of the poorest members of society. If the status of the poorer members of society is improved by precise targeted policies, it may not have much of an impact on other groups and may require only a marginal diversion of spending away from other programs. Still, such social action requires the political will of the majority and a desire on the part of the society as a whole to address the general issue of poverty.

10.5.4   *Religion, social responsibility and governmental attention to poverty and basic needs*

In some loose sense, it may be reasonable to argue that societies where ethical values are promoted more fully within the social fabric are more likely to have a more sympathetic approach to addressing issues of poverty and basic needs. In this regard, the findings of B.E. Moon (1991) that Buddhist societies in Asia achieved higher basic needs provision than other countries based on average relationship between income and basic needs provision are relevant: "It appears that the fine basic needs performance ascribed to Asian countries in general is actually found in only the nine countries coded as Buddhist" (Moon, 1991, pp. 250–252).

Certainly there is more to this than meets the eye. For many years, communist societies supplied a much higher level of basic needs than did capitalist countries at a similar level of income. Furthermore, who is to say that Buddhism carries with it a higher standard for attending to the needs of the poor? There are many anecdotes regarding Thai children that are neglected because society thinks it is their "karma" to be born in this lifetime with a defect due to sins carried over from a past life. Furthermore, income distribution has deteriorated in Thailand in recent years as the gap between Bangkok and the rural provinces has widened.

Nevertheless, the social context is very important in determining the way in which the society addresses the need for providing relief for the poor as well as basic needs. Social safety nets are provided in most European countries to a much wider extent than they are in the US. These differences can be explained by a political consensus that has been arrived at to adopt a more communitarian approach to social justice in Europe than in the US. Advocates of the US system stress the importance of providing incentives to work and the flexibility that the US system has in adjusting to shifting demand patterns. The period of euro sclerosis in Europe is pointed to as a negative side effect of a social system that is characterized by labor markets that are rigid and inflexible and which protects its citizenry from the time they enter the world until the time they leave it.

The point of this discussion is simply to point out that there are social choices to be made and how the society makes them will be conditioned by its attitudes toward social justice and economic and political freedom. In Asia and even in the West, for many years the Japanese system was applauded for its attention to communitarian values and the responsibility that managers had toward their employees. The ability to reach decisions through consensus, wait patiently for a promotion, work ceaselessly to achieve the company's objectives and the dedication of employees toward their employer were also pointed to as highly desirable communitarian traits. Bottom-up management was applauded and many Western companies copied caring customer relations.

However, in recent years, as the Japanese economy has floundered, these same values have been ridiculed for leading to bureaucratic gridlock and a frustrating, even maddening, ability to decide not to decide on any policies that have not been accepted by the society. Policies that could lift the economy out of the doldrums have been rejected because they would fracture the political consensus.

The bottom line, in our view, is not to let the pendulum swing too much in one direction or the other. The circle of influence where altruism and cooperative motives are strongest begins in the family. There are obvious reasons for this, both from a sociobiology point of view and from the point of view of getting along with those around us. The strength of these motives diminishes as those we come in contact with are further removed from the family. In early times when agriculture was much more important, the village group was probably much more central to life than the company is now for most employees in the West. Yet in Asia, loyalty to the firm and to the family is still strong, perhaps as a carryover from the agricultural setting which they have only recently abandoned.

Nevertheless, no matter what the nuance of attachments and relationships there are in individual societies and cultures, there is no doubt that the circle of close altruistic association diminishes as day-to-day contact with a person or group lessens. How individual societies deal with this will depend on a wide array of factors that is difficult to pinpoint.

The relevant point for public policy is that many of the values that economists have traditionally relied upon exclusively in the past to make recommendations regarding the thrust and focus of public policy need to be broadened and adjusted, to take into account the wider values that incorporate an ethical and more broadly based approach to these issues and problems.

10.6 Do People Follow Their Moral Compass?

Some authors argue that individuals follow a kind of moral progression or can be pigeon-holed into different categories of moral reasoning (see Kohlberg, 1981; White, 2002; Maslow, 1968). According to Kohlberg, the lowest stage is dominated by self-interest. At the next highest level, people see the importance of human interactions and value others to some extent as expressed through empathy for family members and sharing responsibility. At the highest level, all human life is sacred and people strive not to violate others' rights as a tenant for all actions. Others have confirmed a relationship between moral reasoning and moral behavior. Asch (1951) found that peer pressure led subjects to give wrong answers to questions that the subject was actually aware of. There are numerous other studies where peer pressure caused subjects to answer against their better judgment or to actually cause harm to others at the urging of those controlling the experiment (see shock experiment in the 1950s, Milgram, 1974; and also the work of Zimbardo, 1975, which deals with a simulated prison). Then there is the fictitious account of children's behavior on a deserted island in *Lord of the Flies*, William Golding's powerful novel. Milgram conjectured that people of lower status relinquished control to those of higher status, while Zimbardo suggests that there is evil in everyone.

These studies also relate to the pogroms and other cases of genocide alluded to earlier, when we were discussing social capital. In any event, this kind of evidence suggests that various social variables can overwhelm an individual's moral judgment and dominate ethical behavior. In the public sector, there are fewer studies of moral consistency. However, there is one study reported by White (2002), which suggests that moral development is hindered by rigid hierarchy. This would be consistent with the observation that many of the morally repugnant acts reviewed earlier were carried out by soldiers and others in a rigidly controlled environment. However, the situation is not that simple. Ethical decision making and the consistency of these decisions will depend on a host of factors including upbringing, social circumstances and pressure from colleagues and associates. The resulting social interaction will help to determine the moral stance of those involved. We can say, however, that the studies carried out so far do suggest that while rigid hierarchies will lead to more consistent dynamics in perceived moral behavior, they may contribute to a lack of resistance to changing norms that are imposed from above. Witness the difficulties of the mutineers who go to trial in *The Caine Mutiny* and the demise of Billy Budd in the Melville novel of the same title.

Bibliography

Anand, P. (2001) Procedural Fairness in Economic and Social Choice: Evidence from a Survey of Voters. *Journal of Economic Psychology*, 22, 247–270.

Andreoni, J. and J.H. Miller (2002) Giving According to GARP: An Experimental Test of the Consistency of Preferences for Altruism. *Econometrica*, 70(2), 737–753.

Arrow, K. (1951) *Social Choice and Individual Values.* New Haven, Connecticut: Yale Press.

Asch, S.E. (1951) Effects of Group Pressure upon the Modification and Distortion of Judgments. In H. Guetzkow (ed.), *Groups, Leadership and Men.* Pittsburgh, PA: Carnegie University Press.

Binmore, K. (1994) *Game Theory and the Social Contract.* Cambridge: MIT Press.

Bronfenbrenner, M. (1985) Income Distribution and Economic Justice. *Journal of Economic Education*, Winter, 35–51.

Buchanan, J. (1975) *The Limits of Liberty: Between Anarchy and Leviathan.* Chicago: University of Chicago Press.

Burrows, P. and G. Loomes (1994) The Impact of Fairness on Bargaining Behavior. *Empirical Economics*, 19, 201–221.

Choi, J.J., D. Laibson and B.C. Madrain (2005) Are Empowerment and Education Enough? Underdiversification in 401(k) Plans. *Brookings Papers on Economic Activity*, 2, 151–213.

Dworkin, R. (1981) What is Equality? Part 2: Equality of Resources. *Philosophy and Public Affairs*, 10(1), 283–345.

Eckel, C.C. and P.J. Grossman (1996) Altruism in Anonymous Dictator Games. *Games and Economic Behavior*, 16, 181–191.

Economist (2006, 6 April) The New Paternalism. http://www.economist.com [Retrieved 17 September 2006].

Elster, J. (1992) *Local Justice: How Institutions Allocate Scarce Goods and Necessary Burdens.* New York: Russell Sage Foundation.

Financial Times (2006, 3 April) Hong Kong's Air Pollution Cuts Its Appeal. http://www.ft.com [Retrieved 4 May 2006].

Frank, R. (1988) *The Passions within Reason: Prisoner's Dilemmas and the Strategic Role of the Emotions.* New York: W. W. Norton.

Frey, B.S. and A. Stutzer (2001) Outcome, Process and Power in Direct Democracy. *Public Choice*, 107, 271–293.

Friedman, M. (1968) The Role of Monetary Policy. *American Economic Review*, 58(1), 1–17.

Frohlick, N. and J.A. Oppenheimer (1992) *Choosing Justice: An Experimental Approach to Ethical Theory.* Berkeley: University of California Press.

Gordon, S. (1976) The New Contractarians. *Journal of Political Economy*, 84(3), 573–590.

Hayek, F.A. von (1944) *Road to Serfdom.* Chicago: The University of Chicago Press.

Hobbes, T. (1651) *The Leviathan.* Malmesbury.

Hoffman, E. and M.L. Spitzer (1985) Entitlements, Rights, and Fairness: An Experimental Examination of Subjects' Concepts of Distributive Justice. *Journal of Legal Studies*, 14, 259–297.

Jasso, G. (1999) How Much Injustice Is There in the World? Two New Justice Indexes. *American Sociological Review*, 64(1), 133–168.

Kahneman, D., J.L. Knetsch and R. Thaler (1986) Fairness as a Constraint on Profit Seeking: Entitlements in the Market. *American Economic Review*, 76, 728–741.

Kleugel, J. and E.R. Smith (1986) *Beliefs about Inequality: Americans' Views of What is and What Ought to.* Chicago: Aldine Publishing Co.

Kohlberg, L. (1981) *Essays in Moral Development: The Philosophy of Moral Development*, Vol. 1. New York: Harper & Row.

Kolm, S.C. (1985) *Le Contrat Social Libéral: Philosophie et Pratique du Libéralisme.* Paris: Presses Universitaires de France.

Konow, J. (2003) Which is the Fairest One of All? A Positive Analysis of Justice Theories. *Journal of Economic Literature*, 41, 1188–1239.

Lamont, J. (1994) The Concept of Desert in Distributive Justice. *The Philosophical Quarterly*, 44, 45–64.

Lamont, J. (1997) Incentive Income, Deserved Income, and Economic Rents. *Journal of Political Philosophy*, 5, 26–46.

Lamont, J. (2006) *Stanford Encyclopedia of Philosophy.* Distributive Justice. http://plato. stanford.edu/entries/justice-distributive [Retrieved 31 January 2006].

Ledyard, J.O. (1995) Public Goods: A Survey of Experimental Research. In J.H. Kagel and A.E. Roth (eds.), *The Handbook of Experimental Economics* (pp. 111–194). Princeton, NJ: Princeton Press.

Little, I.M.D. (2002) *Ethics, Economics, and Politics: Principles of Public Policy.* Oxford: Oxford University Press.

Locke, J. (1690) The Second Treatise of Government. http://oregonstate.edu/instruct/ phl302/texts/locke/locke2/2nd-contents.html [Retrieved 3 June 2006].

Marx, K. (1875, 1993) Critique of the Gotha Programme. In A. Ryan (ed.), *Justice.* Oxford: Oxford University Press.

Maslow, A. (1968) *Toward a Psychology of Being.* Princeton, NJ: Van Nostrand.

McClosky, H. and J. Zaller (1984) *The American Ethos: Public Attitudes Toward Capitalism and Democracy.* Cambridge: Harvard Press.

McNutt, P.A. (1993) The Samarian's Dilemma: Public Choice versus Private Rights. *International Journal of Social Economics,* 20(1), 51–63.

Milgram, S. (1974) *Obedience to Authority: An Experimental View.* New York: Harper and Row.

Mill, J.S. (1861, 1979) *Utilitarianism.* Indianapolis and Cambridge, MA: Hackett Pub. Co.

Miller, D. (1976) *Social Justice.* Oxford: Clarendon Press.

Miller, D. (1992) Distributive Justice: What the People Think. *Ethics,* 102, 555–593.

Moon, B.E. (1991) *The Political Economy of Basic Human Needs.* Ithaca: Cornell University Press.

New York Times (2006, 17 September) Fortune's Fools: Why the Rich Go Broke. http://www.nytimes.com [Retrieved 17 September 2006].

Nozick, R. (1974) *Anarchy, State and Utopia.* New York: Basic Books.

Olson, M. (1965) *The Logic of Collective Action, Public Goods and the Theory of Groups.* Boston: Harvard University Press.

Pareto, V. (1906, 1971) *Manual of Political Economy.* New York: Augustus M. Kelley.

Persson, T. and G. Tabellini (1994) Is Inequality Harmful for Growth? *American Economic Review,* 84(3). 600–621.

Rawls, J. (1971) *A Theory of Justice.* Cambridge, Mass.: Belknap Press of Harvard University Press.

Reder, M. (1975) Corruption as a Feature of Government Organization: Comment. *Journal of Law and Economics,* 18, 607–609.

Rothschild, K.W. (1993) *Ethics and Economic Theory: Ideas, Models and Dilemmas.* Aldershot: Edward Elgar.

Ruffle, B. (1998) More is Better but Fair is Fair: Tipping in Dictator and Ultimatum Games. *Games and Economic Behavior,* 23, 247–265.

Samuelson, P.A. (1937) A Note on the Pure Theory of Consumer's Behavior. *Economica,* 5(17), 61–71.

Schokkaert, E. and L. Lagrou (1983) An Empirical Approach to Distributive Justice. *Journal of Public Economics,* 21, 33–52.

Sen, A. (1983) Liberty and Social Choice. *Journal of Philosophy,* 80(1), 5–28.

Sen, A. (1995) Rationality and Social Choice. *American Economic Review,* 85(1), 1–24.

Sunstein, C.R. and R.H. Thaler (2003) Libertarian Paternalism is Not an Oxymoron. Preliminary draft, 4 March 2003. University of Chicago, University of Chicago Law Review.

Sutherland, S. (1994) *Irrationality: Why We Don't Think Straight!* New Jersey: Rutgers University Press.

White, F.A. (2002) A New Scale: Goal Setting and Behaviour Questionnaire (SGBQ). *Educational Psychology,* 22(3), 285–304.

Widerquist, P. (2003) Public Choice and Altruism. *Eastern Economic Journal*, 29(3), 317–337.

Yaari, M.E. and M. Bar-Hillel (1984) On Dividing Justly. *Social Choice Welfare*, 1(1), 1–24.

Zimbardo, P.G. (1975) Transforming Experimental Research into Advocacy for Social Change. In M. Deutsch and H.A. Hornstein (eds.), *Applying Social Psychology: Implications for Research, Practice and Training*. Hillsdale, NJ: Erlbaum.

Author Index

Subject Index

Printed in the United States
By Bookmasters